The often emotional debate over the impact of structural adjustment on the poor in Africa has been confused by the complexity of economic reforms and their inconsistent implementation, the diversity of prior conditions, and confounding effects of external shocks. Going beyond simple "before and after" comparisons, Professors Sahn, Dorosh, and Younger isolate from other factors the effect of specific policy measures associated with adjustment programs. The analysis draws primarily on the experience of ten African countries: Cameroon, The Gambia, Ghana, Guinea, Madagascar, Malawi, Mozambique, Niger, Tanzania, and Zaire. It combines description of policy reforms and survey data, and quantitative simulations using multimarket and computable general equilibrium (CGE) models. The authors suggest that contrary to common belief, adjustment policies – in particular trade and exchange rate, fiscal, and agricultural reforms – do not harm the poor in Africa. Reforms in fact usually benefit the poor slightly, but alone are insufficient to reduce poverty significantly.

STRUCTURAL ADJUSTMENT RECONSIDERED

Structural Adjustment Reconsidered

Economic Policy and Poverty in Africa

DAVID E. SAHN
Cornell University

PAUL A. DOROSH
Cornell University

STEPHEN D. YOUNGER
Cornell University

CAMBRIDGE
UNIVERSITY PRESS

PUBLISHED BY THE PRESS SYNDICATE OF THE UNIVERSITY OF CAMBRIDGE
The Pitt Building, Trumpington Street, Cambridge CB2 1RP, United Kingdom

CAMBRIDGE UNIVERSITY PRESS
The Edinburgh Building, Cambridge CB2 2RU, United Kingdom
40 West 20th Street, New York, NY 10011-4211, USA
10 Stamford Road, Oakleigh, Melbourne 3166, Australia

First published 1997

Printed in the United States of America

Typeset in Times Roman

Library of Congress Cataloging-in-Publication Data

Sahn, David E.
Structural adjustment reconsidered : economic policy and poverty in
Africa / David E. Sahn, Paul A. Dorosh, Stephen D. Younger.
p.   cm.
ISBN 0-521-58451-5
   1. Structural adjustment (Economic policy) – Africa, Sub-Saharan.
2. Africa, Sub-Saharan – Economic policy. 3. Poverty – Africa, Sub-
Saharan. I. Dorosh, Paul Anthony. II. Younger, Stephen D. III. Title.
HC800.S23   1997
338.96 – dc21   96-40018
                                                                          CIP

*A catalog record for this book is available from
the British Library*

ISBN 0-521-58451-5 hardback

CONTENTS

TABLES AND FIGURES

Tables

Figures

ACKNOWLEDGMENTS

We would like to express our appreciation for the underlying financial support of the U.S. Agency for International Development for the research presented in this book. We are particularly grateful for the commitment to the research and unwavering support of Jerome Wolgin, the chief economist in the Africa Bureau. He ensured that we had the time, resources, and intellectual space with which to explore complex and controversial issues. We also appreciate the support of Yoon Joo Lee, Leonard Rosenberg, and Jay Smith, who served as project officers at USAID during the course of our research.

While the authors of this book were the principal investigators of the research project, numerous others participated in the effort and helped collect the data, develop the models, and conduct the analyses synthesized in this volume. Of particular note are the contributions of Harold Alderman, Jehan Arulpragasam, Nancy Benjamin, René Bernier, R. Sudharshan Canagarajah, Peter Glick, Boniface Essama-Nssah, Jaikishan Desai, Paul Higgins, Cathy Jabara, Mattias Lundberg, Sarah Lynch, Bradford Mills, Carlo del Ninno, Alexander Sarris, Gerald Shively, Shankar Subramanian, Erik Thorbecke, wa Bilenga Tshishimbi, Rogier van den Brink, and Yves Van Frausum. In addition, a number of other researchers contributed to this effort. These include Chris Barrett, David Blandford, Kajal Budhwar, Deborah Friedman, Madeleine Gauthier, Lisa Genetian, Steven Haggblade, Solomane Koné, Steven Kyle, Blaine Lewis, Jeffrey Maton, Lemma Merid, Natasha Mukherjee, Per Pinstrup-Andersen, Grant Scobie, David Shapiro, Kenneth Simler, Elizabeth Stephenson, Hamid Tabatabai, Platon Tinios, Marjatta Tolvanen, Marc Tomjlanovich, and S. Zografakis.

Many African collaborators and institutions also made invaluable contributions to the research effort in their countries. In particular, we wish to thank:[1]

---

[1] Institutional affiliations are those at the time the research was conducted.

in Cameroon – Hakoua Ambroise, Gerard Djophant, and André Ngassam (Ministère du Plan); in The Gambia – Abdoulie Sireh Jallow and Rohey Wadda (Ministry of Finance and Economic Affairs); in Ghana – Charles Jebuni (University of Ghana), S. A. Laryea-Brown (Fudtech, Ltd.), Wayo Seini (Institute for Social, Statistical and Economic Research), and Seth Terkper (National Revenue Secretariat); in Guinea – Mammadou Barry, Kader Kondé, and Sokouvogui Vohou (Ministère de la Santé); in Madagascar – Armand Roger Randrianarivony and Christian Rasolomanana (Institut National de la Statistique), Philippe Rajaobelina and Eugene Razakanaivo (Ministère de l'Economie), Fidèle Rabemananjara (USAID/Madagascar), Tovonahary Rabetsitonta (Office Statistique et Informatique pour la Programmation du Développement), and Jacques Roland Rakotoarizony (Société d'Assistance Technique et Gestion); in Malawi – Wycliffe Chilowa (Center for Social Research), Graham Chipande, Roy Kayinya, and Jeff Malaga (Ministry of Economic Planning and Development); in Mozambique – Duma Salamao Cumbane and Iolande Fortes (Food Security Department, Ministry of Commerce); in Niger – Ousmane Samba-Mamadou (Université de Niamey) and Maidaji Abdou (Ministère du Finance et du Plan); in Tanzania – H. K. R. Amani, W. E. Maro, and Mboya S. D. Bagachwa (Economic Research Bureau, University of Dar es Salaam); in Zaire – Mohammed Ben Seria, Kamiantako Miyamueni, Kalondji Ntalaja, and Muhindo Rugishi (Institut National de la Statistique).

Finally, we appreciate the assistance of Ingrid Satelmajer and Roberta Spivak, who edited and prepared this manuscript, and Carolyn Schofield, Wendy Merrill, Anne Inman, Isabel Gardner, and Pilar Garcia for their administrative support of the research.

1

Introduction

Over the past decade, African economies have performed poorly. Economic growth has been slow or nonexistent, and poverty remains widespread. The apparent correlation between these discouraging economic and social outcomes and the increased prevalence of structural adjustment programs sponsored by the international financial institutions (IFIs), the World Bank and International Monetary Fund (IMF), during the 1980s has led many to question the efficacy and appropriateness of the economic reforms pursued. Further, influential critics argue that, regardless of the macroeconomic outcomes, the poor suffer a disproportionate share of the hardships associated with key macroeconomic and sectoral policy reforms. Critics also see orthodox adjustment policies as too oriented toward achieving short-term macroeconomic stability and, therefore, in addition to adversely affecting the poor, as inappropriate to address Africa's economic failures. In this book, we synthesize the results of a large body of empirical analysis for Africa and address these issues: do the trade and exchange rate, fiscal, and agricultural sector policy reforms, which many economists advocate, harm the poor?

Africa's economic crisis

Prior to discussing how this book informs this question, we describe first the evolution and magnitude of the economic and social crisis that gripped Africa prior to economic policy reform, and the resulting adjustment programs and policies. During the early 1980s, Africa's acute economic failures increased dramatically. Gross domestic product (GDP) per capita in Africa grew by less than 1 percent from 1979 to 1992, a weak performance similar to that in Latin America and the Middle East. By contrast, growth in South Asia, and especially East Asia and the Pacific, far surpassed that in Africa (Table 1.1). As both a reflection and a consequence of Africa's poor economic performance, exports have stagnated, savings and investment have declined, and

1

Table 1.1. *Annual growth rate of real per capita GDP (%)*

	1972–1978	1979–1985	1986–1989	1990–1992
Sub-Saharan Africa[a]	2.76	0.65	0.79	0.62
South Asia	1.88	2.38	3.09	2.26
East Asia and Pacific	4.41	2.05	5.70	4.75
Latin America and Caribbean	2.33	-1.09	0.54	0.87
Middle East and North Africa	2.40	-0.85	-1.80	2.24

[a]Exclusive of South Africa.
Source: World Bank 1995c.

Table 1.2. *Sub-Saharan African export shares*

Commodities	1975	1980	1985	1990
Share in world export				
All commodities	2.1	2.6	1.5	0.9
Food, live animals, beverages, tobacco	3.8	4.1	3.7	2.2
Crude materials, oils, fats, mineral fuels	4.1	4.8	3.1	2.4
Manufactured goods, machinery,				
transport equipment	0.5	0.9	0.3	0.2
Share in developing countries export				
All commodities	8.8	8.8	5.9	4.0
Food, live animals, beverages, tobacco	21.1	13.3	11.1	8.1
Crude materials, oils, fats, mineral fuels	8.2	9.0	7.7	7.1
Manufactured goods, machinery,				
transport equipment	6.6	7.8	1.7	1.1

Source: United Nations, various years.

labor productivity growth has lagged far behind other developing regions. The weakness of export growth has been due to a lack of diversification into new, competitive industries and a loss of market share for traditional exports. Exports of primary products still represented approximately 80 percent of Africa's exports in the 1980s, as they did in the 1960s, while overall export growth lagged behind other regions of the world. As a consequence, Africa's share of developing country and world exports fell by more than one-half between 1975 and 1990 (Table 1.2). Africa's market share for agricultural and food exports also declined acutely, dropping from 21 to 8.1 percent of developing country exports between 1975 and 1990.[1] By 1990, Africa's share of

[1] As exceptions, Africa's tobacco and tea exports increased their market shares in world exports.

Table 1.3. *Gross domestic investment (% of GDP)*

	1972–1978	1979–1985	1986–1989	1990–1992
Sub-Saharan Africa	24.2	20.7	17.8	16.9
South Asia	18.3	21.6	23.4	23.5
East Asia and the Pacific	25.1	27.6	32.1	33.4
Latin America and the Caribbean	23.8	21.4	20.6	19.6
Middle East and North Africa	27.8	25.4	22.8	25.1
Europe and Central Asia	—	29.8	30.4	28.5
World	24.5	23.2	23.2	22.5

Source: World Bank 1995c.

Table 1.4. *Trends in labor productivity in agriculture*

	Average annual percentage growth		
	1961–1973	1973–1980	1980–1990
Sub-Saharan Africa	0.6	-0.9	0.8
Latin America	1.8	2.8	1.7
South and Southeast Asia	1.3	2.0	1.9

Source: Singh and Tabatabai 1993.

developing country exports of manufactured goods fell to an alarming 1.1 percent, from 7.8 percent in 1980. Investment-to-GDP ratios were comparable with those of East Asia and the Pacific and higher than those of South Asia during the mid-1970s. However, a steady decline in Africa in contrast with the increase in Asia resulted in gross domestic investment as a share of GDP being less than half that of East Asia and the Pacific in 1990–1992, and nearly half that of South Asia (Table 1.3). Likewise, as shown in Table 1.4, growth in labor productivity, particularly in agriculture, lagged behind other regions of the world (Singh and Tabatabai 1993). This slow growth was the result of a decaying physical infrastructure, a failure to adopt new technology, a scarcity of productive inputs, and a depletion of natural resources, all of which were manifestations of low savings rates and misallocated investment.

These discouraging economic trends have a wide array of human consequences. The incidence of poverty rose in Africa during the 1970s, in contrast to other regions of the developing world (Singh and Tabatabai 1993). Improvements in infant mortality, life expectancy, and other measures of health have lagged behind other regions of the developing world during the past two decades (World Bank 1993d). Poverty is widespread and living standards are dismally low: one in ten children dies before his or her first birthday, average life expectancy is only around fifty-three years (UNDP 1993), and the rate of malnourished children persistently remains at 30 percent (ACC/SCN 1992). The human consequences of Africa's dismal economic performance are severe.

The root causes of Africa's economic and social crisis, which in turn led to the adjustment policies we examine in this book, have been the subject of ongoing debate. We will not, however, join that debate in this book. Rather than sort out the role of exogenous shock or domestic policy in precipitating declines in economic performance and living conditions, we address the more narrowly defined question of what happens to Africa's poor when governments pursue orthodox trade and exchange rate, fiscal, and agricultural policy reforms. In adopting this focus, we recognize that most countries embarked on the process of economic reform during the 1980s with financing from the IFIs accompanied by policy conditionality. Capital inflows in the form of policy-based lending increased rapidly during the 1980s, reaching extraordinarily high levels: between 1987 and 1991, net official development assistance and external transfers to the low-income, debt-distressed countries in Africa represented 15.4 percent of the countries' real GDP and 75 percent of real imports (World Bank 1994c). The importance of this aid gives bilateral donors and IFIs considerable clout in the design of policy, although it is not clear how effectively their lending fosters policy reform and, subsequently, economic growth (Husain and Faruqee 1993; Mosley, Harrigan, and Toye 1991). Even less established, however, is the effect of policy change on poverty and income distribution, the issue we address.

Broadly speaking, policy-based conditionality assumes two forms: short-run stabilization attempts to establish internal and external macroeconomic equilibrium and longer-run structural adjustment programs to address structural problems in an economy that underlie macroeconomic disequilibria. The former almost always includes exchange rate devaluation and aggregate demand restraint, especially through reduced fiscal deficits. In practice, these types of stabilization programs are associated with the IMF. The latter involves efforts to liberalize trade and exchange rate policies, improve the efficacy of government spending and tax policies, and free markets for agricultural inputs and products. More efficient resource allocation will engender increased productivity and output in the economy, thus improving internal and external balance. At a more practical level, the distinction between stabilization and structural adjustment is tenuous. Both jointly endeavor to improve the balance between aggregate supply and demand, and each employs similar instruments. For example, devaluation of the local currency will simultaneously reduce excess demand for imports and also permit less restrictive trade policies. While stabilization programs hold the former as an objective, the latter is a key component of an outward-looking, export-oriented growth strategy. Likewise, reductions in public spending associated with stabilization efforts simultaneously reduce budget deficits and release resources for private investment that affects the level and structure of output. Despite this congruence, certain types of policies associated with structural adjustment, like trade reform, may worsen the balance of payments in the short term and make the achievement of macroeconomic stability more difficult. Also, structural adjustment programs certainly are associated with a wider range of reforms (e.g., agricultural market liberalization or privatization of public enterprises) than stabilization efforts. Nonetheless, little is to be gained by pursuing the distinction between stabilization and structural adjustment, particularly in light of the policy-oriented focus of this book. In addition, the three critical policy areas we focus on – trade and exchange rate, fiscal, and agricultural policy – are associated with both stabilization and structural adjustment.

In our analysis, we assess the impact of the individual policies themselves, not the role of the IFIs in promoting them or the effect of adjustment programs in the broader sense of a whole package of policies. Thus, although issues like policy performance – how well governments adhere to loan conditions, and how committed they are to policy change – are important when assessing the role of the IFIs, they fall outside the domain of this study. Instead, we explore the growth and equity effects of observed changes in policy, as well as alternative policies contemplated but not undertaken.

Little consensus exists on the impact of policy reform on African economies in general, and on the poor in particular. Debate over basic questions about the appropriateness of adjustment policies in addressing the balance-of-payments and general economic crisis in many sub-Saharan African countries in the early 1980s is grounded in the disagreement over the cause of Africa's economic crisis. The IFIs and donors argue that failed policy, rather than external shocks, is the main cause of Africa's problems. They further assert that fiscal balance, trade liberalization, and "getting the prices right," particularly in agriculture and the foreign exchange market, are the appropriate and requisite reforms to improve the current account, increase growth and employment, and reduce inflation. Important critics disagree with such assertions. They view policy instruments like exchange rate devaluation as ineffective instruments for promoting exports, with adverse consequences like inflation and a misallocation of foreign exchange (Stewart 1992). Likewise, others believe, indiscriminate import liberalization contributes to the availability of cheap competitive consumer goods, while devaluation drives up the prices of essential inputs and capital goods (Cornia, van der Hoeven, and Lall 1992). Others criticize fiscal balance, seeing it emphasizing too much short-term stabilization measures instead of underlying structural weaknesses (Taylor 1993). Among other negative effects, austerity and declining capital accumulation reduce investment in and diversification of production and prove an obstacle to achieving the intended efficiency gains of adjustment policies.

Critics also see reforms as adversely affecting agriculture, often the most critical and distorted sector of many African economies. Jamal (1993) indicates that liberalization policies, including the elimination of subsidies on fertilizer, adversely affect productivity and hamper the shift from land-abundant to input-intensive agriculture. Similarly, critics have seen price reform as favoring export crops to the detriment of the traditional food crop sector (Stewart 1994). Wagoa (1992) argues that the export crop bias that results from adjustment policies adds to foreign debt arrears that contribute to balance-of-payments vulnerability. At the same time, Cornia (1994) points out that adjustment programs not only neglect critical agricultural issues such as unequal land distribution, but in fact exacerbate the problems by encouraging unconstrained land markets in the expectation that efficient private markets will spontaneously replace traditional tenure systems. Stewart (1994) likewise blames adjustment programs for accelerating deindustrialization by their promotion of wholesale privatization and unfettered markets.[2]

Most relevant to this book and, perhaps, to the bulk of Africa's population, however, is the contention that the adverse effects of adjustment policies fall disproportionately upon the poor (Cornia, Jolly, and Stewart 1987; UNECA 1989). We examine this assertion, an important one for several reasons. First, the early indications that adjustment policies hurt the poor have resonated widely. A widespread perception exists among the nongovernmental organizations and other individuals and institutions whose major concern is with the well-being of the poor that adjustment policies have worsened income distribution and poverty. The sensitivity of the World Bank in particular to such assertions has resulted in two somewhat inconsistent responses: one, numerous efforts to discount such assertions through a wide array of studies and publications; two, the design, implementation, and financing of compensatory programs intended to mitigate the purported social costs of adjustment. Neither the critics of adjustment policies nor their proponents (within and without the IFIs), however, have satisfactorily addressed the fundamental question of how reforms affect the poor.

In part, this failure to deal convincingly with the impact of adjustment policies reflects the fact that public policies rarely have unambiguous effects on economic growth or income distribution. Instead, they are filtered through a variety of social and economic institutions before they reach households. Macroeconomic and sectoral policies, in particular, have complex links with

---

[2] Additionally, critics like Stewart (1992) argue that credit market liberalization has also contributed to deindustrialization. That is, financial sector liberalization contributes to a decrease in credit available to small enterprises (especially in agriculture) with poor credit histories and lack of collateral. Stewart (1992) also sees foreign privatization of parastatals, in situations with insufficient private domestic markets, as leading to adverse domestic outcomes, due to lack of domestic familiarity with new technology.

household-level outcomes. Not only are these policies generally designed to achieve macroeconomic rather than poverty objectives, but the analytical requirements to relate such policy measures to household-level outcomes are great.[3] To understand how a particular adjustment policy affects the poor, we need to trace a complex path accounting for direct and indirect effects. In doing so, we must recognize the mediation of policy change by various economic institutions and account for other exogenous influences before we can understand the distributional and poverty effects, which are our main focus.

For the three policy areas we examine in this book, the pathways that link policy change to income distribution and poverty are perhaps most direct for fiscal policy. Governments spend on economic and social services that households access and enjoy. Likewise, households directly pay various types of taxes or are indirectly affected by levies on products. The underlying concern with fiscal policy reform is that it may result in reduced spending on services received by the poor, decrease their earnings through declines in public employment and official wages, and increase the taxes they pay in the name of reducing deficits (see, e.g., Cornia, van der Hoeven, and Lall 1992). With trade and exchange rate policy, reforms primarily affect the welfare of households as a result of changes in relative prices and in access to rents associated with various sorts of rationing and licensing when prices are controlled. The underlying objective of setting the relative price of tradables (exports and imports) to nontradables (goods and services produced or offered for own-consumption or the domestic market) to be consistent with opportunity costs is to increase the efficiency of resource allocation and thereby to raise output in the economy. Pursuit of such policies, however, increases the prospect of reducing employment and/or lowering wages in previously protected industries and increasing prices of important tradable goods in the consumption bundle of the poor. This prospect has led to the conclusion that such policy measures have adverse social consequences. With agricultural policy, the elimination of food subsidies will supposedly hurt consumers, including many poor households that are net producers of food. Contraction of state marketing agencies will potentially leave poor producers, particularly in remote areas, without access to remunerative prices for their output. At best, critics view the rural poor as not sufficiently engaged in the marketing of their output to benefit from the shifting urban rural terms of trade (Jamal and Weeks 1993). We will examine whether the trade and exchange rate, fiscal, and agricultural policies at the heart of the orthodox approach to structural adjustment inherently harm the poor, either by

---

[3] Even for more direct policy alleviation efforts that are not the subject of this book (e.g., food-for-work projects), determining the effects on households becomes complex because of the changes in labor market conditions, asset ownership, and so forth, that such interventions cause.

reducing aggregate GDP, making the distribution of income more unequal, or reducing the benefits connected to government expenditure.

Research approach

Labels hinder much of the debate on structural adjustment and economic reform, as they often are ideologically based and not sufficiently specific to identify the domain of the discourse. As a result, those examining the impact of adjustment often confuse the prescriptive with the analytical and fail to distinguish the process of adjustment from the state of economic crisis. They forget even what ends are being sought through reform or obscure them among the rhetoric of the debate. We therefore seek to avoid examining "structural adjustment" programs in a generic sense, given the divergent political and ideological connotations of the process and the fact that adjustment programs embody a wide range of policy changes, implemented in dramatically different contexts, in response to a variety of prior conditions. In fact, we would argue that the broad range of policy changes associated with adjustment programs contributes to the dissonance over the impact of such operations. Likewise, the fact that the countries that implement such policies have huge differences in economic structure and preconditions contributes to the confusion over the effect of adjustment programs on poverty. We will therefore be country-specific, focusing our analysis of the effects of trade and exchange rate, fiscal, and agricultural policies on ten countries: Cameroon, The Gambia, Ghana, Guinea, Madagascar, Malawi, Mozambique, Niger, Tanzania, and Zaire. Thus, rather than condoning or condemning "adjustment" in some broad and necessarily abstract sense, this book evaluates the impact of specific policy changes in specific country circumstances. Only after analyzing several different countries will we attempt to arrive at generalizations regarding the impact of specific changes in policy on poverty and income distribution in Africa.

The emphasis that we place on different policies in different contexts varies according to two factors. First, not all policy changes in this book are equally relevant to all the countries we examined. For example, we limit the empirical investigation of the impact of retrenching government workers, discussed in Chapter 4, to Ghana and Guinea, two of the three countries in our sample that substantially reduced the size of the public sector during the late 1980s, when the research was being designed and implemented.[4] Second, data problems precluded constructing certain types of models or examining specific policy questions. For example, in Guinea and Mozambique, the absence of reliable national accounts, an input–output table, and rural household survey data limited our attention to policy impacts on urban households. In addition, such data

---

[4] The third was The Gambia, where lack of survey data prevented research on the topic. See de Merode 1992.

constraints preclude our addressing in a comprehensive and consistent fashion how certain policy changes, such as devaluation of the currency, affect poverty and income distribution in all countries.

The body of research on adjustment policies that this book synthesizes was conducted under a Cornell University study funded largely by the U.S. Agency for International Development (USAID). We intended, in our choice of countries for this study, to cover a wide range of contexts and experiences, although consent of the governments also influenced our selections. The country-specific research was conducted between 1989 to 1993 and consisted of three distinct phases. First, we examined the evolution of the economic crisis and the process of economic policy change and presented descriptive statistics that detail trends in the performance of macroeconomic and market-level outcomes based on accessible information sources. A first compendium volume from this first research project, *Adjusting to Policy Failure in African Economies*,[5] reports on these efforts. Based on this initial assessment of the structure of the economies and nature of the economic distortions, we identified salient policy issues that were (or seemed like they would be) central to the reform process.[6] To address the implications of policy change in these critical areas, we collected and analyzed a variety of survey data and built analytical models to explore the impact of policy change on income distribution and poverty. The first results of our efforts to model the impact of particular policies in a country-case study context are in a second volume, *Economic Reform and the Poor in Africa*.[7] We now build on those previous works and many additional journal articles and working papers to provide a coherent synthesis, organized by policy issues, of the Cornell University research on this theme.[8]

Our approach to research on adjustment policies and poverty differs from previous work in two important ways. First, we attempt to provide a solid microeconomic basis for our macroeconomic conclusions and to establish a coherent analytical link between macroeconomic policies and microeconomic outcomes. We thus rely heavily on a variety of household and enterprise surveys to help us understand the complexities of African economic structures and institutions.[9] There is little solace to be found in the quantity or quality of survey data in Africa. Even when data exist, they are often not publicly available;

---

[5] Sahn 1994.

[6] Changes in the national political situation in Zaire derailed that country's economic reforms and significantly lessened the immediate applicability of our research.

[7] Sahn 1996.

[8] A large number of researchers contributed substantially to the body of knowledge synthesized by the authors herein, as discussed in the acknowledgments. We reference their works throughout.

[9] These data sources include surveys conducted during the course of our research (such as the integrated household surveys in Conakry [Guinea], The Gambia, Maputo [Mozambique], and Tanzania; farm surveys in Ghana and Madagascar; enterprise sur-

when available, they are not necessarily current. Nonetheless, the data available to us do allow extensive analysis of consumer, producer, and market behavior in countries, including issues such as the causes of market failures, the role of parallel markets as the source of consumer goods and the outlet for farmers' commodities, and the distribution of rents associated with rationed goods. Lack of such microeconomic detail can lead to erroneous conclusions about the impact of adjustment policies.

Second, we compare the economic consequences of adopting certain policies rather than alternative policy measures by employing a variety of empirically based analytic tools. Comparison of specific policy measures with specific counterfactuals allows us to distinguish correlation of certain policies and economic outcomes from causation. This approach distinguishes itself from the considerable amount of research on adjustment in Africa that compares a base year with a recent year, notes a decline (increase) in some indicator of living standards, and concludes that "adjustment" caused that decline (increase). Another line of research proceeds in a similar fashion, but uses a base year "before adjustment" to compare with another year "after adjustment." Yet another approach compares adjusting countries' performance, using categories such as strong, weak, and nonadjusting countries, or early, intensive adjusters as compared with late, weak adjusters; those who use this method have arrived at conflicting views on adjustment.[10] All of these approaches treat "adjustment" as an integral entity consistent in their design and intent across countries and fail to account for the fact that many other shocks influence economic performance and the severity of poverty. Furthermore, "before and after" approaches fail to appreciate that most African countries undertake adjustment policies at a time of declining living standards. African governments do not pursue adjustment programs on a whim or on the advice of IFIs. Rather, most are forced to change economic policies by external shocks (often severe) and/or significant economic deterioration brought about by poor domestic policies. These extreme circumstances, which drive countries to reform, surely influence the often unfavorable "before and after" evaluations of adjustment. Our research avoids these analytical errors by evaluating

veys in Tanzania and Conakry; and retrenchment surveys in Ghana and Guinea), as well as existing data bases made available to us (such as the Côte d'Ivoire Living Standards Survey, the Cameroon and Zaire household budget surveys, the Ghana Living Standards Survey, and the Malawi cash-cropping survey). Citation of these surveys throughout this book identifies results of calculations made from data contained therein.

[10] Mosley and Weeks (1993) discuss the many problems of this comparative approach. The radically different assessments such classification has generated are perhaps best exemplified by the contentious interchange between the World Bank and UNDP (1989) and the UNECA (1989).

only policies actually changed, and by examining their impact exclusive of other shocks, positive or negative, in the economies we study. In a phrase, we concentrate on comparing economic outcomes "with or without" policy changes rather than "before and after" any point in time.

By framing our discussion around the impact of policy change, we do not address the importance of noneconomic factors, such as drought, civil strife, resource constraints, and the sociocultural context in determining income distribution and economic performance. In a given context, these factors may be of equal or greater importance than economic policy, the primary domain of this book. Furthermore, by concentrating on the question of the economic impact of alternative policy scenarios, we avoid the distracting, albeit important, issue of implementation. Numerous authors, including internal evaluators of the World Bank, express concern about the failure to actually undertake reform, despite a rhetorical commitment to do so. In examining this failure, a body of literature pays particular attention to the question of how to develop political coalitions in support of reform (see, e.g., Callaghy and Ravenhill 1993; Widner 1994; Haggard and Webb 1994a). Because reform's benefits generally materialize slowly, while its negative effects are usually immediately apparent, adjustment quickly becomes unpopular. Relatively influential and affluent people in particular become critical, as they no longer benefit from rents and poorly targeted government subsidies. As a result, as many country experiences illustrate, conditions to which governments and the international community agree will often subsequently be circumvented or ignored during implementation. Therefore, governments and donors should address the "internalization" and "ownership" issues of policy change at the same time that they weigh its economic impacts.[11]

Although such considerations of the political economy of the reform process are largely outside the purview of this book, they nonetheless imply that there are two equally important aspects of successful policy reform: arriving at the appropriate set of policies to improve growth and reduce poverty and developing the consensus and institutional capacity to ensure their implementation. Through concentrating on the effects of alternative policy design, we inform the former, and do not extensively address the determinants of implementation or the political economy of decision making. Thus, this book will influence the policy-making process to the extent that it changes perceptions about the appropriateness and impact of policy change and, in particular, elucidates winners and losers, thereby possibly altering the ideas in good currency about adjustment policies.

---

[11] For further discussion on the slow pace of policy change, the failure to sustain reforms, and the importance of ownership, see, for example, Gallagher 1991; World Bank 1993a; Husain and Faruqee 1993; and Mosley et al. 1991.

Country context

Although the ten countries we explore in this book differ in many ways, they also share common features that facilitate comparative analysis. The low levels of GNP per capita listed in Table 1.5 suggest the extreme poverty of almost all the countries in the sample, the exception being Cameroon, whose real GNP per capita greatly exceeds those of other countries in this study. Likewise, all the countries export only a few primary products, such as minerals in Cameroon, Guinea, Niger, and Zaire, or a couple of agricultural products in the other countries studied. Agriculture is generally the most important sector of the economy, with more than one-half of the labor force engaged in agriculture in all cases. The level of urbanization is also relatively low, falling below 33 percent of the population in all countries. Growth performance is mixed across periods and among the countries represented (Table 1.6). Noteworthy improvements in growth rates between the early and late 1980s took place in some countries (The Gambia, Ghana, and Tanzania), in contrast to the situation in Cameroon, which witnessed a dramatic decline in its terms of trade in 1986. Overall, terms of trade for the countries studied have fallen quite markedly in the 1980s and 1990s, compared with those in the 1970s. Figures on social indicators make clear the level of human deprivation in the countries examined (Table 1.7). Life expectancy at birth remains only fifty-two, lower than any other region of the world. Infant mortality rates range from 64 per 1,000 in Cameroon to 148 in Mozambique, high levels that in part reflect problems like low adult literacy, inadequate primary health care, and lack of access to safe water. Nonetheless, a decline in infant mortality occurred during the 1980s in all countries for which data are available, despite the poor overall economic performance. Analysts often explain the apparently anomalous improvement in these social indicators concurrent with poor economic performance by the success of targeted interventions such as oral rehydration, low-cost hand pumps, and improved immunization coverage. Other explanations include past investments in social infrastructure that is only partly eroded when economies perform poorly and the questionable quality of both the economic and social indicators available.

Although we extensively discuss trade and exchange rate, fiscal, and agricultural reforms in the following chapters, it is nonetheless worth highlighting the wide range of the adjustment experience and the context in which the countries in this book have undertaken reform. Cameroon's per capita GDP, as indicated earlier, is substantially higher than all the other countries in our study. Some social indicators reflect this fact: infant mortality, for example, declined markedly during and after the rapid economic growth of the early 1980s, resulting in Cameroon having the lowest level of infant mortality among the countries in the sample. Other indicators of living standards in Cameroon are also relatively high; 78 percent of the population, for example, has access to sanitary facilities.

Although the country's abundant, high-quality land resource base has certainly contributed to its relative economic success, Cameroon's economic standing is largely due to its position as an oil exporter. Oil accounts for over 60 percent of the total exports. A further important characteristic of Cameroon is its membership in the CFA (Communauté Financière Africaine) zone. Prior to the devaluation of the CFA in 1994, Cameroon was unable to use the exchange rate as a policy instrument and, as such, was forced to rely on fiscal austerity in order to address unsustainable account imbalances when oil prices plummeted.

Niger is the other country we study in detail that belongs to the CFA zone. It relied heavily on fiscal austerity to cope with the particularly adverse terms-of-trade shocks of the 1980s that followed a period of excessive and unsustainable government borrowing. Heightened vulnerability to this shock, as in Cameroon, came from Niger's extreme reliance on exports of a single product, in this case uranium, which comprised approximately two-thirds of the country's total export value. Beyond these commonalities, few others exist between Niger, the only Sahelian country included in this study, and its much wealthier neighbor, Cameroon. The scarcity of arable land in Niger, a reliance on livestock, as well as sizable economic impacts of frequent policy changes by its large and unpredictable neighbor, Nigeria, are also distinguishing characteristics. Niger's social indicators are far worse than Cameroon's and generally fall below the mean for sub-Saharan Africa as a whole.

Guinea, another West African nation that once used the CFA franc, quit the CFA zone at independence. Like Cameroon and Niger, it depends highly upon the export of nonagricultural products, with bauxite and alumina composing nearly three-quarters of total exports. Guinea's early abandonment of the CFA meant greater autonomy over monetary and exchange rate policy. In practice, this freedom resulted in acute distortions that contributed to the virtual collapse of the economy, with the exception of the export enclave of bauxite and alumina, which remained under the control of transnational corporations. The disincentive to produce for the market and the barriers to trade were in part manifested in a return to reliance on subsistence, particularly in the area of food production, where three-quarters of the labor force is engaged. This concentration of the labor force in agriculture contrasts with the fact that agriculture composes less than 15 percent of the country's exports and less than one-quarter of GDP. Excessive state controls, rent seeking, and severe price distortions contributed to the collapse of commercial agriculture, an extremely narrow tax base, and the inability to meet even the most modest expectations in terms of the provision of public goods and essential social and economic services. When reform finally began in the mid-1980s, it was swift and dramatic, particularly in its impact on the real exchange rate. Likewise, Guinea embarked on a relatively serious effort to reduce the size of the public sector payroll and to eliminate many parastatal institutions. Nonetheless, the legacy of prior pol-

14

Table 1.5. *Summary of economic indicators (most recent year available)*

Country	Population (midyear) in thousands 1992	GNP per capita (US$) 1992	Exports as % of GDP 1991	Major exports 1991	Major exports as share of total 1991[a]	Agriculture as % of GDP 1992	% of labor force in agriculture 1992	Urban population as % of total 1992
Cameroon	12,198	820	11.0	Crude oil Cocoa Coffee	60.6 11.8 11.2	22.3	53.0	42.0
Gambia	908	370	45.1	Groundnut products Fish Cotton	11.3 2.6 0.2	20.4	81.0	24.0
Ghana	15,959	450	16.0	Cocoa & products Gold Timber	26.6 39.6 13.3	42.5	52.0	35.0
Guinea	6,116	510	15.0 23.7	Bauxite Alumina Diamonds	55.2 17.6 10.8	24.4	75.0	27.0
Madagascar	12,827	230	14.0	Coffee Vanilla Cloves	9.2 15.1 7.5	33.3	77.0	25.0
Malawi	10,356	220	24.0	Tobacco Tea Sugar	75.6 8.0 6.2	28.3	73.0	12.0

Mozambique	14,872	70	21.6	Shrimps Cashew nuts Cotton	37.4 9.9 5.4	32.3	82.0	30.0
Niger	8,252	280	17.0	Uranium Live animals Cowpeas	66.2 12.0 2.2	38.8	87.0	19.0
Tanzania	27,829	110	18.0	Coffee Cotton Manufacturers	23.1 18.8 18.5	61.4	81.0	22.0
Zaire	39,882	203	10.4	Copper Cobalt Diamonds	35.8 18.0 12.9	44.5	62.0	29.0
Africa (w/o S. Africa)	641,044	482	25.9	—	—	—	64.0	29.0
Africa (w/ S. Africa)	680,944	530	26.0	—	—	21.0	—	—

*Data for Cameroon, Ghana, and Guinea are from 1990, 1993, and 1992, respectively.
Sources: World Bank 1993d, 1994c; IMF 1993a, 1994a, 1994b, 1994c; UNDP 1993.

Table 1.6. *Growth rates and the evolution of terms of trade*

Country	Average GDP growth rate[a]				Terms of trade (1987=100)[b]		
	1972–1978	1979–1985	1986–1989	1990–1992	1972–1978	1979–1985	1986–1989
Cameroon	6.5	9.4	-0.7	-6.3	165	147	92
Gambia	5.3	4.7	3.8	2.9	170	120	108
Ghana	0.3	-0.1	5.0	4.0	136	112	95
Guinea	–	–	4.0	3.3	150	138	99
Madagascar	-0.6	0.4	2.7	-0.9	114	94	110
Malawi	5.9	2.3	2.3	1.0	170	131	102
Mozambique	–	-3.2	4.3	-0.7	–	91	92
Niger	-0.1	-0.6	1.4	0.5	160	124	121
Tanzania	3.5	1.3	6.5	4.1	127	106	101
Zaire	-0.5	1.6	1.5	-6.7	165	119	111
Sub-Saharan Africa	3.4	1.9	2.8	0.5	135	117	101

[a]Data for The Gambia 1990–1991 only; for Guinea 1987–1989 only; and for Mozambique 1981–1985 only.
[b]Data for Mozambique are an average of 1980 and 1985 only.
Source: World Bank 1994c.

Table 1.7. *Summary of social indicators*

Country	Infant mortality rate (per thousand) 1980–1982	1990–1991	Vaccination coverage 1980–1982	1990–1992	Adult literacy rate (%) 1992	Life expectancy 1992	Population with access to medical services 1985–1991	Population with access to safe water (%) 1988–1991
Cameroon	91	65	12	50	57	56	41	54
Gambia	157	135	80	92	30	45	90	77
Ghana	99	84	25	55	63	56	60	54
Guinea	159	137	46	41	27	44	40	64
Madagascar	134	115	21	47	81	51	65	20
Malawi	166	146	63	85	45	44	80	53
Mozambique	154	150	36	52	34	44	39	24
Niger	148	127	15	24	31	46	30	55
Tanzania	120	115	62	84	55	51	80	51
Zaire	112	97	–	–	74	52	40	33
Africa[a]	128	106	36	61	53	52	59	45

[a]Excluding South Africa.

Sources: Berg et al. 1994 for infant mortality and vaccination data; UNDP 1993 and World Bank 1994c for rest of table.

icy failures manifests itself in high infant mortality and low adult literacy levels, and in a relatively slow rate of improvement in those levels.

The effort at economic reform in Guinea's West African neighbor, Ghana, was dramatic and shared many characteristics. Perhaps most visibly similar was the massive devaluation of the local currency after a virtual collapse of much of the formal economy. Ghana, like Guinea, also undertook important measures to retrench public sector workers. The Ghanaian economy, however, differs in many important respects from Guinea, and so too responded more positively to the reforms instituted, as witnessed by the rate of economic growth during the latter half of the 1980s and the early 1990s. For example, in addition to having a substantially larger population, agriculture represents a much higher share of GDP in Ghana, and an agricultural export, cocoa, is an important source of incomes and export earnings. Although Ghana suffered from the decline in world prices for cocoa in the late 1980s, economic hardship was offset by increases in foreign capital inflows from donors and the international financial institutions. Ghana's social indicators are much better than Guinea's, with the adult literacy rate nearly two times higher and the infant death rate nearly one-half less.

The Gambia is the final West African country in our sample. It is distinguished by its small size (less than one million inhabitants in 1992) and its heavy involvement in reexports to its inland neighbors, particularly Senegal, as well as exports of domestically produced groundnuts. As a consequence, exports are a much higher share of GDP in The Gambia than in other countries in the sample. This export dependence probably contributes to the fact that, unlike Ghana and Guinea, The Gambia never allowed its exchange rate to get radically out of line. Since embarking on its economic recovery program, The Gambia's growth performance has strengthened. The improvement in its terms of trade during the early 1990s undoubtedly played a role in this. When one examines a range of social indicators in The Gambia, however, the only encouraging figures are the high vaccination coverage and access to health services. These numbers, unfortunately, have not translated into better health outcomes: infant mortality is high at 135 per 1,000, even after having fallen by 8.7 percent during the latter half of the 1980s.

Mozambique and Malawi are the two southern African countries in our sample. In each, approximately three-quarters of the labor force is engaged in agriculture, which represents around one-third of GDP, and the infant mortality rates in the two countries are the highest among the sample countries highlighted in this book, with little improvement noted during the past decade. Beyond these facts, the contrast between these two countries is quite striking. Mozambique is sparsely populated, with abundant land resources and excellent harbors. Years of destructive civil war, however, have had harsh consequences for the economy, infrastructure, and well-being of the Mozambican population. Malawi, by contrast, is a landlocked country characterized by acute land scarcity and a long period of political stability under authoritarian rule. Perhaps the most important contrasts between Mozambique and Malawi, however, exist in the area of economic policy. Until the recent efforts at economic reform, the socialist state in Mozambique assumed a prominent role in a controlled economy, investing in state farms and factories, rationing their output, and maintaining a grossly overvalued exchange rate that completely discouraged any private sector exports through official channels. By contrast, Malawi's exchange rate was one of the least overvalued in Africa since independence. Furthermore, relative to most other countries in Africa, Malawi's fiscal policy has been restrained. The state, however, was extensively involved in promulgating a legal and regulatory framework that fostered the growth of a dualistic agricultural sector where favored outward-looking estates existed in conjunction with a smallholder sector against which there was heavy discrimination. In Malawi, as in Mozambique, the actions of the parastatal grain marketing agency contributed to high levels of taxation for traditional agriculture and endeavored to ensure low and stable prices to maize consumers, particularly in urban areas. However, the controls and restrictions on marketing were much less severe and distortionary in Malawi. These differences meant that policy changes made in Mozambique were much more dramatic than in Malawi, where the economic crisis was not so severe and the reform measures adopted were not such abrupt departures from past economic policies. This was particularly true in the area of trade and exchange rate reforms, but also applied to fiscal and agricultural policies.

Like its neighbors Malawi and Mozambique, Tanzania has a history of extensive parastatal involvement in both its staple commodity, maize, and in export crop marketing. And the country relies heavily on agriculture as a source of employment and export earnings. Like Malawi, Tanzania has been politically stable, although the state's socialist policies led to considerably greater economic distortions. Like Ghana and Guinea, exchange rate controls in Tanzania contributed to extensive overvaluation and rationing and to large-scale diversion of economic activity, particularly exporting, from official to parallel markets. And as in Guinea and Mozambique, efforts to collectivize agriculture failed and contributed to food insecurity and shortages. Tanzania, however, received exceptional donor financial support, despite the most egregious economic distortions and a protracted period through the mid-1980s lacking in strong commitment to economic reform. Nonetheless there have been some signs of improvement in the late 1980s and early 1990s. Despite the government's historical emphasis on promoting social development in Tanzania, performance as measured in social indicators is at best mixed relative to other countries in the sample. For example, adult literacy and access to safe water are only slightly above 50 percent. While vaccination coverage is 85 percent and access to health services is also high at 80 percent, infant mortality remains at 115 deaths per 1,000 births, a figure that improved little during the period of economic stagnation in the 1980s.

Madagascar, an island nation of nearly thirteen million inhabitants, is anomalous in that its rice economy is in many ways more similar to southern Asia than to the African continent. Traditional paddy farmers predominate, owning and cultivating the vast majority of the land. However, the country's GDP growth rates and levels of social indicators are similar to its continental neighbors. Like Guinea, Madagascar once belonged to the CFA zone and withdrew over differences with the French. From an economic policy perspective, perhaps the most important events occurred in the late 1970s, when the push toward socialism brought increasing state controls and state involvement in the economy. Like Cameroon, and to a lesser extent The Gambia and Niger, Madagascar borrowed heavily in foreign commercial credit markets in order to finance a surge in public and parastatal investment. This infusion of foreign capital failed to yield high returns. The borrowing, however, saddled the country with a significant debt burden and no means to pay it off when prices of its major exports declined and world capital markets tightened. After a protracted period of gradual economic reforms and declining per capita incomes, Madagascar experienced positive real GDP per capita growth in 1989 and 1990, only to suffer declines again in the early 1990s when political instability led to policy reversals and reduced capital inflows. Still one of Africa's poorest countries, social service provision remains low, as exemplified by extremely low rates of vaccination coverage and access to safe water and sanitary facilities.

We included Zaire in our research, the final of our ten sample countries, in part due to its size, with its population of forty million inhabitants second only to Nigeria in Africa. It also arguably has the greatest water, land, and forest endowment in sub-Saharan Africa. Furthermore, in the mid-1980s there were early signs of progress on the reform agenda, a fact overshadowed by the economic anarchy and political disintegration that gripped Zaire in the first half of the 1990s. While the state's fiscal excess was clearly the most detrimental to economic and social outcomes, there was failure to reform the policy framework of virtually all aspects of the economy. Nonetheless, we do endeavor to glean some lessons from a country where, despite its overwhelming dependence on mineral exports, agriculture, although long neglected, remains the backbone of the economy, vital to the needs of the poor. Likewise, some lessons emerge from Zaire's complete failure to control public expenditure and reign in money creation. This fiscal irresponsibility lies at the heart of Zaire's other policy failures, including an overvalued exchange rate, the decimation of physical infrastructure, the collapse of the formal financial sector, and the corruption of public enterprises, which at best serve a small group of politically powerful interests.

The distinctive and diverse nature of countries in this book provides the basis for generalizations about the impact of policy changes as applied in differing circumstances, especially countries' economic structures and their situation prior to policy changes. We examine whether specific types of policy reforms, applied in different contexts, further imperil the poor and vulnerable and why (or why not). Our approach, we believe, provides the correct basis for arriving at recommendations for future efforts to promote economic reform and reduce poverty. Nonetheless, in relying heavily on case studies and then synthesizing results across countries to arrive at generalizable conclusions, we recognize that particular experiences in other African countries may not be consistent with our general findings.

Organization of the book

We organize the remainder of this book as follows. In Chapter 2, we discuss the most salient features of poverty in Africa, giving a description largely based on household data. By profiling the poor, we provide the context for understanding how various policy changes affect the well-being of the poor. Furthermore, characterizing the poor prior to discussing policy is in keeping with the microeconomic, "bottom-up" approach to our research: it is necessary to understand how the poor earn their income, gain access to basic needs, and allocate their expenditures. In Chapter 3, we then discuss the effect of trade and exchange rate reform on household welfare. We use empirically based models to capture the complex paths from policy reforms to household welfare. These models capture shifts in household consumption, factor utilization, earning behavior, and so forth, in response to policies that alter relative prices and contribute to a reduction and redistribution of rents, which were characteristic of most prereform regimes that engaged in foreign exchange rationing. The subject of Chapter 4 is the effect of economic reforms on the state's role in collecting revenues and providing economic and social services and employment. Fiscal imbalances must be addressed, but the question arises of whether prudent fiscal policy threatens the poor. In particular, we focus on the degree to which changes in patterns of taxation and expenditures jeopardize vulnerable groups in society. Chapter 5 focuses on reforms in agricultural input and product markets. Sectoral reforms in agriculture, especially those that alter incentive structures and realign prices, are key components of many adjustment programs. We examine how such market liberalization affects the poor as mediated by the prices paid by consumers and received by producers of both domestic food products and export crops. We also discuss the income distribution effects of such changes. Finally, Chapter 6 presents a brief summary and conclusions, including implications for the future development agenda in Africa.

2

Poverty in Africa

Assessing the impact of adjustment policies on Africa's poor requires an understanding of the context in which such reforms take place. In this chapter, we set the stage for the remainder of the book by discussing different approaches to defining poverty. Next, we present some generalizations about the nature and characteristics of poverty in Africa, derived from household survey data.

Defining the poor

Poverty has many manifestations, including high rates of infant mortality, low levels of literacy, and limited access to safe water and medical facilities. The figures in Table 1.7 reinforce the deplorable conditions much of Africa's population confronts and show poverty's multifaceted nature. Since it is not possible to capture all these indicators of living standards in a single measure, we employ low or inadequate consumption per capita as the primary indicator of poverty. Consumption expenditure is generally acknowledged to be the best available measure of utility since it is the closest approximation to the concept of permanent income. The use of consumption to rank household well-being is consistent with a "welfarist" definition of poverty, where it is measured in terms of money-metric utility.[1]

Broadly speaking, there are two methods for defining a poverty line and thus differentiating between the poor and nonpoor. One method is commonly referred to as the "absolute" approach. The poor are those who, given the con-

---

[1] Implicitly, welfarist measures (i.e., money metric utility) assume that all individuals have identical utility functions, in contrast with a nonwelfarist definition of poverty, where preferences and behavior of households, such as use and availability of nonmarket goods, determine outcomes such as nutrition and health. See Deaton and Muellbauer 1980 for a discussion of these and other issues pertaining to the measurement of welfare.

sumption patterns in their society, are unable to afford essentials, such as adequate nourishment, deemed necessary for full and active participation in society.[2] Alternatively, the "relative" definition of poverty defines the poor as the segment of the population below some arbitrarily defined cutoff, such as the bottom quintile of the income or expenditure distribution, or an income level that is 30 percent of the median. Here, the standard of comparison is the higher welfare of other members of society. Using a relative poverty measure has an important advantage: it dispenses with the many subjective and political judgments that need to be made in designating a bundle of basic needs.

The major shortcoming in relying on relative poverty measures is that it precludes poverty comparisons across countries. Indeed, this type of comparison is of interest and has been attempted elsewhere. The most analytically rigorous attempt was the recent estimation of the population living on less than one dollar per person per day for sub-Saharan African countries where there was sufficient data (Chen, Datt, and Ravallion 1993). We find these results interesting (Table 2.1) in their indication of the general magnitude of deprivation in terms that are readily accessible and understandable: over half the population in the countries examined consumes less than one dollar per person per day. We would argue, however, that cross-country comparisons require a fair amount of caution in interpretation. We question, for example, the finding that the share of the population that is poor in Ghana is only slightly greater than in Botswana, and that in Kenya, the incidence of poverty is twice that in Ghana. In light of the difficulty and inherent inaccuracy in defining comparable poverty lines across different populations, we resort primarily to relative measures, acknowledging fully, for example, that the poor in Cameroon may be less deprived in terms of an objective indicator of basic needs (such as dollars per capita calorie intake or quality of shelter) than the poor in Zaire.

In relying primarily on relative definitions of poverty, we also often group households by socioeconomic characteristics in order to develop functional classifications of poor and nonpoor households. In this case, various groups of households, such as small producers in the Savannah, or nonwage workers in the city, are classified as poor, while other groups (e.g., urban civil services workers) are classified as nonpoor. Although welfare varies considerably within groups designated as poor or nonpoor, the group's expenditures are generally lower than households or individuals in alternative socioeconomic groups (e.g., urban formal-sector wage workers). In practice, the challenge is to divide the population into relatively homogeneous functional groups (with some being defined as poor and others nonpoor) and thereafter to determine how policy change affects the income of these groups. This categorization by functional groups is particularly appropriate with groups that share common

[2] See Greer and Thorbecke 1986; Ravallion 1994.

Table 2.1 *Population living on less than one dollar per person per day in sub-Saharan Africa in 1990*

Country	Population (million)		Percentage
	Total	With less than $1/day	
Botswana	1.3	0.2	15.42
Ghana	14.9	3.0	20.44
Tanzania	24.5	10.8	44.16
Zimbabwe	9.8	3.9	39.71
Kenya	24.2	10.4	42.92
Uganda	16.3	11.3	69.17
Mauritania	2.0	0.6	30.22
Senegal	7.4	4.2	56.19
Côte d'Ivoire	11.9	2.4	20.17
Ethiopia	51.2	35.4	69.13
Zambia	8.1	6.8	84.88
Rwanda	7.1	5.4	76.41
Guinea-Bissau	1.0	0.7	75.68
Lesotho	1.8	0.7	40.87
All survey countries	181.3	95.9	52.89
Sub-Saharan Africa	475.3	251.4	52.89

Source: Chen, Datt, and Ravallion 1993.

characteristics – for example, small-subsistence producers, or export crop producers specializing in a particular crop with similar sources of income, asset ownership, and income levels. Defining functional groups in this way allows them to be incorporated into economic models designed to analyze the impact on the poor of adjustment policies, such as trade and exchange rate reforms and certain agricultural liberalization policies. We use this approach extensively in Chapters 4 and 5, where we discuss the nature of the socioeconomic groups represented in computable general equilibrium and multimarket models in some detail.

In focusing on the impact of adjustment policies on the poor, we examine outcomes in terms of changes both in their incomes and in income distribution. Our concern with equity, as well as poverty, emanates from, first, the important distributional effects of many adjustment policies discussed in this book. Regardless of growth, changes in income distribution that result from reform will have an impact on poverty. Second, inequality is a serious problem in Africa. This is clearly shown in the high Gini coefficients for fifteen African countries reported in Table 2.2. Among nine of the fifteen entries, the Ginis

Table 2.2. *Gini index for selected African countries*

Country	Period	Gini index (%)
Botswana	1985/1986	54.6
Côte d'Ivoire	1985	44.7
Côte d'Ivoire	1988	34.6
Ethiopia	1981/1982	32.6
Ghana	1987/1988	35.9
Ghana	1988/1989	36.9
Guinea-Bissau	1991	56.2
Kenya	1981/1982	57.5
Kenya	1992	54.4
Lethoso	1986/1987	56.2
Malawi	1992	65.0
Nigeria	1985	39.0
Nigeria	1992	44.0
Rwanda	1984	28.9
Senegal	1991	54.1
Tanzania	1991	59.2
Uganda	1989/1990	33.0
Zambia	1991	43.5
Zimbabwe	1990/1991	56.9

Sources: Sen 1994; World Bank 1995a.

are greater than 50, and only in seven countries are the coefficients less than 40. Overall, therefore, Africa is a continent with substantially higher inequality than Asia, although similar to that found in Latin America. But of even greater importance is, third, that the impact of a policy change on the poor will be determined not only by the rate of growth, but how income distribution changes as a result of reform. Studies confirm that growth leads to poverty reduction; they also indicate a wide range in the responsiveness of poverty to growth (Fields 1989; Lipton and Ravallion 1995; Bruno, Ravallion, and Squire 1995). Thus, both the initial level of growth and income distribution, and how they are affected by policy change, are critical determinants of the impact of economic reform.

Although we do address interhousehold income inequality, we do not address inequality within the household. That is, throughout this book we generally focus on the impact of policy reform on household poverty, not accounting for intrahousehold allocation. Collective models of the household where decision makers have different preferences, and where there is not a unique household welfare index to be interpreted as a utility function, clearly are incompatible with the unitary model generally employed in this book.[3] Thus, to the extent that intrahousehold inequalities differ in types of households or household groups, ranking of households by per capita expenditures may not be identical to rankings derived from individual-level consumption information. While we acknowledge this drawback, availability of data and analytical tractability focus our attention on measuring the welfare of household units.

Characteristics of the poor

Striving to identify features of poor households and understanding why people are poor in Africa are necessary in understanding the impact of policy change on poverty. Household survey data, not aggregate statistics such as infant mortality rates and incidence of malnutrition, serve as the basis for characterizing the poor. Both the quality and quantity of such survey data remain limited in Africa, despite recent initiatives to address this deficiency.[4] In light of the paucity of reliable, comprehensive, and representative surveys from a large number, or even necessarily a representative sample, of countries, we present broad generalizations based on the available household data that are consistent with less quantifiable observations in other countries.

Poverty profiles in a number of African countries show that poverty is concentrated among larger households, polygamous households, refugees, households where the head is older, and households with high dependency ratios.[5] These characteristics are not directly relevant, however, in determining how the policy issues discussed in this book will impact income distribution and household welfare, although they are noteworthy and certainly relevant to the design of targeted transfer and poverty alleviation schemes and the provision of social services such as family spacing programs. Of greater concern, particularly in the realm of fiscal policy reforms, is that poor households characteristically are composed of persons with lower educational attainment and have limited access to clean water, sanitation facilities, and health services, both curative and preventive.

Other characteristics of the poor are more important in determining the differential impact of economic reforms, such as the gender of the head of household and the share of income accruing to women. While these factors that

---

[3] For a fuller treatment of alternative models of the household, see Folbre 1986 and Alderman, Canagarajah, and Younger 1995.

[4] Most prominent among them is the World Bank's Living Standards Measurement Survey Program and the Social Dimensions of Adjustment Project.

[5] For examples of poverty profiles from which these generalizations derive, see Lynch 1991 for Cameroon; Glewwe 1988 for Côte D'Ivoire; Jabara, Lundberg, and Jallow 1992 for The Gambia; Boateng, et al. (n.d.) for Ghana; del Ninno 1994 for Guinea; Mukui 1994 for Kenya; Sahn and del Ninno 1994 for Mozambique; World Bank 1993c for Uganda; and Tabatabai 1993 for Zaire.

Table 2.3. *Regional distribution of poor households for selected countries*

	Share of the national poverty		
	Urban/large	Urban/small	Rural
		(%)	
Cameroon	12.5	0.0	87.5
Côte d'Ivoire (1985–1986)	6.7	17.0	76.3
Côte d'Ivoire (1987–1988)	4.6	16.9	78.5
Gambia	34.0^a	—	66.0
Ghana (1989)	4.7	19.5	75.8
Ghana (1992)	6.0	22.0	72.0
Guinea-Bissau	14.0^a	—	86.0
Kenya	10.0^a	—	90.0
Lesotho	7.5	2.5	90.0
Madagascar	7.3	4.4	88.2
Malawi	2.0	0.0	98.0
Tanzania	2.9	7.3	89.8
Uganda	8.0^a	—	92.0
Zambia	2.0^a	—	71.0

^{a}All urban is included under urban/large when no breakdown between large and small cities is available.

Sources: Cameroon: Lynch 1991; Côte d'Ivoire: Government of Côte d'Ivoire 1985; Gambia, Guinea-Bissau, Kenya, and Zambia: World Bank 1994b; Ghana: World Bank 1995d; Lesotho: World Bank 1994a; Madagascar: Dorosh, Bernier, and Sarris 1990; Malawi: World Bank 1990; Tanzania: Tinios et al. 1994; Uganda: World Bank 1993c.

impoverish and disempower women are generally not caused by economic reforms, they are nonetheless distinguishing characteristics of the poor, and will therefore condition the welfare impact of adjustment measures.

Issues such as where the poor live and how they earn their income are most pertinent, however, to evaluating the broad range of policies associated with adjustment programs and how they affect household incomes. Perhaps the most striking feature of Africa's poor is that they are predominantly rural. Table 2.3 shows the distribution of the poor between the urban and rural areas, where the poor are defined in terms of being in the bottom end of the per capita expenditure distribution.[6] In most countries, the share of the poor in rural areas

---

[6] All these numbers are derived from household survey data, although the cutoff points used for the poverty line differ. Using these data for cross-country comparisons would

Table 2.4. *Incidence of households that are poor, by region in selected African countries*

Country	Urban/large	Urban/small	Rural
		(%)	
Cameroon	1.5	29.5	48.7
Côte d'Ivoire (1985–1986)	1.0	2.3	57.4
Côte d'Ivoire (1987–1988)	1.4	31.7	51.2
Gambia	51.0[a]	–	66.0
Ghana (1989)	21.9	33.7	46.7
Ghana (1992)	23.0	28.1	33.9
Guinea-Bissau	25.0	23.0	58.0
Kenya	20.0[a]	–	41.0
Lesotho	28.1	26.8	54.0
Madagascar	18.0	26.0	37.0
Malawi	10.0[a]	–	63.0
Tanzania	26.5	34.6	59.3
Uganda	38.0[a]	–	57.0
Zaire	32.1[a]	–	75.6
Zambia	25.0[a]	–	73.0

[a] All urban is included under urban/large, as no breakdown of large and small cities is available.

Sources: Cameroon: Lynch 1991; Côte d'Ivoire: Grootaert 1995; Gambia, Guinea-Bissau, Kenya, and Zambia: World Bank 1994b; Ghana: World Bank 1995d; Lesotho: World Bank 1994a; Madagascar: Dorosh, Bernier, and Sarris 1990; Malawi: World Bank 1990; Tanzania: Tinios et al. 1994; Uganda: World Bank 1993c; Zaire: Tabatabai (1993).

is 80 percent or more, while the lowest share represented, two-thirds, is in The Gambia. The overwhelming share of the poor residing in rural areas results from two factors: the relatively low share of the population in urban areas, and the considerably higher incidence of poverty in rural as compared with urban areas. Table 2.4 portrays this latter point by showing, for example, that the incidence of poverty in Douala and Yaoundé is only 1.5 percent, rising to 48.7 percent in rural areas of Cameroon. In Malawi, the poverty incidence increases more than sixfold between Lilongwe and the countryside.[7]

> therefore be especially inappropriate. The household survey data do, however, permit accurate comparisons of the poverty incidence across regions within a country.
>
> [7] One cautionary note is that we base many of the comparisons in Table 2.4 on expenditures that are not deflated across regions owing to the lack of regional deflators. In many instances, we would expect this to overstate the difference between rural and urban poverty incidence.

Table 2.5. *Real agriculture GDP per capita index (1987 prices, 1980–1982 average = 100)*

Country	1975–1977	1980–1982	1989–1991
Cameroon	81	100	75
Gambia	102	100	75
Ghana	94	100	81
Guinea	—	100[a]	98
Madagascar	115	100	96
Malawi	110	100	92
Mozambique	—	100	88
Niger	100	100	89
Tanzania	114	100	102
Zaire	108	100	98
Unweighted average[b]	103	100	89

[a]For Guinea, 1986=100.
[b]Exclusive of South Africa.
Source: World Bank 1994d.

Since the poor are concentrated in rural areas, the impact of adjustment on poverty is still mostly determined by what happens to rural smallholders and the rural self-employed outside of agriculture, whose welfare is linked closely with the performance of, and incentive structure in, agriculture. However, rapid rural-to-urban migration will no doubt alter this poverty profile in the years ahead. Combined with the fact that political economy factors would dictate that governments and donors cannot ignore a widespread decline in urban income as a result of reforms, we thus also carefully consider how urban households, both rich and poor, will be impacted by the process of adjustment.

Rural poor

In the years of economic stagnation that precipitated the need for adjustment, the agricultural sector's weak performance was an underlying cause of stagnating incomes that contribute to persistent rural poverty. Table 2.5 shows that, exclusive of South Africa, agriculture GDP per capita has been declining since the mid-1970s. The failure of agriculture is further manifested in the fact that per capita food production has been falling in eight of the ten countries studied (Table 2.6). Although there is considerable variation between countries, and data on food production and agriculture in Africa are of poor quality, there seems little doubt that the weak performance of agriculture, coupled with a population growth of nearly 3 percent, has left rural incomes stagnant at best in the preadjustment years. As we discuss in Chapter 5, this picture has not been altered appreciably by efforts at economic reform.

Table 2.6. *Food production per capita index (1980–1982 average = 100)*

	1964–1966	1980–1982	1988–1990
Cameroon	113	100	91
Gambia	133	100	82
Ghana	120	100	97
Guinea	98	100	102
Madagascar	107	100	96
Malawi	102	100	92
Mozambique	116	100	96
Niger	92	100	115
Tanzania	107	100	96
Zaire	105	100	97
Unweighted average	109	100	96

Source: World Bank 1993b.

There are many reasons why agriculture has failed to perform the vital role as a leading sector in Africa's economic development. The proximate cause is the failure, despite growing resource constraints, to adopt yield-increasing agricultural technologies. Instead, most increases in agricultural output have been a result of land extensification (Cleaver and Donovan 1994). More importantly, the poor performance of agriculture and the absence of technological innovation reflect failed policy. This failure applies to the absence of enabling investments by the state, but also the discriminating pricing and marketing policies discussed in Chapter 5 that discouraged private sector agents from adapting improved technologies.[8]

Beyond the stagnation of output, the lack of technological change in Africa has had three additional consequences. First, Africa's agriculture is characterized by a relatively low level of commercialization and, as a corollary, is highly subsistent. Table 2.7 illustrates this characteristic by showing the poor's share of food consumption (which generally averages two-thirds of the total value of expenditures) that is in the form of consumption of own-production. These figures show that the rural poor rely relatively little on marketing and commercial agriculture and are largely insulated from the market in their role as consumers. Nonetheless, prices do matter, particularly in light of the important role that agriculture plays in determining rural incomes, as will be discussed further.

---

[8] For a discussion of the role of the state in fostering technological change through an improved policy framework and agricultural research, see Mellor, Delgado, and Blackie 1987.

Table 2.7. *Share of expenditures on food among the rural poor in selected countries*

Country/region	Total food share	% food home produced	% food purchased
Côte d'Ivoire			
Forest	0.65	60	40
Savannah	0.70	63	37
Ghana			
Forest	0.72	51	49
Savannah	0.73	70	30
Madagascar			
Coast	0.59	86	14
Plateau	0.65	86	14
South	0.62	87	13
Malawi			
South	0.62	61	39
Gambia			
Regional	0.63	31	69
Tanzania			
All	0.71	51	49

Source: Dorosh and Sahn 1993.

A second important consequence of the lower level of commercialization of agriculture is that the poor, with their generally smaller holdings and fewer productive assets, are not likely to use any modern inputs, particularly fertilizer. In fact, data from 1980 indicate that fertilizer use per hectare of arable land in Africa was only 90 kilograms per hectare in Africa, in contrast to 743 in India and 2,777 in China (Cleaver and Donovan 1994).

Third, few forward and backward linkages exist between agriculture and the rest of the economy. More specifically, Haggblade, Hazell, and Brown (1989) find that rural agricultural growth multipliers are only 60 percent the level observed in Asia. In part, this finding is explained by agroclimatic conditions that preclude cost-effective irrigation on a scale seen in Asia. In addition, factors such as Africa's lower population density limit scale economies for business activities and reduce the diversity of consumption patterns in nonfood goods. However, the lower multipliers in Africa are also due to policy factors, including distorted trade and pricing policies, inadequate productive infrastructure, and the low levels of technological innovation and input utilization.

Despite the high degree of self-sufficiency and the weak linkages in rural Africa, the rural poor (and nonpoor) still rely heavily on direct earnings from

Table 2.8. *Agriculture income shares of poor rural households disaggregated into tradables and nontradables in selected countries*

Country/region	Share of agriculture income		
	Nontraded food	Traded food	Export crops
	(%)		
Ghana			
Forest	70	18	12
Savannah	73	26	1
Tanzania			
All	61	35	4
Côte d'Ivoire			
Forest	41	14	45
Savannah	46	32	45
Malawi			
South	24	53	23
Madagascar			
Coast	46	23	31
Plateau	69	30	1
South	58	36	6

Source: Dorosh and Sahn 1993.

agricultural production. Land is therefore a critical asset, determining household welfare and coming under increasing pressure due to rising population densities and environmental degradation. Besides agriculture, incomes from wages and self-employment are also important and are becoming more so as liberalization increases commercialization and population pressures mount. Thus, despite the high degree of self-sufficiency, the poor are active participants in markets as sellers of their labor, but, even more important, as agricultural producers. Results of household surveys indicate that not only do the poor sell agricultural output, but that tradable products, both export and food crops, constitute a significant share of their agricultural earnings (Table 2.8). In some cases the poor are net purchasers of food grains, although, in many instances, even the poor sell more than they purchase. The implication is that increases in the price of export crops will usually raise incomes of an important subset of the rural poor, and this is the case in many instances for food crops as well. Even where the poor are net purchasers of certain agricultural products, increased demand for off-farm labor and higher wages that generally follow improved producer incentives will often contribute to higher overall incomes for the rural poor.

Table 2.9. *Côte d'Ivoire: sectoral distribution of employed population by per capita expenditure quintile of household of residence, by region*

Region/sector	Per capita expenditure quintile[a]					
	1	2	3	4	5	All
	(%)					
Rural						
Self-employment	98.7	98.7	97.9	94.6	94.6	97.8
Private wage	1.2	0.9	1.6	3.7	3.9	1.7
Public wage	0.1	0.4	0.5	1.7	1.6	0.5
Abidjan						
Self-employment	53.8	43.1	28.9	30.1	24.1	37.8
Private wage	37.9	43.1	47.1	44.1	39.2	42.2
Public wage	8.3	13.8	24.0	25.8	36.7	20.0
Other cities						
Self-employment	84.5	79.4	70.2	68.8	36.1	70.1
Private wage	12.0	15.6	12.8	15.6	26.9	16.0
Public wage	3.5	5.0	17.0	15.6	37.0	13.8
All						
Self-employment	96.6	92.6	88.5	76.4	47.4	85.0
Private wage	2.8	5.7	7.5	14.8	29.8	9.5
Public wage	0.6	1.7	4.0	8.8	22.9	5.5

[a]Quintiles based on expenditure distribution for the national sample.
Source: Government of Côte d'Ivoire 1985.

The rural poor also fail to gain access to products that are sold in markets with dual-price regimes. The case of food subsidies, as we discuss in Chapter 5, illustrates how the poor are rationed out of official markets. Even worse, there are costs to the rural poor of the cheap food policies pursued to the benefit of urban households. Simply, farmers are characteristically taxed so that urban consumers can have access to low-cost foodstuffs.

The final two characteristics of the rural poor that have important effects on the impact of adjustment programs is that they are predominantly self-employed and, as such, do not rely in any meaningful way on public or even formal sector employment. Tables 2.9 through 2.13 illustrate this point for Côte d'Ivoire, Ghana, Guinea, Madagascar, and Tanzania. In all five countries, more than 90 percent of the rural workers are self-employed, reflecting the dominance of own-account agriculture and, to a lesser extent, small and microenterprises in the service sector and manufacturing. Public and parastatal

Table 2.10. *Ghana: sectoral distribution of employed population by per capita expenditure quintile of household of residence, by region*

Region/sector	Per capita expenditure quintile[a]					
	1	2	3	4	5	All
			(%)			
Rural						
Self-employment	95.9	92.0	91.1	85.6	80.7	91.4
Private wage	1.9	2.6	4.6	4.5	8.0	3.5
Public wage	2.2	4.5	4.2	9.9	11.3	5.1
Abidjan						
Self-employment	57.1	58.8	45.5	55.7	42.9	48.9
Private wage	42.9	17.7	25.5	23.7	32.1	27.5
Public wage	0.0	23.5	29.1	20.6	25.0	23.6
Other cities						
Self-employment	81.9	76.6	74.1	62.8	56.1	69.8
Private wage	9.6	9.5	12.6	14.8	19.1	13.3
Public wage	8.5	13.9	13.3	22.4	24.8	16.9
All						
Self-employment	93.7	88.5	84.1	75.0	62.2	82.9
Private wage	3.2	4.5	7.9	10.1	18.2	7.7
Public wage	3.1	7.0	8.0	15.0	19.6	9.4

[a]Quintiles based on expenditure distribution for the national sample.
Source: Government of Ghana 1987.

sector employment are negligible among the rural poor – for example, comprising 2.2 percent of the jobs in the bottom quintile in Ghana, and 0.1 percent in Côte d'Ivoire and Guinea. Even among those rural workers at the upper end of the income distribution, public employment is limited, albeit much higher than at the lower end. For example, in Guinea, the share of workers in the upper quintile who are parastatal or public sector employees is 7.8 percent, in contrast to 0.1 percent in the bottom quintile. Similarly, the share of rural workers in the bottom quintile in Madagascar who engage in wage employment is less than 2 percent, in contrast to 30 percent in the top quintile of the income distribution. The contrast between the shares of workers employed by the state in rural and urban areas is also prominent. The nearly 30 and 20 percent of the work force employed by the state in Dar es Salaam and Abidjan, respectively, are far higher than the 4.1 and 0.5 percent in rural Tanzania and Côte d'Ivoire,

Table 2.11. *Guinea: sectoral distribution of employed population by per capita expenditure quintile of household of residence, by region*

Region/sector	Per capita expenditure quintile[a]					
	1	2	3	4	5	All
	(%)					
Rural						
Self-employment	99.8	99.5	97.8	97.5	88.2	99.1
Private wage	0.1	0.2	0.4	0.6	3.9	0.3
Public wage	0.0	0.3	1.8	1.9	7.8	0.6
Parastatal wage	0.0	0.0	0.1	0.0	0.0	20.1
Conakry						
Self-employment	81.0	76.8	72.3	70.9	52.6	65.8
Private wage	16.7	14.0	15.4	15.9	27.3	19.4
Public wage	0.0	8.1	9.6	10.6	15.8	11.8
Parastatal wage	2.4	1.1	2.7	2.6	4.3	3.0
Other cities						
Self-employment	96.4	91.7	89.4	86.3	77.9	89.4
Private wage	2.3	4.6	4.7	7.6	7.1	5.1
Public wage	0.9	3.3	4.4	5.1	12.1	4.5
Parastatal wage	0.4	0.4	1.5	1.0	2.8	1.1
All						
Self-employment	99.0	95.2	87.3	79.9	60.7	88.2
Private wage	0.66	2.7	6.3	10.9	21.2	6.4
Public wage	0.2	1.9	5.0	7.5	14.5	4.4
Parastatal wage	0.11	0.2	1.4	1.7	3.7	1.1

[a]Quintiles based on expenditure distribution for the national sample.
Source: Government of Guinea 1994.

respectively. Although not shown, women are particularly unlikely to be engaged in wage labor markets, both in the public and private sectors.

Furthermore, the rural poor have only limited access to subsidized social services, including education and public health services. With regard to education, Table 2.14 points out both the low level of education and the strong correlation between education of the household head and the welfare of households in rural areas. The large differences in education attainment between countries are noteworthy. In the case of Niger, for example, most household heads in rural areas are illiterate (over 90 percent), as opposed to a rate of only 25 percent in Tanzania. The limited access to health care services

Table 2.12. *Madagascar: sectoral distribution of employed population by per capita expenditure quintile of household of residence, by region*

Region/sector	Per capita expenditure quintile[a]					
	1	2	3	4	5	All
	(%)					
Rural						
Self-employment	99.3	98.2	95.7	93.5	83.3	95.6
Private wage	0.6	1.4	3.3	4.4	10.6	3.1
Public wage	0.2	0.4	1.0	2.1	6.2	1.4
Antananarivo						
Self-employment	87.3	85.8	83.4	63.4	45.5	62.7
Private wage	2.3	4.2	10.2	25.6	57.6	27.4
Public wage	0.8	1.2	2.2	5.0	18.6	9.9
Other cities						
Self-employment	88.4	90.1	85.3	75.6	61.3	75.8
Private wage	5.5	6.9	15.0	25.0	47.6	16.9
Public wage	0.2	1.4	2.5	6.5	15.1	7.4
All						
Self-employment	98.6	97.3	93.7	88.0	69.7	90.9
Private wage	1.2	2.2	5.0	9.0	19.3	6.5
Public wage	0.2	0.5	1.2	3.0	11.0	2.7

[a]Quintiles based on expenditure distribution for the national sample.
Source: Government of Madagascar 1993.

and public education reflects the fact that the state historically has failed to give priority to the types of primary health and education activities that are most meaningful for the poor, male and female alike. Instead, resources were misallocated to curative care, hospital construction, and higher education, as discussed in Chapter 4. This failing, coupled with poor management, lack of physical infrastructure, and shortage of key commodities that rely on scarce foreign exchange, has impeded the development of efficient social services in rural Africa. This neglect has had particularly harsh consequences for women and children.

Urban poor

Turning next to the urban poor, we find that although poverty is less severe than in rural areas, it nonetheless is a burgeoning problem, especially as the urban centers swell. The urban poor are concentrated in the nonwage sector, being primarily self-employed workers in enterprises with one or two per-

Table 2.13. *Tanzania: sectoral distribution of employed population by per capita expenditure quintile of household of residence, by region*

Region/sector	Per capita expenditure quintile[a]					
	1	2	3	4	5	All
			(%)			
Rural						
Self-employment	97.9	94.8	93.8	92.8	91.9	94.8
Private wage	0.5	1.0	1.7	1.4	1.1	1.1
Public wage	1.4	4.1	3.9	5.3	6.2	3.7
Parastatal wage	0.2	0.2	0.7	0.5	0.8	0.4
Dar es Salaam						
Self-employment	71.6	72.2	60.6	55.8	45.5	50.4
Private wage	17.9	9.6	19.0	20.3	21.1	20.4
Public wage	0.0	11.3	8.0	10.1	17.4	14.4
Parastatal wage	10.5	6.9	12.4	13.8	16.0	14.8
Other cities						
Self-employment	91.1	81.8	81.4	74.5	66.6	77.2
Private wage	2.3	7.0	6.7	10.4	11.9	8.4
Public wage	5.0	9.3	9.3	11.9	15.8	11.4
Parastatal wage	1.6	1.9	2.6	3.2	5.7	3.3
All						
Self-employment	97.1	92.3	90.3	86.2	76.1	89.4
Private wage	0.7	2.1	3.2	4.7	7.9	3.4
Public wage	1.8	5.0	5.2	7.3	11.2	5.7
Parastatal wage	0.4	0.5	1.3	1.8	4.8	1.6

[a]Quintiles based on expenditure distribution for the national sample.
Source: Government of Tanzania/World Bank 1995.

sons.[9] Especially worrisome, however, is that the urban poor are also more vulnerable to external and policy shocks. The cushioning effects of consumption from own-agricultural production are much less, just as reliance on markets for consumption is greater than in rural areas. Likewise, although not universally true, the urban poor in some preadjusting economies (e.g., Madagascar and Zambia), unlike the rural poor, did get access to food subsidies. Thus, to the extent that reforms eliminated poorly targeted entitlements without installing new initiatives with improved targeting, the urban poor stood to lose. However, for the most part, the poor in the cities relied on parallel market prices, so

[9] See, for example, Glick and Sahn 1993; Tabatabai 1993; Sahn and del Ninno 1994.

Table 2.14. *Household expenditure quintile by schooling of the household head in rural areas*

Country/education level	Per capita expenditure quintile					
	1	2	3	4	5	All
	(%)					
Central African Republic						
Illiterate	85	83	80	72	68	77
Completed primary	15	17	19	27	28	22
Completed secondary	0	0	1	1	4	1
Ghana						
Illiterate	53	48	41	44	35	44
Completed primary	40	44	51	46	50	47
Completed secondary	7	7	8	10	15	10
Guinea						
Illiterate	47	37	35	31	31	35
Completed primary	48	54	53	53	49	51
Completed secondary	5	9	11	15	20	12
Guinea-Bissau						
Illiterate	86	83	81	76	73	80
Completed primary	14	16	16	22	23	18
Completed secondary	1	0	3	2	4	2
Kenya						
Illiterate	47	37	41	32	27	36
Completed primary	44	50	46	51	46	47
Completed secondary	9	13	14	17	27	17
Niger						
Illiterate	94	94	96	95	90	94
Completed primary	5	5	4	4	4	5
Completed secondary	1	0	0	1	6	2
Nigeria						
Illiterate	72	73	64	57	49	63
Completed primary	23	22	25	30	29	26
Completed secondary	5	6	12	13	22	11
Sierra Leone						
Illiterate	67	58	62	61	86	68
Completed primary	5	8	7	8	6	7
Completed secondary	28	34	31	31	8	25
South Africa						
Illiterate	53	43	37	36	17	28
Completed primary	37	41	44	41	39	40
Completed secondary	10	16	19	23	43	31
Tanzania						
Illiterate	34	30	23	22	21	25
Completed primary	61	61	70	70	68	66
Completed secondary	5	8	7	9	4	8
Uganda						
Illiterate	47	37	35	31	31	35
Completed primary	48	54	53	53	49	51
Completed secondary	5	9	11	15	20	12
Zambia						
Illiterate	81	65	61	44	96	55
Completed primary	19	35	39	56	67	45
Completed secondary	0	0	0	0	0	0

Source: World Bank 1995b.

any change in official prices, including elimination of implicit subsidies, did not harm them. The poor's inability to extract rents in the form of access to official food prices was also characteristic of their not enjoying the rents from foreign exchange rationing, subsidized credit, and other such distortions that existed prior to reform.

Regarding employment, as noted earlier, urban workers were more likely than rural ones to be engaged in public sector enterprises or as civil servants (Tables 2.9–2.13). Twenty percent of the workers in Abidjan and 24 percent of the labor force in Accra are engaged in the public sector, while the share of workers in Dar es Salaam who are either public sector or parastatal workers is 31.2 percent. Other cities also have a large share of public sector workers, but the share is around one-third less than in both Abidjan and Accra, the capital cities. In Antananarivo, the rate is 10 percent; in Conakry, it is 11.8 percent, with another 3 percent being parastatal wage workers. In Tanzania, public sector employment remains high, at 11.1 percent overall in urban areas excluding the capital, although parastatal employment is much higher, at 14.8 percent of the workers in Dar es Salaam, relative to 3.3 percent in other cities. The data also reveal a marked increase in public sector employment across the expenditure quintiles: for example, in Côte d'Ivoire, 37.0 percent of the workers in cities other than Abidjan in the upper expenditure quintile, in contrast to 3.5 percent in the lowest quintile.

Next, we examine patterns of employment by gender in capital cities. To do so, we calculate new expenditure quintiles for households in the capital cities (i.e., where 20 percent of all urban households are in each quintile). Important distinctions emerge in terms of sector of employment (Table 2.15).[10] For example, the self-employed in the cities are mostly women. More specifically, in Maputo and Conakry, the share of women workers who are self-employed is approximately 80 percent, whereas for men it is 27 and 35 percent, respectively. Statistics for Accra indicate that the share of women who are self-employed is three-quarters, with this figure being closer to two-thirds in Abidjan and Dar es Salaam. Antananarivo has the lowest share of self-employed women workers, 58 percent. Male public sector workers are distributed relatively evenly across the urban-only expenditure quintiles in Maputo, Conakry, and Accra, although this is not the case in Abidjan or Antananarivo, and to a lesser extent Dar es Salaam, where the share of workers in the public sector is much higher in the upper expenditure quintiles. In contrast, female public sector workers are concentrated in the upper end of the expenditure distribution in all five capitals, while female workers in the bottom quintile are

---

[10] In the previous tables, we compare sector of employment in different regions using the national expenditure quintiles. In Table 2.15, the expenditure distribution is specific to the capital city, enabling us to look at relative welfare within the major urban areas.

Table 2.15. Sectoral distribution of employment, by gender and per capita expenditure in selected African capital cities

Capital city/sector	Men: per capita expenditure quintile[a]						Women: per capita expenditure quintile					
	1	2	3	4	5	All	1	2	3	4	5	All
	(%)						(%)					
Abidjan												
Self-employed	27.3	22.2	12.5	23.0	25.2	21.8	80.3	77.3	55.0	43.8	23.1	62.0
Private wage	68.2	62.5	59.4	54.0	39.6	57.6	7.6	11.4	27.5	25.0	38.5	18.8
Public wage	4.6	15.3	28.1	23.0	35.9	20.6	12.1	11.4	17.5	31.3	38.5	19.2
Accra												
Self-employed	22.8	26.9	41.2	23.3	23.3	27.6	81.8	82.6	84.2	57.1	63.6	76.4
Private wage	38.6	50.0	25.5	44.2	48.8	41.2	4.6	6.5	10.5	21.4	9.1	9.6
Public wage	38.6	23.1	33.3	32.5	27.9	30.9	13.6	10.9	5.3	21.4	27.3	14.0
Antananarivo												
Self-employed[b]	83.2	63.4	48.9	39.9	33.1	56.4	87.0	75.9	68.9	54.1	37.5	69.0
Private wage[c]	14.0	31.3	37.7	42.0	37.0	31.1	12.8	22.1	26.7	30.9	37.3	23.8
Public wage	2.8	5.3	13.3	18.1	29.8	12.5	0.3	2.0	4.3	15.0	25.3	7.2
Conakry												
Self-employed	36.7	37.9	35.7	34.4	30.2	35.0	91.0	88.6	78.5	63.6	45.7	78.0
Private wage	37.3	33.5	36.7	33.8	32.8	35.0	4.2	3.2	8.7	8.6	18.1	7.0
Public wage	26.0	28.6	27.6	31.8	37.0	30.0	4.8	8.2	27.8	27.8	36.2	15.0

Dar es Salaam

Self-employed	56.1	44.6	48.8	39.2	35.0	45.2	81.5	67.7	69.7	48.7	41.1	62.1
Private wage	21.7	27.9	26.1	26.6	21.6	24.8	7.4	12.3	7.4	13.8	12.9	10.7
Public wage	10.7	8.4	11.8	17.8	20.7	13.6	5.8	12.0	12.8	26.9	24.1	16.1
Parastatal wage	11.4	19.1	13.4	16.4	22.7	16.4	5.3	8.0	10.1	10.7	21.9	11.1

Maputo

Self-employed	27.3	26.5	21.7	30.0	31.9	27.4	84.2	86.3	86.7	72.3	59.3	79.0
Private wage	34.6	33.9	37.4	30.3	31.6	33.6	10.6	7.7	6.8	11.6	13.0	9.8
Public wage	38.1	39.6	40.9	39.7	36.5	40.0	5.2	6.0	6.5	16.1	27.7	11.2

ᵃExpenditure quintiles are based on urban-only income distributions.
ᵇIncludes part-time workers who receive wages working for other households, e.g., general agriculture workers in smallholder agriculture.
ᶜIncludes parastatal enterprises.
Sources: Accra: Government of Ghana 1987; Abidjan: Government of Côte d'Ivoire 1985; Antananarivo: Government of Madagascar 1993; Conakry: Glick and Sahn 1993; Dar es Salaam: Government of Tanzania/World Bank 1995.
Maputo: Sahn and del Ninno 1994;

Table 2.16. *Predicted entry probability for self-employment and wage employment, by level of education for Conakry and Maputo*

	Self-employment		Wage employment	
	Men	Women	Men	Women
Conakry				
None	.25	.22	.22	.02
Primary	.13	.13	.24	.06
Secondary	.08	.10	.36	.13
University	.03	.04	.34	.42
Maputo				
None	.29	.45	.38	.06
Primary	.23	.49	.53	.09
Secondary	.18	.31	.52	.21
University	.05	.17	.78	.37

Sources: Glick and Sahn 1997; Sahn 1993.

disproportionately concentrated in self-employment. For example, in Maputo and Conakry, 84 and 91 percent of the women workers in the lowest quintile are self-employed. By contrast, 59 and 46 percent of women in the upper quintile are self-employed. In Antananarivo, the share of the women in the labor force from the upper expenditure quintile who are public wage workers is one-quarter, compared with only 1 percent of the women in the bottom quintile. Across the quintiles, the share of self-employed women workers falls by more than half. In general, then, as income increases, the share of self-employed women declines and wage employment increases, especially in the public sector. Among men, no such pattern is found. Instead, the distribution of workers between self-employed, private wage, and public wage workers displays no general trend across expenditure quintiles.

In exploring the underlying factors that determine in which sector individuals work, we estimated multinomial logit models for Conakry and Maputo. Instead of modeling labor market behavior as a dichotomous choice of whether or not to work, we model labor market choices in a polychotomous framework. This approach not only avoids the specification bias of the dichotomous choice model, but allows us to assess the relative importance of human capital and other factors in determining how participants are sorted into different sectors of the labor market. We can thereafter analyze the process of wage formation in a labor market that is not homogenous, thereby ensuring that the nonrandom selection of workers into segments of the labor market is the basis for accurate wage functions.

Results from Conakry and Maputo (Table 2.16) show the probabilities of being engaged as a wage or a self-employed worker, disaggregated by level of education. These probabilities, derived from the multinomial logit model of labor market participation, show that as education increases for both men and women, so does the probability of being in the wage sector. Conversely, the probability of being a self-employed worker declines as education increases, as in Conakry, where among men, the probability of being self-employed is 0.25 for men with no education, and 0.03 for men who completed university. At all education levels, the probabilities of being in the wage sector are substantially lower for women than men. For example, in Maputo, the probability of a man with primary education being a wage worker is 0.53, versus 0.09 for a woman. Thus, the table illustrates the importance of human capital endowment and gender in determining both participation and sector of employment in urban areas.

Regarding earnings, a growing body of evidence shows that education is a critical determinant of household welfare. Statistics that relate the educational achievement of the household head to the household's expenditure quintile indicate the importance of schooling (Table 2.17). For example, in Ghana, the share of households in the bottom quintile headed by someone who is illiterate is 36 percent, versus 11 percent for those in the highest quintile. The comparable numbers in Guinea are 27 and 4 percent, respectively. But more compelling than these figures are several studies from Africa that use more formal econometric techniques to estimate returns to human capital. They show that the returns to education and experience are quite high.[11] For example, the results from Guinea shown in Table 2.18 are particularly informative since they uniquely distinguish the role of schooling in different sectors of the labor market: private wage labor, public wage labor, and self-employment. For men, schooling significantly affects earnings in every sector of the labor market. This impact is particularly marked for self-employment where, relative to no schooling, completing secondary schooling implies a doubling of wages, while university graduates nearly triple their earnings. Public sector wage compression is also observed for men, but not for women, for whom the returns to education are greater in this sector. For women who are self-employed, the returns to education are positive, raising earnings by around 30 percent. Earnings also increase further for women with secondary education, although the small number of women included in this group limits our ability to interpret this coefficient.

---

[11] See, for example, Appleton, Collier, and Horsnell 1990 for Côte D'Ivoire and Alderman et al. 1995 for Ghana where wage and earnings functions are estimated. Likewise, a number of essays that estimate household welfare functions, or model the determinants of poverty, also indicate the importance of education. See, for example, Glewwe 1988; Sahn and del Ninno 1994; del Ninno 1994; and Tabatabai 1993.

Table 2.17. *Household expenditure quintile by schooling of the household heads in urban areas*

| Country/education level | \multicolumn{6}{c}{Per capita expenditure quintile} |
	1	2	3	4	5	All
			(%)			
Central African Republic						
Illiterate	72	58	49	40	40	51
Completed primary	26	38	45	46	40	39
Completed secondary	2	4	6	14	20	10
Ghana						
Illiterate	36	29	20	23	11	23
Completed primary	46	52	54	53	46	50
Completed secondary	19	19	26	24	43	27
Guinea						
Illiterate	27	15	9	10	4	12
Completed primary	47	51	52	44	33	44
Completed secondary	26	34	39	46	63	44
Guinea-Bissau						
Illiterate	51	48	36	32	28	39
Completed primary	36	39	50	43	41	42
Completed secondary	13	13	14	26	31	19
Kenya						
Illiterate	16	8	8	8	13	11
Completed primary	45	43	37	37	30	37
Completed secondary	38	49	55	55	57	53
Niger						
Illiterate	94	91	83	78	59	79
Completed primary	4	7	11	14	14	11
Completed secondary	2	2	6	8	27	11
Nigeria						
Illiterate	55	42	36	26	21	35
Completed primary	26	35	39	32	29	32
Completed secondary	19	24	28	42	50	33
Sierra Leone						
Illiterate	62	60	59	54	63	57
Completed primary	30	32	33	34	29	32
Completed secondary	8	8	8	11	8	9
South Africa						
Illiterate	26	17	11	7	5	10
Completed primary	42	40	28	18	7	21
Completed secondary	31	43	61	75	87	69
Tanzania						
Illiterate	24	17	22	15	12	17
Completed primary	66	66	64	64	63	64
Completed secondary	11	17	14	21	25	18
Uganda						
Illiterate	27	15	9	10	4	12
Completed primary	47	51	52	44	33	44
Completed secondary	26	34	39	46	63	44
Zambia						
Illiterate	27	13	7	7	4	10
Completed primary	73	87	92	91	89	87
Completed secondary	1	0	1	2	7	2

Source: World Bank 1995b.

Table 2.18. *Conakry: returns to education by sector and gender*

	Male			Female[a]	
	Public wage	Private wage	Self-employment	Public wage	Self-employment
	(%)			(%)	
Primary	33	28	31	81	29
Secondary	50	77	99	127	39
University	105	146	273	263	—

[a]There were too few female workers in the private wage sector to estimate a robust set of parameters.
Source: Glick and Sahn 1997.

Table 2.19. *Characteristics of enterprises by gender of proprietor in Conakry*

	Men	Women
Enterprise type (%)		
Retail commerce	45.8	92.5
Small industry	19.0	3.2
Construction and utilities	1.7	13.7
Other	2.6	21.5
All	100.0	100.0
Finances (GF)		
Revenue	644,354	183,521
Expenses	368,611	108,662
Capital	46,751	4,638
Materials	293,772	96,835
Other	28,088	7,189
Net revenue	275,743	74,859

Source: Mills and Sahn 1993a.

While these figures are indicative of labor markets that reward human capital accumulation, most of the poor have little schooling and rely primarily on self-employment; in addition, the majority of self-employed women are from the poorest households in African cities, a pattern that again does not apply to self-employed men, who are distributed relatively evenly across the expenditure categories. This latter finding reflects the heavy concentration of female-headed enterprises in small-scale retail commerce, which has lower use of capital inputs and credit and lower gross and net revenues. Table 2.19 illustrates this point for Conakry (Mills and Sahn 1993a), where most female-headed enterprises (over 90 percent) are in retail commerce; this is the case for less than half of the enterprises headed by men. Female-headed enterprises in Conakry also only have one-tenth the capital inputs, Guinea francs (GF) 4,638, as male-headed enterprises, GF 46,751. Again, this pattern has been observed in a range of environments, including Dar es Salaam, where the current asset value of female-headed enterprises in 1991 was Tanzanian shilling (Tsh) 208,000, versus Tsh 730,700 for male-headed enterprises; and where the male-headed firms are nearly four times more profitable than female-headed firms (Bagachwa, Sarris, and Tinios 1993).

In combination, one of the key elements to the well-being of the poor is reform that fosters an environment where commerce and microenterprises in both rural and urban areas can flourish. Conversely, the poor are unlikely to lose significantly from public or formal wage sector layoffs. Women in poor households are particularly immune from any effects, since they are largely engaged as self-employed workers. However, this is not to say that those who are redeployed do not become a new class of poor, an issue we discuss in Chapter 4 of this book.

While these generalizations provide some insight into the poor's role in the economy as producers, consumers, and beneficiaries of government spending, the fact remains that the poor constitute a large and diverse group in Africa. Even particularly vulnerable groups, such as female-headed households, are characterized by considerable heterogeneity.[12] And while understanding who the poor are is the first step in our analysis, the real challenge is to explore in greater detail the impact of specific policies on the poor, moving beyond the empirically based, albeit stylized, facts presented here. In doing so, however, we limit our purview to the role of economic policy, recognizing the wide range of political, social, and cultural forces that contribute to poverty. Thus, it is to the specifics of policy change and the implications for growth and income distribution that we now turn.

---

[12] For example, it is crucial to distinguish between the case of a female household head with no young children who is receiving substantial remittances (possibly from the husband or son), and a widowed or abandoned female head with young children and no external means of support. Likewise, there are differences between de facto female headship, where the self-declared male head is absent from the household for a majority of time, and de jure female headship, where the woman is generally both the legal and customary head, with the man playing essentially no role in providing for the household's financial and other needs. For further discussions see, for example, Kennedy and Haddad 1994.

3

Trade and exchange rate policy reforms

Trade and exchange rate policy reforms are probably the most controversial aspect of structural adjustment programs in sub-Saharan Africa.[1] In part, the controversy arises because these policy reforms have large effects on the economy and, in particular, on income distribution. Moreover, for many government decision makers, the debate regarding the appropriate long-term development strategy – import substitution versus outward-oriented trade policy – remains unsettled. But perhaps the most important reason why trade and exchange rate policy reforms arouse such heated debate is that these policy changes often appear to be imposed from outside, as conditions for needed foreign financing by the World Bank, the International Monetary Fund, or other donors.

This chapter analyzes the impacts of trade and exchange rate policy reforms on macroeconomic performance, income distribution, and poverty. In this chapter, we first discuss the role of trade and exchange rate policy in overall development strategies and a summary of the basic analytics of exchange rate determination in the African context. Next, we explore the effectiveness of policy reforms in terms of major macroeconomic objectives, real exchange rate

[1] Trade policy, narrowly defined, includes measures such as trade taxes and quotas that change the relative prices of tradable goods; exchange rate policy encompasses choice of nominal exchange rate regimes and accompanying macroeconomic policy measures that change the relative prices of tradables to nontradables. The two types of policies are clearly linked. For example, trade policies affect real exchange rates by altering demand and supply of nontradables in the economy (see, e.g., Dornbusch 1974) and, together with exchange rate policies, determine real prices of individual tradable commodities. Moreover, in most non-CFA countries in sub-Saharan Africa, import quotas and licensing, mechanisms that effectively ration foreign exchange, have been an integral part of exchange rate policy. Thus, as in Thomas and Nash 1991, we make no attempt in this chapter to maintain a sharp distinction between trade and exchange rate policy reforms. See Helleiner 1994 for a contrasting view.

depreciation, and levels of exports. We also discuss the performance of the industrial sector during reform periods. In order to highlight the importance of the context in which reforms take place and the varying degrees of success of actual trade and exchange rate policy reforms, we describe case histories of individual countries in some detail.

Following our overview of the macroeconomic impacts of trade and exchange rate policy reform, we analyze the impacts of trade and exchange rate policy reform on household income distribution and poverty. We present estimates of economic rents associated with restrictions on foreign exchange together with a set of counterfactual simulations using computable general equilibrium (CGE) models. Here, we argue that policy reforms leading to real exchange rate depreciation tend to have positive impacts on real incomes of the poor, especially the rural poor. A brief summary concludes the chapter.

Trade orientation and development strategies

From independence to the early 1980s, most countries in Africa adopted import substitution policies in an effort to spur industry and economic growth. Pessimism over the long-run terms of trade of primary exports relative to manufactured imports and a belief that protection of domestic industries would spur wider economic growth provided the rationale for these policies. The trade and exchange rate policy reforms advocated by Western donors in the 1980s entailed a sharp reversal in development strategy. These policies were designed to spur exports and economic growth through shifts in relative prices and liberalization of commodity and foreign exchange markets.[2] To support this more outward-oriented approach, proponents of reform argued on the basis of a combination of both economic theory and historical evidence.

The intellectual foundation for the import substitution strategy that was widespread in sub-Saharan Africa prior to reforms derived from the research of Prebisch (1950) and Singer (1950), who argued that the medium- to long-run terms of trade favor industrialized products and the countries that produce them. If the price of raw materials and commodities in international markets declines relative to the price of manufactured goods over time, countries that do not industrialize will become increasingly poorer relative to industrial countries. By producing import substitutes domestically, a developing country could avoid the negative effects of the terms-of-trade shifts. Even though some import-substituting "infant" industries might have high initial costs and need

[2] See *Accelerated Development in Sub-Saharan Africa* (World Bank 1981) for an early and influential statement of these arguments. This document, often referred to as the Berg report, after its major author, generated considerable debate especially in regard to its call for large exchange rate devaluations. Edwards (1993) summarizes the ensuing debate and Wilson (1993) discusses French support and recommendations for adjustment policies.

temporary protective import tariffs, over time they would become efficient and produce at costs competitive with goods on the world market.

The case for an outward-oriented approach for Africa draws largely on the concept of comparative advantage, which dates back to David Ricardo in the early nineteenth century. According to this theory, international trade leads to specialization and higher incomes for trading countries. In the basic two-country, two-goods formulation with constant costs of production, incomes in both countries rise as each country produces more of the good for which it is relatively more efficient and trades for the good for which it does not have comparative advantage. Thus, total output produced in the two countries increases, enabling potentially greater consumption in each country.[3]

This basic model of comparative advantage presents a static framework, but the static gains in efficiency potentially translate into higher savings, more investment, and increased growth. Moreover, proponents of outward-oriented development strategies argue that increased openness to trade promotes technical change through incentives to remain competitive and become familiar with new technologies developed abroad. A wide range of theoretical models illustrates potential gains from trade resulting from these dynamic as well as static effects.[4]

Empirical evidence on both the long-run trends in the terms of trade and country-specific experiences with development policies sheds light on the debate but is not conclusive. The evidence on the long-run terms of trade is mixed and depends crucially on the choice of time period for the analysis.[5] African countries enjoyed the benefits of a commodity boom in the 1970s that raised prices of major exports (such as petroleum in Nigeria, Cameroon, and Gabon; uranium in Niger; copper in Zaire and Zambia; coffee in Tanzania, Madagascar, and Côte d'Ivoire; and cocoa in Côte d'Ivoire and Ghana). Buoyant export earnings and widely available commercial bank loans helped to mitigate the adverse effects of real exchange rate appreciations linked to high inflation and inappropriate exchange rate policies. With foreign exchange available for capital investments and imported intermediate inputs, large industrial parastatals were established in many countries, including Cameroon, Madagascar, and Tanzania.

The subsequent fall of agricultural commodity prices in the early 1980s, together with a rise in oil prices and tighter world credit markets, aggravated the adverse effects of real exchange rate appreciation on the trade balance, however, and were major factors in balance-of-payments crises in most sub-Saharan African countries outside the CFA (Communauté Financière

---

[3] See Jones and Neary (1984) for a more detailed discussion of the theory.

[4] Corden (1984) and Helleiner (1992) present overviews of these dynamic issues.

[5] See Cuddington (1992); Sapsford, Sarkar, and Singer (1992); Reinhart and Wickham (1994); and León and Soto (1995) for recent discussions of the empirical evidence.

Africaine) zone. Under pressure from international donors, and with little room to maneuver because of balance-of-payments constraints, most countries in sub-Saharan Africa undertook trade liberalizations (including the lowering of import tariffs and export taxes and elimination of import quotas) and exchange rate reforms (devaluation and no rationing of foreign exchange) as part of stabilization and structural adjustment programs. In theory, these policy reforms would improve producer incentives for tradables (both exports and competitive import substitutes) and thus encourage increased use of domestic factor resources (land, labor, and capital) in these sectors, enabling a growth in exports and real incomes.

Part of the rationale for these outward-oriented policies is a more sanguine view of long-run commodity prices and Africa's comparative advantage in production. However, even with a fall in the relative price of exports to imports (the barter terms of trade), the purchasing power of exports (the income terms of trade) need not decline if exports increase in volume. The scope for increasing exports of agricultural products facing price-inelastic world demand, such as cocoa and coffee, is limited since an increase in total exports by all developing countries threatens to reduce world prices and total incomes for all exporters. Nonetheless, African countries as a group saw a decline in their market shares of cocoa, coffee, and other major exports in the 1980s, suggesting that some scope for increased foreign exchange revenues existed. Moreover, export-oriented strategies need not focus mainly on traditional exports or even primary products. Over time, the composition of developing countries' exports, particularly those in Asia, has shifted toward manufactured goods. This shift, together with the potential for intraindustry specialization, suggests that a general export pessimism is unfounded (Bhagwati 1988).

The success of outward-oriented development strategies in a number of countries in Asia and Latin America also lends support to an outward-oriented approach (see Little, Scitovsky, and Scott 1970; Krueger 1978; Bhagwati 1978; and the review by Edwards 1993). Asian countries that grew rapidly kept their real exchange rates relatively stable[6] and avoided trade and exchange rate policies that lead to large premiums on parallel markets for foreign exchange. Lewis and McPherson (1994) show that for most of the 1970–1990 period, parallel market premiums for a seven-country sample of rapidly growing Asian countries were small, averaging 4 percent from 1986 to 1991. Real exchange rates were generally stable or slowly depreciating: the coefficient of variation in the real exchange rate using the official exchange rate was 17.9 percent for

---

[6] Equilibrium real exchange rates are not completely stable over time, but are a function of terms-of-trade shocks, technical change, and other exchange rate "fundamentals" (Edwards 1989). Thus, even under an ideal exchange rate policy, one would expect some variation in real exchange rates. Moreover, as Lewis and McPherson (1994) argue, stability in real exchange rates itself contributes to economic growth.

the 1970–1990 period (22.9 percent using the parallel exchange rate). In contrast, as we describe in the rest of this chapter, many African countries avoided depreciations in nominal exchange rates, thus allowing their real exchange rates to appreciate and reducing price incentives for production of tradable goods.[7]

In summary, the major goals of trade and exchange rate policy reforms in Africa involved macroeconomic considerations: to increase economic openness and, in so doing, to promote domestic production of tradables and economic growth. Apart from short-term efforts at stabilization aimed at easing balance-of-payments crises in the initial stages of policy reform, the major purpose of trade and exchange rate policy reform was not to reduce unsustainable current account deficits in the short to medium run. In fact, reform was often accompanied by increased foreign capital inflows, mainly through official grants and loans, implying a widening of the current account deficit, as will be discussed.[8] Before discussing case histories of trade and exchange rate policy reform, however, we first present a theoretical framework that emphasizes the role of foreign exchange rationing in explaining the outcomes of reform in Africa.

Basic analytics of trade and exchange rate policy reform in Africa

In implementing import-substitution development policy, governments in sub-Saharan Africa protected domestic industries through a combination of import tariffs and import licensing, while imposing heavy taxes on agricultural and mining exports. As we will discuss in detail, nominal exchange rates were in many cases fixed relative to a major international currency (e.g., the U.S. dollar or French franc) for long periods of time. For many countries outside the CFA franc zone, where rules of the monetary union limited inflationary financing of deficits, government budget deficits led to increased domestic money supplies and general inflation.

Prices of tradable goods (especially export goods) tended not to rise along with the general price level, however, since the border price, evaluated using the official exchange rate, remained tied to world prices. Thus, the relative price of nontradable goods to tradable goods rose – that is, the real exchange

---

[7] In a sample of nine non-CFA zone African countries, Lewis and McPherson (1994) report that parallel market premiums averaged 93 percent from 1986 to 1991, real exchange rates appreciated substantially in the 1970s, and average coefficients of variations on real exchange rates for the 1970–1990 period were 37.7 and 35.3 percent, using official and parallel exchange rates, respectively.

[8] Note that the African experience contrasts sharply with that of most Latin American countries, where reducing current account deficit was a major goal of trade and exchange rate policy reform.

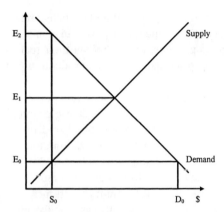

Figure 3.1. Foreign exchange market with and without rationing.

rate appreciated. As real prices of export goods fell, thus reducing export incentives, foreign exchange earnings declined. At the same time, demand for imported goods in official markets, priced using the official exchange rate, increased. This imbalance between foreign exchange supply from export earnings and foreign exchange demand for imports was often resolved through rationing of foreign exchange, stricter import licensing requirements, and higher import tariffs.[9]

Exchange rate devaluations under foreign exchange rationing
Exchange rate devaluations have been a central part of most stabilization and structural adjustment programs outside the CFA zone. However, the economic implications of devaluations are vastly different under rationed and nonrationed foreign exchange markets, as illustrated in Figure 3.1. Here, we express the exchange rate as units of domestic currency per unit of foreign currency and hold fixed the domestic prices of nontradable goods, so that the changes in the nominal exchange rate reflect equivalent changes in the real exchange rate. In the absence of rationing, if we assume long-term net capital inflows are zero,[10] equilibrium in the foreign exchange market requires an

---

[9] Collier (1991) points out that African countries avoided trade retaliation from developing countries in spite of the trade restrictions imposed, in part because of their use of foreign exchange rationing to control imports rather than tariffs, which are easily quantifiable.

[10] In many countries, foreign capital inflows, either in the form of excessive borrowing or mounting arrears on foreign debts, were not sustainable prior to devaluations. In these cases, trade and exchange rate policy reform led not only to the removal of foreign exchange controls outlined in Figure 3.1, but to reductions in the level of net capital inflows to new equilibrium levels, as well. To bring about equilibrium in the foreign exchange market, with a decline in net capital inflows, would require a real depreciation beyond that due directly to the liberalization.

exchange rate of E_1 so that supply of foreign exchange (from exports and transfers from abroad) equals demand for foreign exchange (for imports and transfers to the rest of the world). If the government devalues the exchange rate to a point such as E_2, suppliers of foreign exchange (net producers of tradables) enjoy a higher price (in terms of domestic currency) for the foreign exchange and increase their supply (i.e., export earnings and transfers from abroad) in response. Conversely, the devaluation harms net consumers of foreign exchange and they reduce their demands for foreign exchange (for imports and transfers to the the rest of the world) in response. The result is a trade surplus (or, more accurately, a current account surplus).

More typical in Africa, however, is for governments to set the official exchange rate below E_1, at a rate such as E_0. At this overvalued rate, demand for foreign exchange exceeds supply and the government must ration the existing supply, S_0. Such rationing may occur through explicit import licensing requirements and quotas, limitations on access to foreign exchange for travel abroad, as well as less transparent processes of allocating foreign exchange. What is clear is that, at this official exchange rate, a strong incentive exists for a parallel market to develop since net consumers of foreign exchange would be willing to pay E_2 (the marginal value of foreign exchange) if the supply of foreign exchange is constrained to S_0.[11] This premium paid for foreign exchange on the parallel market implies that importers fortunate enough to get access to foreign exchange at the official exchange rate will earn a rent: they can sell their goods at domestic prices that are determined by the scarcity value of foreign exchange, or the parallel exchange rate, E_1, while buying at the official exchange rate, E_0.

Under foreign exchange rationing, the effects of a devaluation may be very different than in nonrationed foreign exchange markets. A devaluation from E_0 to any level less than or equal to E_1 will have little direct effect on prices in the domestic economy since prices of most tradable goods depend on the market-clearing parallel exchange rate, not the inframarginal official one. To the extent

---

[11] Exactly how this incentive affects the foreign exchange markets depends on the ease with which exporters and importers can evade the official market and operate in the parallel market. The existence of alternate supplies of foreign exchange on the parallel market also affects parallel market exchange rates. Typically, African governments have access to certain flows of foreign exchange such as foreign borrowing, aid flows, and exports from enclave mining industries, none of which are easily diverted to the parallel market. The government uses this foreign exchange for its own needs or sells it to parastatals or selected individuals at the official exchange rate. Foreign exchange from parallel market exports and transfers combines with foreign exchange diverted from the official market to supply the parallel market. The parallel exchange rate adjusts to equilibrate the supply of foreign exchange in the parallel market with the demand for foreign exchange not satisfied in the official market. See Kiguel and O'Connell 1995 for a review of various models of parallel markets for foreign exchange.

that some exports are sold in official markets, an inframarginal devaluation of the official exchange rate may permit an increase in the domestic price of these export goods.[12] In general, though, a devaluation insufficient to eliminate the need for foreign exchange rationing will likely have little impact on relative prices for most producers and consumers, and thus on the outward orientation of the economy. Moreover, the maintenance of a rationing system for foreign exchange will likely result in a continuing misallocation of foreign exchange, away from its most productive uses.

Given that many relative prices remain unchanged, the income distribution consequences of a devaluation starting from a point of foreign exchange rationing depend on who was receiving the rents before the devaluation and who receives the benefits of the higher official exchange rate.[13] As we will argue, the poor are unlikely to benefit from foreign exchange rents and, thus, unlikely to lose from the devaluation. On the other hand, they may be exporting goods in the official market, especially if they are producing traditional agricultural exports where marketing is tightly controlled by a public sector monopoly, so the devaluation might benefit the poor on this count. Of course, the marketing board must raise the local currency prices it pays farmers in line with the devaluation for this benefit to pass through to the poor, something that rarely happens in Africa.

In sum, to understand the redistributive impact of devaluation in Africa, we must know more than which households are net exporters and which are not. When countries severely ration foreign exchange, understanding who must sell tradable goods at the official exchange rate and who is allowed to buy them at that rate is more important than understanding the impact of relative price changes in official markets, which are, in many cases, inframarginal. Answers to these questions are highly country-specific and depend on the structures of the economies, their political economies, external shocks in the pre- and postadjustment period, and the degree to which reforms were implemented. We thus now turn to an empirical investigation of trade and exchange rate policy reforms in our sample countries, beginning with the macroeconomic aspects of these policy reforms.

Macroeconomic aspects of policy reforms

The evidence from the ten countries in our sample suggests that trade and exchange rate policy reforms enjoyed at least limited success in changing relative prices in official markets for foreign exchange. However, only in one country (Ghana) were these reforms associated with significant improvements

---

[12] In addition, the redistribution of income resulting from the elimination of rents will lead to a change in the pattern of demand and thus may result in (second-order) effects on domestic prices and output.

[13] See Krueger (1974) for a discussion of the costs associated with rent seeking.

in export and GDP growth; the performance of the other non-CFA zone reforming economies has been somewhat disappointing.[14] As we will argue, the poor macroeconomic performance is due in part to a failure to sustain policy reforms.

We use two measures to evaluate the impact of trade and exchange rate policy reforms. The extent of real exchange rate depreciation achieved, as measured by the official nominal exchange rate deflated by changes in the domestic price level, shows the degree to which changes in trade and exchange rate policy actually changed relative prices in the economy, at least in the official market for foreign exchange. Real exchange rate depreciation is only an intermediate measure of the effectiveness of policy reform, however. The second measure, the change in real exports, indicates whether the ultimate macroeconomic goals of the reforms are achieved. Here, drawing the links between policy reform and macroeconomic performance is much more difficult.

Table 3.1 summarizes episodes of trade and exchange rate policy reform in our ten sample countries during the 1980s. The periods of reform are defined by a sharp change in nominal exchange rates (exchange rate devaluations) over a period of one (e.g., in The Gambia, Guinea, Malawi, and Zaire) to five (e.g., in Ghana) years. In most cases outside the CFA zone, these nominal exchange rate devaluations were accompanied by liberalization of mechanisms for allocating foreign exchange (i.e., the introduction of auctions or open general licensing systems for imports). Note that trade and exchange rate reforms that were not fully implemented also took place in other years in many of these countries. For the eight non-CFA zone countries, nominal exchange rate depreciations, measured by the change in the official exchange rate between the year immediately prior to the reform and the year immediately after the reform, averaged 1,441 percent.[15] For three countries, Ghana, Guinea, and Mozambique, nominal depreciations exceeded 1,000 percent. These extraordinarily large nominal devaluations do not translate into equally large real depreciations, however. Domestic inflation often erodes a substantial amount of the change in the nominal exchange rate. In fact, one criticism of devaluation as a policy instrument holds that it is ineffective because it *causes* a proportional increase in domestic prices so that relative prices, and thus incentives for tradables goods production, do not change at all. Most of the countries in our sample, however, did achieve a real depreciation despite domestic inflation. All of the countries with nominal devaluations greater than 100 percent saw a real

---

[14] Unavailability of trade and national accounts data on Cameroon and Niger for 1995 precluded an analysis of the real side effects of the devaluation of the CFA franc in January 1994.

[15] Here, we express exchange rates in terms of units of local currency per international currency (e.g., cedis per dollar). Thus, a devaluation from 10 to 30 cedis per dollar is described as a 200 percent devaluation.

Table 3.1. *Trade and exchange rate liberalization in sub-Saharan Africa*

Countries	Year of liberalization	Nominal depreciation[a]	Real depreciation[a]	Change in Real exports[a,b]	Change in Industrial value-added[c]
Cameroon	1994	76[d]	32	—	—
Gambia	1986	82	32	17.7	4.8
Ghana	1983–1987	7258	749	6.7	0.8
Guinea	1986	1661	21	14.3	—
Madagascar	1987–1988	137	57	2.7	-0.4
Malawi	1988	25	-12	-0.7	2.4
Mozambique	1987–1988	1743	250	9.3	-0.6
Niger	1994	76[d]	31	—	—
Tanzania	1987–1988	338	111	6.7	1.6
Zaire	1984	287	177	9.9	2.5
Average (all countries)		1168	—	—	—
Average (non-CFA countries)		1441	150	8.3	1.6

[a]Percentage change between the year immediately prior to liberalization and the year immediately after liberalization.
[b]Real exports are measured as the nominal dollar value of exports of goods and services deflated by an index of the dollar prices of imports by developing countries (IMF various years b).
[c]Percentage change in real industrial value added, calculated using averages of the two years immediately prior to liberalization and the two years immediately following liberalization.
[d]Devaluation relative to the the dollar was 76.3 percent. The devaluation relative to the French franc was 100 percent.
Sources: World Bank 1993b; authors' calculations; IMF various years b.

depreciation of at least 20 percent.[16] The two CFA countries, Cameroon and Niger, achieved real exchange rate depreciations of 32 and 31 percent, respectively.[17]

More formally, Younger (1992) uses a time series model of monthly price data to test the hypothesis that the massive devaluations of Ghana's Economic Recovery Program (ERP) caused inflation in that country. The model regresses

[16] We calculate the real exchange rates for Ghana, Guinea, Madagascar, Mozambique, Niger, and Tanzania here by multiplying the official nominal exchange rate by the dollar-denominated import price index for developing countries (IMF various years b), and dividing by the domestic consumer price index. For Cameroon, The Gambia, Malawi, and Zaire, the real exchange rate series (published in IMF various years b) are based on trade baskets for the individual countries.

[17] Real exchange rate depreciations between 1993 and 1995 in Côte d'Ivoire (43 percent) and Senegal (47 percent) were even larger (IMF various years).

inflation on changes in the money supply, changes in the official exchange rate (devaluations), the two major droughts during the sample (1977 and 1983), and two coups d'etat in 1979 and 1981. Each regressor has its own autoregressive moving average (ARMA) lag structure which makes the equation quite flexible. Across a wide variety of equation specifications, none of the estimates finds a large impact of the official exchange rate on prices. The estimated long-term effect of a 100 percent devaluation on prices ranges between 6 and 10 percent. This impact is statistically different from zero in several of the models, but it is relatively unimportant given the size of the devaluation. At the same time, the model accepts the null hypothesis of money neutrality – that is, a 100 percent increase in the money supply leads to a 100 percent increase in prices, suggesting that the rampant inflation of the fixed exchange rate period had much more to do with money creation than devaluation.

Export performance

For the seven non-CFA zone countries listed in Table 3.1 that achieved real exchange rate depreciation,[18] the average gain in real exports of goods and nonfactor services[19] was 8.3 percent per year. Of course, such comparisons of "before" and "after" miss important factors influencing the real exchange rate and exports, such as terms of trade, trade taxes, and climatic conditions.

Achieving more rapid increases in exports and economic growth may require administrative reforms, as well. For example, in Tanzania, despite significant depreciation of the real exchange rate, numerous administrative procedures hindered exports, including requirements for export permits, export licensing by the Board of External Trade, export registration by the central bank, and annual renewal of a business license from the Ministry of Industry and Trade (Lipumba 1993). Inadequate port, transport, and communication facilities also hinder expansion of exports in many countries. Finally, the establishment of associations of traders and firms to facilitate contacts with potential importers, provide market information, and assist in other trading arrangements can help spur exports in the context of an environment of improved price incentives (Thomas and Nash 1991).

Econometric analysis of the relationship between policy reform and export performance in Africa is hampered by data problems including the relatively short time-series involved, the absence of data on parallel market trade, and difficulties in including other relevant contributing factors. Nonetheless, econometric evidence from a sample of sub-Saharan African country data from

[18] Only in Malawi was a major liberalization of foreign exchange markets not associated with a real exchange rate depreciation.

[19] Dollar exports of goods and nonfactor services deflated by the IMF import price index for developing countries (IMF various years b).

1972 to 1987 suggests that over the period a 1 percent misalignment of the real exchange rate (defined as the difference between the actual real exchange rate and an estimated equilibrium real exchange rate) was associated with a .025 percent reduction in real GDP growth and a 0.096 to 0.112 percent reduction in real exports as a share of GDP (Ghura and Grennes 1993). Similarly, Balassa (1990) shows a negative correlation between real exchange rate appreciation and exports in sub-Saharan Africa. Numerous other studies using samples of developing countries outside of Africa have also shown negative relationships between real exchange rate appreciation and both real exports and growth.[20]

Even greater variation is seen in terms of changes in industrial output before and after the policy reforms (Table 3.1). This variation in outcomes might be expected since trade and exchange rate liberalization has both positive and negative effects on industrial real value added. Increased foreign exchange availability (the result of large official capital flows accompanying reforms) enables imports of key intermediate goods and increased prices of competing imports on official markets, both of which tend to spur industrial output. Higher costs of imported inputs, particularly for firms who earlier had access to foreign exchange at official market prices, reduces profitability.

Industrial real value-added increased in The Gambia, Ghana, Malawi, Tanzania, and Zaire, though it fell in Madagascar and Mozambique. It must be remembered, however, that the industrial sector remains small in most countries of sub-Saharan Africa. In spite of the earlier import-substitution policies of the 1960s and 1970s, industry (including mining) accounted for more than 30 percent of GDP in only nine countries, many of these with large mining sectors (Botswana, Congo, Gabon, Guinea, Nigeria, and Zambia). The share of manufacturing in GDP exceeded 20 percent only in Cameroon, Mauritius, Swaziland, Zambia, and Zimbabwe (Table 3.2).

A more detailed breakdown of industrial performance suggests that the short-term consequences of policy reforms were clearly negative for inefficient industries that lost the benefits of trade protection and implicit subsidies arising from access to foreign exchange at official prices. Many of these firms could not produce profitably without subsidies, however, and were later privatized or liquidated as part of adjustment efforts in the 1980s. For example, in Tanzania, inefficient firms (those with negative value-added at social prices in 1985 or domestic resource cost ratios greater than 2.0) contracted their output by 43 and 20 percent, respectively, following the introduction of the ERP in 1986. Relatively efficient firms, mainly textiles, tobacco manufactures, wood and wood products (except furniture), paper and paper products, rubber products,

---

[20] See Dollar 1992, Edwards 1988, and Frenkel and Khan 1990. Comparing average performance for various groups of African countries, Mosley and Weeks (1993) also find that real exchange rate depreciation was associated with higher investment, export growth, and real GDP growth from 1980 to 1990.

Table 3.2. *Industrial and manufacturing output in sub-Saharan Africa*

	Industrial real value-added			Ind/ GDP[a]	Manf/ GDP[b]
	1972– 1974	1980– 1982	1990– 1992	1990– 1992	1990– 1992
Cameroon	62.2	115.6	115.2	29.8	21.6
Gambia	77.3	78.4	99.4	12.1	5.5
Ghana	117.6	88.5	89.2	16.8	9.4
Guinea	—	—	—	31.7	4.2
Madagascar	98.1	87.5	82.8	12.7	7.6[c]
Malawi	97.0	99.9	106.9	20.5	13.7
Mozambique	—	96.3	66.3	13.6	—
Niger	49.7	100.2	71.2	18.3	6.6
Tanzania	106.0	95.7	85.9	14.4	7.7
Zaire	115.2	97.0	62.6	17.9	6.1

[a]Share of industrial value-added in GDP (percent).
[b]Share of manufacturing value-added in GDP (percent).
[c]1988–1989.
Sources: World Bank 1994d; IMF 1993c, 1995d, 1994c; UNDP and World Bank 1989.

and nonmetallic products, increased their output by 24 percent between 1985 and 1988 (Ndulu and Semboja 1994).[21]

Again, the before and after changes in exports and industrial output presented here describe historical changes, but do not necessarily show causality. A lack of response in exports (or, conversely, a large increase in exports) following a change in policy may be due to exogenous factors outside the realm of policy such as weather, movements in international prices, and political crises. Changes in exports may also be the result of ineffective implementation of policy (continuing licensing regulations, etc.). A major purpose of the following discussion of individual country experiences is to highlight these exogenous factors and implementation issues, which are country-specific and are difficult to capture in econometric analyses with short time-series data.

Country experiences

In summarizing the individual case histories of the ten countries included in the study, we define three broad groups: non-CFA countries with

---

[21] Prior to reforms, Madagascar's industrial sector was also heavily protected and inefficient, with an average domestic resource cost ratio of over 2.0 (Greenaway and Milner 1990). Similarly, Cameroon's industry was dominated by large, inefficient, capital-intensive parastatals (Willame 1986).

severe exchange rate distortions prior to liberalization, non-CFA countries with moderate exchange rate distortions, and the CFA countries. For ease of comparison, we show the evolution over time of exchange rate indices and levels of trade in the same format for each of the ten countries in Figures 3.2 to 3.11.

We show exchange rate indices on a logarithmic scale so that equal distances measured on the vertical axis represent equal *percentage* changes in the index.[22] Nominal official exchange rate indices are equal to 100 in 1975.[23] We calculate parallel exchange rate indices relative to the level of the nominal official exchange rate in 1975.[24] Thus the gap between the parallel and official exchange rate indices measures the percentage premium in the parallel foreign exchange market. We calculate the real exchange rate index using the official exchange rate adjusted for world and domestic inflation.[25]

Three measures of trade performance are also shown: imports of goods and nonfactor services,[26] total exports, and exports excluding the major export commodity (a measure that indicates the extent of export diversification). In each case, we express trade levels in terms of real 1980 dollars, using the IMF's index of average prices of developing countries' imports as a deflator. The deflated values of trade thus capture both changes in quantity and changes in the terms of trade (as measured by changes in the price of a country's exports or imports relative to the average price of imports for developing countries).[27] We use the same deflator for both exports and imports so that the difference between imports and exports reflects the balance-of-trade deficit.

Countries with severe distortions in foreign exchange markets prior to reforms

In five of the countries – Ghana, Guinea, Mozambique, Tanzania, and Zaire – distortions in exchange rate markets (as measured by the premium on foreign exchange in the parallel market) exceeded 100 percent prior to liberal-

---

[22] For example, the distance between 100 and 200 on the vertical scale is the same as the distance between 200 and 400 or 1,000 and 2,000.

[23] The official exchange rate index (IOER) is: $IOER_t = (OER_t/OER_{1975}) * 100$, where OER_t is the nominal official exchange rate in year t.

[24] The parallel exchange rate index (IPER) is: $IPER_t = (PER_t/OER_{1975}) * 100$, where PERt is the nominal parallel exchange rate in year t.

[25] The real exchange rate (RER) is: $RER_t = OER_t * PW^t/CPIt$, where PW^t is the dollar price index of imports by developing countries (IMF various years a). The real exchange rate index (IRER) is: $IRER_t = (RER_t/RER_{1975}) * 100$, where PERt is the nominal parallel exchange rate in year t.

[26] Imports of goods and nonfactor services exclude interest payments on foreign debt, considered a factor service in the balance of payments.

[27] Note that these measures differ from real exports and imports of goods and nonfactor services shown in national accounts, which represent the quantity of trade at base-year prices. The national accounts figures thus reflect only quantity changes and not terms-of-trade changes.

Table 3.3. *Estimated economic rents from foreign exchange restrictions*

Countries	Year of liberalization	Premium before (%)	Premium after (%)	Implicit rent before (mill $)	Rent per capita ($)
Gambia	1986	-5	9	-5	-6
Ghana	1983–1987	2143	25	748	57
Guinea	1986	1177	3	533	106
Malawi	1988	13	30	75	10
Madagascar	1987–1988	25	5	106	10
Mozambique	1987–1988	4156	51	287	19
Tanzania	1987–1988	405	74	908	40
Zaire	1984	117	2	1027	33
Average		1004	25	460	34

Sources: World Bank 1993b; authors' calculations.

ization (Table 3.3). Among these five countries, however, the degree of success in eliminating these distortions and in spurring exports differed markedly.

Ghana: Trade and exchange rate reforms in Ghana, largely implemented over five years (1983–1987), were most successful. The government undertook these reforms only after the near collapse of the economy, however, because of earlier experiences with devaluations. When General Acheampong overthrew the Busia government in 1972, one of the reasons he gave was his predecessor's decision to devalue the cedi. This public statement made it politically impossible for the Acheampong government to devalue. Accelerating domestic inflation combined with a fixed nominal value of the cedi quickly led to a highly overvalued exchange rate. By 1978, the premium on the parallel market was 400 percent, and the spread widened to 2,000 percent in 1982. The extreme overvaluation of the cedi led to a huge excess demand for foreign exchange in the official market, a problem that the government resolved through severe rationing. While an ad hoc licensing system supposedly directed foreign exchange to priority imports, even importers of favored items often could not get foreign exchange for lack of supply. Despite sharp declines in exports, particularly after world cocoa prices fell in 1981 (Figure 3.2), and the chaos in the foreign exchange markets, successive governments stubbornly refused to devalue, convinced that devaluation was the kiss of death for any Ghanaian regime. Nevertheless, the critical drought of 1981–1983 left the country with little option but to accept a Washington-style adjustment package.

The ERP began in April 1983, with a 900 percent devaluation of the cedi. While apparently extreme, that devaluation still left the official exchange rate

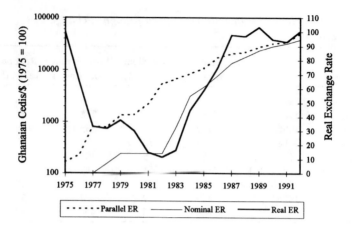

Figure 3.2a. Ghana: exchange rate fluctuations (real, nominal, and parallel).

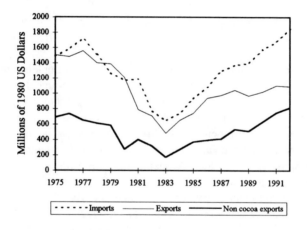

Figure 3.2b. Ghana: real exports and imports for goods and nonfactor services.

(about 25 cedis per dollar) at a fraction of the parallel rate (Figure 3.2a). Foreign exchange rationing continued as before, though it became less severe as there were more dollars to distribute, largely from multilateral lenders. As the reform process continued, Ghana devalued its exchange rate in large steps again in 1984, 1986, and 1987, resulting in a cumulative depreciation of 7,258 percent, from 2.75 cedis per dollar in 1982 to 154 cedis per dollar in 1987 (Figure 3.2a).[28] As a result of the devaluations, the real exchange rate, which had

[28] See Pinto 1990 for a discussion of Ghana's exchange rate management during this period.

appreciated by 88.6 percent between 1975 and 1982, depreciated sharply and by 1987 was only 2.3 percent below its 1975 level.[29] Subsequently, the government adopted an auction system, which eventually brought the official and parallel rates to within a few percent of one another by 1990. Throughout the process, Ghana gradually dismantled the licensing system, first by selectively moving items from a restricted list to an open general license list and eventually by abandoning licensing altogether. At present, the government maintains only a short negative list of import restrictions, all for noneconomic reasons. Other current account transactions are unrestricted.

Comparing the year prior to reforms (1982) with the year after reforms were completed (1988), real exports increased by 48 percent, an average of 6.7 percent per year over the period.[30] By 1988, real exports were 34 percent higher than in 1982. Although the value of cocoa exports declined after 1987 due to a decline in world prices,[31] other exports increased to allow total exports to remain constant. Noncocoa exports increased by $221 million (1980) between 1987 and 1990. Gold exports accounted for 28 percent of the increase ($61 million [1980]), with the remainder coming from other diverse exports.[32]

Guinea: Guinea's major trade and exchange rate liberalization took place later than Ghana's, beginning only in 1986, but had equally dramatic effects on the market for foreign exchange. At independence in 1960, Guinea withdrew from the CFA franc zone, established its own currency – the Guinea franc (between 1971 and 1984) – and adopted a centrally planned development strategy. From 1973 to 1985, the official exchange rate was fixed at Guinea syli (GS) 20.46 per dollar. Price controls were imposed on most major commodities, holding down measured inflation, but import demand greatly exceeded foreign exchange supply at the official exchange rate. Given the shortage of foreign exchange, imports were tightly controlled through quantitative restrictions and high tariffs. But price controls and the large premium for foreign exchange on the parallel market discouraged

---

[29] Given that Ghana's terms of trade and macroeconomic situation had changed in the intervening period, the difference in real exchange rates between 1975 and 1987 is not in itself an indication of a disequilibrium in the foreign exchange market in the latter year. See the discussion of equilibrium real exchange rates in Krumm 1993.

[30] Although we caution against inferring causality from this correlation, in Ghana's case it is difficult to see what factor other than policy changes might explain the growth of exports.

[31] The volume of cocoa exports actually increased during this period, mitigating the effects of the decline in world prices on the value of cocoa exports.

[32] Macroeconomic management since 1990 has been less successful in Ghana, though the problems have been mostly ones of fiscal balance (discussed in the next chapter). Continued nominal depreciations have prevented a real exchange rate appreciation, and exports have continued to grow at a rate comparable to that of the late 1980s.

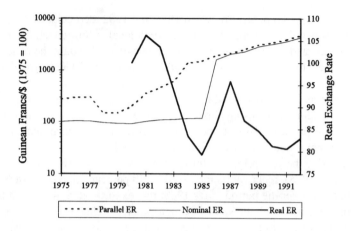

Figure 3.3a. Guinea: exchange rate fluctuations (real, nominal, and parallel).

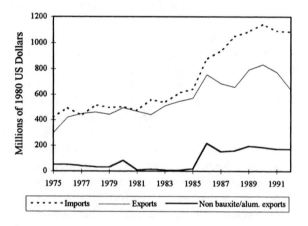

Figure 3.3b. Guinea: real exports and imports including net services and private transfers.

nonmining exports in the official market, so foreign exchange revenues came almost exclusively from bauxite and alumina exports. By 1985, the parallel exchange rate reached Guinea franc (GF) 311 per dollar: the premium on the parallel market was thus 1,420 percent.

As part of economic reforms undertaken by Guinea's Second Republic following the death in 1984 of the country's first president, Sekou Touré, the government sharply devalued the currency and liberalized trade. Between the last quarter of 1985 and the first quarter of 1986, the nominal exchange rate was devalued by 1,700 percent (Figure 3.3a). Also as part of the reforms, import licensing was abolished and tariff rates were simplified and reduced.[33] Massive domestic inflation (as measured using official prices) ensued as prices were decontrolled, but overall, between 1985 and 1987, the real exchange rate depreciated by 21.0 percent.[34] In response to the increased incentives in the official market, nonaluminum exports (mainly gold and agricultural) rose from $18.0 to $188.0 million between 1985 and 1986 and rose to $230.9 million dollars in 1989, equal to 30.3 percent of exports (Figure 3.3b). Much of this increase in recorded exports may represent a shift from parallel to official markets, rather than an increase in total exports. Unfortunately, lower world coffee prices beginning in 1990 helped to cut nonmining exports in half, so that nonmining exports averaged only $114.0 million from 1990 to 1992. Nonetheless, Guinea's overall real GDP growth averaged 3.7 percent per year over the postreform period, 1987 to 1992 (Arulpragasam and Sahn 1996).

Mozambique: Like Ghana and Guinea, Mozambique's trade and exchange rate policy reforms had major effects on the foreign exchange market, but war and drought hampered efforts to increase real exports. Mozambique's balance-of-payments problems in the early 1980s were the combined result of a civil war, a prolonged drought from 1982 to 1985, and bad economic policies, including large fiscal deficits and attempts at centralized control of prices and marketing. The government rationed foreign exchange and import licenses and controlled export receipts. While inflation raised the domestic price level by 221.9 percent between 1980 and 1986, the nominal exchange rate was allowed to depreciate by only 24.7 percent, so that the real exchange rate appreciated by 61.2 percent over the period (Figure 3.4a). Parallel market exchange rates ranged from Meticais (Mt) 1,450 to 1,950 per dollar from 1984 to 1986, 3,300 to 4,800 percent above the official nominal exchange rates (Dorosh and Bernier 1994a).

While the war continued, major economic reforms began with the Economic Rehabilitation Program adopted in 1987. Mozambique undertook two large

---

[33] This rapid liberalization took place in several steps. In October 1985, a second window for foreign exchange was established. Shortly thereafter, in January 1986, the syli was replaced by the Guinean franc (GF) at par, and a large devaluation of the currency was announced (from GF 20.46 per dollar to GF 300 per dollar). By June 1 of that year, the first and second windows for foreign exchange were unified. See Arulpragasam and Sahn (1996) for other details of the process.

[34] We calculate this relatively small real exchange rate depreciation using Guinea's GDP price deflator as a measure of annual domestic inflation. Using the consumer price index (which unfortunately begins only in late 1985), the initial real depreciation was 2,200 percent (Arulpragasam and Sahn 1996). Because the consumer price index is dominated by goods for which prices were controlled prior to the liberalization, this second measure of the real exchange rate overstates the extent of the real depreciation in overall economy.

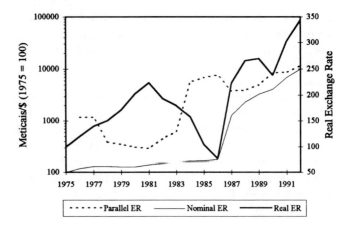

Figure 3.4a. Mozambique: exchange rate fluctuations (real, nominal, and parallel).

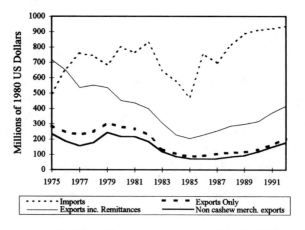

Figure 3.4b. Mozambique: real exports and imports (merchandise trade and remittances).

devaluations of 80 and 50 percent in 1987, raising the nominal exchange rate to Mt 289.4 per dollar, while large injections of foreign aid inflows sharply reduced the parallel exchange rate from Mt 1,950 per dollar in 1986 to Mt 975 per dollar in 1987. Exports (mainly prawns and cashews) increased by an average of 15.9 percent per year in dollar terms from 1987 to 1991 (Figure 3.4b). Contributing to the recovery were large flows of foreign aid, which averaged 47.9 percent of GDP over the period.

Finally, in 1992, a major trade liberalization was undertaken, and with foreign exchange no longer allocated through an import licensing system, the premium on the parallel market for foreign exchange fell to 17.3 percent. And in June 1993, the official and secondary market exchange rates were unified,[35] making the official exchange rate market-determined for the first time in Mozambique's history.[36]

Tanzania: Trade and exchange rate liberalizations in Tanzania have been more gradual and, until 1992, less complete than in the preceeding three countries. For Tanzania, a combination of long-term foreign capital inflows and high world coffee prices during the mid-1970s financed the country's import needs, and the country's third five-year plan (1976–1981) included several large import-intensive industrial and infrastructural projects (such as the Tanzania–Zambia railroad project). In the late 1970s, however, a decline in world coffee prices reduced export earnings, while increased imports for military goods needed for the war with Uganda in 1978 and 1979 raised demand for foreign exchange and contributed to a balance-of-payments crisis. The government was slow to respond to these developments, and imports remained high in 1980 and 1981, even after the war's end (Figure 3.5b). In 1982, the country's first structural adjustment program failed to win IMF approval because tight import controls were maintained and only small devaluations (10 percent in March 1982, 20 percent in June 1983) were undertaken (Sarris and van den Brink 1994).

Major trade and exchange rate liberalizations in Tanzania were a central part of the Economic Recovery Program, adopted in August 1986.[37] The Tanzanian shilling (Tsh) was devalued from Tsh 17 per dollar to Tsh 190 per dollar between 1986 and 1990, reducing the premium on foreign exchange in the parallel market from 809 percent at the end of 1986 to 56 percent at the end of 1990 (Figure 3.5a). In the wake of these policy changes, noncoffee exports doubled between 1986 and 1992, from $162.9 to $337.5 million.[38] The increase in total exports of goods and nonfactor services was smaller, however (only 25.4 percent), because a decline in world coffee prices led to a $125.2-million decline in coffee export revenues from 1986 to 1992 (IMF 1994b).

[35] A legalized secondary market for foreign exchange was established in late 1990.

[36] More important for long-term recovery, a peace accord was signed in October 1992, and elections held in 1994.

[37] Prior to the ERP, an own-funded import scheme was instituted in 1985, which allowed individuals to use their own foreign exchange (with no questions asked about its origin) to import goods on the official market. As a result, private foreign exchange from parallel market exports and other sources funded a large increase in official imports, and the ratio of official imports to GDP grew from 15.6 percent in 1985 to 28.4 percent and 40.4 percent in 1986 and 1987.

[38] Much of this increase was due to exports of cotton, which rose from $30.4 to $97.6 million from 1986 to 1992 (IMF 1994b).

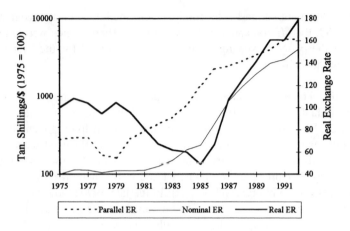

Figure 3.5a. Tanzania: exchange rate fluctuations (real, nominal, and parallel).

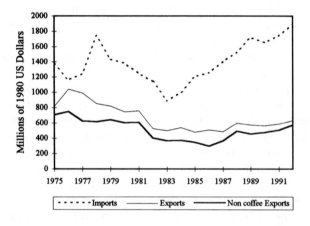

Figure 3.5b. Tanzania: real exports and imports for goods and nonfactor services.

Further reforms liberalizing the trade and exchange system were instituted in 1992 and 1993. These included the introduction of foreign exchange bureaus in 1992, the unification of the official and open market exchange rates through weekly foreign exchange auctions beginning in August 1993, and the virtual elimination of import and export licensing, registration, and permit requirements.

Zaire: While each of the above four countries enjoyed a measure of success in implementing policy reforms and promoting exports, no sustained macroeconomic reforms have taken place in Zaire in spite of a succession of stabilization and structural adjustment programs. Rather, balance-of-payments problems, which began in 1975 with a nearly 40 percent fall in the world price of copper (Zaire's major export) have plagued the economy through much of the past two decades. Contributing to the crisis in the early 1970s was massive foreign borrowing for investment projects in 1972 and 1973. From 1976 to 1982, Zaire negotiated seven separate agreements for financing from the IMF, yet large deficits financed by credit expansion fueled inflation, which averaged 40 percent per year over the period. Despite several devaluations of the currency over this period, the real exchange rate appreciated sharply, and the premium on the parallel market for foreign exchange averaged 176 percent (Figure 3.6a).

In 1983, an IMF-sponsored stabilization plan focusing on exchange rate devaluation, trade reform, and price liberalization was undertaken. A combination of a 77.5 percent devaluation of the zaire and tighter fiscal policy that reduced inflation from 101.0 percent in 1983 to 14.5 percent in 1984 resulted in a substantial depreciation of the real exchange rate. Thereafter, depreciation of the nominal official exchange rate was linked to market transactions in a secondary foreign exchange market. Exports rose by 18.6 percent in 1984, but fell in 1985 and 1986 as fiscal deficits and domestic inflation increased, while export incentives fell. A structural adjustment program that began in 1987 failed due to lack of fiscal discipline, and loan disbursements were suspended by donors in both 1988 and 1990. From 1989 to 1993, increased deficit spending by the government amid an uncertain political situation led to hyperinflation,[39] rapid currency depreciation, and destruction of capital. Over this period, real GDP declined by 33.8 percent and exports fell by 48.0 percent in dollar terms (IMF 1994c) (Figure 3.6b).

Countries with moderate distortions in foreign exchange markets

In contrast to the massive distortions in the foreign exchange markets prior to reforms in the five preceding countries, exchange rate distortions in Madagascar, Malawi, and The Gambia were much smaller. Real exports responded positively to reforms in Madagascar and The Gambia, though only in the latter country was a liberalized trade regime sustained.

Madagascar: Madagascar undertook significant trade and exchange rate policy reforms in 1987 and 1988, five years after initial stabilization efforts. In the late 1970s, Madagascar benefited from high world prices of its major agricultural exports: coffee, cocoa, and vanilla. During this time the Malagasy government launched an ambitious investment program funded

---

[39] The hyperinflation eventually led to the introduction of a new currency, the new zaire, which replaced the old zaire at a parity of 1 new zaire = 1 million old zaires in October 1993.

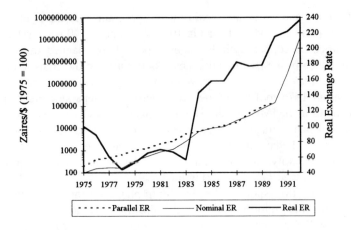

Figure 3.6a. Zaire: exchange rate fluctuations (real, nominal, and parallel).

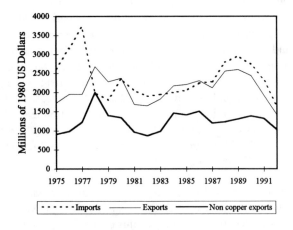

Figure 3.6b. Zaire: real exports and imports for goods and nonfactor services.

mainly by foreign commercial borrowing. Imports of capital goods soared in 1979 and 1980 (Figure 3.7b). Unfortunately, export earnings fell sharply during the investment boom as world coffee prices fell and as an appreciating real exchange rate (caused in part by the surge in foreign capital inflows) reduced export incentives. World credit markets tightened in the early 1980s and Madagascar's short-term loans came due, forcing an abrupt halt to the investment boom and the adoption of an IMF-sponsored stabilization in 1982.

A number of policy reforms, including liberalization of domestic rice marketing, decontrol of prices, reductions in government spending, and exchange rate devaluations, were undertaken gradually beginning in 1982. However, the

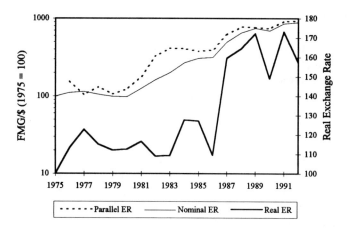

Figure 3.7a. Madagascar: exchange rate fluctuations (real, nominal, and parallel).

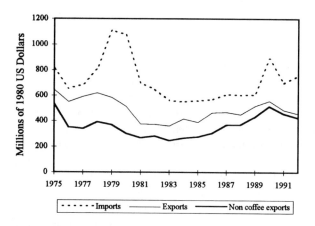

Figure 3.7b. Madagascar: real exports and imports for goods and nonfactor services.

government did not implement major trade reforms – in particular, liberalization of the import licensing system – until 1987 and 1988. In the aftermath of these reforms, which included a 137 percent nominal devaluation (and a 57 percent real devaluation) of the Malagasy franc relative to the dollar in 1987 and 1988 (Figure 3.7a), real exports increased by 14 percent between 1986 and 1989 (an average of just 2.7 percent per year). More important, growth in real GDP per capita was positive in both 1989 and 1990, the first increases in real per capita incomes since the unsustainable investment boom of 1978 to 1980.

Unfortunately, beginning in 1991, economic growth faltered as political turmoil, related to an eventual transition to a new government, led to strikes, disruptions in aid flows, and reversals of earlier policy changes. In particular, the transitional government reversed trade and exchange rate policy reforms and reimposed controls on foreign exchange. Finally, after the installation of a new government in 1993, trade and exchange rate liberalization began anew with a devaluation of the Malagasy franc from FMG 1,900 to 3,400 per dollar in May and June of 1994.

Malawi: Unlike most other African countries, Malawi maintained a relatively liberal trade and exchange rate regime throughout the 1960s and 1970s. At independence, nominal exchange rates were pegged to the British pound, then in 1973 to a weighted average of the pound and the U.S. dollar, and in 1975 to the Special Drawing Right (SDR). Conservative fiscal policy limited aggregate demand and domestic inflation, so that the real exchange rate did not appreciate dramatically as in other non-CFA countries with fixed nominal exchange rates (i.e., Guinea and Zaire) (Figure 3.8a). Exports of tobacco and other agricultural products contributed to growth in real GDP that averaged 6.3 percent per year from 1974 to 1979.

Malawi's balance-of-payments situation deteriorated after 1977 as its terms of trade declined by 40 percent while foreign borrowing financed a surge in imports from 1978 to 1980 (Figure 3.8b).[40] As in Madagascar, much of the increase in imports was due to greater government development expenditures (which rose from 5.5 percent of GDP in 1977 to 13.8 percent of GDP in 1981).[41] The debt service ratio (interest and amortization as a percentage of the value of exports of goods and services) rose from 10.0 percent in 1977 to 26.8 percent in 1981 (and later to 40.0 percent in 1986).[42] Initial reform efforts in the early 1980s were stymied by drought and the war in neighboring Mozambique, which shut down traditional low-cost rail links and forced land-locked Malawi to use higher-cost routes to South Africa and Tanzania for exports and imports.[43] In the face of foreign exchange shortages, Malawi replaced its liberal trade and exchange rate regime with quantitative restrictions on imports. A series of discrete devaluations from 1982 to 1987 prevented major changes in the real exchange rate, but failed to restore equilibrium in the balance of payments.

[40] Average imports in 1978–1980 were 28.5 percent higher than in 1977 in quantity terms (calculated from data in Sahn, Arulpragasam, and Merid 1990) and 68.6 percent higher in dollar terms (calculated from data in Pryor 1988).

[41] Sahn et al. 1990.

[42] Pryor 1990.

[43] The drought in 1980/1981 and an influx of Mozambican refugees contributed to the balance-of-payments crisis by raising food import needs (Sahn et al. 1990).

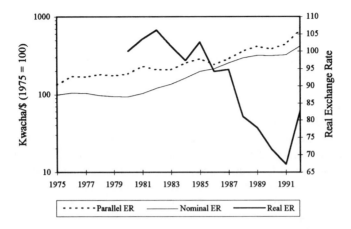

Figure 3.8a. Malawi: exchange rate fluctuations (real, nominal, and parallel).

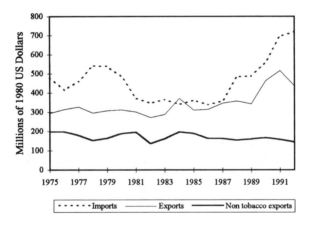

Figure 3.8b. Malawi: real exports and imports for goods and nonfactor services.

Major trade liberalization took place in 1988 with a small 11.6 percent exchange rate devaluation[44] and liberalization of foreign exchange allocation. With domestic inflation of 33.9 and 12.5 percent in 1988 and 1989, respectively, the real exchange rate actually appreciated by 12.2 percent between 1987 and 1989, however. Real imports, funded largely by official transfers, increased sharply, but real exports stagnated until 1990 when tobacco exports rose by 63.2 percent in volume terms (34.5 thousand tons). Nontobacco exports stagnated, however. Foreign exchange controls were reimposed in

[44] We measure nominal exchange rate depreciation from fourth quarter of 1987 to first quarter of 1988 (IMF 1994a).

1992 as donors suspended nonhumanitarian balance-of-payments support to Malawi (because of concerns about governance) and drought reduced agricultural export earnings. After the end of the drought, a national referendum, and the resumption of foreign aid flows in 1993, the government again liberalized the foreign exchange market in February 1994, with the exchange rate determined through weekly auctions for foreign exchange.

The Gambia: For The Gambia, exchange rate and trade policy reforms have been sustained and have contributed to a large increase in real exports since 1986. As in Madagascar and Niger, The Gambia's balance-of-payments problems in the early 1980s can be traced to a surge in development spending (beginning in 1975/1976 as part of the country's first Five-Year Plan), and a decline in terms of trade (due to lower world groundnut export prices) in the early 1980s. Problems were compounded by a drought in 1980 and 1981 that reduced agricultural production and exports and necessitated increased rice imports. Stabilization efforts supported by the IMF included cuts in government imports and, in 1984, a 25 percent devaluation of the dalasi, which had been pegged to the British pound since 1974. But increased development expenditures financed by foreign capital inflows in that year led to a rise in inflation to 22 percent and a 9.3 percent appreciation of the real exchange rate in 1985, more than offsetting the real depreciation achieved in 1984.

As part of the Economic Recovery Program in 1985/1986, the government introduced an interbank market for foreign exchange in January 1986.[45] After an initial depreciation of 49 percent, the dalasi depreciated further so that by October 1986, the spread in the parallel market essentially disappeared (Figure 3.9a). The real exchange rate depreciated by 39.1 percent in 1986 and these improved export incentives were maintained: relative to 1985, the average real exchange rate from 1986 to 1992 was 33.1 percent higher than in 1985.[46] Real exports increased by 135.0 percent between 1985 and 1992 (an average growth rate of 13.0 percent per year) before falling slightly in 1993 (Figure 3.9b).

Much of this growth in exports resulted from increased reexports to neighboring West African countries[47] (the share of reexports in total merchandise exports rose from 71.1 percent in 1987/1988 to 82.1 percent in 1991/1992

---

[45] The Gambian government established foreign exchange bureaus later, in 1990 (IMF 1992a).

[46] These calculations use the estimates of The Gambia's real effective exchange rate from the IMF (various years b). A simpler measure of the real exchange rate uses the average import price for less developed countries as the world price index of tradable goods. By this measure, the real exchange rate depreciated by only 10 percent in 1986 and then appreciated by 12.4 percent in 1987, ending up 3.6 percent below the initial level of 1985.

[47] The Gambia's only land borders are with Senegal. Reexport trade includes both goods sold in Senegal and transit trade to other countries.

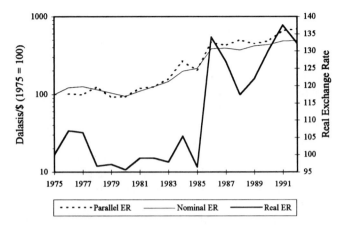

Figure 3.9a. The Gambia: exchange rate fluctuations (real, nominal, and parallel).

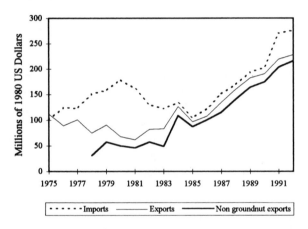

Figure 3.9b. The Gambia: real exports and imports for goods and nonfactor services.

[IMF 1993a]). Since imports are taxed, the reexport trade also accounts for a sizable portion of government revenues (about 20 percent of total government revenues in 1992/1993). Thus, after Senegal reinforced border surveillance and suspended convertibility of the CFA franc in August 1993 (making transactions in the CFA franc less attractive), reexports declined sharply, falling by 34 percent in 1993/1994 (SPA 1994).

The CFA zone

Trade and exchange rate policy reforms in the CFA zone differed markedly from reforms in other African countries. Up until January 1994, the countries of the CFA zone maintained a fixed exchange rate with the French franc at parity of 50 CFA francs per French franc. In 1994, the members of the CFA zone devalued the CFA franc by 100 percent to a new rate of 100 CFA francs per French franc.[48] Throughout the 1980s and early 1990s, however, the countries of the CFA zone lacked the option of an exchange rate devaluation and were left only with trade taxes and quotas as policy levers capable of directly influencing external balances. In practice, more indirect measures were used – expenditure reductions and restrictive credit policies.

Under the arrangements of the CFA zone,[49] member countries are required to deposit 65 percent of their foreign currency holdings in the operations account at the French treasury. In exchange, France guarantees the full convertibility of the CFA franc at a fixed exchange rate by provision of central bank overdrafts on these accounts.[50] Monetary targets for the countries of the West African Economic and Monetary Union (UEMOA) and the Central African Economic and Customs Union (UDEAC) are set by regional central banks,[51] headed by representatives of member countries and the French treasury. Credit by the central banks to member governments is limited to 20 percent of the government's fiscal receipts in the previous year.[52]

Until the adjustment period of the early 1980s, the macroeconomic performance of CFA countries was generally better than that of the non-CFA countries in sub-Saharan Africa. Cross-country regression analysis indicated that the CFA countries had significantly higher growth than other countries in sub-Saharan Africa over the 1960–1982 period (Devarajan and de Melo 1987). Guillaumont, Guillaumont, and Plane (1988) hypothesize that convertibility, monetary discipline, and stability of real exchange rates contributed to commercial openness and greater levels of investment in the CFA zone countries, in part accounting for the higher growth rates.

[48]   The Comorian franc was set at a new parity of CF 75 per 1 French franc.
[49]   The fifteen members of the franc zone are Benin, Burkina Faso, Côte d'Ivoire, Mali, Niger, Senegal, and Togo (all members of the West African Economic and Monetary Union [UEMOA]); Cameroon, Central African Republic, Chad, Congo, Equatorial Guinea, and Gabon (members of the Central African Economic and Customs Union [UDEAC]); the Comoros and France.
[50]   External convertibility of the CFA franc was discontinued for a short time, from August 1993 to January 1994, as balance-of-payments problems linked to adverse movements in the terms of trade threatened the financial viability of the franc zone.
[51]   The Banque Centrale des Etats de l'Afrique de l'Ouest (BCEAO) is the central bank of the UEMOA, and the Banque Centrale des Etats de l'Afrique Centrale (BCEAC) is the central bank of the UDEAC.
[52]   This rule has not prevented the financing of government spending from abroad through commercial bank loans to governments and parastatals (Guillaumont and Guillaumont 1984; Bhatia 1985). Moreover, as in Côte d'Ivoire in the 1970s, the inflow of foreign exchange during periods of high export receipts leads in itself to increases in money supply (Lane 1989).

Difficulties in adjusting the real exchange rate in response to adverse external shocks contributed, however, to a deterioration in the economic performance of franc zone countries in the 1980s (Devarajan and de Melo 1990). Though inflation was kept low, economic growth suffered. Devarajan and Rodrik (1991) conclude that "the costs of maintaining a fixed exchange rate regime in the context of highly variable external terms of trade" resulted in a trade-off between output and inflation that was "a bad bargain for CFA member countries."

With the nominal exchange rate of the CFA franc fixed relative to the French franc prior to 1994, depreciation of the real exchange rate in CFA countries was difficult to achieve. The fall in prices of petroleum, coffee, cocoa, and other key export commodities of CFA countries coincided with an appreciation of the French franc (and thus the CFA franc) against other major currencies. A real depreciation of the CFA franc would thus have required a substantial decline in domestic prices relative to prices of trading partners. Reducing money supply to achieve this goal, however, would have meant a substantial cut in credit to the economy, with potentially disastrous consequences for the formal manufacturing and services sectors.[53]

Up until 1994, a devaluation of the CFA franc, while advocated by the World Bank and IMF, was opposed by the French government. French development officials argued that Africa's exports are either initially priced in dollars or face an inelastic world demand, so that a devaluation would not lead to an increase in the quantity of exports. Moreover, a devaluation would make debt payments more burdensome. The validity of these objections is questionable, at best,[54] leading many observers to suspect that "the resistance to devaluation is largely to protect French political and business interests" (Wilson 1993, 336).[55]

---

[53] Côte d'Ivoire attempted to mimic a liberalizing devaluation in 1984 through an export subsidy of 20 percent on local value-added and standardize effective protection of import competing goods at 40 percent. The reform failed due to numerous exemptions and incomplete coverage of the taxes, a rise in parallel markets to evade taxes, and, ultimately, a sharp deterioration in terms of trade, which forced a lowering of the prices of export crops (cocoa and coffee) in 1989 (Azam and Morrisson 1994).

[54] A real devaluation would permit an increase in the domestic producer prices of exports, spurring production and farmer incomes (see Chapter 5). While total world demand for many of Africa's exports may be price inelastic, many African countries have been losing market share to countries outside of Africa. Though a devaluation would increase the CFA franc value of the debt, it would leave the foreign currency value unchanged, while tending to increase the value of exports and reduce the value of imports in foreign currency terms.

[55] Because French companies with investments in CFA countries faced potential large losses (in French franc terms) with a devaluation, there was massive capital flight out of the franc zone prior to the devaluation.

Both Cameroon and Niger fit the broad patterns of economic boom and decline described here. Favorable terms-of-trade movements in the 1970s and early 1980s boosted economic growth, but later declines in world prices of their exports contributed to economic stagnation and serious fiscal problems in the late 1980s and early 1990s. Few major changes in trade and exchange rate policy took place in these countries prior to 1994.

Cameroon: During the 1970s and early 1980s Cameroon's economy grew rapidly, due first to high prices of its major agricultural exports (coffee and cocoa) in the 1970s and then, after the discovery of oil in 1978, to a surge in petroleum exports. Between 1978 and 1986, real GDP doubled, raising per capita incomes by 57 percent (Blandford et al. 1994). Unlike other developing-country petroleum exporters such as Nigeria and Mexico, Cameroon adopted a conservative fiscal policy during the oil boom years, depositing much of the oil revenues in offshore accounts.[56] By thus limiting the inflationary impact of higher oil revenues on domestic prices, the country to a large extent avoided a sharp appreciation of the real exchange rate and the adverse consequences of reduced production incentives in tradable goods sectors (the so-called Dutch disease).[57] In addition, in an attempt to protect tradable agricultural sectors, the government introduced trade policy measures in the mid-1980s, such as tariffs on imported rice and increases in producer prices of export crops. The government also intervened by promoting foreign investment linked with parastatal enterprises as part of its doctrine of "planned liberalism."[58]

Subsequent declines in export prices of oil, coffee, and cocoa in 1986 and 1987 greatly reduced government revenues, forced cutbacks in public investment and subsidies to parastatals, and led to a sharp increase in foreign borrowing. Cameroon's economic reform program was supported by an initial standby agreement with the IMF in 1988,[59] and a structural adjustment loan with the World Bank in 1989. As world prices fell further, the government sharply cut prices of cocoa and coffee in 1989/1990 to bring domestic prices in line with world prices. In February 1990, Cameroon removed import restrictions on 105 products and abolished import licenses. Despite these reforms, however, continued declines in the terms of trade, sharp cutbacks in govern-

---

[56] This conservative policy was more than justified, given projections that economically recoverable oil reserves were likely to be depleted by the mid-1990s (Blandford et al. 1994).

[57] Benjamin and Devarajan (1986) provide quantitative estimates of the potential adverse consequences of allowing oil earnings to reduce production incentives for nonoil tradable goods.

[58] See Ndongko 1986 and Willame 1986 for two sharply contrasting views of the effectiveness of "planned liberalism."

[59] The government signed a second standby agreement in 1991.

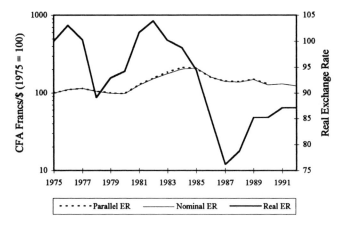

Figure 3.10a. Cameroon: exchange rate fluctuations (real, nominal, and parallel).

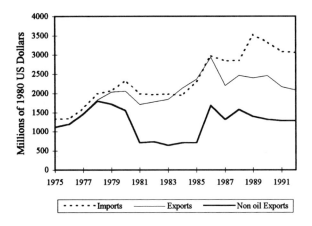

Figure 3.10b. Cameroon: real exports and imports for goods and nonfactor services.

ment investment, and political turmoil contributed to a decline in real per capita incomes of more than 50 percent between 1986 and 1993. Total exports and nonoil exports declined in real dollar terms, while imports remained high (Figure 3.10b) and Cameroon accumulated arrears in payments of interest to its foreign creditors.

Niger: Niger's management of its uranium export earnings stands in sharp contrast to Cameroon's more conservative fiscal policies during the early 1980s. With expected future export earnings boosting its creditworthiness,

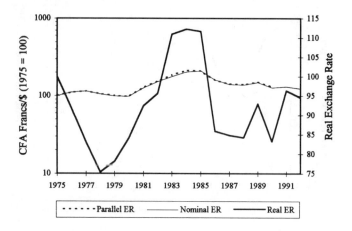

Figure 3.11a. Niger: exchange rate fluctuations (real, nominal, and parallel).

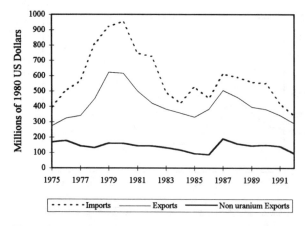

Figure 3.11b. Niger: real exports and imports for goods and nonfactor services.

Niger borrowed heavily in international markets from 1978 to 1982 to fund a massive public investment program in infrastructure, manufacturing, and irrigation. A combination of increasing interest payments on past debt, declining terms of trade, and tighter world credit markets in the early 1980s led to severe fiscal deficits and current account deficits in the balance of payments (Figure 3.11b). The current account deficit (before official transfers) reached 125.8 billion francs, equal to 19.5 percent of GDP and 86.9 percent of exports of goods and nonfactor services in 1982 (World Bank 1993b). Reform efforts supported by the IMF and the World Bank beginning in 1983 helped reduce imports (mainly through cuts in investment expenditures), but drought, a decline in uranium export earnings, and economic recession in Nigeria (a major trading partner bordering Niger to the south) prevented an economic recovery.

While membership in the CFA zone constrained Niger's exchange rate policy, the long, relatively open border with Nigeria made trade tax measures unenforceable. Attempts to tax Niger's cross-border exports of cattle and cowpeas or imports of manufactured goods and gasoline from Nigeria could be easily evaded through unofficial trade. When Nigeria's exchange rate devaluations and macroeconomic reforms led to depreciation of the Nigerian naira – that is, an appreciation of the real exchange rate of the CFA franc relative to the naira – trade policy measures (e.g., import tariffs) were not a feasible policy option. Niger's adjustment efforts thus focused on fiscal reforms, mainly cuts in government expenditures, in an effort to reduce aggregate demand and budget deficits. In part due to political constraints preventing large cuts in the government wage bill, adjustment efforts were largely ineffective in reducing trade imbalances until 1991 and 1992.

Summary of country experiences

The ten country experiences outlined suggest a number of generalizations about trade policy reform in sub-Saharan Africa. First, balance-of-payments crises in the ten countries were the results of a combination of both external shocks and inappropriate domestic economic policies. Some combination of adverse movements in the terms of trade, droughts, tightening of world credit markets, or the effects of war contributed to balance-of-payments crises in all the countries. To a large extent, however, inappropriate economic policies during periods of favorable terms of trade and the absence of negative shocks created latent problems in terms of increasing foreign debt and/or appreciations of the real exchange rate that grew to crisis proportions when external shocks hit. In particular, overly ambitious development plans financed by foreign borrowing in Madagascar and Niger (and, to a lesser extent, in The Gambia, Malawi, Tanzania, and Zaire) led to increases in foreign debt and interest payment obligations, and large fiscal deficits, most notably in Ghana, Guinea, Mozambique, Tanzania, and Zaire, led to domestic money creation, appreciations of the real exchange rate, and excess demand for imports.

Second, policy reform implementation has been difficult to achieve and to sustain. In four of the five countries with massive distortions in foreign exchange markets prior to reform (Ghana, Guinea, Zaire, and Mozambique), trade and exchange rate policy reforms were central aspects of the initial liberalization efforts and were undertaken rapidly. In the countries with smaller initial distortions (Madagascar, Malawi, The Gambia, and the CFA countries) and in Tanzania (where exchange rate reforms were vigorously resisted), substantial liberalization of foreign exchange allocation took place only after years of

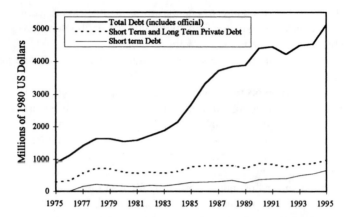

Figure 3.12.   Average real expenditure debt of sample countries, 1975–1995.
Source: World Bank, various years, 1993b; IMF, various years b.

adjustment efforts. Sustaining reforms has proved difficult in the three non-CFA countries in the sample (Madagascar, Malawi, and Zaire) that reimposed foreign exchange controls within five years of major liberalization efforts.

Third, postliberalization gains in real export earnings were mitigated by a decline in world prices of coffee, a major export of Madagascar, Guinea, and Tanzania, and cocoa, Ghana's major export. Only in Ghana and Mozambique, countries for which policy reforms helped improve export incentives, have nontraditional exports increased substantially.

Finally, it is important to note that the trade and exchange rate policy reform did not lead to a long-term decline in trade deficits. Foreign capital inflows increased and the trade deficit widened for most countries after reforms were initiated, as loans from bilateral and multilateral donors increased to support the policy changes. For some countries, such as Madagascar, the increase in official foreign capital inflows came only after stabilization programs. These programs sharply cut back imports that were previously financed by commercial borrowing. Nevertheless, beginning in the mid-1980s, official foreign capital inflows (and foreign debt) rose sharply, more than offsetting the reversal of private capital flows (Figure 3.12). Unlike in Latin America, adjustment in sub-Saharan Africa has not involved a net outflow of capital.

To a large extent, increased capital inflows made policy reform politically acceptable. Liberalization of foreign exchange markets in the absence of large inflows of foreign capital would have required very large depreciations of the real exchange rate. Where this foreign aid supporting liberalization was withdrawn, as in Madagascar and Malawi, trade and exchange rate reforms were reversed.

Implications of reform for income distribution and poverty

A major concern of critics of adjustment in sub-Saharan Africa has been the deleterious impact of exchange rate devaluations on the poor. How various household groups have been affected by these policy reforms depends to a large extent on whether they had access to foreign exchange and imported goods at official prices prior to the policy changes.[60] In general, access to official markets by the poor was extremely limited and, as we will argue, the poor were likely better off *with* trade and exchange rate policy reform than *without* the reforms. In contrast, households that did have access to foreign exchange and imported goods at official markets, generally a small number of urban elite, suffered significant losses of income, a major reason behind their opposition to policy reform.

Excess profits (rents) associated with foreign exchange controls and trade restrictions in sub-Saharan Africa prior to policy reforms were enormous (Table 3.3). In the year immediately preceding reforms, premiums on foreign exchange in the parallel markets exceeded 100 percent in Zaire and Tanzania (i.e., the parallel exchange rate was more than double the official exchange rate) and more than 1,000 percent in Guinea, Ghana, and Mozambique. Devaluations and trade policy reforms that lessened import restrictions reduced these premiums from an average of 1,004 percent in the year preceding the reforms to only 25 percent in the year after the reforms.

The difference between the value of imports as measured at parallel prices and at official prices provides a rough measure of the size of the excess profits associated with trade and exchange rate restrictions. These implicit rents (converted to dollars using the parallel exchange rate) averaged $460 million for the eight country sample in Table 3.3, equivalent to $34 per person.

Of course, these implicit rents were not distributed equally throughout the population. Some of the rents accrued to government agencies that received import licenses and scarce foreign exchange to import capital goods and pay other foreign exchange costs of development projects. Much of the rents, however, went to the small minority of households that obtained imported goods and foreign exchange at official prices for home consumption or for resale in parallel markets.[61] For these households, trade and exchange rate policy reforms represented huge losses of income. Other, nonfavored households gen-

---

[60] In addition, since an overvalued exchange rate also taxes producers of export crops who sell their products on the official market, producers of export crops stand to gain from a real exchange rate depreciation. The model simulations presented here assume that producers are not able to avoid this implicit tax through parallel market exports.

[61] Absence of consumer goods at official prices in rural markets (one evidence that the rural poor do not receive the rents associated with foreign exchange restrictions) is a common feature of African economies that have price and import controls. The resulting adverse consequences on agricultural growth are explored by Bevan, Collier, and

erally purchased their goods in parallel markets and so were not directly affected by the elimination of rents.

How did the changes in the economy associated with policy reforms affect these households that did not have access to foreign exchange and imported goods at low official prices? Neoclassical economic theory suggests that in economies where labor is relatively more abundant than capital, returns to labor will rise with liberalization as production of labor-intensive tradables increases.[62] Though the theory only describes changes in factor incomes (earnings of labor and capital), it implies in the case of sub-Saharan Africa that poor households will tend to gain because labor is the major source of their income.

CGE model simulation

More complicated CGE models overcome the oversimplifications of the basic economic theory by modeling production of various sectors and returns to several factors of production; determining changes in household income through a more detailed mapping from factor incomes to various types of households; and taking into account changes in consumption and prices. Here, we present counterfactual simulations using CGE models of five economies (Cameroon, The Gambia, Madagascar, Niger, and Tanzania) to highlight the impacts of policy changes on poor households.

The five CGE models are neoclassical in structure, following Dervis, de Melo, and Robinson (1982). We base all models on detailed social accounting matrices (SAMs), constructed from data from the national accounts (including input–output tables), household expenditure surveys, and agricultural censuses

Gunning (1990) for Tanzania, Berthélemy (1988) for Madagascar, and Azam and Faucher (1988) for Mozambique.

[62] The Stolper – Samuelson theorem (Stolper and Samuelson 1941) shows these results in the case of a small country with two internally mobile factors of production (labor and capital), producing two goods (the Heckscher–Ohlin model). If labor is the more abundant factor (as is the case in most developing countries), the more labor-intensive good will be exported and the more capital-intensive good will be imported, provided that there is not a demand bias toward consumption of the capital-intensive good that outweighs this production bias.

Imposing a tariff on the imported good will raise its domestic price, resulting in an increase in production of the imported good. Since the imported good is more capital-intensive than the exported good, demand for capital will rise along with total returns to capital. Removal of a tariff brings the opposite result: an increase in total payments to labor. Since the poor in developing countries tend to derive a larger share of their income from labor than do the rich, the implication is that a trade liberalization will help increase the incomes of the poor.

Bourguignon and Morrisson (1989) point out that these results may not hold in models with several goods and factors of production (e.g., various skill levels of labor, sector specific capital), or in the case of imperfect mobility of factors and oligopolies in service and commodity markets. See Chacoliades 1978 and Ethier 1983 for a further discussion of the theorem and its variants.

and other surveys.[63] We generally define household groups according to asset ownership (land and agricultural capital such as cattle) and labor skills of the head of household, characteristics that correspond generally with income level (Table 3.4). By defining relatively homogeneous household groups sharing similar income sources and consumption patterns in this way, it is possible to simulate the effects of policy and external shocks on the average welfare of major subgroups of the poor and nonpoor.

In the models,[64] production is disaggregated into major agricultural, industrial, and tertiary subsectors in a manner reflecting the importance of various subsectors in each country. Value-added is modeled as a constant elasticity of substitution (CES) function of labor of various skilled types and sector-specific fixed capital (including formal and informal nonagricultural capital), and land disaggregated by ecological region (for Cameroon, Madagascar, and Niger) and income level (poor/nonpoor) of farm household. We determine incomes of households according to each household's fixed share of returns to factors of production. We model consumption of each commodity either as a fixed value share of total expenditures (The Gambia and Niger) or by using a linear expenditure system (LES) specification (Cameroon, Madagascar, and Tanzania). Note that we do not analyze within-group variations in household incomes and behavior. Thus, the models provide insights on changes in average incomes of the household groups shown, neglecting intragroup variations.

In all five models, prices and wages clear markets, labor supply is fixed,[65] imports and exports are less than perfect substitutes for local goods, and government spending is exogenous. Total investment in the models is equal to total savings – the sum of households' savings (a linear function of households' incomes), government savings (revenues less recurrent expenditures), and foreign savings. We hold fixed foreign savings (foreign capital inflow) across the model simulations here,[66] so as to facilitate comparison of income

---

[63] See Dorosh and Essama-Nssah 1991, Dorosh et al. 1991, Gauthier and Kyle 1991, Subramanian 1994, Jabara et al. 1992, and Sarris 1994b for complete descriptions of the social accounting matrices and data sources.

[64] Further details of the models are found in the appendix and in Benjamin 1993; Subramanian 1996; Dorosh and Lundberg 1996; Dorosh 1996; Dorosh, Essama-Nssah, and Samba-Mamadou 1996; and Sarris 1996. The Tanzania CGE model used for the simulations in this book was adapted from Sarris 1996 and excludes the financial variables and equations of the original model.

[65] In an earlier version of these simulations of alternative policy responses to terms-of-trade shocks, Dorosh and Sahn (1993) use a nonzero labor supply elasticity to simulate underemployment. This alternative specification does not lead to qualitatively different results.

The Tanzania model simulations do include small variations in total employment due to changes in households' labor-leisure-education choices, but real wages adjust to equate labor supply and demand.

[66] Some of the simulations in Chapter 4 use an alternative savings–investment closure.

Table 3.4. *Household per capita incomes and population, CGE models*

	Population (%)	Per capita income[a]	Share of national income (%)
Cameroon			
Urban nonpoor	10.1	853	21.9
Urban poor	0.9	310	0.7
Rural nonpoor	40.5	564	58.2
Farm	27.8	480	34.0
Nonfarm	12.7	749	24.2
Rural poor	48.5	155	19.1
Farm north	12.7	165	5.3
Farm south	25.6	148	9.6
Nonfarm	10.2	160	4.2
All Cameroon	100.0	393	100.0
Gambia			
Urban nonpoor	8.6	6702	28.3
Urban poor	20.1	2554	25.2
Rural nonpoor	21.4	2061	21.7
Rural poor	49.9	1013	24.8
All Gambia	100.0	2036	100.0
Madagascar			
Urban nonpoor	2.2	877	11.2
Urban poor	14.7	170	14.5
Urban middle income	11.7	181	12.3
Urban low income	3.0	126	2.2
Rural nonpoor	23.5	271	37.1
Rural poor	59.6	107	37.1
Farm plateau	19.9	103	11.9
Farm east coast	20.8	105	12.7
Farm west, south	14.0	118	9.6
Nonfarm	4.9	103	3.0
All Madagascar	100.0	172	100.0
Niger			
Urban nonpoor	3.2	415	16.6
Urban poor	11.3	116	16.5
Large city poor	6.4	160	12.8
Small city poor	4.9	60	3.7
Rural nonpoor	34.1	82	35.2
North	10.4	116	15.1
South	23.7	68	20.2
Rural poor	51.4	49	31.6
North	31.2	49	19.2
South	20.2	49	12.5
All Niger	100.0	80	100.0

Table 3.4. *(cont.)*

	Population (%)	Per capita income[a]	Share of national income (%)
Tanzania			
Urban nonpoor	9.0	4110	28.4
Urban high income	3.2	7424	18.4
Urban middle income	5.8	2254	10.0
Urban poor	3.9	870	2.6
Rural nonpoor	22.7	1726	29.9
Rural high income	4.4	2711	9.1
Rural middle income	18.3	1490	20.8
Rural poor	64.3	799	39.2
All Tanzania	100.0	1312	100.0

[a]Units of incomes are as follows: Cameroon (thousand 1985 CFAF), The Gambia (1990 Dalasis), Madagascar (thousand 1984 FMG), Niger (thousand 1987 CFAF), Tanzania (1976 Tanzanian shillings).
Sources: Dorosh 1994b; Dorosh and Lundberg 1996; Dorosh and Essama-Nssah 1991; Subramanian 1996; and Sarris 1996.

levels across simulations.[67] We make no attempt to model monetary or financial variables, thus confining our analysis to relative price effects (see also Shoven and Whalley 1992 for a detailed discussion of the data needs and the implications of alternative equation specifications in CGE models of this type).

Given these market clearing assumptions, the models do not accurately reflect short-run (less than one year) consequences of adjustment, but may indicate medium-term adjustment to the shocks and policy changes simulated. Moreover, like most other economic models, these do not capture infrastructural changes associated with adjustment. Sizable evidence suggests, however, that markets, particularly labor markets in African economies, generally perform well and that wages are flexible (except in the public sector) (Levy and Newman 1989; Colclough 1991; Hoddintot 1993; Horton, Kanbur, and Mazumdar 1994). Likewise, as discussed in Chapter 4, data from a survey of redeployed government workers in Ghana show that, four months after redeployment, 82 percent of workers still in the labor force (i.e., nonretirees) were employed, though 14 percent of redeployees were involved in only minimal agricultural activities. One year after redeployment, less than 10 percent of workers were unemployed (Younger 1996b). In Guinea, job transitions of government redeployees were also rapid for women, but not for men, who appear to queue for formal sector wage jobs (Mills and Sahn 1993b).

---

[67] An increase in foreign savings will in itself tend to raise real incomes of all households.

Table 3.5. *Niger: real exchange rate adjustment in the CFA zone simulation results (% change from base run)*

	Real exchange rate adjustment	Foreign exchange rationing
Real GDP	-1.8	-1.7
Investment	-23.2	-31.7
Exports	-13.3	-16.1
Imports	-9.9	-12.0
Real exchange rate	9.7	0.0
Household incomes		
Urban nonpoor	-6.5	15.8
Urban poor	-4.8	-7.7
Semiurban	-2.5	-4.8
Rural nonpoor north	-2.3	-4.2
Rural nonpoor south	-2.0	-4.1
Rural poor north	-2.4	-5.2
Rural poor south	-1.8	-4.3
Total	-3.1	-1.4

Source: Dorosh, Essama-Nssah, and Samba-Mamadou 1996.

To illustrate the income distribution implications of trade and exchange rate policy reform, Table 3.5 compares the results of simulations of two alternative policy responses to a terms-of-trade shock in Niger.[68] The first simulation shows the effects of a decline in the world price of uranium exports when the government rations foreign exchange for imports and holds fixed the real exchange rate.[69] The second simulation shows the effects of the same terms-of-trade shock, but with a freely adjusting real exchange rate.

Under both scenarios, real GDP declines as the economy suffers the effects of the terms-of-trade shock. However, with real exchange rate adjustment (a real exchange rate depreciation of 9.7 percent), the decline in exports is smaller because the real exchange rate depreciation improves incentives for export production. Moreover, for the economy as a whole, household incomes are higher, resulting in more savings and investment.

Poor households also fare better under real exchange rate adjustment to a terms-of-trade shock than under foreign exchange rationing. Real incomes of the rural poor decline by 1.8 to 2.4 percent under adjustment compared with

[68] The simulation models the effects of a 25.9 billion CFA franc decline in uranium revenues (equal to 3.9 percent of GDP in 1987), reflecting the fall in uranium export revenues from 1987 to 1990.

[69] We model the rationing of foreign exchange by putting a uniform implicit tariff on all imports, with rents from the implicit tariff accruing to the urban nonpoor households.

Table 3.6. *Madagascar: trade liberalization simulation results*
(% change from base run)

	Year 1	Year 6
Real GDP	2.8	6.6
Investment	19.0	38.0
Exports	7.0	12.9
Imports	5.9	10.9
Real exchange rate	11.8	18.0
Household incomes		
Urban nonpoor	-11.5	-8.3
Urban middle income	-4.5	9.8
Urban low income	2.0	4.8
Rural nonpoor	4.2	6.6
Small farm plateau	2.8	5.3
Small farm east coast	4.3	8.3
Small farm west, south	2.8	5.1
Nonfarm rural poor	2.6	4.2
Total	1.1	3.9

Note: The base run simulates the continuance of import quotas on
manufactured goods and rice at their 1984 per capita levels.
Source: Dorosh 1994b.

4.3 to 5.2 percent without real exchange rate adjustment, since prices of export goods such as cattle and cowpeas rise, spurring production and labor demand. The urban poor benefit due to higher investment spending leading to increased demand for labor and higher returns to informal sector capital. The urban nonpoor, as a group, suffer more under adjustment, however, since these households lose the excess profits (economic rents) associated with rationing.

A CGE analysis of the impacts of Madagascar's trade liberalization in 1987–1988 produces similar results (Table 3.6). Compared with a policy of maintaining foreign exchange restrictions for imports, trade liberalization results in an 11.8 percent depreciation of the real exchange rate in the first year of the simulation, leading to a 7.0 percent increase in exports. Increased economic efficiency and output results in a 2.8 percent increase in real GDP and a 19.0 percent increase in investment. The higher investment, in turn, leads to an even larger gain in real GDP (6.6 percent) by year six of the simulation.

Again, both urban and rural poor gain from the liberalization. The real exchange rate depreciation improves production incentives for tradable goods; agricultural output rises, leading to increased labor demand and higher real incomes of the poor. Producers of export crops, including small farmers on Madagascar's east coast, gain slightly more from the relative price changes than do other rural poor. Nevertheless, the overall increase in economic activity also leads to increased demand for agricultural goods employing rural unskilled labor and for construction, transport, and marketing services employing urban unskilled labor, thus extending the benefits of the liberalization beyond export crop producers only.

As the Niger and Madagascar model simulations suggest, the extent to which the poor benefit from trade and exchange rate policy reform varies according to country. To highlight the role of individual country characteristics, we compare the outcomes of two alternative policy responses to a negative terms-of-trade shock in Tables 3.7 and 3.8. The first policy option modeled is the imposition of quotas on imports to reduce foreign exchange demand (the practice of most economies prior to reform); the alternative is full adjustment of the real exchange rate. For each country, we specify the terms-of-trade shock as a 10 percent reduction in the world price of the major export good,[70] combined with a decline in net foreign capital inflows equal to 10 percent of initial exports.

Imposing quotas in response to a terms-of-trade shock results in a sharp decline in export earnings and real incomes in all five countries. In the absence of adjustment of the real exchange rate, the implicit tariff on imports (equivalent to the premium on foreign exchange for imports in the parallel market) helps reduce import demand and bring into balance supply and demand for foreign exchange. Rents created as a result of the premium on foreign exchange (which ranges from 13.1 percent in Tanzania to 35.1 percent in Madagascar) allow real incomes of the urban nonpoor to rise while real incomes of all other household groups decline.

Structural characteristics of the economies explain the variations in foreign exchange premiums across countries. Most important are the size of the external shock relative to investment spending and overall GDP, and characteristics of export supply (price responsiveness and presence of parallel markets). For all five countries, the external shock (measured in terms of lost foreign exchange earnings) is between 9.7 and 12.0 percent of the initial level of imports. However, for The Gambia (the most open economy considered), the ratio of the shock to GDP is 6.3 percent, compared with 1.7 to 3.5 percent for the other four countries. Given the large reduction in foreign savings and export earnings, total savings in The Gambia declines steeply and, along with it, total investment and demand for services of the labor-intensive construction sector. Real wages for both skilled and unskilled urban workers fall, helping to reduce the price of hotels and other services and permitting an increase in tourism exports. Thus the loss of foreign exchange revenues is partially offset, so that a premium of only 17.0 percent is sufficient to restore equilibrium in foreign exchange markets. In

---

[70] We model reductions in world prices for the following countries' commodities: Cameroon (export crops – mainly cocoa and coffee), The Gambia (groundnuts and groundnut products), Madagascar (export crops – mainly coffee, vanilla, and cloves), Niger (uranium), and Tanzania (export and cash crops – mainly coffee and cotton).

Table 3.7. *Macroeconomic outcomes under alternative trade and exchange rate policies: CGE model simulations (% change)*

| | Terms-of-trade shock with | | |
	Import quotas	Real exchange adjustment	Impact of liberalization
Cameroon			
Real GDP	-1.83	-1.16	0.68
Investment/GDP	-0.89	-1.06	-0.17
Exports/GDP	-2.21	-0.01	2.25
Foreign exchange premium			
(level in %)	26.83	0.00	-26.83
Real exchange rate	0.00	15.66	15.66
Gambia			
Real GDP	-3.55	-2.34	1.25
Investment/GDP	-6.37	-6.26	0.12
Exports/GDP	0.75	2.81	2.04
Foreign exchange premium			
(level in %)	16.97	0.00	-16.97
Real exchange rate	0.00	4.27	4.27
Madagascar			
Real GDP	-2.32	-1.07	1.28
Investment/GDP	-1.03	-0.50	0.54
Exports/GDP	-0.98	0.17	1.16
Foreign exchange premium			
(level in %)	35.10	0.00	-35.10
Real exchange rate	0.00	11.46	11.46
Niger			
Real GDP	-2.94	-2.72	0.23
Investment/GDP	-3.78	-3.10	0.71
Exports/GDP	-1.25	-0.58	0.68
Foreign exchange premium			
(level in %)	14.22	0.00	-14.22
Real exchange rate	0.00	9.16	9.16
Tanzania			
Real GDP	-0.90	-0.52	0.37
Investment/GDP	-2.83	-1.62	1.21
Exports/GDP	-0.55	0.35	0.90
Foreign exchange premium			
(level in %)	13.10	0.00	-13.10
Real exchange rate	0.00	6.11	6.11

Note: Impact of liberalization column gives the percentage change of the given variable in the real exchange rate simulation (column 2) relative to the import quota simulation (column 1).

Sources: Dorosh and Sahn (forthcoming); model simulations.

Table 3.8. *Household incomes under alternative trade and exchange rate policies: CGE model simulations (% change)*

| | Terms-of-trade shock with | | |
	Import quotas	Real adjustment exchange	Impact of liberalization
Cameroon			
Urban nonpoor	21.14	1.85	-15.92
Urban poor	-8.81	-3.79	5.51
Rural nonpoor	-10.09	-2.98	7.91
Rural poor	-10.04	-3.39	7.39
All Cameroon	-3.22	-2.00	1.26
Gambia			
Urban nonpoor	4.32	-0.49	-4.61
Urban poor	-8.75	-1.11	8.37
Rural nonpoor	-6.51	-3.82	2.88
Rural poor	-5.71	-3.09	2.78
All Gambia	-3.78	-2.01	1.84
Madagascar			
Urban nonpoor	16.33	-7.35	-20.36
Urban poor	-13.51	-3.51	11.56
Rural nonpoor	-5.61	-1.62	4.23
Rural poor	-5.25	-0.96	4.53
All Madagascar	-3.23	-2.42	0.84
Niger			
Urban nonpoor	14.33	-7.30	-18.92
Urban poor	-6.68	-3.94	2.94
Rural nonpoor	-4.09	-2.05	2.13
Rural poor	-4.67	-2.11	2.69
All Niger	-1.52	-3.20	-1.71
Tanzania			
Urban nonpoor	3.87	-1.61	-5.28
Urban poor	-2.17	-1.10	1.10
Rural nonpoor	-0.53	-1.47	-0.94
Rural poor	-1.79	-1.02	0.78
All Tanzania	0.32	-1.25	-1.56

Note: Impact of liberalization column gives the percentage change of household income of the real exchange rate simulation (column 2) relative to the impact quota simulation (column 1).

Source: Dorosh and Sahn (forthcoming) and model simulations.

Niger, the initial foreign exchange shock is also relatively large, 3.5 percent of GDP, so that investment demand (and consumer demand) for livestock falls. As a result, the exportable surplus of livestock rises, softening the decline in foreign exchange availability, so that the simulated foreign exchange premium is only 14.2 percent. In contrast, with Madagascar's very closed economy, the shock is a small 1.7 percent of GDP, so there is little impact on savings (and thus total investment). Since investment demand for manufactured imports (which accounts for a large share of total imports) changes little, the bulk of the adjustment must be borne by a reduction in consumer demand. To achieve this shift in demand, a large increase (35.1 percent) in the exchange rate premium (and the price of imported manufactured goods) is required.

The price elasticity of the export good suffering the simulated terms-of-trade shock also significantly affects the results. This elasticity determines the extent of the loss of foreign exchange earnings through a decreased volume of exports. In Niger, uranium export supply is very inelastic so the 10 percent decline in the price of uranium reduces total uranium revenues only by 11.7 percent. The 10 percent decline in world prices of Madagascar's export crops (coffee, vanilla, cloves) reduces export revenues from these crops by 17.1 percent. Finally, where parallel exports are widespread, as modeled for Tanzania, a smaller premium on imported goods is required to restore equilibrium on foreign exchange markets. The premium on foreign exchange in the parallel market leads to a diversion of exports from official exports. Though official exports decline more steeply than in other countries, the total export decline is smaller because of the increase in parallel market exports.

In the simulations of a freely adjusting real exchange rate (column 2 in Tables 3.7 and 3.8), although real GDP still declines, the fall is not as steep as in the case of import quotas. For example, in Madagascar, the real exchange rate depreciates by 11.5 percent and real exports as a share of GDP increase slightly (0.2 percent), compared with declines in real GDP and the export share of 2.3 and 1.0 percent, respectively, in the import quota scenario. The urban nonpoor fare much worse under a liberalized trade and exchange rate regime, however, since there are no quota rents to boost their incomes.

Comparing results of the liberalized trade and exchange rate regime with results under a regime of trade and foreign exchange controls shows the extent to which the poor benefit from trade and exchange rate policy reforms. For all five country simulations, both the urban and rural poor enjoy higher incomes. Two factors explain this result. First, although these five African economies differ in terms of relative importance of agriculture, economic openness, and other factors, they generally share key characteristics: concentration of poverty in rural areas, importance of agriculture and labor incomes for the rural poor, and relatively small manufacturing sectors. In the simulations, as rents formerly acquired by the urban nonpoor disappear, costs of importable goods fall, leading to a more efficient allocation of resources so that demand for unskilled labor (and real wages) rises. Second, because some of the poor are net producers of tradables, the real exchange rate depreciation directly increases their real incomes (e.g., of small farmers producing export crops in Cameroon and Madagascar). Thus, trade and exchange rate liberalization involving elimination of quotas and real exchange rate depreciation both improves macroeconomic performance and marginally increases real incomes for poor households. [71]

Summary

Changes in trade and exchange rate policies have important consequences both for the macroeconomy and for household incomes. In terms of macroeconomic objectives (improving incentives for tradable goods sectors, increasing exports and efficient import substitution, and sustaining GDP growth), these policy reforms have enjoyed only limited success in most countries. Although real exchange rate depreciation has been achieved, exports and GDP growth have responded only in a limited way.

The primary losers from trade and exchange rate policy reform are households and institutions that previously had access to foreign exchange or imports priced at the official exchange rate. Model simulations suggest that other household groups, including the rural poor, tended to benefit from trade and exchange rate reforms as rents were redistributed throughout the economy, price incentives for production of many tradables improved, and payments to unskilled labor, land, and informal sector capital rose. Thus, contrary to much conventional wisdom, the evidence suggests that trade and exchange rate policy reforms in themselves do not harm the poor, but instead tend to raise their real incomes. However, the policy simulations in this chapter by design do not attempt to include the effects of changes in the external environment or changes in other government policies coincidental with trade and exchange rate policy reform, such as droughts, terms-of-trade shocks, cutbacks in government expenditures, and changes in capital flows. [72] For the rural poor, two factors are of particular importance: world prices of agricultural exports and domestic agricultural trade and price policy. We discuss these factors further in Chapter 5.

[71] The result that real exchange rate depreciation tends to benefit the poor is consistent with findings by Schneider et al. (1992), who use a CGE model for Côte d'Ivoire with both real and financial variables developed by Bourguignon, Branson, and de Melo (1989a, 1989b). Model simulations show that a 22 percent real devaluation of the CFA franc in 1981 spurs exports, increases employment, and reduces poverty in both urban and rural areas.

[72] Simulations of the effects of these other factors on economic performance and income distribution have been conducted for the economies of Madagascar (Dorosh 1996), Niger (Dorosh, Essama-Nssah, and Samba-Mamadou 1996), Tanzania (Sarris 1996), The Gambia (Dorosh and Lundberg 1996), and Cameroon (Subramanian 1996).

4

Fiscal policy

Fiscal policy is the second broad area of policy reform encompassed by adjustment programs. Like exchange rate policy, changes in government expenditures and revenues are important for short-run attempts to stabilize the macroeconomy and for longer-run efforts to make key structural changes to the economy. From the point of view of stabilization, economies with serious current account deficits typically have unsustainable fiscal deficits as well. In part, this correlation reflects the fact that, especially in Africa, external shocks (e.g., declines in world commodity prices) that lead to problems on the balance of payments also lead to fiscal imbalances, either through reduced revenues or because the government attempts to compensate the adverse impact of the shock with increased spending. But in part the relationship between fiscal imbalances and current account imbalances is causal: a widening fiscal deficit increases the demand for goods and services in the economy, and some or all of that demand spills over into excess demand for imports over exports. This causal link explains why loans and credits from the IMF and the World Bank are usually conditioned on a reduction in government spending and/or an increase in tax revenues for the duration of the agreement. Beyond the issue of fiscal balance, longer-term adjustment efforts in many African countries also address the structure of public expenditures and taxes, attempting to make the public sector a more efficient provider of essential public services. Many African countries impose taxes that are highly distortionary, especially in the area of trade taxes, and many have an inefficient pattern of expenditures, which tend to be biased toward personnel costs, transfers to state-owned enterprises, and sometimes capital expenditures that have donor financing associated with them.

Policies that attempt to reestablish fiscal balance, change the priorities of public expenditure, or adjust the pattern of taxation are all controversial. The most active debate has been over expenditure cuts. A general perception exists that adjustment programs have demanded draconian cuts in public expenditures that were already woefully inadequate, especially in the social sectors, where public spending per capita is often no more than one or two dollars a year. There has been less international debate over increased taxation, but several notable adjustment programs have increased taxes significantly (e.g., in Ghana and in Uganda) while others have foundered for not doing so (in Cameroon). Once again, the politics of increased taxation are difficult, often because taxes must fall on the formal sector of the economy where political power is concentrated

Understanding the implications of changes in fiscal policy for poverty is complicated by the public goods nature of many public services. It is impossible to quantify the benefits to particular households from expenditures for national defense or maintenance of the public order, for example. Thus, it is equally impossible to say what the importance of reduced military or police expenditures is for the poor. On the other hand, the beneficiaries of some public services, especially health and education services, are more readily identified, enabling us to examine the likely impact of cuts in these areas on the poor. Similarly, household survey information allows us to say something about who pays the taxes. These descriptions overlook the possibilities for tax (and benefit) shifting, however. When governments offer a service or impose a tax, people's behavior changes in response, leading to indirect effects that are quite different than what one might expect. For example, provision of public health clinics might harm private providers, or imposition of a tax on beer might lead people to substitute traditional beverages, to the benefit of their producers.

In this chapter we first evaluate the extent of public expenditure cuts in Africa during the 1980s, arguing that critics have exaggerated their severity in many cases. In this context, we also discuss the attempts at fiscal policy reform in our case study countries. We then examine the incidence of public expenditures – that is, who benefits from them – especially in the social sectors. Here, we examine household-level data to discover which households use public health and education services, and we return to our general equilibrium models to see which households will likely benefit or suffer from reductions in general government spending. We have paid special attention to the issue of public sector retrenchment in the course of our research, and a significant proportion of this chapter discusses surveys of retrenched public sector workers in Ghana and Guinea, again attempting to identify the costs of public sector expenditure cuts for an obviously vulnerable group. Finally, we consider the incidence of different tax policies.

The pattern of government expenditures in Africa

Fiscal deficits

Fiscal deficits are large and persistent in Africa even after including the considerable amount of grant financing available to many countries on the continent. This gap in the governments' finances has been an obvious target for policy reformers. But as Table 4.1 shows, the notion that African economies have been subjected to radical changes in fiscal policy during the 1980s is exaggerated.[1] While overall deficits shrunk in the first half of the decade, 2 to 3 percent of GDP on average, these gains have been sustained only through increased grant financing in the latter half of the decade. Exclusive of grants, the average deficit at the end of the decade was about the same as in 1980, contradicting the notion that most African countries pursued extraordinarily contractionary fiscal policy during the decade. Changes in fiscal policy clearly have been less pronounced and less enduring than exchange rate and trade adjustments, at least on average. Nevertheless, as we noted earlier, most of the controversy surrounding fiscal policies has not been about the deficit, but rather expenditures. It is possible that deficits remained constant despite drastic cuts in expenditures because revenues declined equally drastically, a scenario that has in fact played itself out in some of our case study countries. It is also possible that certain items in the budget, most notably expenditures for foreign debt service, have crowded out others. It is useful, then, to consider separately the behavior of expenditures and revenues, both on average and in individual countries, to understand the extent of fiscal policy adjustments during the 1980s. We address expenditure policy first, returning to taxes later in the chapter.

---

[1] Different sources often report widely varying estimates of the time series used in this chapter. In general, we rely on two sets of data that are internally consistent across the continent: the African Development Indicators (ADI) and the IMF data compiled by Nashashibi and Bazzoni (1993). The latter appear to have the most accurate data, but they begin only in 1980. The African Development Indicators, on the other hand, probably underreport interest expenditures and grant revenues, two items that are important to the debate on overall fiscal policy.

In addition to these sources, CFNPP authors have at times made their own modifications. For example, Blandford et al. (1994) attempt to include the unaccounted oil revenues in Cameroon's fiscal data, as well as the use of offshore funds from previous oil sales, and Younger (1992) adjusts Ghana's fiscal data for the fact that project-related expenditures are excluded from the budget if financed by foreign aid. For the sake of consistency, however, we use only the sources cited above in this chapter, noting in passing any marked differences between these data and our own best estimates.

Table 4.1. *Government finances in Africa*

	1975	1976	1977	1978	1979	1980	1981	1982
IMF data[a]								
Deficit, including grants	—	—	—	—	—	6.6	7.4	7.7
Deficit, excluding grants	—	—	—	—	—	8.9	9.9	9.6
African development indicators[b]								
Deficit, including grants	4.0	4.3	3.9	5.0	4.7	5.6	7.4	7.1
Deficit, excluding grants	5.0	5.3	5.0	6.2	6.0	7.1	9.1	9.1
IMF data[a]								
Total expenditures	—	—	—	—	—	27.5	28.6	28.6
Expenditures net of interest	—	—	—	—	—	25.9	26.9	26.5
Africa development indicators[b]								
Total expenditures	19.7	18.9	20.0	21.2	21.2	24.8	25.9	26.6
Expenditures net of debt service	19.1	18.0	19.1	20.3	20.2	23.5	24.4	24.6
Real net expenditures, $ 1987 pc	61	59	65	54	58	68	74	68
Social sector expenditures								
Education expenditures, % total	—	—	14.7	12.9	12.9	14.0	14.0	14.5
Health expenditures, % total	—	—	5.6	5.2	4.8	4.7	4.8	4.9
Education expenditures, $ 1987 pc	—	—	13.7	13.6	13.1	18.3	19.7	20.2
Health expenditures, 1987 pc	—	—	5.7	5.8	5.4	6.2	6.6	7.1

Table 4.1. *(cont.)*

	1983	1984	1985	1986	1987	1988	1989	1990
IMF data[a]								
Deficit, including grants	6.9	5.5	4.4	5.6	5.4	4.0	3.9	7.7
Deficit, excluding grants	8.8	7.5	7.2	9.9	9.4	8.6	8.6	9.6
African development indicators[b]								
Deficit, including grants	5.8	3.9	4.0	4.3	5.3	—	—	—
Deficit, excluding grants	7.5	5.6	5.8	6.2	7.8	—	—	—
IMF data[a]								
Total expenditures	28.0	27.1	26.7	28.1	28.1	27.4	27.7	27.4
Expenditures net of interest	25.5	24.0	23.3	24.3	24.5	23.7	23.8	23.4
Africa development indicators[b]								
Total expenditures	25.4	24.4	24.6	25.0	26.9	25.4	—	—
Expenditures net of debt service	23.3	21.9	21.6	22.0	23.7	22.4	—	—
Real net expenditures, $ 1987 pc	64	55	55	58	62	58	—	—
Social sector expenditures								
Education expenditures, % total	14.4	13.4	12.9	12.6	12.4	12.6	—	14.5
Health expenditures, % total	4.9	4.9	4.7	4.5	4.7	4.7	—	4.9
Education expenditures, $ 1987 pc	19.5	18.8	17.5	18.5	18.6	19.3	—	20.2
Health expenditures, 1987 pc	6.8	6.7	6.7	6.8	6.9	7.4	—	7.1

[a]IMF data are from Nashashibi and Bazzoni (1993) who rely on the *Government Finance Statistics*, updated by IMF staff estimates. The series are a simple average of 30 countries.

[b]The African Development Indicators are published by the World Bank. Series are a simple average of 21 to 23 countries, depending on the series, except for the series reported in 1987 U.S. dollars per capita (pc), which are total spending in dollars in 21 countries divided by the populations of those countries.

Total expenditures

If we take the early 1980s as a point of reference, it is true that there has been some reduction in government expenditures net of debt service in Africa (Table 4.1). But those reductions have been moderate, 3 percent of GDP on average, and they remain insufficient to eliminate existing deficits. Further, taking the early 1980s as a point of reference, a common practice, is misleading. Government expenditures in these years were unusually high by historical standards. Compared with expenditures in the mid-1970s, fiscal contraction in the 1980s has done little more than deflate the bubble at the beginning of the decade, returning deficits to their mid 1970s levels and leaving expenditures higher than they were a decade earlier.

The surge in government expenditures observed in Table 4.1 often came from temporary access to additional financing (Gelb 1986; Omolehinwa and Roe 1989). In some countries, this increase had to do with commodity price booms during the late 1970s. Because many commodity exports are taxed heavily, these booms temporarily increased government revenues and thus encouraged governments to overextend their expenditures. Once international prices returned to more normal levels (or collapsed as in the case of coffee, cocoa, and petroleum), governments found it difficult to curtail spending and thus ran larger deficits. In other cases, particularly the more creditworthy economies, the availability of international borrowing prior to the debt crisis made it easier to run deficits, and many countries did so, yet that source of financing also proved to be short-lived.[2]

None of these data says anything about adjustment, of course. The data simply describe the average behavior of fiscal variables across the continent. Countries that by some definition "adjusted" may have suffered sharp expenditure reductions while those that did not remained stable. While we try to avoid such distinctions in this book, it is relevant to consider the variance of experience of African countries in addition to the averages, with special interest in the cases of sharp declines in government spending. Table 4.2 shows

----

[2] A common response to the criticism of the boom in government expenditure in the late 1970s and early 1980s is that it is always easy to know that a commodity boom was temporary ex post. Ex ante, many analysts expected commodity prices to stay high and even rise, so the increases in expenditures were justified. Although this argument has some validity in the cases of energy exports (oil and uranium), it was clearly imprudent to inflate spending based on the rise in coffee and cocoa prices, which were clearly associated with a temporary phenomenon (the Brazilian frost). The same is true of extensive commercial borrowing. In any event, the outcome of this debate does not detract from our main point, which is entirely descriptive: expenditures were unusually high in the early 1980s and thus are not a good benchmark for judging future developments, whether they were justified or not.

Table 4.2. *Percent change in real government expenditures per capita 1975–1977 to 1986–1988*

>150	50 to 150	10 to 50	-10 to 10	<-10 to -50	<-50
Total expenditures net of debt service					
Botswana	Burundi	The Gambia	Burkina Faso	Ghana	
Cameroon	Ethiopia	Kenya	Gabon	Liberia[a]	
Chad	Rwanda	Malawi	Swaziland	Mauritania	
Congo[b]	Somalia	Mauritius	Zaire	Nigeria	
Lesoto		Niger		Senegal	
Seychelles		Zimbabwe		Sierra Leone	
				Sudan	
				Tanzania	
				Uganda	
				Zambia	
Education expenditures					
Botswana	Cameroon	Burkina Faso	The Gambia		Nigeria
	Kenya	Ethiopia	Ghana		Sierra Leone
	Lesoto	Malawi	Liberia		Somalia
	Rwanda	Mauritius			Uganda
	Zimbabwe[b]	Niger[b]			Zaire
		Swaziland			Zambia
Health expenditures					
Botswana	Cameroon	Ethiopia	Burkina Faso	Liberia	Somalia
Lesoto	Malawi	The Gambia	Ghana	Nigeria	Uganda
	Rwanda	Kenya		Sierra Leone	
	Swaziland	Mauritius		Zambia	
	Zimbabwe	Niger			
		Zaire			

[a]Includes only 1986-1987;
[b]Includes only 1976-1977.
Source: IMF various years a, various years b; World Bank 1993a.

changes in government expenditure per capita net of debt service from the period 1975–1977 to 1986–1988.[3] Of the thirty cases for which we have data, ten have declines of net spending greater than 10 percent on average during this period. Four – Liberia (-14%), Mauritania (-26%), Sudan (-46%), and Uganda (-24%) – reflect serious civil conflict and a fifth, Nigeria (-45%), reflects dramatic declines in the terms of trade in 1981 and especially 1986. Of the rest, government spending usually declined well before the country began any orthodox attempt at adjustment – Ghana (-11%), Sierra Leone (-18%), Tanzania (-25%), and Zambia (-22%). Only in Senegal (-16%) do expenditures appear to fall sharply as part of an extended adjustment effort during this period.

Expenditures on social services

There are many good arguments in favor of public expenditures on social services, based on both equity and economic efficiency. Thus, one of the strongest criticisms voiced of adjustment programs is that they have forced governments to reduce their role as providers of social services. As with overall government expenditures, however, the gap between the common perception and the data is considerable. On average in Africa, education expenditures per capita increased sharply in the early 1980s, coincident with the general increase in expenditures, and they remained well above the levels of the 1970s for the rest of the decade despite having declined from their peak (Table 4.1). Health expenditures, on the other hand, remained much more stable, both during the bubble and the subsequent stabilization. In neither case, however, have average expenditures on these social services declined to the degree that is commonly presumed.

Table 4.2 shows the percent change in various government spending on health and education expressed in constant U.S. dollars per capita, from the period 1975–1977 to 1986–1988. These amounts vary more than government spending in general, mostly because the base amounts are so small (often no more than one or two dollars per capita). Nevertheless, the story is similar to that for total spending. A few countries with significant civil conflict (Liberia, Mauritania, Somalia, Sudan, and Uganda) have sharp declines, as do a few other economies that fell apart in the early 1980s (Ghana, Sierra Leone, Zambia, and Zaire). But with the exception of The Gambia (in education), and arguably Zambia (in health), the declines are not part of an extended attempt to balance the government's fiscal position.

---

[3] These comparisons are based on the ADI data, the only series that allow us to compare the mid-1970s with the mid-1980s. They divide the annual average for 1986–1988 by the average for 1975–1977.

Experience in case study countries

Because the majority of attention to fiscal policy issues has focused on public spending, it is useful to group our countries according to the magnitude of changes in government expenditures during the 1970s and 1980s. Madagascar and Tanzania witnessed large declines in government spending, following equally large increases made possible by commodity booms and easy access to foreign credit during the late 1970s and early 1980s. Government expenditures also fell precipitously in Guinea, concurrent with the economic crisis that led to political and economic change, and in Zaire, during the early stages of its stabilization program that preceded the virtual collapse of macroeconomic management. In contrast, Ghana implemented adjustment policies only after the near collapse of government spending. Consequently, economic reform included a major increase in real government expenditures. The remaining countries in our sample showed no strong trends in government spending. In The Gambia, Malawi, and Mozambique, however, there were large fluctuations reflecting factors such as terms-of-trade shocks and changes in level of foreign capital inflows. In contrast, Cameroon's and Niger's membership in the CFA zone helped impose fiscal discipline and limit the urgency and magnitude of the consequent cuts in government spending in the wake of terms-of-trade shocks.

Madagascar: Madagascar is a perfect example of a debt-financed boom in government expenditures that ended abruptly when foreign lending collapsed in 1982. Frustrated with two decades of slow growth, the Malagasy authorities began an investment program in the late 1970s which they financed entirely with foreign borrowing, much of it on commercial terms. Overall expenditures rose from under 20 percent of GDP in the mid-1970s to over 35 percent in 1980 (Table 4.3). As Madagascar's debt ratios ballooned, however, foreign creditors became wary of further lending, and the bubble burst as quickly as it had inflated. By 1983, expenditures had returned to about 20 percent of GDP and the deficit was back to 5 percent in the context of a stabilization program supported by the World Bank and the IMF.

At first glance, the episode was little more than a short-lived binge. Yet the accumulation of debts had a lasting impact on the composition of public expenditures. Debt service payments more than doubled as a share of total expenditures, crowding out expenditures on other goods and services (operations and maintenance). In addition, large increases in public employment associated with the investment boom meant that, even though the overall wage bill remained roughly constant as a share of expenditures, public sector salaries declined by half in real terms. Expenditures on health and education also maintained their shares in overall spending, but declined from their peaks in 1980 as a percent of GDP, consistent with the overall contraction of public spending.

Table 4.3. *Madagascar: fiscal data*

	1975	1976	1977	1978	1979	1980	1981	1982	1983
Deficit, incl grants	—	—	—	—	—	14.9	12.0	7.0	5.3
Deficit	3.3	4.1	6.4	4.0	14.3	18.5	15.4	9.1	6.0
Expenditure	—	—	—	—	—	29.6	24.4	19.6	17.9
Expenditure, net of interest	—	—	—	—	—	28.8	23.7	18.7	16.9
Expenditure	17.0	18.8	21.3	24.8	34.0	36.8	30.6	24.3	21.2
Education expenditures	—	—	—	—	—	3.7	3.1	2.9	2.9
Health expenditures	—	—	—	—	—	1.21	0.70	0.73	0.79
Revenue, excl grants	—	—	—	—	—	14.7	12.4	12.2	11.9
Grants	—	—	—	—	—	—	—	0.4	0.7
Revenues, incl grants	13.7	14.7	14.9	20.9	19.7	18.3	15.2	15.2	15.2
Official development assistance	3.7	2.9	2.6	3.4	4.0	5.7	6.5	6.9	5.2
Stock of international debt, $	184	206	296	366	792	1,257	1,612	1,920	2,102
Real expenditure	233.3	251.1	289.2	328.9	495.1	540.7	15.5	325.5	285.2
Real deficit	44.8	55.1	86.4	52.5	208.4	271.8	209.6	122.4	80.7
Real GDP	1,374	1,334	1,358	1,325	1,455	1,470	1,359	1,339	1,346

Table 4.3. (cont.)

	1984	1985	1986	1987	1988	1989	1990	1991
Deficit, incl grants	3.2	3.8	3.4	3.2	3.1	7.4	3.3	6.9
Deficit	4.0	4.7	4.3	4.1	—	—	—	—
Expenditure	17.9	17.2	16.2	18.7	17.1	20.5	16.9	16.3
Expenditure, net of interest	16.4	15.7	14.6	16.6	15.0	17.9	15.4	14.3
Expenditure	21.8	20.8	19.8	22.8	—	—	—	—
Education expenditures	2.8	2.7	2.6	2.5	—	—	—	—
Health expenditures	0.84	0.87	0.80	0.95	—	—	—	—
Revenue, excl grants	13.8	12.9	12.0	14.7	13.1	11.3	11.8	8.5
Grants	0.9	0.5	0.8	0.8	0.9	1.8	1.8	0.9
Revenues, incl grants	17.8	16.1	15.5	18.7	—	—	—	—
Official development assistance	5.2	6.6	9.7	12.5	12.5	13.1	—	—
Stock of international debt, $	2,160	2,460	3,009	3,728	3,638	3,607	3,633	3,715
Real expenditure	298.6	291.3	280.7	327.5	304.1	390.9	—	—
Real deficit	55.2	66	60.8	59	57.2	95.3	—	—
Real GDP	1,369	1,400	1,419	1,439	—	—	—	—

Note: All data as percentage of GDP except international debt data, which are U.S. dollars.

Sources: For deficit, revenues, expenditures, Dorosh and Bernier 1994b, Nashashibi and Bazzoni 1993 for 1980–1991, IMF various years a; for social sector and official development assistance, World Bank 1993b; for debt, World Bank various years.

105

Table 4.4. *Tanzania: fiscal data*

	1975	1976	1977	1978	1979	1980	1981	1982	1983
Deficit, incl grants	9.7	6.5	5.2	7.3	15.6	13.7	9.8	13.6	8.6
Expenditure	32.0	24.4	25.6	28.4	37.1	37.8	33.3	34.5	29.1
Expenditure, net of interest	30.7	23.1	24.4	27.3	35.4	35.7	31.0	32.2	26.6
Education expenditures	3.1	2.9	3.1	3.7	3.7	3.8	3.5	3.9	3.6
Health expenditures	1.74	1.47	1.63	1.84	1.72	1.71	1.61	1.70	1.39
Revenue, excl grants	20.3	16.1	18.3	18.9	18.4	19.7	20.1	18.2	18.7
Grants	2.0	1.9	2.2	2.2	3.1	4.4	3.4	2.7	1.8
Official development assistance	10.9	8.8	9.4	10.6	13.0	13.2	11.9	10.9	9.4
Stock of international debt, $	945	1,354	1,783	1,979	2,168	2,572	2,694	2,985	3,380

Table 4.4. (cont.)

	1984	1985	1986	1987	1988	1989	1990	1991
Deficit, incl grants	9.7	8.2	1.2	1.1	1.4	1.5	2.6	-0.7
Expenditure	29.5	27.1	23.1	24.6	24.7	27.9	27.4	26.8
Expenditure, net of interest	26.7	24.5	21.1	21.2	20.9	23.9	23.8	23.3
Education expenditures	2.8	1.6	1.8[a]	1.8[a]	—	—	—	4.5[b]
Health expenditures	1.32	1.09	1.03[a]	0.86[a]	—	—	—	3.7[b]
Revenue, excl grants	19.8	18.9	14.8	16.3	16.9	19.6	20.6	23.5
Grants	—	7.1	7.1	7.2	6.4	6.8	4.2	4.0
Official development assistance	9.6		13.9	25.6	29.7	32.6	—	—
Stock of international debt, $	3,431	3,867	4,167	4,839	5,139	4,819	6,129	6,460

Note: All data as percent of GDP except international debt data, which are U.S. dollars.
[a]Data from World Bank 1989b. (This series may not be consistent with other data.)
[b]Data from World Bank 1994e. (These are averages for the period 1990–1992 and may not be consistent with other data.)

Sources: For deficit, revenues, expenditures, Nashashibi and Bazzoni 1993 for 1980–1991, IMF various years a for 1975–1979; for social sector and official development assistance, World Bank 1993a; for debt, World Bank various years.

Beyond the mere stabilization of the public finances, fundamental reforms such as public sector retrenchment or public enterprise reform have been noticeably absent in Madagascar as compared with the situation in The Gambia, Guinea, and Ghana. Moreover, after several years of holding deficits to about 4 percent of GDP, spending and the deficit increased substantially in 1989, and the deficit again increased in 1991 due to shortfalls in tax revenue caused by political strife that led to general strikes and the closing of the port, thus reducing tariff receipts.

Tanzania: Tanzania has undertaken its adjustment efforts while abandoning state socialism. Thus government expenditures are not surprisingly a smaller share of GDP now than they were fifteen years ago (Table 4.4). Virtually all of the decline came, however, before the government began its Washington-supported adjustment program. Paralleling Ghana's experience in the late 1970s, lack of revenues, rather than the IMF, forced expenditures to contract. Only in the context of the recovery program, generously financed by donors, did expenditures recover somewhat in the late 1980s. At the same time, the government reduced the deficit to about 2 percent of GDP in 1986 and held it there until recently. In the early years this reflects increased grant receipts rather than an improved revenue effort, though revenues did increase by 6 percent of GDP from 1988 to 1991.

Tanzania's emphasis on equitable distribution did not shield the social sectors in the early 1980s. Reductions in education expenditures were even more precipitous than total expenditures prior to 1985 and appear to have been stable in the period immediately after the adjustment program began. Reductions in the health sector were roughly proportional to overall spending cuts prior to 1985, but they continued to decline after general spending stabilized in 1986. In both education and health, more recent information suggests, expenditures have increased sharply, probably due to donor interest in supporting these sectors.

Guinea: Guinea is generally considered to have made a sustained effort to adjust its fiscal policy in the 1980s, though the lack of reliable data before 1986 hampers our ability to evaluate the extent of these adjustments. Table 4.5 shows a considerable reduction in government expenditures in 1986, the year that the Programme de Redressment Economique et Financier (PREF) began. Although data from earlier years are only rough estimates, expenditures likely did fall given the Second Republic's rejection of Sekou-Touré's doctrinaire socialism. The prior volatility in expenditures reflects both wide fluctuations in real salary expenditures (due to high inflation and infrequent nominal salary adjustments) and availability of funds from the mining industry. Nevertheless, the deficit after 1986 has stayed near 5 percent of GDP with no sign of reductions beyond those experienced in the initial years of the adjustment program.

Table 4.5. *Guinea: fiscal data*

	1975	1976	1977	1978	1979	1980	1981	1982	1983
Deficit	10.5	—	—	—	—	0.3	2.5	4.8	10.4
Expenditure	5.4	—	—	—	—	32.5	34.9	50.0	34.6
Health expenditures	—	—	—	—	—	1.24	1.12	2.10	1.16
Revenue	14.9	—	—	—	—	32.2	32.4	45.2	24.2
Official development assistance	0.0	0.0	0.0	0.0	0.0	0.0	0.0	0.0	0.0
Stock of international debt, $	790	832	914	1,022	1,130	1,117	1,361	1,345	1,329

Table 4.5. *(cont.)*

	1984	1985	1986	1987	1988	1989	1990	1991
Deficit	4.6	23.5	4.9	4.1	7.1	5.0	5.3	4.6
Expenditure	27.7	41.6	20.3	24.3	25.5	24.1	25.2	22.9
Health expenditures	0.94	2.20	0.59	0.53	0.66	0.84	0.73	0.50
Revenue	23.1	18.1	15.4	20.2	18.5	19.0	19.9	18.4
Official development assistance	0.0	0.0	8.7	10.1	10.8	12.7	—	—
Stock of international debt, $	1,226	1,438	1,735	2,036	2,220	2,176	2,478	2,626

Note: All data as percentage of GDP except international debt data, which are U.S. dollars.

Sources: For deficit, revenues, expenditures, Nashashibi and Bazzoni 1993 for 1980–1991, IMF various years for 1975–1979; for social sector Arulpragasam and Sahn 1996; for official development assistance and debt, World Bank various years.

In fact, except for the surges in 1983 and 1985, the deficit does not appear to be higher prior to the reform effort than subsequently.

Within this aggregate picture, however, the government has made several important changes. Thirty percent of public employees were retrenched in an effort to shrink payrolls and reestablish rational pay scales while maintaining the total wage bill under 5 percent of GDP. The government closed many state-owned enterprises, and sold several more to private operators. In more recent years, a concerted effort to raise nonmining tax revenue through more vigilant enforcement and more rational tax schedules has helped offset the effects on government revenue of lower bauxite prices, thus avoiding further public expenditure cuts or increased deficits. Government spending on both health and education has decreased substantially as a share of GDP, though not as a share of overall expenditures. Each sector declined soon after the change in regime, though education has recovered somewhat in more recent years thanks to increased donor support. Spending on health, however, remained depressed through the end of the decade at levels well below African averages.

Zaire: The economic and social chaos that has engulfed Zaire in recent years makes it tempting to ignore this country when considering the impacts of adjustment policies. Nevertheless, the government did make a serious if unsustained attempt to adjust its fiscal accounts in the mid-1970s and again in the early 1980s. The 1970s episode followed a sharp deterioration in the world price of copper, Zaire's leading export and an important source of government revenue. In 1976, the government signed the first in a series of four agreements with the IMF that, among other things, promised to cut public expenditures significantly. While expenditures did indeed decline during the second half of the decade, the government continued to run substantial deficits which caused suspension of successive agreements (Table 4.6). With external financing limited, the government resorted to monetization of the deficit, and inflation soared. Moreover, expenditures began to increase again in the early 1980s, financed in part on commercial terms.

In 1983, another effort by the government to stabilize the macroeconomy led to cuts in government expenditures and an attempt to broaden the tax base through improved enforcement. Revenues did increase substantially from 1983 to 1985, though this was probably linked more to favorable external prices for Zaire's mineral exports than to improved tax administration. Expenditures fell by more than 4 percent of GDP in 1983, but the change lasted only one year. Deficits were soon growing again, and unrestrained recourse to the inflation tax established the basis for the hyperinflation of the 1990s. From 1986 onward, despite continuing consultations with the donors, Zaire has made little or no effort to reestablish fiscal discipline.

Data on social sector spending are suspect, especially those showing steady gains in health expenditures after the collapse in the 1970s. Apart from these increases, the remarkably low levels for these items throughout the period are notable, both in dollars and as a percent of GDP.

Ghana: Ghana is an interesting case because many analysts heralded it as a success in the 1980s and because its history of economic decline and policy reform precedes those of other African economies by five to ten years. In an effort at public-sector-led growth, government expenditures and deficits rose sharply in the early 1970s as compared with rates in the late 1970s or early 1980s in other economies. By the late 1970s serious economic distortions were limiting tax revenues, which, in turn, forced a sharp contraction in government expenditures (Table 4.7). By 1982, government revenues had fallen to only 6 percent of GDP and expenditures to only 12 percent. From 1983 onward, the Economic Recovery Program brought about a notable reversal of the prior decade's economic decline, with fiscal discipline as a cornerstone. Oddly, however, Ghana's adjustment efforts began with a sharp *increase* in government expenditures. The deficit was reduced only because tax revenues increased even more, largely due to the huge exchange rate devaluation which increased the cedi value of imports and brought significant portions of the parallel economy into the formal (and therefore taxed) sector. The overall recovery of government expenditures was accompanied by sharp increases in social sector spending.

After the initial efforts to stabilize the fiscal position, the ERP turned to more difficult structural questions. In particular, the government began to retrench civil servants in 1987 at a rate of about 10,000 per year (or 3 percent of the civil service work force), continuing until 1992. Progress on parastatal enterprises has been delayed, however. On the tax side, the government has shifted the burden of taxes from cocoa excises and import tariffs to the corporate income tax, petroleum excises, and, more recently, a value-added tax.

As Ghana prepared for its first elections since 1978, the country suffered a dramatic reversal of the fiscal discipline that had been the hallmark of the ERP since its inception. The budget surplus of 1.5 percent of GDP in 1991 eroded to a substantial deficit of 4.8 percent of GDP in 1992 as the government raised public sector wages substantially and also reduced its tax effort considerably, both for political reasons. After the elections, the government made a substantial effort to reestablish fiscal control, but succeeded only in halving the deficit in each of 1993 and 1994, mostly through increased taxation.

The Gambia: In the mid-1970s, the government of The Gambia began a concerted effort to accelerate economic development through the public sector. From 1975 to 1985, civil service employment doubled and a large number

Table 4.6. *Zaire: fiscal data*

	1975	1976	1977	1978	1979	1980	1981	1982	1983
Deficit, incl grants	8.4	19.3	7.8	7.8	0.6	0.0	10.5	9.1	3.9
Expenditure	36.9	42.2	32.3	27.5	27.0	12.8	22.6	23.0	17.2
Expenditure, net of interest	35.1	39.2	29.6	25.3	24.7	11.4	18.6	19.2	13.6
Education expenditures	2.0	1.9	2.1	1.5	1.3	2.3	2.7	2.1	1.1
Health expenditures	0.20	0.49	0.56	0.32	0.23	0.30	0.35	0.41	0.35
Revenue, excl grants	25.6	20.0	21.0	16.6	22.1	12.8	12.1	12.1	11.1
Grants	2.9	2.9	3.6	3.1	4.3	0.0	–	1.8	2.2
Official development assistance	2.0	2.0	2.1	2.1	2.8	3.0	3.1	2.6	2.9
Stock of international debt, $	1,804	2,522	3,429	4,213	4,817	4,860	4,976	4,990	5,146

Table 4.6. (cont.)

	1984	1985	1986	1987	1988	1989	1990	1991
Deficit, incl grants	4.9	2.3	6.6	7.9	15.7	4.0	5.4	0.0
Expenditure	24.7	25.4	23.5	25.0	32.4	25.2	25.9	—
Expenditure, net of interest	15.8	15.0	17.6	21.5	27.4	21.3	21.8	—
Education expenditures	0.3	0.4	0.2	1.2	1.1	—	—	—
Health expenditures	0.46	0.55	0.57	0.94	0.76	—	—	—
Revenue, excl grants	16.0	18.6	13.6	13.4	13.2	16.7	16.5	—
Grants	3.8	4.5	3.3	3.7	3.5	4.5	4.0	—
Official development assistance	4.0	4.5	5.5	8.2	6.5	7.3	—	—
Stock of international debt, $	5,150	6,027	7,060	8,744	8,742	8,843	10,215	10,705

Note: All data as percentage of GDP except international debt data, which are U.S. dollars.
Sources: For deficit, revenues, expenditures, Nashashibi and Bazzoni 1993 for 1980–1991, IMF various years for 1975–1979; for social sector and official development assistance, World Bank 1993b; for debt, World Bank, various years.

Table 4.7. Ghana: fiscal data

	1975	1976	1977	1978	1979	1980	1981	1982	1983
Deficit, incl grants	6.4	9.4	8.1	8.4	6.0	4.1	6.4	5.6	2.7
Expenditure	21.7	22.7	19.1	15.1	15.2	11.1	11.0	11.2	8.2
Expenditure, net of interest	20.3	21.2	17.6	12.9	13.3	9.4	9.6	8.9	7.0
Education expenditures	3.6	2.9	2.0	1.8	1.6	2.4	1.8	2.1	1.6
Health expenditures	1.46	1.06	0.76	0.81	0.60	0.76	0.68	0.64	0.59
Revenue, excl grants	15.3	13.3	10.2	6.6	9.2	6.9	4.5	5.5	5.5
Grants	0.0	0.0	0.8	0.0	0.0	0.1	0.1	0.1	0.0
Official development assistance	4.5	2.3	2.9	3.1	4.2	4.3	3.4	3.5	2.7
Stock of international debt, $	730	733	1,075	1,286	1,274	1,314	1,462	1,397	1,598

Table 4.7. *(cont.)*

	1984	1985	1986	1987	1988	1989	1990	1991
Deficit, incl grants	1.9	2.2	-0.2	-0.6	-0.3	-0.7	-0.1	-1.6
Expenditure	10.2	14.0	14.3	14.3	14.3	14.4	13.9	14.9
Expenditure, net of interest	8.9	12.5	12.1	12.9	13.2	13.1	12.5	13.1
Education expenditures	2.0	2.4	3.3	3.3	3.5	3.7	–	–
Health expenditures	0.85	1.31	1.15	1.13	1.22	1.29	–	–
Revenue, excl grants	8.0	11.3	13.7	14.1	13.5	13.6	12.5	15.0
Grants	0.3	0.5	0.8	0.8	1.1	1.5	1.5	1.5
Official development assistance	4.9	4.5	6.5	7.3	9.1	10.5	–	–
Stock of international debt, $	1,898	2,147	2,652	3,134	3,113	3,078	3,296	3,761

Note: All data as percentage of GDP except international debt data, which are U.S. dollars.
Sources: For deficit, revenues, expenditures: Nashashibi and Bazzoni 1993 for 1980–1991, IMF various years for 1975–1979; for social sector and official development assistance: World Bank 1993b; for debt: World Bank various years.

of parastatal enterprises sprang up in many different industries. Expenditures on health and education also increased dramatically, especially in the capital budgets and on the payrolls. Even though government revenues grew considerably during the late 1970s, expenditures far outstripped them, and deficits ran between 5 and 15 percent of GDP (Table 4.8). The government financed these deficits through foreign borrowing and, increasingly, recourse to the inflation tax.

The 1981 drought put even more pressure on the government's fiscal position and was relieved only through exceptional amounts of foreign grant assistance. Nevertheless, when foreign aid returned to more normal levels in 1982, the government had to begin to search for expenditure cuts and balance-of-payments support. The government signed a series of standby arrangements with the IMF from 1982 to 1984. Even though overall expenditures did not decline much in the context of these loans, some sectors, notably health and education, fell sharply, while others, debt service and support to parastatals, increased substantially.

Despite these early efforts to stabilize the economy, The Gambia continued to suffer macroeconomic difficulties, especially in the balance of payments, so a more thorough adjustment effort began in 1986 under the guise of the Economic Recovery Program. The ERP's most important changes in fiscal policy included a significant retrenchment of public sector employees and an effort to reduce transfers to parastatals, thus tackling two of the thornier fiscal problems that affect many African governments. While progress was uneven on both fronts, the ERP did manage to reduce public sector staffing by about 25 percent between 1986 and 1989, and it eliminated more than half of all public enterprises through outright sales, management agreements, or liquidations. These operations at times required extraordinary expenditures on the part of the central government, mostly to absorb bad debts that the public enterprises had accumulated at home and abroad. These expenditures explain entirely the surge in total spending for 1988 and 1989, virtually all of which was financed with donor assistance. Excluding these expenditures, total expenditures have declined slightly, and the overall deficit has been brought under control.

On the revenue side, the government has attempted to move away from taxes on international trade to more general sales and income taxes. De facto, however, the openness of the Gambian economy and the difficulty of taxing domestic informal activities means that the tax structure still relies heavily on international transactions, though taxes on groundnut exports have been eliminated.

Malawi: Malawi has enjoyed a reputation for responsible macroeconomic management – one not entirely consistent with the data. Although Malawi maintained an export-oriented development strategy during the 1970s, fiscal deficits were consistently high, averaging about 6 percent of GDP after grants (Table 4.9). These were financed with borrowing, mostly abroad and on soft terms. As in many countries, Malawi experienced a short-lived surge in expenditures in the early 1980s without a compensating increase in tax revenues, so that the deficit shot up to 12 to 15 percent of GDP after grants. Most of this had to be financed on commercial terms, and the government quickly entered into a series of standby arrangements with the IMF, complemented by several World Bank adjustment credits. The accompanying stabilization program succeeded in returning the deficit to prior levels, about 6 percent of GDP, but spending again surged in the mid-1980s in response to the inflow of refugees from Mozambique, the loss of the rail link to Beira, and financial problems in the parastatal sector. These shocks, combined with rising debt service obligations, forced a more substantial fiscal adjustment in the late 1980s, when the deficit was reduced to about 2 percent of GDP with the help of a large increase in foreign grant financing (to aid Malawi's support of Mozambican refugees), reductions in real civil service wages, other cost controls, and improved management at several important parastatals. In the social sectors, spending on education and health increased substantially in the late 1970s or early 1980s. While this spending later contracted, especially in the 1988/1989 budget, these sectors were protected in the 1981/1982 stabilization.

Mozambique: Very little reliable information is available for Mozambique. What is clear, however, is the overwhelming importance of donors in financing and influencing priorities for public expenditures. Official development assistance to Mozambique has been more than half of GDP since the mid-1980s when the government began an adjustment program that abandoned state socialism as the organizing principle for the economy. While much progress has been made in market reforms, fiscal deficits remain high even after the extraordinary amounts of foreign grant financing (much in the form of food aid) that Mozambique receives (Table 4.10). Thus, the large increase in government expenditures as a proportion of GDP witnessed during the adjustment program reflects that ever increasing donor support is channeled through the budget and that production was in a decimated state due to the war. In the social sectors, education expenditures contracted as a share of GDP along with the general decline in public spending, but had recovered to levels even higher than spending in the early 1980s by the end of the decade. There are no reliable data on health allocations. For both education and health, though, rural services surely have suffered as a consequence of the war.

Cameroon: Until the collapse of oil prices in 1986, Cameroon was often cited as an example where prudent fiscal management contributed to low inflation and rapid growth in Africa. Even though expenditures grew substantially in the late 1970s and early 1980s (Table 4.11), they were financed entirely by

Table 4.8. *The Gambia: fiscal data*

	1975	1976	1977	1978	1979	1980	1981	1982	1983
Deficit, incl grants	2.6	1.3	6.0	9.9	4.5	3.7	4.1	14.6	7.1
Expenditure	18.4	18.4	24.2	36.2	27.2	31.7	36.2	36.3	29.5
Expenditure, net of interest	18.4	18.3	24.0	36.1	27.0	30.8	35.6	34.9	27.6
Education expenditures	1.4	1.9	2.4	2.0	2.7	4.0	4.6	5.3	5.1
Health expenditures	1.22	1.24	2.16	1.95	1.91	2.37	2.23	2.41	2.41
Revenue, excl grants	14.6	16.4	18.2	20.9	19.5	22.2	18.3	18.0	17.4
Grants	1.2	0.7	0.0	5.5	3.2	5.8	13.8	3.7	5.0
Official development assistance	7.2	9.1	13.3	19.6	15.4	23.2	32.2	22.4	20.4
Stock of international debt, $	13	15	40	52	83	137	176	207	212

Table 4.8. *(cont.)*

	1984	1985	1986	1987	1988	1989	1990	1991
Deficit, incl grants	8.0	5.7	-11.3	0.7	7.2	-7.4	0.1	-5.5
Expenditure	34.1	33.5	26.2	36.6	37.1	26.0	29.9	24.0
Expenditure, net of interest	31.3	29.8	22.7	32.0	32.6	21.6	25.8	20.1
Education expenditures	3.8	2.7	2.2	2.0	2.1	2.0	–	–
Health expenditures	2.20	1.76	–	–	–	–	–	–
Revenue, excl grants	20.7	19.0	19.3	23.2	20.7	23.2	21.7	19.8
Grants	5.4	8.8	18.2	10.2	9.2	10.2	8.1	9.7
Official development assistance	32.6	29.0	68.3	42.1	38.6	42.1	–	–
Stock of international debt, $	230	245	270	342	322	342	352	351

Note: All data as percentage of GDP.
Sources: For deficit, revenues, expenditures: Nashashibi and Bazzoni 1993 for 1980–1991, IMF various years for 1975–1979; for social sector and official development assistance: World Bank 1993b; for debt: World Bank various years.

119

Table 4.9. *Malawi: fiscal data*

	1975	1976	1977	1978	1979	1980	1981	1982	1983
Deficit, incl grants	8.4	4.8	4.3	5.2	7.5	16.0	12.7	7.6	7.2
Expenditure	26.5	21.1	21.9	26.8	32.3	39.4	35.7	29.5	28.7
Expenditure, net of interest	25.0	19.7	20.5	24.9	30.0	36.2	30.8	25.1	24.8
Education expenditures	2.1	2.0	2.3	3.0	2.4	3.1	3.9	4.1	3.9
Health expenditures	1.33	1.13	1.08	1.36	1.47	1.91	1.83	1.51	1.96
Revenue, excl grants	15.8	14.7	15.4	18.2	20.8	19.1	19.2	18.6	19.2
Grants	2.3	1.6	2.3	3.4	4.1	4.3	3.8	3.3	2.3
Official development assistance	10.4	9.4	9.8	10.4	13.4	11.6	11.1	10.3	9.5
Stock of international debt, $	260	303	453	591	665	821	812	857	885

Table 4.9. (cont.)

	1984	1985	1986	1987	1988	1989	1990	1991
Deficit, inc. grants	6.0	7.8	9.4	6.6	1.3	2.0	1.7	3.3
Expenditure	28.2	32.2	34.2	29.2	27.9	28.6	25.7	23.8
Expenditure, net of interest	22.3	26.0	27.7	23.2	23.6	24.3	22.4	21.1
Education expenditures	3.4	3.5	3.6	3.1	2.4	2.8	–	–
Health expenditures	2.20	2.15	2.40	1.82	1.42	1.67	–	–
Revenue, excl. grants	19.8	22.1	21.2	19.8	20.7	21.8	19.6	18.4
Grants	2.4	2.3	3.6	2.8	5.9	4.8	4.4	2.1
Official development assistance	13.1	10.0	16.8	23.7	27.4	25.1	–	–
Stock of international debt, $	876	1,018	1,161	1,373	1,345	1,394	1,584	1,676

Note: All data as percentage of GDP except international debt data, which are U.S. dollars.

Sources: For deficit, revenues, expenditures: Nashashibi and Bazzoni 1993 for 1980–1991, IMF various years for 1975–1979; for social sector and official development assistance: World Bank 1993b; for debt: World Bank various years.

121

Table 4.10. *Mozambique: fiscal data*

	1980	1981	1982	1983	1984	1985	1986	1987	1988	1989	1990	1991
Deficit, incl grants	8.3	12.8	6.8	16.1	17.9	12.7	15.7	11.7	11.1	7.5	13.2	4.7
Expenditure	30.2	38.4	39.3	49.1	41.4	27.8	31.2	37.2	44.7	47.6	51.9	51.3
Expenditure, net of interest	30.2	38.4	39.3	49.1	41.3	27.7	30.7	35.3	42.4	44.4	48.6	48.8
Education expenditures	3.7	4.1	4.2	4.5	4.0	3.0	3.0	2.5	3.9	4.8	5.0	—
Revenue, excl grants	19.3	23.2	29.9	29.8	20.7	13.1	13.2	16.1	19.8	23.5	22.3	23.9
Grants	2.6	2.4	2.6	3.2	2.8	2.0	2.3	9.4	13.8	16.6	16.4	22.7
Official development assistance	7.0	6.3	8.5	9.3	10.2	8.8	10.2	44.7	71.3	59.2	—	—
Stock of international debt, $	—	—	—	82	1,365	2,863	3,525	4,261	4,418	4,737	4,740	—

Note: All data as percentage of GDP.

Sources: For deficit, revenues, expenditures: Nashashibi and Bazzoni 1993 for 1980–1991, IMF various years; for education: World Bank 1992b; for debt: World Bank various years.

increased oil revenues. Indeed, Cameroon apparently heeded in part the usual admonition to save income from temporary booms, unlike almost all other mineral exporters in Africa. Cameroon saved part of its oil revenue, it is widely believed, holding it offshore in extrabudgetary accounts called *comptes hors budget* (CHB).[4] Even though foreign borrowing on the strength of future oil revenues would have been an easy source of finance, the government maintained deficits near zero throughout the period during which other African nations generated serious external debt problems.

This sanguine picture of the public finances before 1986 contrasts sharply with the financial problems that followed. The halving of world oil prices was a huge shock, to be sure, costing the economy about 14 percent of its real income and reducing government revenues by about 30 percent. Moreover, the government had just begun a major public investment program, relaxing the restraint that characterized public expenditures in the 1970s and early 1980s. Thus, the fiscal deficit shot up from roughly 0 to 13 percent of GDP in 1987, financed in large part by drawing on the CHB. Even this figure is an understatement, as the government ran up substantial arrears to local contractors, which do not show up as deficit financing in the budget.

Attempts to stabilize the fiscal situation have been halting and incomplete. Despite sharp cuts in capital expenditures, the deficit has held steady at 4 to 6 percent of GDP since the 1988 stabilization. The government has been unable to reduce the deficit below that level, largely because the expenditures that remain, salaries and support to public enterprises, are difficult to cut for political reasons (van de Walle 1994). Similarly, efforts to increase nonpetroleum tax revenues have consistently fallen short of their targets because tax enforcement is lax and, more recently, because political opponents of the government have promoted nonpayment as a form of civil disobedience. These constraints, combined with the inability to use the inflation tax that CFA membership implies, have left the government little option but to accumulate arrears, both domestically and internationally. A more fundamental rethinking of the role and structure of the public sector is clearly in order, but the political hurdles to such an adjustment are high. To date, little progress is evident and Cameroon is mired in a prolonged economic decline.

In the social sectors, spending on health and education increased sharply in the early 1980s, roughly in proportion to the increases in total expenditures but

---

[4] As Blandford et al. (1994) note, it is difficult to know exactly how much the government saved abroad. The government closely guards information on oil sales, distribution of revenues, and allocation of the proceeds, partly for political reasons and partly because such savings violate the CFA agreement – the accounts are not held with the French treasury. Nevertheless, the consistent transfer of resources to the budget from abroad during the mid- to late-1980s indicates that Cameroon initially saved abroad a nontrivial amount of the oil revenues.

Table 4.11. *Cameroon: fiscal data*

	1975	1976	1977	1978	1979	1980	1981	1982	1983
Deficit, incl grants	2.1	2.4	0.1	-1.1	-2.9	-0.4	0.2	-0.2	-3.5
Expenditure	17.8	19.1	16.9	17.4	16.5	16.5	21.7	24.7	23.6
Expenditure, net of interest	17.6	18.8	16.6	16.9	16.3	16.2	21.1	24.0	23.0
Education expenditures	–	2.4	2.1	1.9	1.6	1.8	1.4	2.0	2.6
Health expenditures	–	0.72	0.61	0.61	0.52	0.72	0.51	0.69	0.73
Revenue, excl grants	15.0	15.9	16.2	18.5	19.4	16.9	21.5	24.9	27.1
Grants	0.7	0.8	0.6	0.0	0.0	–	–	–	–
Official development assistance	4.0	4.5	5.3	4.1	4.8	3.5	2.4	2.7	1.6
Stock of international debt, $	420	591	1,057	1,478	2,116	2,513	2,548	2,717	2,739

Table 4.11. (cont.)

	1984	1985	1986	1987	1988	1989	1990	1991
Deficit, incl grants	0.1	3.3	0.4	13.0	6.4	5.1	8.5	8.6
Expenditure	23.3	22.1	23.1	32.0	24.2	21.9	23.1	24.7
Expenditure, net of interest	22.7	21.2	22.2	30.9	22.0	19.9	20.1	20.5
Education expenditures	2.5	3.0	2.5	3.1	3.6	2.4	–	–
Health expenditures	0.96	1.08	0.71	0.83	0.79	0.68	–	–
Revenue, excl grants	23.2	18.8	22.7	19.0	17.8	16.8	14.6	16.1
Grants	–	–	–	–	–	–	–	–
Official development assistance	2.3	1.9	2.1	1.7	2.2	4.2	–	–
Stock of international debt, $	2,722	2,940	3,710	4,039	4,224	4,743	5,990	6,278

Note: All data as percentage of GDP except international debt data, which are U.S. dollars.
Sources: For deficit, revenues, expenditures: Nashashibi and Bazzoni 1993 for 1980–1991, IMF various years for 1975–1979; for social sector and official development assistance: World Bank 1993b; for debt: World Bank various years.

with a lag of one to two years. On the other hand, spending on education and especially health services declined with the first signs of the crisis in 1986, suggesting that these sectors are low priorities for the government. In addition, analysts have noted that the increase in spending was highly concentrated in technical schools and universities in education and hospital construction in health while more basic and equitably distributed services were neglected. More recently, the burden of salaries in these ministries has crowded out expenditures on operations and maintenance, lowering the efficiency of each. Capital spending has all but disappeared.

Niger: Niger is a classic example of a country that used sharp increases in foreign borrowing to leverage a commodity boom into huge increases in government expenditures. Prior to the discovery of uranium deposits in the mid-1970s, Niger's government was very small, spending only 15 percent of GDP (Table 4.12). The exploitation of the uranium mines, combined with a fourfold increase in international prices, increased government revenues modestly, from 13 percent of GDP in 1976 to 15 percent in 1980. But government spending continued increasing as Niger borrowed abroad, on commercial terms, against its (expected) future uranium revenues. Most of the related spending was on the capital account as several large projects were initiated. Unfortunately, the decline of uranium prices and the restrictive borrowing environment of the 1980s forced a quick reversal, with many projects left incomplete. Despite these cutbacks on capital expenditures, however, current expenditures continued to climb, especially for salaries and debt service. By the early 1990s, the wage bill accounted for more than 90 percent of tax revenues. Overall, total expenditures did not contract much, though the growth did subside. Deficits continued to mount until the mid-1980s, when they stabilized at 5 percent of GDP.[5] Spending in the social sectors paralleled general expenditures, with sharp cuts in development expenditures during the 1982–1984 stabilization while current expenditures continued to grow. Later in the decade, several foreign-financed projects in these sectors permitted stronger growth in education and health than in the general budget.

Observations and generalizations

In most of our sample countries, government expenditures do decline, at times dramatically, during the 1980s. However, as with the continent-wide

---

[5] Note that the ADI data show an increase of about 5 percent of GDP in expenditures and the deficit in 1981, as opposed the IMF's 1 percent decline. This jump is reversed in 1982, when the two series are again similar. Dorosh and Bernier (1994b) show even sharper increases in expenditure because their data include extrabudgetary accounts. Fiscal control was lax at the time and individual ministries or parastatals were able to finance projects without the Finance Ministry's approval. As a result, the reported budget data understate true government expenditures and borrowing.

average, spending does not decline below the levels realized before the boom in most countries, and it remains well above those levels in several countries, including some (e.g., The Gambia, Niger) that maintained serious adjustment programs and good relations with the IMF and the World Bank. Three exceptions to this pattern are noteworthy: Tanzania, Guinea, and Ghana. All three countries eschewed a socialist ideology during the 1980s, in the context of an adjustment program financed (in part) by the World Bank and the IMF. In Tanzania and Guinea, government expenditures as a percentage of GDP and in dollars per capita declined considerably during the 1980s and apparently are somewhat below the levels of the 1970s. However, government expenditure declined sharply *before* each country began its sustained adjustment program with the multilateral institutions (1985 for Tanzania, 1986 for Guinea). Because expenditures had reached well beyond what tax revenues and grants could finance in the early 1980s, each country was forced to contract spending before reaching agreement with the World Bank and the IMF. Later agreements accepted the (reduced) level of spending without substantial modification. Ghana is an even more dramatic example of this same phenomenon. Ghana's prolonged economic decline brought government spending to extraordinarily low levels, and it is notable that the IMF and World Bank accepted sharp increases in government spending in the adjustment program that finally began in 1983.

These three cases show that, in Africa, radical declines in government expenditure are not the unique consequence of adjustment programs or adverse external shocks. Limited tax revenues, which often declined substantially in real terms because of exchange rate overvaluation, or cheap official prices forced several countries to contract expenditures. While this is especially discouraging, it is also important to note that the multilateral institutions have been reasonably sensitive to the specific circumstances of these countries and have not, in general, demanded further expenditure cuts as a condition for their support. The acceptance of substantial increases in spending in Ghana's case, for example, was entirely sensible given the decimated public finances of 1983. At the same time, the devaluation and price decontrol of 1983 helped boost revenues to pay for the additional expenditures.

Another fundamental point that emerges from our country cases is the close link between shocks to the terms of trade or the flow of foreign capital and fiscal policy. African governments depend heavily on international transactions for their tax revenue, in the form of import tariffs and royalties from natural resource exports. This dependence yields a high correlation between external shocks and the government fiscal stance. In addition, almost all international loans, commercial and concessional alike, go to the public sector in Africa, often to finance the budget directly. (This contrasts sharply with Latin America where a sizable proportion of loans before 1982, while guaranteed by the government, went to private enterprises.) Thus, each of the major external shocks

Table 4.12. *Niger: fiscal data*

	1975	1976	1977	1978	1979	1980	1981	1982	1983
Deficit, incl grants	–	2.1	1.7	2.3	1.9	2.7	3.5	4.7	6.6
Expenditure	–	14.9	14.7	16.3	16.0	18.9	17.6	19.7	19.1
Expenditure, net of interest	–	14.3	13.8	15.5	14.7	17.8	16.2	17.5	17.0
Education expenditures	–	1.7	1.9	2.3	2.3	3.3	2.0	2.2	2.6
Health expenditures	–	0.54	0.48	0.59	0.62	0.75	0.57	0.51	0.65
Revenue, excl grants	–	12.3	12.8	13.6	14.0	11.7	10.3	11.2	10.9
Grants	–	0.5	0.2	0.4	0.1	4.5	3.8	3.8	1.6
Official development assistance	13.4	12.1	7.5	8.8	8.2	6.7	8.9	13.1	9.8
Stock of international debt, $	112	130	170	606	2,628	863	1,022	957	950

Table 4.12. (cont.)

	1984	1985	1986	1987	1988	1989	1990	1991
Deficit, incl grants	5.1	5.8	3.7	4.4	6.0	6.1	8.2	6.3
Expenditure	19.6	20.4	20.1	20.3	20.9	20.9	23.7	18.4
Expenditure, net of interest	16.9	17.5	17.3	17.4	18.2	18.3	21.4	16.4
Education expenditures	2.6	2.5	2.4	2.5	2.3	–	–	–
Health expenditures	0.79	0.69	0.76	0.85	0.76	–	–	–
Revenue, excl grants	11.1	11.0	11.3	10.5	10.3	10.4	10.1	8.6
Grants	3.4	3.6	5.1	5.4	4.6	4.4	5.4	3.5
Official development assistance	11.0	21.1	16.5	16.3	15.9	14.5	–	–
Stock of international debt, $	956	1,208	1,448	1,697	1,742	1,578	–	–

Note: All data as percentage of GDP except international debt data, which are U.S. dollars.
Sources: For deficit, revenues, expenditures: Nashashibi and Bazzoni 1993 for 1980–1991, IMF various years for 1975–1979; for social sector and official development assistance: World Bank 1993b; for debt: World Bank various years.

to African economies during the 1980s, declining terms of trade and reduced commercial credits,[6] directly affected the funds available to the government, as well as indirectly affected them through reduced imports (which further reduced the tax base). This correlation is important to the debate over whether the causes of Africa's economic crisis are external (terms-of-trade shocks and reduced capital flows) or internal (poor fiscal and pricing policy). Because an external shock will usually strongly affect the government's revenues as well as macroeconomic targets like GDP and the current account, budget deficits tend to increase as revenues decline after the external shock. Nonetheless, an economy whose macroeconomic imbalances are the result of external shocks still must adjust.

A related lesson for governments dependent on the international terms of trade is that attempts to maintain or expand the government's expenditure as a share of GDP when its revenue base declines as a share of GDP can be quite damaging. Even though such a policy might make sense in terms of counter-cyclical macroeconomic management, as resources from its traditional tax base of traded goods shrink compared with GDP, the government must resort to taxes that are more difficult to collect and probably more distortionary (e.g., the inflation tax) and/or borrowing to maintain its share of GDP. The distortions implied by the revised tax system may, in turn, exacerbate the decline in GDP caused by the initial terms-of-trade shock.

Evidence on social sector spending in our case study countries is more difficult to come by and to interpret. Time series are shorter in many cases and often do not span important years (from the perspective of evaluating adjustment programs). Even when data exist, they are more likely to reflect budgets than actual expenditures. Nevertheless, a few generalizations surface. First, in broad terms, spending in these sectors tends to follow overall government spending, both in constant U.S. dollars per capita and as a share of GDP.[7] Second, the share of expenditures going to the social sectors is often positively correlated with total expenditures' share of GDP. That is, as expenditures increased, especially during the boom of the early 1980s, health and especially education often received a growing proportion of public expenditures (at times with a lag of two or three years). Conversely, sharp reductions in overall

---

[6] The exogeneity of reduced commercial bank lending is debatable. Presumably countries that accumulated foreign debts rapidly in the late 1970s should have recognized that their excessive borrowing was going to make creditors reluctant to lend further. Nevertheless, even countries with exemplary debt management like Colombia or Cameroon found themselves cut off from commercial credits when the debt crisis hit. For these countries, it is reasonable to consider the shock as exogenous.

[7] Again, the fact that these data often reflect budget figures rather than actual expenditures is important. Budget shares tend to have significant inertia as fiscal planners find it convenient (and uncontroversial) to maintain the same shares as in previous years.

expenditures almost immediately dictated even more extreme reductions in social sector expenditures, indicating that many governments view (de facto) these sectors as marginal in the sense that their financing depends on resources that remain after financing other sections of the budget. Finally, refusal to accept orthodox adjustment measures in no sense benefits the social sectors. In fact, the steepest declines in both education and health expenditures – in Ghana in the 1970s, in Tanzania and Zaire in the early 1980s – occurred at times when countries were at odds with the multilateral agencies. Not only do absolute expenditures on social services decline, their shares of the total also collapse in most cases. On the other hand, many countries with sustained adjustment programs during the 1980s – The Gambia (after 1985), Malawi, Madagascar, and Niger – appear to have protected their social sectors in the sense that the shares remain stable or increase despite general budget cuts, albeit after a reduction that reversed (in part) the run-up in expenditures that preceded each country's macroeconomic crisis. To some extent, the protection of these sectors probably reflects donors' preferences for them and the consequent propensity to direct aid flows toward them.

The incidence of public expenditures

In the debate over adjustment policies, critics tend to view increases in government spending in general and the social services in particular as beneficial for the poor. Indeed, the previous section reinforces that tendency. But whether public expenditures are good for the poor depends on the incidence of those expenditures; that is, who actually receives the benefits.[8] In general, that is difficult to determine. Many public services – defense, maintenance of law and order, establishing and enforcing the rules of the game in commerce – do not have easily identifiable beneficiaries. Even in the case of public services where beneficiaries are distinguishable, empirical work requires household-level information from representative surveys that, until recently, have not been available in Africa.[9] Nevertheless, we have made progress in some countries and for some budget items. The most important is the area of social services, where we can complement the use of sectoral budget data with household survey data to examine households' use of public services in different strata of the income distribution. Another area to which we devote considerable attention is

---

[8] More broadly, it also depends on the incidence of the taxes used to finance those expenditures, an issue we address later in this chapter.

[9] At the time of our work, the type of multipurpose national household surveys needed for this analysis were available only in Côte d'Ivoire, Ghana, Guinea, Madagascar, and Tanzania. Our project undertook comparable surveys in Conakry, Guinea, and Maputo, Mozambique. More recently, several governments have begun integrated multipurpose household surveys modeled after the World Bank Living Standards Measurement Surveys. These include surveys for The Gambia, Madagascar, Niger, Nigeria, Sierra Leone, South Africa, Uganda, and Zambia.

public employment, a theme that has become a major focus of adjustment policy. Again, by examining who public employees are and where their households are in the income distribution, we can begin to gauge the incidence of public employment and, conversely, the welfare consequences of retrenchment programs. Finally, in a broader context, we can use our CGE models to examine the impact of general reductions in government expenditures.

Methodology

The most general method for comparing the incidence of public expenditures is to test for "welfare dominance" (Yitzhaki and Slemrod 1991). Yitzhaki and Slemrod (1991) construct "concentration curves," diagrams that are similar to Lorenz curves[10] in that they plot households from the poorest to the wealthiest on the horizontal axis against the cumulative proportion of expenditures for all households from the poorest up to household n. They then prove that for any social welfare function that favors an equitable distribution of income, changing the structure of expenditures by slightly increasing expenditures on a service x and reducing those on a service y by just enough to keep total expenditures constant will improve social welfare when x's concentration curve is everywhere above y's.[11] The intuition is straightforward. If poorer households tend to consume more of a particular public service, say primary education, and less of another, say university education, then reducing expenditures on the latter to pay for more of the former will improve the distribution of welfare. Yitzhaki and Slemrod (1991) refer to this as "welfare dominance" because of the analogy with the concept of second-order stochastic dominance in the finance literature. The concentration curve for primary education is above that for university education because poorer households consume a larger percentage of total primary education services than they do of university education services.

It is also insightful to compare each service's concentration curve with two benchmarks: the Lorenz curve for expenditures and the 45 degree line. Analogous to the tax literature, we can say that an expenditure is progressive if it benefits poorer households more than wealthy ones, relative to their expenditures, and regressive if it does not. At the same time, public expenditures are often held to a higher standard than taxes in their being considered well tar-

---

[10] A Lorenz curve plots all households in the sample from poorest to the richest on the horizontal axis versus cumulative household income (expenditure) as a proportion of all households' total income (expenditure).

[11] Yitzhaki and Slemrod (1991) actually develop the argument in terms of commodity taxes, but it is equally applicable to expenditures, or combinations of taxes and expenditures. Technically, the argument also requires that the efficiency consequences of the expenditure/tax change be at least neutral, that is, that the efficiency of the allocation of resources not worsen with the change. This condition is more difficult to identify in practice, but we will usually assume that it is satisfied in our discussion.

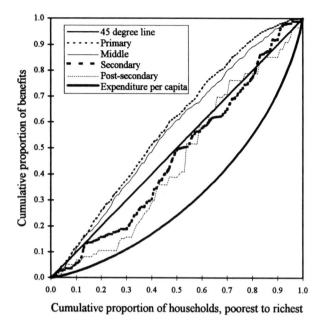

Figure 4.1   Ghana: concentration curves for public school attendance, by level. *Source:* Government of Ghana 1987.

geted to the poor only if the benefits go disproportionately to the poor in absolute terms, not relative to income. In that sense, a well-targeted public expenditure has a concentration curve that is above the 45 degree line (concave rather than convex), while those above the Lorenz curve but below the 45 degree line are progressive and those below the Lorenz curve are regressive.

While its generality makes the criterion of welfare dominance attractive, its practical application can be problematic, especially in samples where relatively few households are benefiting from the expenditures in question. The criterion requires that one curve be everywhere above another, but, in practice, the curves for many expenditures tend to cross, yielding inconclusive results. Consider Figure 4.1, which gives an example of concentration curves for public school attendance in Ghana. A cursory examination suggests that public spending on primary and middle schools is generally well targeted to the poor: their concentration curves lie above both the household expenditures Lorenz curve and the 45 degree line.[12] Spending on secondary schools appears to be progressive, but not well targeted to the poor. Nevertheless, we cannot establish

[12] We caution that we are assuming that the subsidy received by all students at a given level of schooling is the same. If poorer households receive lower-quality services, the curve would be less progressive.

welfare dominance among any of the concepts presented in the graph (except for the 45 degree line and household expenditures): the concentration curves cross at least once for each of them. The combination of noise in the data and a certain lumpiness of the benefits we are interested in – not all households have a child in school or have need for public health services – makes it very likely that the curves will cross, especially near the ends. When the dominance tests are inconclusive, we can draw conclusions only by being more specific about the importance of each household in the social welfare function.[13] For example, if we rank social services by their Gini coefficients, we will always have an ordering, but it comes at a price: comparing Gini coefficients for different concentration curves implicitly accepts a particular social welfare function, that of the Gini formula, and choice of another welfare function might yield a different ordering.

Yitzhaki (1983) provides a middle ground between the normative generality (and consequent indeterminancy) of the welfare dominance approach and the precision (and lack of normative generality) of the Gini coefficient. He shows that an extended Gini coefficient can adjust the weight given to poorer households and thus give a clearer notion of how more progressive social welfare functions would rank expenditure items. The coefficient is defined as:

$$G(v) = -v * Cov\{e,[1 - F(e)]^{(v-1)}\}/\bar{e}, \quad v > 1$$

where e measures households' use of an expenditure item; F(e) is the cumulative distribution of households ranked from the poorest to the richest; $\bar{e}$ is mean use of the item; and v is a parameter that affects the weighing of each household's welfare in the social welfare function. In particular, G(2) yields the traditional Gini coefficient, while values of v greater than 2 yield measures that give greater weight to the use of the item by poorer households. Thus, by calculating the extended Gini coefficient for increasing values of v, we can gain a sense of how more progressive social welfare functions rank the value of a given public service. As an example, consider Figure 4.1 once again. Here, the concentration curves for all items cross. However, Table 4.13 shows that even for values of v up to 10, which gives extraordinary weight to the poorest households in the sample,[14] Yitzhaki's measure maintains an ordering of public primary, public middle, 45 degree line, public secondary, and household expenditures. Thus, for concentration curves that cross only near the extremes,

---

[13] Recall that if one distribution is welfare dominant over another, then the first will be preferred to the second under *any* social welfare function that favors progressivity.

[14] Yitzhaki (1983) shows that the extended Gini gives a weight of $v*(v - 1)*(1 - F)^{(v-2)}$ to each point in the concentration curve where F is the household's position in the cumulative distribution. For v=10, the weight for the ordinate at the 10th percentile is 43 million times the weight for the ordinate at the 90th percentile.

Table 4.13. *Examples of extended Gini coefficients for use of public schools in Ghana*

v-parameters	Public primary school	Public middle school	45 degree line	Public secondary school	Public postsecondary school	Per capita household expenditures
2	-0.169	-0.130	0	0.064	0.103	0.382
4	-0.236	-0.170	0	0.177	0.280	0.573
6	-0.239	-0.156	0	0.235	0.375	0.643
8	-0.228	-0.129	0	0.267	0.416	0.683
10	-0.212	-0.101	0	0.286	0.432	0.708

Source: Government of Ghana 1987.

it is impossible to reverse the obvious ordering without placing huge weights on the welfare of a very few of the poorest households and near-zero weights on the wealthiest.

In the remainder of this chapter, we employ both the concepts of welfare dominance and the extended Gini coefficient to examine the welfare implications of public expenditures and taxes. The techniques require household survey data, of course. Here, we use such survey data from Côte d'Ivoire (the Côte d'Ivoire Living Standards Survey), Ghana (the Ghana Living Standards Survey), Guinea (Integrated Survey of Households' Living Conditions), Madagascar (1993 Permanent Household Survey), Maputo (the Maputo Integrated Food Security Survey), and Tanzania (the Human Resource Development Survey). Côte d'Ivoire is not one of our case study countries, but given the scarcity of household survey information in Africa, we include it in this analysis.

The incidence of social sector spending

Each survey reports information on households' use of a variety of public services, including public education at different levels and public health services such as hospitals, clinics, and maternity centers. We have not attempted to put a monetary value on these services. Instead, we simply count the number of students, number of hospital visits, and the like, per household. This does not alter the concentration curve for an individual service as long as the value of the subsidy inherent in the service is the same for every recipient: putting a monetary value on the service will enter the numerator (cumulative value) and the denominator (total value) symmetrically. It does, however, impede the summation of different services (e.g., creation of a concentration curve for all education expenditures). To gauge the overall impact of public expenditures on education, for example, we cannot simply average the concentration curves for primary, secondary, and postsecondary education. We need to weight that average by the importance of each item in the overall welfare of households, which requires attaching monetary (or utility) values to each type of schooling. While it is feasible to devise weighting schemes at a broad sectoral level by using, for example, budget shares of each level of schooling (Verghis and Demery 1994; Demery et al. 1995), doing so at the household level is a difficult task. In theory, one could estimate the value of the public service to the household using techniques similar to those of Gertler and van der Gaag (1990), subtract any fees paid, and derive a net benefit for the household. We have not pursued that strategy, but that different households surely receive different benefits from apparently comparable public services highlights the importance of our assumption to the contrary. It seems likely, for example, that rural schools and clinics provide lower-quality services than urban institutions. Because urban households are wealthier, this implies a bias favoring wealthier households that the concentration curves and Gini coefficients will not capture. Also, this information tells us nothing about the efficiency with which the government provides these services, and we will assume throughout the analysis that marginal changes in expenditures from one category to another do not have efficiency costs.

Despite these caveats, examining households' reported use of services does give us some indication of who the beneficiaries are and, of course, who would suffer if services were cut. This is an area where information has been sorely lacking in Africa (Jimenez 1989). Beginning to uncover usage patterns should help improve policy making by targeting services to those who most need them.

We consider first the use of public health care facilities. To begin, the private sector plays a substantial role in the provision of health services. Furthermore, donors also finance large shares of health expenditures for both public and private services. Public expenditures on health, as a percent of the total, range from a high of 39.7 percent in Guinea to 8.5 percent in Zaire, among the countries highlighted in this book (Table 4.14). Thus, our findings on the incidence of public health spending must be considered in the context of the great importance of the private provision of health care.

For the few African countries where we can make the distinction, the majority of public health expenditures go either to hospitals or administration. Much less is dedicated to primary and preventative medicine, services that are more likely to reach the poor, especially in rural areas (Table 4.15). Thus, nothing suggests that the poor are major beneficiaries of publicly provided health care expenditures. Nevertheless, Figures 4.2 to 4.7 show that public health expenditures, even those for hospitals, are progressive, though they are not well targeted to the poor. Also, except for Côte d'Ivoire, the concentration curve for private health services lies above the Lorenz curve for per capita expenditures. This combination contradicts a common notion that public health services are inferior goods that the poor consume but wealthier households avoid because

Table 4.14. *Public and private health sector expenditures and foreign aid as a share of the total health expenditures*

Country	Public	Private	Aid
		(%)	
Cameroon	26.4	61.7	11.9
Gambia	28.3	20.7	51.0
Ghana	35.0	51.8	13.2
Guinea	39.7	40.3	20.0
Madagascar	29.0	49.6	21.4
Malawi	35.0	41.7	23.3
Mozambique	21.0	25.7	53.3
Niger	24.5	31.3	34.1
Tanzania	14.4	31.6	54.0
Zaire	8.5	64.8	26.7
All Africa	43.8	46.6	9.2

Source: World Health Organization 1994.

they can afford higher-quality private care. If that were true, the concentration curves for public health services would be well targeted to the poor, but private health services would fall below the Lorenz curve. An alternative interpretation is that because publicly provided health services are rationed, some households from all strata must seek private health care – not because it is superior, but because it is their only option. This interpretation, combined with a low income elasticity of demand for health care in general, is consistent with the results in these these samples.

The welfare ordering of the different services is usually consistent with what one would expect: the concentration curves suggest that private care is the most concentrated, followed by public hospital care, and finally other public care. Exceptions exist, however. In Guinea, private health care appears to be no more concentrated than other public services. This may be due to the limited availability of public health services, which leads the poor to rely on private care, especially traditional medicine. In Maputo, we find that public hospitals are more progressive than other public facilities. That this is only an urban sample may explain this anomaly. In particular, urban and rural clinics may offer different services, and the urban poor tend to rely on hospitals for a wide range of outpatient services, whereas the rural poor do not, because no hospitals are available to them. We also note that private health care appears to be as concentrated as public care in Ghana.

Table 4.15. *Health sector expenditures in Africa*

Country	Health sector expenditure shares	
	Primary	Other[a]
Angola[b]	6	94
Benin[c]	30	70
Burundi[d]	20	80
Chad[c]	19	81
Comoros[c]	25	75
Côte d'Ivoire[d]	34	65
Ethiopia[c]	24	76
Ghana[d]	23	77
Guinea[c]	34	66
Guinea-Bissau[c]	48	52
Kenya[c]	21	79
Lesotho[d]	14	86
Madagascar[d]	18	81
Malawi[c]	30	–
Namibia[c]	43	67
Senegal[d]	58	42
Tanzania[c,e]	31	69

Note: Figures are from most recent year that data are available.
[a]Other includes district, provincial and other hospitals, and administration not directly related to the delivery of primary health and related preventive care services.
[b]Development expenditures only.
[c]Total expenditures.
[d]Recurrent expenditures only.
[e]Data divided into hospital (69 percent), preventive (6 percent), and other (25 percent).
Sources: Sahn and Bernier 1995; Hammer, Pyatt and White 1996.

The Gini coefficients generally fall in the same order as the concentration curves (Table 4.16). Putting very high weight on the welfare of the poorest households (v = 10) does not reverse these rankings in any case. Thus, the data support the popular notion that governments would do well to concentrate their expenditures in nonhospital services, especially if rationing of public services is important. By redirecting expenditures from expensive, intensive services available to only a few people toward less expensive primary care, governments could ease the rationing of the latter and probably make their distribution more equitable.

Table 4.16. *Extended Gini coefficients for use of public and private health services*

v-parameter	Other public	Private care	Public hospital	Total per capita expenditures
Côte d'Ivoire				
2	0.044	0.456	0.203	0.512
4	0.267	0.697	0.403	0.690
10	0.350	0.861	0.572	0.798
Ghana				
2	0.087	0.189	0.218	0.382
4	0.196	0.314	0.393	0.573
10	0.253	0.443	0.545	0.708
Guinea				
2	0.048	0.033	0.375	0.495
4	0.105	0.049	0.638	0.686
10	0.186	0.093	0.822	0.802
Madagascar				
2	0.049	0.378	0.289	0.482
4	0.112	0.550	0.450	0.660
10	0.226	0.648	0.542	0.779
Tanzania				
2	0.083	0.324	0.283	0.418
4	0.157	0.507	0.431	0.594
10	0.239	0.618	0.521	0.712
Maputo				
2	0.117	0.159	0.040	0.428
4	0.239	0.227	0.058	0.593
10	0.326	0.360	-0.076	0.705

Notes: All measures are per capita. The data for Tanzania and Madagascar are weighted.
Sources: Government of Mozambique/CFNPP 1992; Government of Guinea 1994; Government of Côte d'Ivoire 1985; Government of Ghana 1987; Government of Tanzania/World Bank 1995.

The national surveys show an important urban bias in hospital services (Table 4.17), but no significant differences by gender for either hospitals or clinics. Use is higher for urban than for rural residents in every quintile, with a more marked difference in rural areas between use by lower versus upper quintiles, reflecting the difficulty that poor people in rural areas have in reaching hospitals. Use of other public facilities (mostly clinics and maternity facilities) is much more balanced, both within and between urban and

Table 4.17. *Proportion of the population using health facilities in the past month by per capita expenditure quintile*

	Quintile				
	1	2	3	4	5
	(%)				
Public hospital					
Côte d'Ivoire					
All	2.8	4.0	5.4	6.9	6.1
Rural	2.6	2.9	4.3	4.9	8.7
Urban	3.9	6.5	6.9	8.3	5.6
Ghana					
All	2.5	4.6	5.4	6.9	8.4
Rural	1.9	3.9	3.8	5.9	6.4
Urban	4.9	6.2	8.0	8.0	9.4
Guinea					
All	1.1	3.4	6.0	8.1	11.7
Rural	0.4	1.4	2.4	3.7	8.4
Urban	3.7	5.2	7.1	8.6	11.9
Madagascar					
All	1.0	0.9	0.9	1.4	1.4
Rural	1.0	0.8	0.8	1.3	0.9
Urban	1.3	2.0	1.5	1.5	1.9
Tanzania					
All	1.1	1.2	1.5	2.7	3.1
Rural	0.6	0.5	0.8	1.2	1.0
Urban	4.4	3.7	3.3	5.1	4.8
Other public facilities					
Côte d'Ivoire					
All	6.5	6.7	7.3	8.2	6.8
Rural	6.6	7.3	7.8	9.4	7.5
Urban	6.0	5.3	6.6	7.3	6.6
Ghana					
All	2.5	3.6	4.4	5.8	3.3
Rural	2.6	3.6	5.4	6.6	4.0
Urban	2.3	3.8	2.7	5.0	2.9
Guinea					
All	4.5	5.3	5.0	5.3	5.4
Rural	5.0	6.7	9.1	9.9	18.1
Urban	2.9	4.0	3.8	4.9	4.7
Madagascar					
All	1.3	2.2	2.7	3.4	3.6
Rural	1.3	2.3	2.5	3.4	3.3
Urban	1.6	1.6	2.8	3.5	4.0
Tanzania					
All	3.2	3.8	4.2	4.7	4.6
Rural	3.5	4.3	5.0	6.1	6.6
Urban	1.3	1.8	2.1	2.3	2.9

Table 4.17. *(cont.)*

	Quintile				
	1	2	3	4	5
			(%)		
Private facilities					
Côte d'Ivoire					
All	0.2	1.1	1.1	2.5	3.8
Rural	0.2	1.1	0.8	1.0	1.1
Urban	0.0	1.0	1.6	3.5	4.4
Ghana					
All	4.4	5.5	5.7	7.6	11.3
Rural	3.7	5.1	5.8	7.2	9.4
Urban	4.5	6.3	5.4	7.9	12.2
Guinea					
All	4.3	3.7	3.8	4.4	4.9
Rural	4.8	5.3	6.9	9.7	3.0
Urban	2.5	2.9	3.9	3.1	5.0
Madagascar					
All	0.7	1.2	1.5	2.0	3.4
Rural	0.7	1.1	1.4	1.6	3.2
Urban	1.0	1.1	2.1	3.5	3.9
Tanzania					
All	1.6	2.5	3.0	5.6	7.7
Rural	1.6	2.5	2.7	5.0	6.4
Urban	1.1	2.4	3.5	6.4	8.8

Sources: Government of Côte d'Ivoire 1985; Government of Ghana 1987; Government of Tanzania/World Bank 1995; Government of Guinea 1994; Government of Madagascar 1993.

rural areas, though these services usually receive a much smaller share of overall health sector budgets. One might expect, then, that the urban-only surveys in Maputo would show more equitable distribution, but that is not the case. Overall, use of public health services in this city is extremely low, even when compared with data from the national samples, suggesting that rationing of services is as serious a problem in these cities as it is in the entire population of the other countries.

Turning our attention to public education, the data are more encouraging than those for the health sector. On average half of the education budget goes to primary schools (Table 4.18), which are more likely to benefit the poor. On a per pupil basis, however, funding favors secondary and especially university students. For the twenty-two countries with available data, per pupil expenditures for secondary students average almost five times as much as those for

Table 4.18. *Education sector expenditures in Africa*

Country	Education sector expenditure shares			Per pupil education expenditures[a]		
	Primary	Secondary	University	Primary	Secondary	University
	(%)					
Benin	54	27	18	100	252	1,988
Burkina Faso	46	24	29	—	—	—
Cameroon	42	25	33	100	—	—
Central African Republic	54	25	21	—	212	1,677
Chad	68	29	3	100	—	—
Côte d'Ivoire	52	33	15	—	306	1,794
Gambia	49	39	12	100	230	—
Ghana	86[b]	—	14	—	—	4,120
Guinea	36	32	32	100	306	4,362
Kenya	49	25	25	100	578	—
Madagascar	72[b]	—	28	—	—	—
Malawi	45	18	37	—	—	—
Mozambique	37	43	20	100	628	9,344
Nigeria	81[b]	—	19	100	337	6,017
Senegal	48	26	25	100	210	1,867
Tanzania	56	16	27	—	—	—
Togo	38	34	27	100	325	3,370
Zambia	45	31	24	100	608	11,985
Zimbabwe	55	30	14	—	—	—
Average	48[c]	29	22	—	—	—

Note: Figures are from most recent year that data is available;
[a]Indices: primary = 100.
[b]Primary and secondary combined.
[c]Average excludes Ghana, Madagascar, and Nigeria.
Source: Sahn and Bernier 1994.

primary students. For university students, per pupil expenditures are fifty times those for primary students.

Public primary education is highly progressive and well targeted to the poor in most of the household survey samples (Figures 4.1 and 4.8–4.12). In Côte d'Ivoire and Guinea, even though the concentration curves for public primary schools fall below the 45 degree line in the lower expenditure deciles, their Gini coefficients are close to zero. At first sight, this result is not surprising: households with many children are by definition poorer in terms of per capita expenditures because the denominator is large, and they are also the households likely to benefit from public schools. Nevertheless, the data do suggest that, unlike

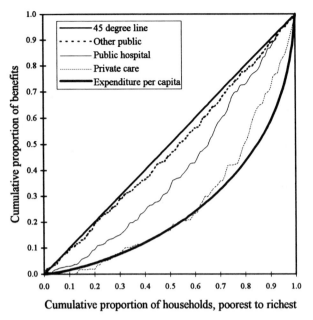

Figure 4.2. Côte d'Ivoire: concentration curves for use of public and private health services. *Source:* Government of Côte d'Ivoire 1985.

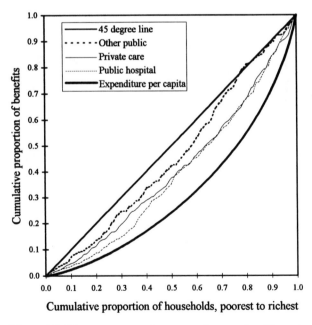

Figure 4.3. Ghana: concentration curves for use of public and private health services. *Source:* Government of Ghana 1987.

143

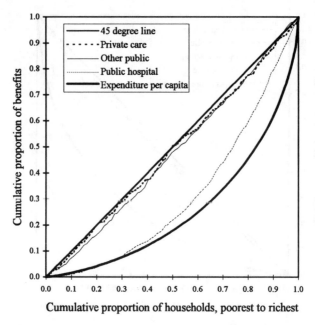

Figure 4.4. Guinea: concentration curves for use of public and private health services. *Source:* Government of Guinea 1994.

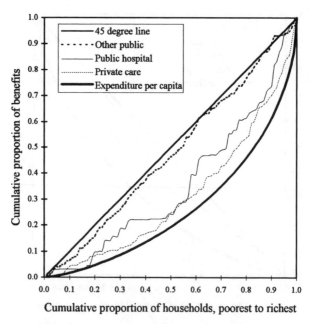

Figure 4.5. Madagascar: concentration curves for use of public and private health services. *Source:* Government of Madagascar 1993.

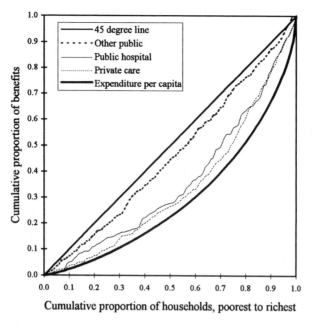

Figure 4.6. Tanzania: concentration curves for use of public and private health services. *Source:* Government of Tanzania/World Bank 1995.

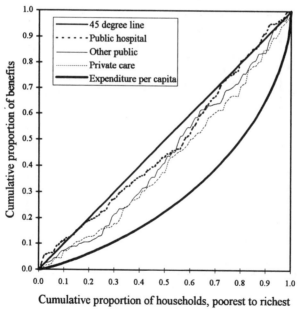

Figure 4.7. Maputo: concentration curves for use of public and private health services. *Source:* Government of Mozambique/CFNPP 1992.

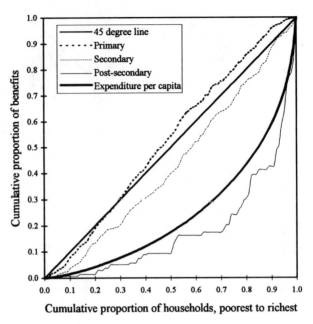

Figure 4.8. Côte d'Ivoire: concentration curves for public school attendance, by level. *Source:* Government of Côte d'Ivoire 1985.

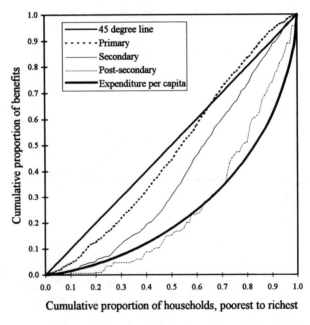

Figure 4.9. Guinea: concentration curves for public school attendance, by level. *Source:* Government of Guinea 1994.

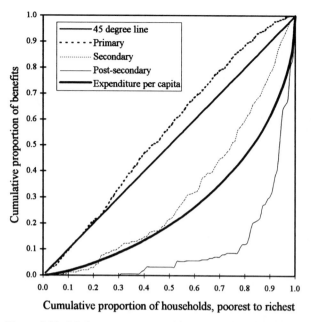

Figure 4.10. Madagascar: concentration curves for public school attendance, by level. *Source:* Government of Madagascar 1993.

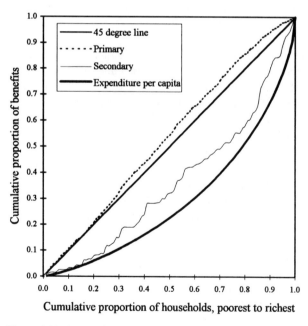

Figure 4.11. Tanzania: concentration curves for public school attendance, by level. *Source:* Government of Tanzania/World Bank 1995.

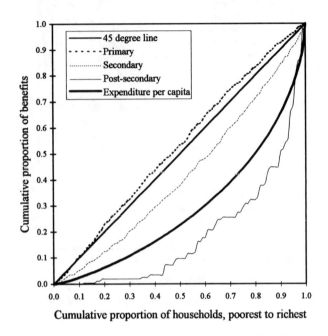

Figure 4.12. Maputo: concentration curves for public school attendance, by level. *Source:* Government of Mozambique/CFNPP 1992.

public health care, families from all income strata take advantage of public schools. Moreover, public primary education's dominance of other public services does not change if one ranks households by a weighted per capita expenditure measure in which each child from 0 to 6 years old is counted as 0.3 adult equivalents, from 7 to 12 as 0.6 adult equivalents, and from 13 to 17 as 0.9 adult equivalents. Although the concentration curves shift downward somewhat, especially for public primary education, they remain above the 45 degree line.

Secondary schooling in all the samples is less progressive than primary education, as one might expect, but its concentration curve remains close to the 45 degree line in Ghana and to a lesser extent Côte d'Ivoire, but not in the other samples. Only with postsecondary education is the distributional impact mixed, with regressive expenditures in Côte d'Ivoire, Madagascar, and, to a lesser extent, Guinea, but very progressive results in Ghana and Tanzania. These results, however, are based on very few observations[15] and may also be

---

[15] Specifically, forty-nine students in Côte d'Ivoire, fifty-two in Ghana, forty-six in Conakry, and sixty-three in Maputo. In Tanzania, only nineteen were included in the survey, so we exclude postsecondary students from the analysis.

Table 4.19. *Extended Gini coefficients for use of education*

v-parameter	Private primary	Private secondary	Public primary	Public secondary	Public post-secondary	Expend -itures
Côte d'Ivoire						
2	0.348	0.363	-0.054	0.131	0.636	0.512
4	0.565	0.617	-0.011	0.267	0.799	0.691
10	0.678	0.780	0.152	0.467	0.883	0.798
Ghana						
2	0.027	0.185	0.169	0.064	0.103	0.382
4	0.070	0.369	-0.236	0.177	0.280	0.573
10	0.126	0.454	-0.212	0.286	0.432	0.708
Guinea						
2	0.354	—	0.053	0.229	0.471	0.495
4	0.681	—	0.210	0.498	0.760	0.686
10	0.920	—	0.419	0.729	0.920	0.802
Madagascar						
2	0.196	0.607	-0.100	0.366	0.788	0.482
4	0.322	0.814	-0.099	0.618	0.947	0.660
10	0.479	0.928	-0.010	0.818	0.992	0.779
Tanzania						
2	-0.093	0.256	-0.068	0.276	—	0.418
4	-0.183	0.500	-0.078	0.439	—	0.594
10	-0.024	0.703	-0.063	0.595	—	0.712
Maputo[a]						
2	—	—	-0.054	0.166	0.617	0.428
4	—	—	-0.074	0.288	0.844	0.593
10	—	—	-0.047	0.410	0.949	0.705

[a]Data for Maputo are for all schools.
Sources: Government of Ghana 1987; Government of Mozambique/CFNPP 1992; Government of Guinea 1994; Government of Côte d'Ivoire 1985; Government of Tanzania/World Bank 1995; Government of Madagascar 1993.

confounded by the surveys' not correctly associating university students who are away from home with their household.

Table 4.19 shows that the welfare ordering of expenditures for public education meets one's expectations: the extended Gini coefficients for public primary schooling are lowest, followed by secondary and then postsecondary schooling. Public schooling is also more progressive than private, the exception being primary schools in Tanzania where the sample size for private primary is very small. Also, the extended Gini coefficients for education expenditures, especially for primary and secondary schools, are usually lower than those for health expenditures, indicating that their incidence is more progressive.

Table 4.20. *Côte d'Ivoire: proportion of eligible persons attending public school by gender or area and per capita expenditure quintiles*

	Quintile				
	1	2	3	4	5
	(%)				
All					
Primary	36.0	44.2	49.3	45.9	41.6
Secondary	15.3	16.3	21.0	21.7	19.8
Postsecondary	0.3	1.2	1.0	2.1	3.3
Male					
Primary	46.5	54.6	58.6	54.4	45.9
Secondary	27.8	32.6	40.3	34.6	36.2
Postsecondary	0.7	3.1	1.4	3.8	3.9
Female					
Primary	32.9	45.0	47.7	46.2	44.7
Secondary	12.9	11.6	15.2	23.0	17.4
Postsecondary	0.0	0.0	1.1	1.2	3.7
Urban					
Primary	38.9	42.6	54.3	41.2	39.3
Secondary	21.4	21.6	23.1	24.9	21.1
Postsecondary	0.0	1.9	1.6	3.0	3.8
Rural					
Primary	35.4	44.8	45.2	53.6	52.6
Secondary	13.7	13.1	18.7	15.8	6.3
Postsecondary	0.4	0.8	0.5	0.7	0.0

Source: Government of Côte d'Ivoire 1985.

Household survey data also reveal that enrollment rates differ markedly for boys and girls in a number of countries (Tables 4.20–4.25). Particularly noteworthy are the gender differences in Guinea. They occur for all levels of education and for all expenditure quintiles. Differences are also more pronounced for secondary and postsecondary education and for households in the lower end of the expenditure distribution. Côte d'Ivoire has a similar, albeit less dramatic, pattern of gender differences at all levels of schooling. We also find gender differences in enrollments in Ghana for middle, secondary, and postsecondary school, although not for primary school. In the other national samples, no clear gender-specific patterns occur, and in Maputo, male enrollments are only higher for postsecondary education, a

Table 4.21. *Ghana: proportion of eligible persons attending public school by gender or area and per capita expenditure quintiles*

	Quintile				
	1	2	3	4	5
	(%)				
All					
Primary	50.7	53.5	54.3	53.5	42.3
Middle	29.4	34.1	32.3	35.4	33.7
Secondary	8.0	8.8	12.4	11.3	14.2
Postsecondary	1.1	2.1	2.3	2.4	3.1
Male					
Primary	63.4	64.5	63.0	62.8	52.5
Middle	44.0	44.2	38.6	51.5	49.3
Secondary	12.4	19.4	22.2	20.8	28.0
Postsecondary	3.4	5.9	7.7	7.6	3.6
Female					
Primary	50.1	55.4	57.8	56.6	42.4
Middle	28.6	37.6	43.9	36.2	38.3
Secondary	6.7	3.5	8.5	9.5	9.2
Postsecondary	2.1	3.3	3.8	3.2	8.6
Urban					
Primary	60.3	54.0	54.5	52.1	36.8
Middle	5.2	14.6	17.3	20.0	21.9
Secondary	5.2	8.6	12.7	15.8	16.9
Postsecondary	2.6	6.3	3.3	4.0	4.7
Rural					
Primary	47.9	53.3	54.1	54.8	55.4
Middle	28.7	31.4	29.6	29.0	20.4
Secondary	8.7	8.8	12.1	7.1	9.2
Postsecondary	0.8	0.3	1.8	1.0	0.0

Source: Government of Ghana 1987.

pattern that exists across all expenditure quintiles. Distinctions also appear between urban and rural areas, being most pronounced for secondary and postsecondary school. Among the national samples, regional differences are greatest in Guinea. Results from Ghana, Madagascar, and Tanzania show marked urban bias in secondary and postsecondary school, but not primary school.

Table 4.22. *Guinea: proportion of eligible persons attending public school by gender or area and per capita expenditure quintiles*

	Quintile				
	1	2	3	4	5
			(%)		
All					
Primary	21.2	38.3	48.7	56.0	53.6
Secondary	8.8	19.6	32.5	33.5	41.7
Postsecondary	0.9	3.4	6.2	8.0	16.4
Male					
Primary	27.2	46.9	56.9	64.0	56.0
Secondary	11.9	26.9	42.5	46.3	50.9
Postsecondary	1.8	4.4	8.1	10.5	23.6
Female					
Primary	14.3	28.6	40.6	48.0	51.4
Secondary	4.2	9.8	18.4	19.5	34.1
Postsecondary	0.0	2.4	4.3	5.6	9.8
Urban					
Primary	32.6	48.0	52.1	57.8	53.9
Secondary	20.6	26.9	37.5	35.9	42.2
Postsecondary	1.2	5.3	7.4	8.3	17.0
Rural					
Primary	17.5	26.2	36.1	36.0	44.8
Secondary	3.7	7.3	7.3	3.0	11.1
Postsecondary	0.8	0.6	0.0	3.8	0.0

Source: Government of Guinea 1994.

The incidence of public employment

Public employment has become an important issue in fiscal policy in Africa. Most African governments have far too many employees, a problem that complicates both overall fiscal stability and the allocation of resources within a given budget (see, e.g., Lindauer and Nunberg 1994). Yet any attempt to reduce the size of the public sector involves the politically and socially difficult question of retrenchment. Here, too, critics express concerns about the impact on poor households and the potential for impoverishing a large and politically influential segment of the working population through layoffs. But the fact that in most African economies a significant proportion of government expenditures produces no useful services receives much less concern. This waste includes wages that, while technically pertaining to the various min-

Table 4.23 *Madagascar: proportion of eligible persons attending public school by gender or area and per capita expenditure quintiles*

	Quintile				
	1	2	3	4	5
	(%)				
All					
Primary	36.2	49.1	52.8	55.3	43.5
Secondary	2.1	8.9	14.3	22.6	31.1
Postsecondary	0.0	0.5	0.7	1.1	11.1
Male					
Primary	36.9	47.6	50.4	56.7	44.9
Secondary	2.1	10.3	13.2	23.4	32.5
Postsecondary	0.0	1.0	0.8	1.2	9.3
Female					
Primary	35.4	50.7	55.3	53.6	42.3
Secondary	2.2	7.5	15.4	21.6	29.6
Postsecondary	0.0	0.0	0.7	1.0	13.2
Urban					
Primary	60.9	58.4	61.1	57.1	35.7
Secondary	13.2	21.0	22.5	34.7	39.0
Postsecondary	0.0	2.3	1.0	3.9	18.1
Rural					
Primary	34.6	47.8	50.4	54.3	53.0
Secondary	1.1	6.7	11.5	15.3	17.4
Postsecondary	0.0	0.2	0.6	0.0	1.8

Source: Government of Madagascar 1993.

istries and state-run enterprises, are essentially transfer payments to nonproductive employees. As such, no one benefits other than the workers who receive the salaries. As with social services, household survey data can shed light on who benefits from these wage payments by identifying households that include public sector employees and the earnings they receive from those jobs.

Figures 4.13 to 4.18 show the concentration curves for total compensation from public and private sector wage employment in our household surveys.[16] In all but one of the national samples, the concentration curves fall well below the Lorenz curve for expenditures per capita, indicating that public and private wages are distributed less equitably than expenditures. In Tanzania, the con-

---

[16] The data for Maputo are for wages only. No wage data are available for Tanzania, so the data are dummy variables for holding a public or private wage job.

Table 4.24. *Tanzania: proportion of eligible persons attending public school by gender or area and per capita expenditure quintiles*

	Quintile				
	1	2	3	4	5
			(%)		
All					
Primary	58.9	65.2	66.9	68.8	71.4
Secondary	1.8	3.4	4.7	4.3	8.6
Postsecondary	0.7	1.9	0.6	0.6	0.0
Male					
Primary	59.3	61.7	63.3	70.9	69.8
Secondary	1.7	5.0	4.7	4.5	9.0
Postsecondary	0.8	2.3	0.0	1.2	0.1
Female					
Primary	58.4	68.7	70.9	66.8	73.1
Secondary	1.8	1.9	4.8	4.1	8.3
Postsecondary	0.6	1.6	1.0	0.1	0.0
Urban					
Primary	72.2	69.3	69.0	72.9	69.2
Secondary	2.5	5.5	9.0	6.4	10.8
Postsecondary	0.0	0.0	0.1	0.4	0.0
Rural					
Primary	57.1	64.1	65.9	66.3	74.1
Secondary	1.7	2.7	2.7	2.9	6.2
Postsecondary	0.7	2.3	0.8	0.7	0.0

Source: Government of Tanzania/World Bank 1995.

centration curves are close to the Lorenz curve, but those data are for public and private job holding, not the wages that come from those jobs. Since wages are more concentrated than job holding, it is probably also true that public and private wages are distributed less equitably than expenditures in Tanzania. In the urban sample of Maputo, however, the curves are all quite close. These differences reflect the unsurprising urban bias of expenditures on wages and salaries, in both the public and private sector.[17] Thus from a national perspective, if we view salaries as transfer payments, or at least payments that include a significant wage premium relative to work in the private sector, they are regressive. The proximity of the concentration curves for public and private

[17] Similar graphs for Abidjan and Accra also have concentration curves that are very close to the Lorenz curve.

Table 4.25. *Maputo, Mozambique: proportion of eligible persons attending public school by gender or area and per capita expenditure quintiles*

	Quintile				
	1	2	3	4	5
	(%)				
All					
Primary	73.1	78.6	82.5	83.5	92.4
Secondary	35.6	39.3	47.4	59.0	72.5
Postsecondary	4.9	2.4	11.9	23.8	57.0
Male					
Primary	72.8	78.0	84.5	82.9	92.1
Secondary	39.8	39.9	44.0	61.0	64.7
Postsecondary	9.5	5.4	18.6	37.7	75.9
Female					
Primary	73.4	79.2	80.3	84.2	92.6
Secondary	31.3	38.8	51.2	57.1	78.9
Postsecondary	1.6	0.0	6.0	11.6	37.7

Source: Government of Mozambique/CFNPP 1992.

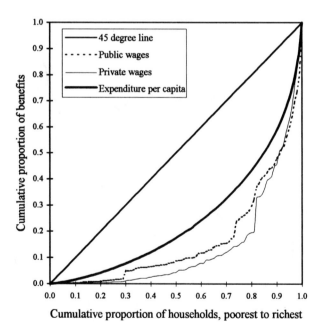

Figure 4.13. Côte d'Ivoire: concentration curves for public and private wage employment earnings. *Source:* Government of Côte d'Ivoire 1985.

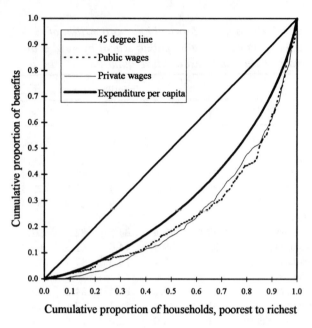

Figure 4.14. Ghana: concentration curves for public and private wage employment earnings. *Source:* Government of Ghana 1987.

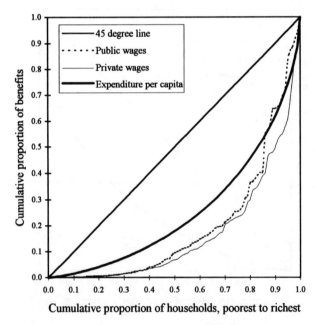

Figure 4.15. Guinea: concentration curves for public and private wage employment earnings. *Source:* Government of Guinea 1994.

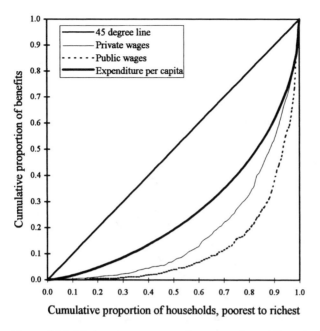

Figure 4.16. Madagascar: concentration curves for public and private wage employment earnings. *Source:* Government of Madagascar 1993.

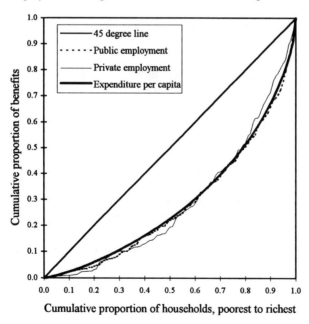

Figure 4.17. Tanzania: concentration curves for public and private wage employment earnings (curves based on number of workers, not earnings). *Source:* Government of Tanzania/World Bank 1995.

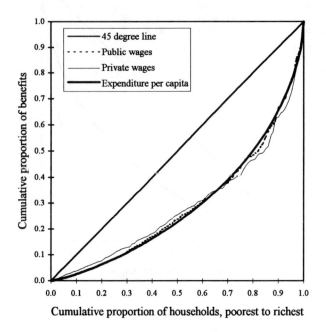

Figure 4.18. Maputo: concentration curves for public and private wage employment earnings. *Source:* Government of Mozambique/CFNPP 1992.

wage earnings shows that the key distinction does not appear to be public earnings versus private, but wages versus self-employment.

Although the results for expenditures on social services generally suggest that public spending on education and health is progressive, these results on salaries suggest that it is not. For example, consider a doctor who works for a public hospital. If she provides genuinely useful health services for her patients during the course of the day and earns a salary commensurate with the value of those services, she is in no sense a beneficiary of public spending. She is simply selling useful services at a fair market rate, and the fact that the government is the purchaser (in favor of the patients) is irrelevant. The true benefit incidence of these expenditures is for the patients who received the services, and the analysis of social sector expenditures in the previous section is appropriate for understanding who is gaining from public health expenditures on hospitals. On the other hand, if the doctor does not provide useful services for whatever reason (lack of medicine, electricity, etc.; absenteeism; lack of demand) and spends her time at an alternative activity (private practice or leisure), then she is the beneficiary of the expenditure on her salary, which is a transfer payment. In this case, the concentration curves presented here, not those on use of public hospitals, are relevant for understanding the incidence of public expenditures. While these survey data cannot reveal who provides useful services and who does not, the marked difference in the concentration curves for most social services and for public employment highlights the importance of making the distinction when judging the overall progressivity of public expenditures.

General equilibrium consequences of expenditure reductions

Since tax and benefit shifting make it difficult to identify the beneficiaries of many types of government expenditures, we cannot determine the overall incidence of all government expenditures by using household survey data alone. We do have available a complementary research strategy, however. With general equilibrium models, we can identify the change in real incomes for different households that results from an across-the-board reduction in public expenditures, the sort of fiscal "belt-tightening" that many critics of adjustment programs argue falls disproportionately on the poor.

What are the general equilibrium effects of changes in government spending on household incomes and, in particular, poor households? Simulations using CGE models for Cameroon, The Gambia, Madagascar, Niger, and Tanzania indicate that cuts in government spending affect government workers and the urban population most severely, with little short-term effects on other households (Table 4.26). A 10 percent reduction in real government expenditures reduces demand for skilled labor and thus leads to lower real wage rates for skilled labor, especially in Madagascar and Niger, where the government is a major employer of skilled labor. Real incomes of the urban nonpoor in Niger fall by 7.7 percent. In Madagascar, where the government workers are among the middle class (here included under the broad category of urban poor), real incomes of the urban poor decline by 3.1 percent.

For those households not directly employed by the government, however, the biggest effect of the decline in government spending is the potential for increased investment as savings in the economy are freed up. Real investment increases in all four countries, by 0.71 to 2.23 percent of GDP. To the extent that private investments raise output in subsequent years, and that these investments are in labor-intensive activities, the poor stand to gain from the decline in government recurrent expenditures. There is thus a trade-off, not only between current and future consumption, but also between concentrated benefits for a few workers in the current period and potential widespread, but smaller (on a per capita basis), benefits for the broader population in the future.

The preceding simulations assume that available savings constrain private investment in the sample countries, not a shortage of profitable investment opportunities. However, given the uncertainty surrounding the political and economic climate in adjusting countries, private investment may be slow to respond to increased financial capital. Thus, in Table 4.27, we examine the effects of a cut in government expenditures with private investment fixed,

Table 4.26. *General equilibrium impacts of a reduction in government spending: model simulations*

	Percentage change[a]				
	Cameroon	Gambia	Madagascar	Niger	Tanzania
Real GDP	0.03	-0.38	-0.20	-0.18	-0.08
Consumption/GDP	-0.09	-0.32	0.00	-1.13	0.10
Total investment/GDP	0.85	1.26	0.71	2.23	1.90
Government recurrent expenditures/GDP	-0.65	-1.32	-0.92	-1.33	-1.57
Government revenue/GDP	0.05	0.03	0.32	-0.01	0.81
Exports/GDP[b]	0.07	0.16	0.10	0.12	0.52
Imports/GDP[b]	0.07	0.16	0.10	0.12	0.52
Change in foreign savings/ base year exports	0.00	0.00	0.00	0.00	0.00
Real exchange rate	0.41	0.29	0.58	0.84	0.98
Real wage rates					
Skilled labor	-1.97	-0.36	-8.32	-11.40	-4.78
Semiskilled labor	-0.52	0.48	-3.83	—	—
Unskilled labor	0.16	-0.02	0.64	0.31	0.00
Real income					
Urban nonpoor	0.11	-0.76	0.93	-7.66	-0.45
Urban poor	-0.78	-0.97	-3.12	-0.96	-0.20
Rural nonpoor	-0.28	0.14	0.04	-0.66	0.15
Rural poor	-0.11	0.05	0.56	-0.44	0.50
Small farm - export oriented	—	—	0.67	-0.49	—
Total	-0.16	-0.42	0.00	-1.75	0.11

[a]Percentage change relative to a base simulation with an adjustable real exchange rate.
[b]Exports and imports valued at the base simulation real exchange rate.
Sources: Model simulations.

allowing foreign savings (the trade deficit) to vary. Under this alternate model closure, the cut in government spending reduces aggregate demand in the economy, leading to a decline in imports and a reduction in the trade deficit (a decrease of foreign savings). Real GDP declines slightly in each country as aggregate demand falls. While the prices of tradable goods are tied to the fixed nominal exchange rate, the prices of nontradable goods fall due to reduced aggregate demand. As a result, the real exchange rate depreciates (the price of tradables relative to nontradables rises), spurring exports and reducing imports. In the highly open Gambian economy, where the level of shares of both exports and imports each exceeds 50 percent of GDP, a small change in the real exchange rate (1.01 percent) is sufficient to improve the trade balance by 1.77 percent of GDP. Given smaller initial shares of trade in GDP and relatively price-inelastic exports and imports, the necessary changes in the real

Table 4.27. *General equilibrium impacts of a reduction in government spending with fixed private investment: model simulations*

	Percentage change[a]				
	Cameroon	Gambia	Madagascar	Niger	Tanzania
Real GDP	-0.24	-0.97	-0.99	1.55	-0.51
Consumption/GDP	-0.57	-0.57	-1.80	-2.22	-0.55
Total investment/GDP	0.00	-0.85	-0.46	-0.86	-0.40
Government recurrent expenditures/GDP	-0.65	-1.32	-0.91	-1.33	-1.57
Government revenue/GDP	0.72	0.00	0.63	-0.18	0.71
Exports/GDP[b]	0.61	1.06	1.21	0.87	1.84
Imports/GDP[b]	-0.46	-0.71	-0.98	-1.95	-0.63
Change in foreign savings/ GDP	-1.07	1.77	-2.18	-2.82	-2.47
Real exchange rate	4.39	1.01	12.21	7.72	3.68
Real wage rates					
Skilled labor	-4.35	-1.36	-14.39	15.22	-6.23
Semiskilled labor	-2.91	0.37	-7.87	—	—
Unskilled labor	-0.48	0.06	-0.84	-1.94	0.09
Real income					
Urban nonpoor	0.59	-1.01	-9.64	-12.48	-1.73
Urban poor	-3.31	-1.41	-6.66	-3.95	-1.01
Rural nonpoor	-1.44	-0.26	-1.70	-2.07	-0.82
Rural poor	-1.43	-0.15	0.11	-1.98	-0.32
Small farm - export oriented	—	—	0.67	-1.71	—
Total	-0.99	-0.74	-2.65	-3.96	-0.87

[a]Percentage change relative to a base simulation with an adjustable real exchange rate.
[b]Exports and imports valued at the base simulation real exchange rate.
Sources: Model simulations.

exchange rate to bring about equilibrium in the external accounts are larger in Niger (7.72 percent) and Madagascar (12.21 percent). The real exchange rate depreciation in Cameroon of 4.39 percent is similar in relative magnitude to that of Madagascar, given that the demand shock (total cut in government spending as a share of GDP) in that country is more than twice as large as that modeled for Cameroon. For Tanzania, the small real exchange rate depreciation is partly due to the large share of government investment expenditures, which are modeled as noncompetitive imports. The reduction in government spending directly reduces imports of investment goods, without directly affecting demand or prices of domestic investment goods. Real wages fall more than in the flexible investment scenario since investment-led demand is lower. In general, all household groups suffer more severe real income declines than under the flexible investment scenario in Table 4.26. This outcome is to be expected since the reduction in foreign capital inflows (foreign savings) under the alternate closure contributes to a further reduction in aggregate demand and incomes. Nonetheless, the change in model closure does not affect the main distributional result: declines in real incomes are generally larger for urban groups than for rural groups, who benefit from the real exchange rate depreciation (through higher agricultural incomes) and suffer less from cuts in government spending on wages. This real exchange rate effect is especially pronounced for the rural poor in Madagascar, particularly small farmers producing export crops, whose real incomes actually rise by 0.67 percent despite the decline in foreign savings and government expenditures.[18]

Public sector retrenchment programs

While government spending in excess of revenues has caused considerable macroeconomic problems in Africa, the allocation of public expenditures across different budget items is distorted, at times so much so that the government cannot provide the basic public services that it should. One important cause of these inefficiencies is the public sector's employment practices. Driven in part by the widely held notion that the public sector should lead their countries' development efforts, and in part by political patronage, African governments and their agencies increased staffing levels at a rapid pace after independence; most continue to do so. These practices cause macroeconomic problems as the wage bill increases and fiscal deficits grow, but the problems often run much deeper. Once governments reach the limit of what they can finance through tax revenue, aid, and the inflation tax, they must reduce other expenditures to make wage payments. Typically, capital spending goes first. Even though significant amounts of foreign aid can help protect this item, it is not uncommon for struggling African governments to neglect completely capital expenditures so that donors finance virtually all of the capital budget. If eliminating locally financed capital expenditures is insufficient, expenditures for operations and maintenance come next. These reductions tend to make public sector employees less productive as they do not have the appropriate equipment or materials with which to work.

In the most extreme cases, governments have to cut public sector real wage rates to support the ever growing number of employees. In essence, the total wage bill reaches its maximum, and further increases in the number of employees must be "financed" by reducing each employee's pay. The apparently paradoxical result is that although the wage bill causes serious fiscal problems, earnings in the public sector are low relative to the private (formal) sector (Lin-

---

[18] Real incomes of the urban nonpoor in Cameroon also increase in this scenario because (1) wages from government employment compose a small share of their real incomes, (2) no decline in government investment (a source of income-generated demand for construction and other services) is modeled in this case, and (3) these households enjoy some of the revenues from the increase in real exports.

dauer and Nunberg 1994). Furthermore, since such cuts usually begin with the highest paid civil servants, salary scales become compressed and skilled employees with good opportunities elsewhere leave, further reducing the productivity of the public sector. Thus, a second paradox results: although the public sector suffers from excess employment, many skilled posts become difficult to fill. Employees who remain may take second jobs after hours, or even during regular working hours. Recognizing that public salaries are no longer sufficient to provide employees with a decent living, superiors find it difficult to object to absenteeism. In the end, the government is left with a large number of low productivity employees—its most skilled employees having left or devoted their attention to other occupations.

Africa policy makers understand the gravity of this scenario and many African governments have instituted some sort of policy action to address overstaffing. Nunberg (1994) cites twenty-five African countries with one or more World Bank structural adjustment credits dedicated in part to public sector employment practices. Nevertheless, very few governments have made progress at unwinding this chain of events, largely because any solution must begin with (often dramatic) reductions in public sector staffing levels. While several governments have been willing to study staffing levels, accept voluntary departures, eliminate ghost workers, and enforce retirement rules, even the most authoritarian regimes shy away from actually laying off employees, a policy option seen as politically risky and inhumane. Of the cases Nunberg (1994) reviews, only a handful of countries laid off a nontrivial number of public sector employees. Behind these reservations is a strong belief that retrenched public sector employees could not find other gainful employment if they were laid off, so that retrenchment would either leave them destitute or create a politically volatile population concentrated in the capital city.

Despite the almost universal reluctance to retrench, a few African governments have risked public sector layoffs as part of the structural adjustment programs of the 1980s. Ghana and Guinea, the two most notable cases in Africa, are where we have studied retrenchment.[19] In Ghana, more than 60,000 civil servants left the public sector between 1987 and 1992 through enforced retirements, ghost removal, voluntary departures, and involuntary layoffs. This reduction was approximately 20 percent of the previous number of employees, and the layoffs continue at a rate of approximately 10,000 per year. In Guinea, the retrenchment program was more short-lived, but the government used a similar combination of mechanisms to remove 30,000 public employees from the payrolls between 1985 and 1989, 30 percent of the previous total.

While there are many interesting and important fiscal, administrative, and

---

[19] Several countries that plan deep cuts in public employment have begun retrenchment programs recently (e.g., Uganda and Tanzania), but we have no information about their implementation.

political questions about retrenchment, we will limit our discussion to the welfare consequences of retrenchment for the affected employees and their households.[20] In particular, we explore the labor market experiences of former public sector employees in terms of their ability to find other gainful employment and their earnings once they do so. We also examine the extent to which retrenched workers are poor relative to their compatriots, both before and after their layoff. This is important information for policy makers concerned about the poverty consequences of retrenchment programs, and it also figures into the debate over the implications of adjustment for poverty. While much of this book argues that the vulnerability of African populations, especially the poor, to adjustment policies is exaggerated, the case of retrenchment is the most likely counterexample to this argument and, as such, is an important area of research in the poverty consequences of adjustment.

Labor market experience and welfare of redeployees[21]

In light of the importance of public sector retrenchment, Cornell University undertook two household-level surveys of the families of former public sector employees, one in Conakry (in conjunction with our larger household welfare survey) and a second in Ghana.[22] These surveys permit us to address several empirical questions about the consequences of retrenchment:

1. How quickly will former public sector employees find new jobs, if at all?
2. If employees find new work, how will their new earnings compare with those of the public sector?
3. Will former public sector workers, whether employed or not, fall into poverty as a result of having been retrenched?

---

[20] Mills et al. (1994) discuss the fiscal impact of retrenchment programs, the political problems that governments in Ghana and Guinea faced, and a variety of administrative considerations that contribute to the success of such programs. More generally, Lindauer and Nunberg (1994) provide a useful survey of the issue of pay and employment reform in Africa.

[21] "Redeployment," a term coined by the government of Ghana, refers to the retrenchment process. While largely euphemistic, it has worked its way into the lexicon, and we use it here to refer to both the process and the affected workers, "redeployees."

[22] See Mills and Sahn 1995 for a general description of the Conakry survey and an overview of its results. See Alderman, Canagarajah, and Younger 1994 for the same information about the Ghana survey.

Table 4.28. *Spells without work for redeployees in Ghana and Guinea (% of redeployees)*

Country	Months not working after redeployment					
	<1	1–12	13–24	25–48	>48	Median
Ghana						
All	67	19	7	6	1	1
Female	41	37	11	10	1	2
Male	63	26	5	5	1	1
Guinea						
All	26	11	15	13	35	24
Female	39	13	13	3	32	12
Male	23	11	16	15	35	25

Sources: CFNPP 1990, 1992.

Spells without work following retrenchment:　　Table 4.28 shows that the labor market experiences of the retrenched workers in Conakry and Ghana were quite different. In Conakry, the median spell of unemployment before finding a first postretrenchment job was approximately two years, and a significant number of former public sector employees had not found work several years after their retrenchment. In Ghana, on the other hand, reabsorption into the labor market was rapid, with half of retrenched civil servants finding work within one *month*, and 80 percent within a year of being laid off. In part, this difference reflects differing degrees of "moonlighting" while in the public sector. In Ghana, about half of the retrenched civil servants held a second job while in the civil service, almost always in the informal sector or agriculture. Virtually all of these employees continued to work at that second job after being laid off, and on average, they increased the hours per week dedicated to it from 16 to 39. This group, then, had an easy means of shifting employment with little loss of time. But even for the remaining workers, the transition has been much smoother than in Conakry. Although these survey results cannot fully explain this difference, we suspect that the different structure of the labor markets in the two countries explains some of it. In Ghana, despite the statist tendencies of economic policy in the 1960s and 1970s, the informal sector remained active and important; in Guinea, however, the Sekou-Touré regime worked hard to stamp out that sector, apparently with success. Given that the public sector accounts for a great deal of formal sector employment, new formal sector jobs are relatively scarce when the government is retrenching public sector workers. Former public sector employees must turn to other employment opportunities, and there are probably many more of these in

Ghana than Guinea. In fact, the share of working redeployees in Ghana engaged either in self-employment activities or farming is 80 percent, whereas for Conakry it is only 35 percent.

One important qualification to the Ghana data is the incidence of second job holding after retrenchment. Even though redeployees found *some* work quickly, they often took much longer to find a second job. Indeed, many continue to work their former second job and no other. If we consider that there are more employment states than employed or not working, the experience of Ghanaian redeployees is not as optimistic as the previous paragraph suggests. For example, suppose that employment state is defined by the number of jobs held: zero, one, and two or more. Under this definition, although a large number of redeployees were working within one year of redeployment, less than half had actually recovered their initial state at that time (Younger 1996b).[23]

There are important differences between the labor market transitions of men and women in both countries. To begin, a disproportionate number of redeployees are women. In Ghana, women represent 35 percent of redeployees but only 21 percent of civil servants. In Conakry, the outcomes are more balanced, with women constituting 25 percent of redeployees and 22 percent of civil servants. However, excluding retirements (which were much more important in Guinea than in Ghana), the share of laid-off public sector workers who were women was 32 percent, suggesting a bias similar to Ghana's. In neither case, however, do these differences appear to be the result of explicit discrimination (Alderman, Canagarajah, and Younger 1994; Mills and Sahn 1995). Instead, they reflect the use of a "last-in first-out" rule in the criteria for selecting employees for layoff. Because female recruitment is a fairly recent phenomenon, women have fewer years of civil service experience than men and are thus more vulnerable to this rule. Thus, even though this rule is viewed as a fair way to select employees for involuntary layoff, governments interested in reducing gender discrimination in public employment may want to modify the rule to protect some or all female employees.

Once laid off, Ghanaian men had easier transitions than did women (Table 4.28), largely because more men than women were moonlighting while in the civil service: 52 percent of men carried over a job held prior to redeployment and thus had no spell without work, whereas only 37 percent of women did so. Among redeployees who had to search for new work, men were still more likely to have a very short spell without work (one month or less) than women were, but the other spells are comparable. In Conakry, women actually enter new employment faster than men, a surprising result to which we will return.

---

[23] The results are biased by the fact that some redeployees are censored: we interviewed them only x months after redeployment and thus cannot say what their state is at x+1 and greater months after redeployment. This bias is more severe as the lag grows with 27 percent of redeployees censored at twelve months and 49 percent at twenty-four.

The distribution of new jobs between sectors is more clearly different for men and women in both countries. Table 4.29 gives the result of a multinomial logit function estimating the probability of employment in Ghana in three different sectors: self-employment (including agriculture), wage work, and underemployment in agriculture.[24] "Not working" is the default category. The results show that gender did not influence the probability of a redeployee being either self-employed or underemployed at the time of the survey, but that female redeployees have a significantly lower probability of finding wage work. Because wage employees earn more than the self-employed and underemployed, this selection into wage work is an important gender difference yielding lower overall earnings for women.

In Conakry, retrenched women actually began new work almost twice as quickly as men. Yet Mills (1994) develops and tests a model in which this result is logical, given the discrimination against women in the formal wage sector. Suppose that it is more difficult to find work in the formal sector in general, and more difficult for women than men.[25] Because women know that their probability of employment in the formal sector is low, they more readily accept less remunerative work in the informal sector, where entry is not as difficult. Men, on the other hand, have a stronger incentive to shun informal employment, hoping to find a formal sector job. Therefore, if most employment opportunities are in the informal sector, women will take up new jobs more quickly than men even though they are discriminated against in the formal sector. Mills and Sahn (1993b) show that for female redeployees in Conakry, there is a dramatic difference in entrance probabilities by sector. Whereas the cumulative probability that a man will enter either the wage or nonwage sector is roughly comparable, the probability that a woman will enter the informal sector reaches 80 percent in two years, while the probability that she will enter the wage sector is low and rises more slowly than that for males. Given that informal sector employment is less attractive than a wage job, women generally experience less favorable labor market transitions than men in Conakry despite the fact that their unemployment spells are shorter.

Cumulating the transitions to employment from the time of retrenchment to the time of the survey, we find that the rapid acquisition of new work in Ghana gives redeployees a degree of labor force participation that is virtually identical to the general population,[26] with 89 percent employed and only 3 percent

---

[24] The final category is important in interpreting the earnings results reported here and reflects the fact that some redeployees, while technically farming, are not doing so very intensively. See Alderman et al. 1995 for a more detailed justification of this category.

[25] Mills and Sahn (1995) find support for both of these propositions in the Conakry labor market.

[26] For each survey, we compare redeployees to the general population older than the youngest redeployee, which is twenty-one for Ghana and thirty for Guinea.

Table 4.29. *Multinomial logit equation for sector of current employment*

Regressor	Self-employed			Wage employment			Underemployed farmer		
	Beta	t-stat	d(Prob)	Beta	t-stat	d(Prob)	Beta	t-stat	d(Prob)
Constant	-1.58	-1.11	-0.32	-3.26	-1.72	-0.37	-5.50	-2.37	-0.31
Total employment experience	0.26	2.80	0.05	0.49	3.31	0.06	0.38	2.59	0.02
Total experience²(x10⁻²)	-0.39	-2.63	-0.08	-0.99	-3.30	-0.11	-0.51	-1.83	-0.03
Civil service job experience[a]	-0.12	-1.15	-0.02	-0.22	-1.55	-0.03	-0.37	-2.39	-0.02
Civil service job experience²(x10⁻²)[c]	0.17	0.73	0.03	0.47	1.30	0.05	0.62	1.69	0.03
Urban resident[a]	-0.59	-0.97	-0.12	0.13	0.16	0.01	0.46	0.57	0.03
Central region[a]	-0.34	-0.68	-0.07	-0.30	-0.50	-0.03	0.10	0.13	0.01
Ashanti region[a]	-0.60	-1.48	-1.12	-1.17	-2.29	-0.13	0.52	0.79	0.03
Age>55	-0.76	-1.68	-1.15	-0.42	-0.80	-0.05	-0.95	-1.30	-0.05
Dependency ratio	0.20	0.43	0.04	-0.59	-1.06	-0.07	0.30	0.44	0.02
Gender=female	0.14	0.34	0.03	-2.04	-3.54	-0.23	0.67	0.97	0.04
Dependecy ratio x gender	0.56	0.88	0.11	2.05	2.49	0.23	0.61	0.69	0.03
Logarithm of severance pay	0.12	2.08	0.02	0.12	1.64	0.01	0.06	0.69	0.00
Logarithm of unearned income	-0.14	-3.70	-0.03	-0.21	-4.00	-0.02	-0.10	-1.55	-0.01
Primary education	2.60	1.76	0.52	-0.13	-0.07	-0.01	2.89	1.45	0.16
Middle education	0.12	0.16	0.02	-1.12	-1.24	-0.13	-1.01	-0.84	-0.06
Secondary and higher education	-1.37	-1.41	-0.27	-2.30	-1.88	-0.26	1.04	0.53	0.06
Primary x years since redeployment	-0.90	-1.97	-0.18	-0.44	-0.77	-0.05	-1.51	-2.11	-0.08
Middle x years since redeployment	-0.16	-0.60	-0.03	-0.07	-0.20	-0.01	-0.38	-0.93	-0.02
Secondary x years since redeployment	0.52	1.18	0.10	0.73	1.47	0.08	-1.63	-1.31	-0.09

Nonagricultural second job[a]	2.31	3.03	0.46	2.25	2.76	0.26	-0.54	-0.41	-0.03
Agricultural second job[a]	1.77	3.89	0.35	0.65	1.16	0.07	2.88	4.59	0.16
Time since redeployment	0.23	0.25	0.05	0.94	0.85	0.11	1.73	1.14	0.10
Time since redeployment^2	0.00	0.02	0.00	-0.12	-0.66	-0.01	-0.19	-0.74	-0.01
Redeployed in 1987	0.17	0.16	0.03	0.33	0.26	0.04	-1.57	-1.00	-0.09
Redeployed in 1988	-0.11	-0.10	-0.02	-0.79	-0.57	-0.09	-0.62	-0.34	-0.03
Redeployed in 1989	-0.29	-0.28	-0.06	-0.64	-0.52	-0.07	-0.52	-0.31	-0.03
Redeployed in 1990	0.26	0.37	-0.05	-0.25	-0.29	-0.03	0.83	0.65	0.05

[a]These variables are measured as of the time of redeployment. All others are measured at the time of the survey.

Source: Younger, Canagarajah, and Alderman 1995.

Table 4.30. *Labor force status of retrenched public sector workers and sector of employment for those working*

	Ghana		Conakry	
	Rede-ployees	General population > 21	Rede-ployees	General population > 30
Status				
Working	83	89	60	64
Inactive	14	8	24	29
Unemployed	3	3	16	7
Sector				
Wage	21	—	65	—
Self-employment	39	—	36	—
Agriculture	39	—	—	—

Source: Mills and Sahn 1993b; Alderman, Canagarajah, and Younger 1994.

Table 4.31. *Change in monthly earnings for working redeployees in Ghana and Guinea*

Country	Average change in earnings (%)
Ghana	
Formal	-1
Informal	-41
Guinea	
Wage	118
Self-employment	102

Sources: Alderman, Canagarajah, and Younger 1994; Mills and Sahn 1993b.

unemployed, in the technical sense that they are actively seeking but have not found work (Table 4.30). In Conakry, the survey showed only 60 percent of redeployees working, compared with 64 percent of the general population currently employed. The unemployment rate for redeployees, however, is more than double that of the general population.

Earnings of retrenched public sector workers: Turning to our second question, the results for earnings of redeployees in Ghana and Guinea are almost exactly the reverse of those for unemployment spells. Table 4.31 shows that in

Ghana total earnings of former civil servants now employed in the informal sector (the vast majority) declined by 40 percent between the time of their retrenchment and the survey date, while those in the formal sector (less than 20 percent of all redeployees) have remained constant. In Conakry, on the other hand, earnings of retrenched workers, whether wage workers or self-employed, more than double. This latter result, which is counterintuitive, is probably due to the fact that real wages in general have been rising in Conakry since the time of the retrenchments, which occurred just after the Guinean economy had "bottomed out" at the end of the Sekou-Touré regime. In fact, real public sector wages increased by 118 percent between 1986 and 1989, indicating that laid-off workers in Conakry have had wage increases similar to those who remain in the public sector.[27] In Ghana, on the other hand, retrenchments, which began in 1987, did not take place until well after the economic recovery began in 1983. Thus, the general increase in wages has been less pronounced since the layoffs than in Conakry.

The sharp decline in earnings is alarming in Ghana. To explore the issue further, we have estimated earnings functions for the change in earnings for retrenched workers between the last month in which they worked in the civil service and the time of the survey, reported in Table 4.32.[28] The estimating equation is :

$$\ln(\gamma_{cu}) - \ln(\gamma_{cs}) = X\beta + Z_{cu}\gamma_{cu} - Z_{cs}\gamma_{cs} + U\delta + \epsilon$$

where y is the redeployee's earnings; X is a vector of time-invariant regressors that affect his or her earnings; Z is a vector of time-varying determinants of earnings; and U is a vector of regressors that are applicable and/or available only for the current period (the sector of current employment). The subscripts indicate time, with cu being the time of the interview and cs being the month just prior to redeployment. The β coefficients equal the difference of the coefficients in the current and former earnings functions ($b_{cu} - b_{cs}$). Note that these earnings functions must be corrected for sector selection, based on a model such as that in Table 4.29. Alderman, Canagarajah, and Younger (1995) find that current earnings functions for redeployees in different sectors are not significantly different except for the constant, so that pooling the different sectors into one earnings function is acceptable as long as a dummy variable for each sector is included in the regression. These are the U variables in the regression. The dummy, in turn, is endogenous because it depends on the sector selection,

---

[27] These figures do not account for the significant increase in education levels of public sector workers during the same period, in part because retrenched workers were not as educated as those who stayed and in part because new hires have had more education. See Mills et al. 1994.

[28] The time difference is not constant: redeployments occurred between 1987 and 1991, while the interviews occurred between May 1991 and January 1992.

Table 4.32. *Ghana: regressions for change in earnings (current earnings less earnings before redeployment)*

Regressor	Model 1 Beta	Model 1 t-stat	Model 2 Beta	Model 2 t-stat	Model 3 Beta	Model 3 t-stat	Model 4 Beta	Model 4 t-stat
Time invariant regressors								
Constant	0.02	0.03	-0.34	-0.59	-0.66	-3.29	-0.73	-3.84
Civil service job experience[a]	0.02	0.46	0.01	0.15	–	–	–	–
Civil service job experience^2(x10^{-3})[a]	-0.04	-0.40	-0.03	-0.27	–	–	–	–
Urban resident[a]	0.37	2.15	0.23	1.26	0.28	1.65	0.43	2.78
Central region[a]	-0.50	-3.03	-0.25	-1.46	-0.29	-1.89	-0.53	-3.75
Ashanti region[a]	-0.28	-1.89	0.15	0.84	0.11	0.69	-0.09	-0.71
Gender=female	-0.30	-1.78	0.28	1.25	–	–	–	–
Primary education	0.11	0.54	0.43	1.81	–	–	–	–
Middle education	0.00	-0.03	0.18	0.95	–	–	–	–
Secondary and higher education	0.24	1.09	0.19	0.85	–	–	–	–
Redeployed in 1987	0.33	1.32	0.04	0.15	–	–	–	–
Redeployed in 1988	0.07	0.30	0.10	0.42	–	–	–	–
Redeployed in 1989	0.05	0.23	-0.05	-0.26	–	–	–	–
Redeployed in 1990	-0.26	-1.33	-0.17	-0.88	–	–	–	–

Time varying regressors

Total employment experience[b]	-0.30	-2.46	-0.38	-3.10	-0.10	-1.78	-0.07	-1.33
Total experience^2(x10^{-2})[b]	0.20	0.78	0.39	1.52	-0.13	-1.14	-0.16	-1.47
Age>55[b]	0.15	0.53	0.03	0.10	0.07	0.28	0.14	0.55
Dependency ratio[b]	-0.26	-0.78	-0.05	-0.16	-0.06	-0.23	-0.29	-1.30
Dependency ratio x gender[b]	0.33	0.74	-0.07	-0.15	-0.15	-0.52	0.06	0.24
Total employment experience[a]	0.29	2.59	0.34	3.13	–	–	–	–
Total experience^2(x10^{-2})[a]	-0.25	-0.97	-0.36	-1.45	–	–	–	–
Age>55[a]	-0.19	-0.62	-0.10	-0.34	–	–	–	–
Dependency ratio[a]	0.12	0.45	0.13	0.48	–	–	–	–
Dependency ratio x gender[a]	-0.04	-0.11	0.01	0.04	–	–	–	–
Wage sector	–	–	1.99	3.34	1.15	3.44	0.46	4.10
Underemployed	–	–	-0.88	-1.31	-1.44	-2.71	-1.37	-7.04

[a]These variables are measured as of the time of redeployment.
[b]These variables are measured as of the time of the survey. In the restricted equations, they are the difference between this variable's value at the time of the survey and the time of redeployment.

Source: Alderman, Canagarajah, and Younger 1995.

so it is instrumented by the logit probability of ending up in a particular sector for each worker, as estimated in Table 4.29.

The second column reports the full model. As one can see, most of the β coefficients are not significantly different from zero, and most of the γ's are close to equal and opposite. Formally, we reject an F-test for equality of all the γ's and all the β's equal to zero, however, indicating that there are differences in the earnings functions before and after retrenchment. But we accept a similar test for equality of the all the γ's and all the β's equal to zero except the constant and the variables that indicate a redeployee's location before redeployment: urban versus rural residence and the region of residence. That is, the change in earnings is not due to different returns to human capital variables or to different decisions concerning participation in the labor market, but rather is a downward shift in the earnings function, with the size of the shift depending on a redeployee's residence before redeployment and the sector in which she or he is currently working. Thus, redeployees' earnings are lower after redeployment not because their human capital (including job-specific experience) is worth less, nor because they decide to work fewer hours. Instead, they have lost a fixed amount associated with working in the civil service, which is most probably a rent associated with public employment.[29]

The third column reports the results of a model that imposes these restrictions. Use of the restrictions improves the t-statistics substantially, largely because several of the regressors are highly correlated. The intercept is significantly different from zero and is large: other things equal, the earnings function shifts down by 48 percent of preredeployment earnings. This shift is somewhat less for redeployees who lived in urban areas prior to redeployment, and somewhat greater for those from Central Region. More importantly, the function actually shifts up for those currently employed as wage workers, while it shifts down by a huge amount, 88 percent, for currently underemployed farmers.

Although the estimates in column three are not biased by the endogeneity of sectoral choice (because the dummies for current sector are instrumented), there is some risk in using them for predictions at probability one. Ideally, the logit estimates for sector selection would yield bimodal distribution of predicted probabilities, one near zero (for workers not actually in the sector) and another near one (for those who are). However, the observed distribution is unimodal, with the observations for actual wage earners or underemployed farmers trailing off to the right. While these estimates may more accurately represent the impact of a marginal change in the likelihood of being in a sector

---

[29] Alderman et al. (1995) discuss, and dismiss, the possibility that the changing intercept reflects the loss of a good job match.

Table 4.33. *Change in earnings after redeployment as a proportion of preredeployment earnings*

	Sector of current employment		
	Wage employment	Self-employment	Underemployed
Estimates based on Model 3 (instrumented sector dummies)			
Urban	0.51	-0.52	-0.89
Cases	85	253	32
Rural	0.14	-0.64	-0.91
Cases	5	49	5
Estimates based on Model 4 (sector dummies)			
Urban	-0.17	-0.48	-0.87
Cases	85	253	32
Rural	-0.46	-0.64	-0.91
Cases	5	49	5

Source: Alderman, Canagarajah, and Younger 1995.

on earnings, predictions far away from that mean may not be accurate. Therefore, we include a fourth column in which the sector dummies are not instrumented. These estimates are potentially biased from the endogenous sector choice, but may be more useful for predictions.

Given the comparatively straightforward nature of the differences in earnings, it is easy to calculate redeployees' earnings losses after redeployment from the restricted models. The expected value for the logarithm of monthly earnings in the civil service for those individuals currently employed is 9.75 (or 17,150 1991 cedis per month) compared with only 9.08 currently. That is, for those redeployees currently working, earnings fell after they were redeployed on average by 48 percent of their previous earnings. This, however, is a mean over a heterogeneous group. Table 4.33 shows the shift in earnings for redeployees by former residence and current sector of employment, based on the restricted estimates of the difference functions in Table 4.32. The few redeployees who have found work in the wage sector have fared reasonably well, but the remainder – even those who are currently fully employed – have suffered substantial declines in income. For the underemployed farmers, earnings have all but disappeared.

Alderman et al. (1995) also test the change in earnings by estimating two separate earnings equations, one for the time of the survey and one just prior to redeployment, and then comparing the coefficients across equations. The results are less striking, but consistent with those of the difference equation.

Table 4.34. *Distribution of redeployees' households in per capita income quintiles for the general population*

	Quintile				
	1	2	3	4	5
	(%)				
Ghana per capita income					
Before redeployment	4	28	26	21	20
Current	20	26	23	16	14
Conakry per capita expenditure					
Current civil servants	15	18	18	26	23
Current redeployees	26	23	18	16	17

Sources: Mills and Sahn 1993b; Alderman, Canagarajah, and Younger 1994.

More importantly, they yield an interpretation of the difference between earnings for male and female redeployees. Earnings for working female redeployees in Ghana are lower than those for men, but this difference is due entirely to the selection process, which sorts men into wage labor jobs and women into self-employment. Within any sector of the labor market (wage labor, self-employment, and underemployed farming), women's earnings are comparable with men's after controlling for human capital and household composition.[30] Yet, because wage workers generally earn more than nonwage workers, women's overall earnings are lower.

The poverty consequences of retrenchment

Since former civil servants in Ghana have significantly lower earnings and redeployees in Conakry have had difficulty finding new work, concerns about the poverty implications of retrenchment merit attention. In particular, has retrenchment created a new class of poor? Consider first the case of Ghana. Table 4.34 shows the proportion of retrenched workers' households in each per capita income quintile for the Ghana Living Standards Survey (GLSS) household survey. Redeployees' households would be similar to Ghanaian households in general if the distribution were 20 percent per quintile. Even though most redeployees came from the lower echelons of the civil services, it was highly unlikely that a redeployee's household was in the lowest quintile before retrenchment, while more than a proportionate share were in the second and third quintiles. This is consistent with the fact that households

---

[30] Formally, the coefficient on gender in the earnings functions is always insignificantly different from zero.

with public sector employees tend to be better off than the general population in Ghana, as in the other countries we have studied. After retrenchment, the situation is worse, with 20 percent of redeployees' households in the lowest quintile at the time of the survey and a more than proportionate share in the second and third quintiles. Thus, relative poverty clearly increased among these households. Nevertheless, the distribution of retrenched workers' households does not differ significantly from that of the general population, indicating that poverty, while increasing for this particular group, is not much worse for them than it is for the Ghanaian population in general.

In Conakry, the survey does not allow us to compare incomes before and after retrenchment, although we can compare the per capita expenditures (a better measure of welfare) of retrenched workers' households with those of public sector employees who still hold their jobs (Table 4.34). These results show that retrenched workers' households are overrepresented in the lower two quintiles, while current civil servants are about equally as likely to be in the upper two quintiles. Nevertheless, the disparity does not account for differences in skill levels between present and former public sector workers. In fact, a regression of household expenditures on households' human capital and composition for the entire Conakry sample shows that, after accounting for these other characteristics, having a household member who was retrenched has no impact on household welfare relative to the general population (Table 4.35). In this case, it is also important to recall that the survey is for Conakry only, where households are likely to be better off than in rural areas. Thus, while retrenched workers' households may be slightly poorer than the population of Conakry, they are probably not worse off than Guineans in general.

Implications for policy

The most common concern about public sector retrenchment programs is that the social costs for the affected workers will be too great to justify the benefits to the government budget. Our research indicates that, in both Ghana and Guinea, household welfare has declined after retrenchment and that there are more poor households among laid off workers than there were prior to retrenchment. In this sense, they are a vulnerable group. Nevertheless, poverty is not extraordinarily severe among retrenched workers' households in either country, and most retrenched workers' households are not poor, at least relative to other households in the same country. Thus, while recognizing the significant losses that many families incurred in Ghana and Guinea, we should also acknowledge that these families suffer losses from a relatively privileged position. Further, the data presented earlier on the relative welfare of households with public employees in Maputo and in Côte d'Ivoire suggest that in those countries as well, public sector workers are better off than the population in general.

Table 4.35. *Conakry: a reduced form model of household welfare*

	Dependent variable in per capita household expenditures	
	Parameter estimate	T-statistic
Household head		
Age	-0.0743	-2.63[a]
Age^2	0.0013	2.24[a]
Age^3	-0.000007	-1.99[a]
School	0.0359	5.34[a]
School^2	-0.00074	-1.82[a]
Other household members		
No. of males with primary education	0.081	0.78
No. of males with secondary education	0.0520	1.70[b]
No. of males with university education	0.0827	1.53
No. of females with primary education	0.1049	5.08[a]
No. of females with secondary education	0.1543	4.38[a]
No. of females with university education	0.2338	3.62[a]
No. of children under 6	-0.1095	-9.62[a]
No. of children between 6 and 14	-0.0720	-7.60[a]
No. of males between 15 and 20	-0.0685	-3.34[a]
No. of females between 15 and 20	-0.0562	-2.91[a]
No. of males between 21 and 65	-0.0497	-2.57[a]
No. of females between 21 and 65	-0.0670	-4.03[a]
No. of elderly	-0.0556	-1.11
Season (July-September=0)		
January-March	0.0782	4.01[a]
April-June	0.1482	6.43[a]
October-December	-0.0415	-1.85[b]
Assets (100,000 GF)		
Farm	-2.77E^{-8}	-0.01
Business-financial	0.00011	3.05[a]
Ethnicity (Susa, Other=0)		
Fula	0.0505	1.69[b]
Mandinka	0.1138	3.32[a]
Forestiere	0.2751	4.81[a]
No. of public sector departees	0.0196	0.48
Intercept	11.7335	26.16[a]
Model Statistics	45.32[a]	
F-ratio	0.419	
R-square	N=1725	

[a]Significant at the 5 percent level.
[b]Significant at the 10 percent level.
Source: Mills and Sahn 1993.

On these grounds, we are tempted to conclude that there is little reason to target retrenched workers as an especially disadvantaged segment of the population as did, for example, the Program to Mitigate the Social Costs of Adjustment (PAMSCAD) in Ghana. Some of these workers are poor, and more so than before being laid off, but they are no poorer, on average, than their neighbors. Nevertheless, we must also recognize that this group will suffer peculiar, if temporary, costs associated with finding new work, and it is entirely appropriate to mitigate these costs. Further, to the extent that a protracted spell of unemployment represents a broader cost in terms of the waste of a country's human resources, attempting to minimize the spell is an appropriate public policy.

Unfortunately, programs directed at this problem have a poor track record in Africa (see Mills et al. 1994). To begin, administrative capacity is, almost by definition, weak in governments that require massive retrenchment. Thus, for example, the programs to retrain and retool redeployed workers in Ghana required almost four years to get off the ground. Further, the irony of creating a new bureaucracy (the Ministry of Mobilization in Ghana, the Bureau d'aide à la reconversion des agents de la fonction publique [BARAF] in Guinea) to reduce the existing one is apparent. Finally, while special loan programs to help retrenched workers start their own businesses are popular, their performance is poor. First, loan repayment rates are usually abysmal: the "loans" end up as grants. Because the loans are often much larger than regular severance pay, this additional transfer skews the distribution of benefits in the overall severance package toward loan recipients. While there is little household-level information on the recipients of loans (the survey we conducted included only two beneficiaries of the BARAF program), several authors report on the general sense that employees in the upper echelons tend to receive the majority of such loans. (See Mills et al. 1994; Kingsbury 1992; and Karp-Toledo 1991.)

The one policy to aid laid-off workers that appears to work well and have low administrative costs is severance pay in cash. Any country can easily make severance payments if it has a centralized, computerized payroll (which it should have before starting a retrenchment program; otherwise, it is too easy to undercut the program with massive rehiring). Further, by making severance pay more generous for those with low public sector salaries – the most likely to become poor – this policy can address concerns for the poorest workers with low administrative costs. Finally, we note that in Ghana, where severance was paid lump-sum, a significant amount of severance pay went to savings, particularly for those who are currently self-employed. In Guinea, on the other hand, the government strung out severance payments over an extended period, and people invested much less. Given that most small businesses (potential and extant) are likely to be credit-constrained in Africa, having access to a large amount of cash can be very helpful in starting or expanding an enterprise.

One other aspect of redeployees' labor history should be noted. Since the transition to new work was especially easy for redeployees who already held a second job, programs that successfully target this group for layoff can minimize the social costs of unemployment. For example, announcing that a full eight-hour work day will be required may encourage "daylighting" workers with good opportunities outside the public sector to volunteer for retrenchment if there is some incentive (severance pay) to do so.

The incidence of taxes and tax reform

While adjustment policies for public expenditure have received a great deal of attention, and have been subject to a great deal of criticism, changes in tax policy have gone largely unnoticed. Yet in many African countries, the level of public expenditure is not unreasonably high. Rather, the main fiscal problem is a lack of revenue (and a poor allocation of the existing resources). This is particularly true of the economies that suffered serious economic collapse before entering their adjustment programs. The most striking example is Ghana. As Table 4.36 shows, tax revenue declined precipitously in the decade before the ERP began, and spending was eventually pulled down with it. During the ERP and under the conditionality of the IMF and the World Bank, government spending actually increased quite substantially, as we have seen. Yet the deficit was quickly reduced to zero because of the recovery of tax revenues. In Madagascar, on the other hand, tax revenues have declined persistently during the past fifteen years while efforts at fiscal stabilization have concentrated on expenditure control, often unsuccessfully.

Increased tax revenue is an important part of the adjustment story in Ghana, and seemingly would be desirable in Madagascar, where expenditures are not exceptionally high. Yet this approach to fiscal stabilization begs the same question as expenditure cuts: who suffers (or would suffer) when taxes are raised? To answer this, we examine the incidence of the taxes in Ghana and Madagascar. Table 4.37 shows the extended Gini coefficients for several major taxes in the two countries. Note that because we are now addressing tax rather than expenditure incidence, a higher extended Gini coefficient is more progressive. In particular, taxes with a coefficient greater than the coefficient for expenditures per capita are progressive, and vice versa.

To estimate tax incidence, we assume that income earners pay direct taxes on their incomes and that consumers bear the burden of excise and sales tax on goods that they consume.[31] For example, even though the tobacco excise is levied on firms, we assume that it is paid by households who report buying cigarettes, because the firms include the tax in their price. This reasoning is con-

---

[31] Younger (1996a) discusses the methods for calculating taxes paid by different households in Ghana, and Younger et al. (1996) discuss Madagascar.

Table 4.36. *Madagascar and Ghana: taxes as percentage of GDP*

	1978–1980	1981–1983	1984–1986	1987–1989	1990–1991	1992–1994
Madagascar						
Export crop taxes	5.69	7.42	6.58	4.63	1.69	0.86
Import duties	4.96	3.16	3.18	4.05	3.90	3.82
Domestic indirect taxes	3.33	3.25	3.08	2.64	1.94	2.39
Direct taxes	2.58	2.15	2.03	1.56	1.51	1.64
Other revenues	1.13	0.82	0.41	1.14	1.38	0.79
Total revenue	15.47	11.99	12.85	13.00	10.16	9.27
Total expenditures	20.09	14.42	16.06	17.51	16.49	19.27
Deficit	4.62	2.43	3.20	4.51	6.33	10.00
Ghana						
Explicit and implicit taxes on cocoa	17.30	5.62	6.63	3.76	1.50	0.79
Import duties and sales taxes	1.45	1.13	2.12	3.89	4.31	4.14
Other indirect taxes	1.20	1.63	2.35	2.38	3.30	4.12
Personal and corporate income taxes	1.48	1.31	2.10	3.36	2.47	2.43
Other taxes, nontaxes, and grants	0.75	0.86	2.20	2.41	2.68	3.81
Total revenue and grants	9.25	5.73	11.51	14.88	14.12	15.29
Total expenditure plus net lending	17.71	11.39	12.82	14.34	13.29	18.93
Deficit	8.46	5.67	1.31	-0.55	-0.83	3.64

Notes: Ghana fiscal data before 1983 are midyear, for the year ending in the year noted. Last column includes 1992–1993 only for Ghana.

Sources: Younger 1993; Younger et al. 1996.

Table 4.37. *Ghana and Madagascar: extended Gini coefficients for tax categories*

v-parameter	Export duties[a]	Petroleum excises	Gasoline excises	Kerosene excises	Nonpetroleum excises	Sales tax	Value-added tax	Income and property tax	Expenditures per capita
Ghana									
2	0.24	0.38	0.58	0.27	0.38	0.41	—	0.46	0.38
4	0.41	0.57	0.77	0.42	0.52	0.59	—	0.66	0.57
6	0.49	0.64	0.82	0.47	0.57	0.65	—	0.74	0.64
8	0.54	0.68	0.85	0.51	0.59	0.68	—	0.78	0.68
10	0.57	0.71	0.86	0.53	0.60	0.70	—	0.80	0.70
Madagascar									
2	0.20	—	0.96	0.29	0.67	—	0.64	0.85	0.48
4	0.48	—	0.99	0.46	0.85	—	0.79	0.97	0.66
6	0.62	—	0.99	0.53	0.90	—	0.83	0.99	0.72
8	0.67	—	0.99	0.58	0.92	—	0.85	0.99	0.76
10	0.70	—	0.99	0.61	0.93	—	0.036	0.99	0.78

[a]Cocoa for Ghana, vanilla for Madagascar. Gasoline excises include indirect effects through public transport.
Sources: Government of Ghana 1987; Government of Madagascar 1993.

sistent with assuming perfect competition in the relevant industries. The one case where we go beyond this simple assumption is with gasoline because only a small proportion of all gasoline sales go to final consumers. Most is used for transport. Therefore, we assume that the gasoline excise is paid by final consumers of gasoline and final consumers of transport services, where the amount of the latter that is taxed is equal to a fairly standard input–output coefficient of 0.2. In addition, to calculate overall petroleum tax incidence in Ghana (which includes diesel as well as gasoline and kerosene), we use a weighted average of the gasoline incidence, the kerosene incidence, and the expenditure's Lorenz curve (for diesel), where the weights are the actual proportions of refinery production of the three fuels.[32] Finally, we assume that cocoa and vanilla producers bear the burden of their respective export taxes, a reasonable assumption given that virtually all production is exported.

Table 4.38 shows two clearly regressive taxes in both countries, the cocoa or vanilla export duties and the kerosene excise tax. Farmers producing export crops tend to be poorer than the population in general, even though they are better off than other farmers, so taxing them is highly regressive. Similarly, kerosene is a fuel largely used almost equally by poor and nonpoor households alike. The tax on gasoline, on the other hand, is quite progressive in both countries, even after including the indirect impact on transportation services, so that overall, the petroleum duties in Ghana are neutral. The government's increasing reliance on these taxes in recent years has brought protests that they are unfairly prejudicial to the poor, a complaint that, on average, is not supported by the data, but which is certainly true for kerosene duties. The same general argument would apply to Madagascar if it were to raise petroleum taxes, a policy that has been debated recently.

Economists often argue for reliance on sales, value-added, and income taxes, all of which are more broad-based and less distortionary than specific excises. In both countries, all of these taxes are progressive, though not as progressive as the gasoline excise. The sales tax in Ghana and the value-added tax (VAT) in Madagascar fall mostly on imports and on production of the formal sector. Poorer households, especially those in rural areas, tend not to consume these goods, which makes the tax progressive. The income tax is also levied almost exclusively on formal sector wage and capital income. The fact that formal sector employees tend to be better off than the general population explains this tax's progressivity.

With this information in hand, consider the development of major tax categories over time in Ghana and Madagascar shown in Table 4.36. Both governments have reduced explicit and implicit export taxes significantly as part of

---

[32] We lack sufficient data to do the same calculation for Madagascar.

Table 4.38. *Ghana and Madagascar: measures of tax incidence*

Tax	Proportion of tax paid by poorest 30% of households	Progressivity coefficient[a]	Number of households paying this tax
Ghana			
Cocoa taxes, implicit and explicit	0.19	-0.14	383
All direct taxes on households	0.08	0.07	2,579
Sales taxes	0.11	0.03	3,034
All nonpetroleum excise duties	0.13	-0.00	2,737
Petroleum excise duties	0.09	0.07	3,034
Duties on kerosene	0.16	-0.12	2,658
Duties on gasoline[b]	0.05	0.19	2,731
All taxes combined for			
1977/1978	0.17	-0.10	—
1981/1982	0.14	-0.05	—
1987	0.12	-0.00	—
1990	0.11	0.03	—
Poorest 30% of households' share of expenditures	0.11	—	3,034
Madagascar			
Vanilla taxes, implicit and explicit	0.09	-0.26	103
Direct taxes on households	0.01	0.37	723
Value-added taxes	0.05	0.16	4,491
Nonpetroleum excise duties	0.02	0.22	2,074
Petroleum excise duties			
Duties on kerosene	0.15	-0.19	3,936
Duties on gasoline	0.01	0.41	2,194
Poorest 30% of households' share of expenditures	0.09	—	4,500

[a]The progressivity coefficient measures the area between the Lorenz curve for per capita expenditures and that for per capita tax payments.
[b]This includes the indirect effect of gasoline prices on transport costs.
Sources: Younger 1993; Younger et al. 1996.

their adjustment efforts. This has helped to make the tax system more progressive in Ghana and Madagascar. The main difference is that Ghana replaced these revenues with other more progressive taxes, while Madagascar did not. Nevertheless, that the taxes have shifted toward wealthier households is encouraging.

While we do not have comparable information for other countries, it is important to note that the most regressive tax in Ghana and Madagascar is, notably, export duty. Taxes on agricultural exports are quite common in

Africa, as we show in the next chapter on agriculture and adjustment. Econo-mists have long argued against such taxes on efficiency grounds, but if the pat-tern we observe in Ghana and Madagascar is more general, a strong case exists for reducing these taxes in terms of social equity as well.

Conclusion

We can summarize the results of this chapter in two broad conclu-sions: the behavior of public expenditures during the 1980s is at odds with the common perception of drastic cutbacks, and the incidence of those expendi-tures is usually disappointing. On the history of public expenditures, we simply wish to set the record straight. Although expenditures net of debt service have fallen in many African countries since the early 1980s, critics have exagger-ated the extent of that decline both absolutely and relative to historical norms. Further, it is difficult to find a correlation between orthodox adjustment pro-grams and fiscal retrenchment. Government spending net of debt service declined about 3 percent of GDP on average in the early 1980s and, after some fluctuation, stabilized at about 24 percent of GDP on average. Total spending changed little over the decade, so the notion that debt service has crowded out other expenditures is accurate, at least on average, but again, the extent is less than is commonly believed. Moreover, expenditure levels were historically very high in the early 1980s, having run up by 5 or 6 percent of GDP during the late 1970s when commodity prices were high and countries easily obtained international credit. Thus, any comparison with the early 1980s is inherently unfavorable. If we extend the horizon back to the mid-1970s, it is the high expenditures of the late 1970s and early 1980s that appear anomalous, not the "austere" budgets that followed.

In the social sectors, where concern about fiscal policy's impact on poverty is concentrated, the story is broadly similar. Expenditures on education and health increased as a share of GDP and on a per capita basis in the late 1970s, only to retreat in the mid-1980s. For education, the bubble was more accentu-ated than for general expenditures, with a sharper increase and also a sharper decline, while health expenditures were more stable throughout the period. In both cases, expenditures as a share of the total and as a share of GDP were about the same in the mid-1980s as they were in the mid-1970s.

This descriptive information, based on the continent, says little about the impact of adjustment programs on expenditures, of course. There is a wide variance around the average in Africa, and it is possible that those countries undertaking adjustment programs are also those with declines in expenditures. But the data do not support that hypothesis. Rather, the most striking correla-tion takes place between serious civil conflict and large declines in expendi-tures. Rarely did expenditure reductions in adjustment programs do any more than deflate the bubble of the late 1970s. In fact, two of the sharpest declines in expenditures among our case study countries, Ghana and Tanzania, occurred before those countries accepted orthodox policy packages.

Our second main point is more important. Whatever their level of expenditures, African governments do not spend their resources in a socially progressive way. Expenditures on health and education, two public expenditures whose justification depends in part on redistributive arguments, are biased against the poor, especially in rural areas. Although poor households constitute the majority of beneficiaries of some public services, most notably primary education and nonhospital health services, those services are also chronically underfunded in comparison to other less equitable ones. Furthermore, that the quality of the services is surely worse in rural areas where the poor reside suggests that our results, based on simple attendance data, are overly optimistic. To some extent, it makes sense to concentrate the provision of services in urban areas. African health and education ministries have extremely small budgets and thus cannot provide a wide range of service to all citizens. The concentration of potential beneficiaries in urban areas makes them the logical site for a hospital or university. What does not make sense, however, is to concentrate the subsidies there. In fact, while the only public hospital may necessarily be in a city, the fact that its probable beneficiaries are better off than the population in general argues against subsidizing its services.

We recognize that this message is not new. An emphasis on the importance of primary care in health and universal primary education has been widely accepted for twenty years for reasons of equity and efficiency (because these are the services with the highest public goods content). What our work does bring to the debate is information on the substantial distance between that rhetoric and the African reality. Despite the publicly stated intentions of governments and donors, they are not concentrating their efforts on the delivery of primary services to the poor. The discouragement that these results bring is only heightened by the recognition that governments in other developing countries do much better (e.g., see Selowsky 1979, for Colombia, Meerman 1979, for Malaysia, or Younger and Sahn, 1995, for the Caribbean). Thus, fiscal policy's harm to the poor is not so much in the commonly misperceived cuts in overall social sector budgets, but rather in the concentration of those expenditures' benefits among the middle and upper classes.

Our work on public employment and public sector retrenchment comes to similar conclusions. Public sector employees receive significantly higher incomes than other comparable households in their respective countries, and this premium is not explained by higher skills, experience, and so on. Rather, public employees receive substantial rents which are, again, distributed inequitably. Although the use of public employment as a form of political patronage is universal, in some African countries it appears to have reached such an extreme that it displaces the ostensible motive, the provision of public services.

For policy makers, the most important implication of our work is that the rancorous debate over the increase or decrease of social sector expenditures by a few cents per capita is less important than an improved allocation of the resources that are spent. Similarly, rather than focusing on the welfare costs to retrenched public employees, a more constructive policy debate would address the question of the staffing that African governments need to provide public services efficiently. We recognize that the political economy considerations that make these issues important will also make them difficult to resolve. But giving them prominence in the debate can only help.

5

Agriculture and food markets

The agricultural sector remains at the heart of most African economies. Most of the labor force still is engaged as agricultural workers. Agriculture is generally the most important sector in GDP. In general, private consumers devote over 50 percent of their total expenditures to food. This share is even higher (often exceeding two-thirds of the consumption bundle) for urban and rural poor households. The share of exports from agricultural products is also extremely high, with the exception of countries with a particularly important mineral export (such as Cameroon [petroleum], Guinea [bauxite], Niger [uranium], and Zaire [copper and diamonds]) (Table 5.1). The poor rely even more on agriculture and food markets than the population in general. As discussed in Chapter 2, this dependence is because Africa's poor are concentrated in rural areas and their incomes largely derive from own-farm production, wages earned as paid agricultural laborers, and incomes earned in processing and marketing agricultural products. Finally, because women farmers are the primary producers of food in most countries, agricultural policies can potentially have large impacts on the welfare of women and children.

Policies that discriminate against agriculture have been major contributors to the economic crisis in Africa. State monopolies in export crop marketing and related export price controls have had particularly deleterious effects on export performance and the balance of payments. High rates of explicit and implicit export crop taxation contribute to stagnating production and diversion of output to parallel markets with high transaction costs. Intervention in staple food trade is also common, especially in eastern and southern Africa. Such intervention characteristically pursues cheap food policies for urban consumers by implicitly taxing farmers, a transfer of resources that harms the rural poor. Moreover, the government generally rations food subsidies, without favorable distributional effects. In some cases, food subsidies contribute significantly to

Table 5.1. *Structural features of study countries, early 1980s*

Countries	Share of agriculture in GDP[a]	Share of labor employed in agriculture	Share of food in private consumption	Share of exports in GDP	Share of agriculture in total exports	Major agriculture export crop(s)
			(%)			
Cameroon	28	70	55	20	42	Coffee/cocoa
Gambia	41	84	58	30	24	Groundnuts
Ghana	57	65	64	25	64	Cocoa
Guinea	31[b]	81	51	31	3	Coffee
Madagascar	32	81	60	12	77	Coffee/vanilla
Malawi	37	83	61	25	86	Tobacco
Mozambique	59	85	73	23	51	Cashew/cotton
Niger	31	91	56	23	31	Groundnut/cotton
Tanzania	53	80	68	20	63	Coffee/cotton
Zaire	31	72	71	39	8	Coffee/palm kernel

[a]1980–1982 average.
[b]1985–1986 average.
Source: World Bank 1993b.

fiscal deficits, illustrating the interaction between major microeconomic distortions and macroeconomic stability.

Policy reforms in agricultural export and food markets are designed to reduce or eliminate the bias against the agricultural sector. The nature and effectiveness of these reforms have varied substantially across sub-Saharan African countries because of significant differences in the structures of the agricultural economies of the region as well as in the extent of distortions and commitment to reform. In this chapter we analyze policy reforms in export crop and food markets. For each of these two areas of reform, we examine broad characteristics related to their importance in the overall economies of the sample countries, the level of distortions prior to reform, the extent to which reforms have changed real prices of agricultural products, the consequences of reform for income distribution and the welfare of the poor, and, briefly, the private sector's capacity to respond to the state's withdrawal from food and agriculture markets.[1] We conclude the chapter with a discussion of why, in spite of the substantial change in many agricultural markets, observed supply response to date has been so limited and what complementary measures may be needed to achieve greater gains in output.

Agricultural export policy reforms

Macroeconomic distortions and government interventions in export crop marketing in Africa contributed to declining real producer prices, stagnating production, reductions in official exports, and increased smuggling in the 1970s and early 1980s. In response, agricultural policy reforms, in conjunction with changes in trade and exchange rate policy, were designed to improve producer incentives and thus spur production, exports, and economic growth. Increases in real producer prices of export crops tend to lead to a more equal income distribution as well, since small farmers account for a large share of export crop production in most African countries. The extent to which these reforms succeed in their objectives depends not only on government policy, however, but also on prices of export commodities in world markets, which are beyond the control of individual countries.

The place of agricultural exports in national economies

Agricultural exports are a major source of foreign exchange earnings and tax revenues in many sub-Saharan African countries. As a result, changes in pricing policy and terms of trade that affect levels of production and export also can have major implications for foreign exchange earnings, government revenues, and the budget deficit. Through these macroeconomic channels, changes in export pricing policy also affect real incomes throughout the econ-

---

[1] For more on the private sector's response, see Jebuni and Seini 1992; Berg 1983; and von Braun and Puetz 1987.

Table 5.2. *Agricultural export duties in selected countries*

Country	Average export duties (% of total excluding grants)		
	1975–1977	1980–1992 avg.	1990–1992
Cameroon	12.0[a]	7.9[a]	1.2[a]
Gambia	10.4[a]	5.3[a]	0.1[a]
Ghana	27.0[a]	12.5[a]	9.2
Madagascar	15.3[b]	9.3	6.7
(including other taxes)[c]	24.5[b]	17.0	10.4
Tanzania	8.6[a]	3.1[a]	0.0[a]

[a]Total export duties.
[b]Madagascar 1977–1979 average instead of 1975–1977.
[c]Includes extrabudgetary net receipts of the National Consolidated
Equalization Fund (Fonds National).
Sources: For 1975–1977 and 1980–1982, World Bank 1993b; for
Cameroon and The Gambia, IMF 1992a; for Ghana, IMF 1993b; for
Madagascar, World Bank 1984, 1986, IMF 1989, 1993c; for Tanzania IMF
1994b.

omy. Moreover, since many of the poor in sub-Saharan Africa produce agricultural exports, changes in prices affect their incomes directly.

For five of the sample countries listed in Table 5.1, agricultural exports account for over 50 percent of export earnings. Furthermore, one or two crops account for the vast majority of agricultural exports in these countries, making them extremely vulnerable to adverse movements in the terms of trade of these commodities. This structure reflects the comparative advantage and colonial heritage of these tropical countries, as well as the underdevelopment of nonagricultural export sectors, due in part to trade and exchange rate policies biased against the tradable goods sector. Agricultural exports are much less important sources of foreign exchange in countries with large mineral export sectors, such as Cameroon, Guinea, Niger, and Zaire.

Tax revenues from export crops accounted for over 10 percent of government revenues in the late 1970s in four of the study countries: Cameroon, The Gambia, Ghana, and Madagascar (Table 5.2). Export taxes, predominantly from cocoa, accounted for over one-quarter of government revenues in Ghana in the 1975 – 1977 period. Including implicit tax revenues captured by export crop marketing boards in Madagascar,[2] export taxes on agricultural products

[2] These figures include the net receipts of the National Consolidated Equalization Fund (Fonds National Unique de Péréquation – FNUP), which includes implicit taxes on vanilla (and until 1989 on coffee, cloves, and other agricultural exports, as well).

accounted for a similar amount: nearly 25 percent of government revenues. Large taxes on mineral products in Guinea, Niger, and Zaire have minimized the importance of agricultural export tax revenues in these countries. In Malawi and Mozambique, explicit export taxes have been low, though in Mozambique, indirect taxation of agricultural exports before liberalization measures in the late 1980s was very high.

One reason for the high levels of taxation of agricultural exports in the countries shown in Table 5.2 is that trade is relatively easy to tax, as compared with general taxes on sales or income taxes, which require a more sophisticated and expensive tax administration. In addition, export supply of agricultural products, particularly tree crops, is price inelastic in the short run, so that production and foreign exchange earnings are little affected by moderate changes in producer prices. Export crop pricing policy in many countries has reflected this "export pessimism" – a belief that increases in producer prices through reduced taxation or a real exchange rate depreciation would have little positive effects on production or exports. As many African countries discovered, however, excessive taxation of export crops led to substantial declines in production over time as farmers invested less in purchased inputs (pesticides, fungicides, fertilizer), labor for crop maintenance, and other inputs. In addition, high taxation encouraged smuggling to neighboring countries and other means of avoiding tax. The steep decline in Ghana's export tax revenues in the 1980–1982 period largely reflects production declines and smuggling. As discussed later, declines in export taxes in other countries (and in Ghana beginning in the late 1980s) reflect reductions in export tax rates, often forced by declining world prices.

Adverse movements in the terms of trade greatly affected those countries dependent on export crops for a large share of foreign exchange earnings and tax revenues. Beginning in the mid-1980s, world prices for cocoa and especially coffee fell sharply (Figure 5.1), significantly reducing export earnings for Côte d'Ivoire, Ghana, Madagascar, Tanzania, and other African countries. For Malawi, a large increase in transport costs due to the closing of marketing links through Mozambique had a similar effect of reducing export prices for tobacco and other products. The extent to which these external price shocks and coincidental macroeconomic reforms affected real producer prices, however, was determined by agricultural trade and price policy.

Policy impacts on producer prices

Producer prices are determined by the interaction of world prices, the exchange rate, and agricultural pricing policy. This is shown in equation 5.1, where the price of an export good (P_e) is equal to the world price measured in foreign currency (PW_e) multiplied by the nominal exchange rate (ER), less export taxes (tx):

$$P_e = ER * PW_e * (1 - tx) \tag{5.1}$$

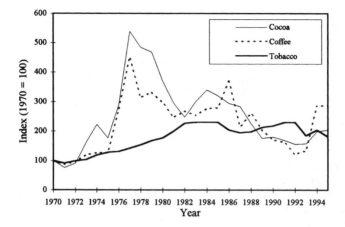

Figure 5.1. World prices of major agricultural export crops (index of f.o.b. prices in U.S. dollars). *Sources:* Alderman 1991; Dorosh, Bernier, and Sarris 1990; Jaeger 1992b.

Dividing by the consumer price index (CPI) gives a measure of the real price of the export good:

$$P_e/CPI = ER * PW_e * (1 - tx)/CPI \qquad (5.2)$$

Regrouping the terms on the right-hand side of the equation and multiplying and dividing by PW (the average world price of tradable goods) gives:

$$P_e/CPI = (ER * PW/CPI) * (PW_e/PW) * (1 - tx). \qquad (5.3)$$

Thus, the real price of the export good can be decomposed into the product of three terms: the real exchange rate (ER $*$ PW/CPI), the real price of the export good in world markets (PW$_e$/PW), and export taxes (1 − tx), which drive a wedge between the border price of the export good and the domestic price.

Prior to reforms, many countries fixed producer prices in nominal terms, ostensibly for the purpose of stabilizing farmer incomes but, as we will show, resulting in large levels of taxation for farmers. In terms of equation 5.1, fixing P_e at a level different from the border price[3] resulted in a total direct taxation of exports of tx.[4] In addition, African export farmers were indirectly taxed through the overvaluation of the exchange rate, which lowered the border price

---

[3] The border prices for export crops presented in this chapter include an adjustment for transport and marketing costs to the producer level. Thus, the border price P_b is defined as: $P_b = ER * PW_e - trans$, where trans is a measure of transport and marketing costs from farm gate to the port (f.o.b.) price.

[4] This implicit taxation includes both explicit export taxes as well as profits received by marketing boards.

Table 5.3. *Real producer prices of major export crops (average 1980 – 1982 = 100)*

Country (major export crop)	Years		
	1975–1977	1980–1982	1989–1991
Cameroon (cocoa)	73	100	49
Gambia (groundnuts)	121	100	79
Ghana (cocoa)	167	100	177
Guinea (coffee)	76	100	117
Madagascar (coffee)	138	100	104
Malawi (tobacco)	105	100	113
Mozambique (cashews)	84	100	199
Niger (cowpeas)	110	100	120
Tanzania (coffee)	274	100	99
Zaire (coffee)	61	100	—
Unweighted average (not including Zaire)	128	100	117

Sources: Arulpragasam and Sahn 1996; Blandford et al. 1994; Dorosh, Bernier, and Sarris 1990; Dorosh and Bernier 1994; Donovan 1993; Jabara 1990; Jaeger 1992b; Government of Niger 1993; IMF 1993a, 1993b, 1993c, 1994b, 1994d; World Bank 1994d.

measured in domestic currency.[5] As shown later, in most of the non-CFA countries in our sample, this indirect taxation far exceeded direct taxation prior to reforms.

As will be discussed, the effectiveness of policy change differed among the countries examined, and few countries succeeded in significantly raising real producer prices of export crops. In the case of Ghana, Guinea, and Mozambique, real producer prices of major export crops increased substantially after adjustment (Table 5.3). In Madagascar, The Gambia, Tanzania, Malawi, and Zaire, improvements were limited by adverse terms-of-trade movements and incomplete or delayed reforms. In Cameroon and Niger, membership in the CFA zone helped limit the prereform distortions in export crop prices and

[5] Krueger, Schiff, and Valdès (1988) measure the indirect effects of trade and exchange rate policy by comparing an estimated equilibrium exchange rate to the official exchange rate. In this chapter, we use the spread between the parallel exchange rate and the official exchange rate as a measure of indirect taxation through distortions in the foreign exchange market. In situations where the official exchange rate is seriously out of alignment, both methodologies produce similar results (see, e.g., Dorosh, Bernier, and Sarris 1990).

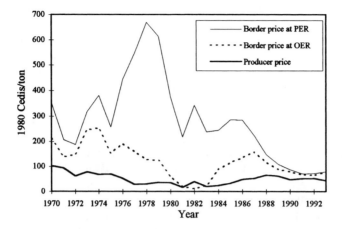

Figure 5.2. Ghana: real cocoa prices, 1970–1992. PER = parallel exchange rate; OER = official exchange rate. *Sources:* Alderman 1991 and authors' calculations.

abundant mineral resources lessened the importance of export crops for generating foreign exchange earnings, so that reforms were of lesser significance to these economies although still of importance to poor producers.

Countries with large improvements in producer incentives

In Ghana the historical emphasis on industrialization through import substitution had as its corollary the squeezing of the agricultural sector. A broad set of policies, ranging from the grossly overvalued exchange rate to inefficient provision of inputs and marketing of outputs, was most directly adverse to export agriculture, particularly cocoa producers. The Cocoa Marketing Board (Cocobud), in fact, stands out as a story of corruption and patronage (Bates 1981). Originally intended to shield domestic producers from the volatility of world cocoa markets, Cocobud instead became an important mechanism for taxation of farmers, since producer prices were set far below border prices. From 1971 to 1975, direct taxation of cocoa, measured by the difference between the border price at the official exchange rate and the producer price set by the government, averaged 56.9 percent (Figure 5.2). The large surge in world cocoa prices from 1976 to 1979 coincided with a period of high domestic inflation and fixed nominal exchange rates in Ghana, so that despite the increase in world prices, real border prices measured at the official exchange rate actually fell by 47.2 percent. Moreover, the huge difference between border prices at parallel exchange rates and official domestic producer prices encouraged smuggling, reducing government tax revenues. With the decline in world cocoa prices in 1980, explicit export tax revenues fell sharply because of the smaller price spread between producer prices and border prices at official exchange rates. The total rate of taxation, measured by the difference between the border price at the parallel rate and the producer price, remained high, however. This indirect taxation of exports through the mandatory surrender of foreign exchange at the official exchange rate was the counterpart of the implicit rents received by those who bought foreign exchange at the low official exchange rate.

The Economic Recovery Program (ERP) that commenced in 1983 marked the reversal of years of declining output in agriculture in Ghana. Real producer prices of cocoa rose substantially with trade and exchange rate liberalization, although explicit taxation on cocoa exports remained high. The series of devaluations of the cedi between 1983 and 1987 eliminated much of the spread between parallel and official exchange rates and raised substantially the real border price of cocoa (measured at official exchange rates). These exchange rate reforms, coupled with a reduction in direct taxation of cocoa exports allowed real producer prices of cocoa to rise by 154 percent between 1983 and 1987. Despite these reforms, direct taxation remained high, at 74.6 percent of the producer price in 1987 and 33.2 percent in 1991. Moreover, Cocobud retained its monopoly on cocoa exports, though in 1994 the government legalized domestic purchases of cocoa by private firms.

Increases in real producer prices had positive effects for lower-income households. As noted in Chapter 4, cocoa taxes in Ghana fall disproportionately on lower-income households because cocoa farmers are poorer than the population in general. Based on the share of cocoa taxes in their total expenditures in 1987, reducing the rate of taxation on cocoa from the actual 1987 level of 69.7 to 10 percent of the producer price would increase real incomes of cocoa producers in the bottom 30 percent of the national income distribution by 22.2 percent. This represents a sizable income gain for the 11.3 percent of poor households in Ghana who are cocoa farmers.[6]

Economic reform resulted in large changes in real producer prices of agricultural exports in Guinea, as well. Despite abundant land and water resources, the export agricultural sector in Guinea has been among the worst performers in Africa since independence. The level of state control and intervention in Guinea's agriculture has, not coincidentally, been perhaps greater than all the other countries discussed in this book. The state endeavored to be the legal proprietor of all land, to control virtually all production decisions, and to be the monopsonistic marketer of both export and food crops.

More specifically, Guinea's First Republic depressed the official producer price of exports as part of a broader effort to gain a large share of the value-

---

[6] These calculations are based on the Ghana Living Standards Survey (Government of Ghana 1987) data and cocoa tax information from the IMF 1993b. See also Younger 1993.

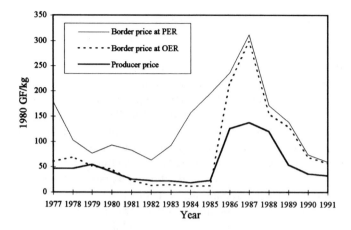

Figure 5.3. Guinea: real robusta coffee prices, 1977–1991. PER = parallel exchange rate; OER = official exchange rate. *Source:* Arulpragasam and Sahn 1996.

added of all productive sectors. Prior to liberalization in 1985, nominal producer prices of major exports increased only slightly, not nearly keeping pace with inflation. Though direct taxation measured at the grossly overvalued official exchange rate was small, nominal protection coefficients evaluated at the parallel exchange rate were only 0.12 for coffee, 0.33 for palm kernels, and 0.33 for groundnuts in the years just prior to reform (Arulpragasam and Sahn, 1996). In response to the worsening incentive structure, the volume of exports plummeted for all major crops during the First Republic. For example, coffee exports, which averaged over 10,000 between 1960–1965, fell to just 580 metric tons (MT) between 1980–1985, while palm kernel exports fell by two-thirds, and banana exports effectively ceased altogether in the 1980s after being 43,000 MT in 1960–1965.

The Economic Recovery Program that marked the beginning of Guinea's Second Republic brought about many changes in policy that affected agriculture, but none as important as the trade and exchange rate policy reforms, discussed in Chapter 3. Between 1985 and 1986, the nominal protection coefficients (NPCs) for coffee, evaluated at the parallel exchange rate, jumped from 0.12 to 0.53 (Figure 5.3). In turn, official coffee exports increased 46-fold between those two years, and have continued to increase by an average rate of close to 40 percent through 1992. Undoubtedly, this increase is due largely to the rechanneling of products from parallel markets to official markets. In spite of these increases in coffee and other commodities, the volume of agricultural exports remains below those observed prior to the adoption of the discriminatory policies of the First Republic. Nonprice factors, such as poor transportation and marketing infrastructure, inadequate irrigation and extension services, and various legal and administrative obstacles to exports, remain as impediments to export growth.

As in Ghana and Guinea, distortions in macroeconomic policies and fixed producer prices resulted in extremely high levels of taxation for producers of export crops in Mozambique. Following independence in 1975, Mozambique's government attempted to control marketing for all crops, at least on the wholesale level. Dislocations associated with the war and the flight of Portuguese settlers, low producer prices, shortages of consumer goods to rural areas, and other marketing problems helped to reduce agricultural exports in the postwar period. With cashew nut exports in 1979 being 42 percent below the preindependence (1973) level and cotton exports down by 68 percent,[7] the government raised nominal producer prices for these two crops by 43 and 69 percent, respectively, in 1980. Domestic inflation eroded the gains in real prices, however, and despite later nominal price adjustments, the real prices of cashew and cotton were at postindependence lows in 1986.

As part of Mozambique's ERP begun in 1987, producer prices of cashews were increased substantially, so that from 1987 to 1992, real prices of cashew averaged 2.9 times their 1986 level. Cotton prices were also increased substantially to 77 percent above their 1986 level, but still 20 percent below the 1980 level.[8] In the wake of these price increases, exports of these crops increased substantially, though other factors, particularly improvements in rural security, played important roles in the export recovery. Exports of cashews averaged 5,200 tons per year between 1988 and 1992, more than 60 percent greater than the 1985 and 1986 levels, but still far below the 16,700 tons exported in 1982. Similarly, cotton exports have recovered from a near total collapse in 1986, but by 1992 were still only 48 percent of their 1981 level.[9]

Little data are available on rural incomes in Mozambique because of the problems of rural security prior to the end of the civil war in 1992, so it is difficult to determine distributional consequences of increases in export crops. Nonetheless, all of cashew production and 47 percent of cotton production in 1991 derived from family farms,[10] mostly in eastern and northern Mozambique, suggesting that increases in prices of these export crops benefited at least a segment of the country's rural poor.[11]

---

[7] Comissao Nacional do Plano 1988 reported in Kyle 1994.

[8] Dorosh and Bernier 1994a.

[9] Computed from World Bank 1988 and IMF 1992b.

[10] Ministry of Agriculture estimates, cited in Dorosh and Bernier 1994a.

[11] Data from a survey in Nampula province in northern Mozambique in 1991 showed that in the cotton-growing district of Monapo 56 percent of smallholder households grew cotton, with cotton accounting for 20.4 percent of gross household income. Cashews were cultivated by more than half of smallholders in both Monapo and

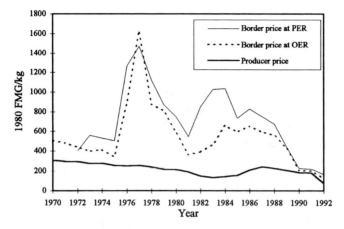

Figure 5.4. Madagascar: real coffee prices, 1970–1992. PER = parallel exchange rate; OER = official exchange rate. *Sources*: Dorosh, Bernier, and Sarris 1990; Dorosh and Bernier 1991.

Countries with limited increases in export crop prices

In Madagascar, adverse terms-of-trade movements prevented export crop liberalization from raising real producer prices. In particular, the government heavily taxed coffee producers under the guise of a price stabilization fund until the liberalization of trade in export crops in the late 1980s. Direct taxation was particularly high from 1976 to 1980, as official producer prices were kept low while world coffee prices rose sharply (Figure 5.4). In the early 1980s, however, world coffee prices declined. The plight of Madagascar's coffee farmers was made worse by rapid domestic inflation coupled with a fixed nominal exchange rate, so that the real border price of coffee declined, reducing revenues for the stabilization fund and justifying low producer prices to mitigate the loss of revenues. Nonetheless, the total rate of taxation remained high. [12]

Nominal exchange rate devaluations in the mid-1980s reduced the rate of indirect taxation, closing the gap between the border prices measured at the official exchange rate and the border prices measured at the parallel exchange rate, but the devaluations did not lead to an increase in the producer price of coffee, which had fallen by 54.2 percent in real terms between 1974 and 1983 (Dorosh, Bernier, and Sarris 1990). Instead, the revenues of the stabilization fund increased as the border price rose while the real producer price fell. Trade and exchange rate liberalization in 1987 and 1988 essentially eliminated the

Angoche districts, but accounted for only 8.7 (Monapo) and 13.7 (Angoche) percent of gross household incomes in these districts (MOA/MSU/UA 1992).

[12] Calculations of indirect taxation on Malagasy agriculture using an estimated equilibrium exchange rate provide similar results to those presented here, which use the parallel exchange rate to calculate the border price (see Dorosh et al. 1990).

spread between official and parallel exchange rates through 1990, but the continued decline in world prices prevented an increase in real producer prices in spite of the elimination of explicit export taxes and liberalization of export crop marketing. Thus, the potential increases in real coffee prices for Malagasy farmers from trade and exchange rate policy reforms were prevented first by agricultural pricing policy in the mid-1980s, which kept producer prices low, and later by the decline in world coffee prices in the late 1980s.

Computable general equilibrium (CGE) model simulations for Madagascar indicate that taxes on the country's major exports (coffee, vanilla, and cloves) reduced real incomes of households throughout the economy (Dorosh 1994b). With a 10 percent increase in the export tax on these products, total exports fall by 3.0 percent in dollar terms in year 1 and 3.7 percent in year 6. This reduction in export earnings necessitates a real exchange rate depreciation of 3.6 percent in year 1 (5.4 percent in year 6) to restore external equilibrium (Table 5.4). In spite of this depreciation, however, agricultural production falls by 0.5 percent in year 6. The tax policy does increase government revenues by 1.2 to 1.4 percent over the six years simulated, which provides additional funds for investment. However, since real GDP and household incomes fall as a result of the reduced export incentives and earnings, total savings and investment rise by only 0.3 percent. Small farmers on the east coast, where these export crops are mainly grown, suffer real income declines of 1.2 percent, though reduced economic efficiency and export earnings lead to lower real incomes for all household groups, and average household incomes fall by 1.3 percent in year 6.

Terms-of-trade movements also hindered The Gambia's early efforts at export crop liberalization. Prior to liberalization of groundnut marketing in 1989/1990, the GPMB (Gambia Produce Marketing Board) held a monopoly on groundnut purchases. The GPMB procured groundnuts through the Gambia Cooperative Union (GCU) or from licensed buying agents, who purchased groundnuts from farmers at a set guaranteed producer price. The GPMB then exported the groundnuts as unprocessed nuts or as groundnut cake and oil.

To increase foreign exchange earnings, the Gambian government raised groundnut prices by 23.5 percent between 1979/1980 and 1982/1983. Unfortunately, a decline in world prices of groundnuts in 1982/1983 left the GPMB costs in excess of world market prices, necessitating a government subsidy for the GPMB (Jabara 1994). Though the transfers to the GPMB did not show up as explicit trade subsidies, they were essentially negative taxes on exports that drove a wedge between the producer price and border price and in effect raised the realized export price received by the GPMB.[13] Given the inefficiencies of

---

[13] Similarly, the profits that accrued to the Ghanaian Cocoa Board in the mid-1970s due to the substantial size of the spread between purchase and export prices relative to actual marketing costs represented an implicit direct tax on cocoa producers.

Table 5.4. *Madagascar: CGE model simulations of an increase in the agricultural export tax*

	Base level*	Percent change	
		Year 1	Year 6
GDP	2,010	-0.8	-1.0
Consumption	1,672	-1.0	-1.2
Total investment	169	0.3	0.3
Private investment	95	0.4	0.5
Public investment	74	0.0	0.0
Government consumption	184	0.0	0.0
Government revenues	209	1.2	1.4
Real exchange rate index	100	3.6	5.4
Exports (mill $)	389	-3.0	-3.7
Imports (mill $)	474	-2.4	-3.0
Foreign savings (mill $)	85	0.0	0.0
Sectoral production			
Agriculture	810	-0.4	-0.5
Industry	833	-0.1	-0.1
Services	1,168	-0.5	-0.5
Public administration	217	0.0	0.0
Total production	3,028	-0.3	-0.4
Household incomes			
Urban high income	871	-1.4	-1.9
Urban middle income	119	-1.2	-1.3
Urban low income	92	-1.4	-1.6
Small farm plateau	89	-0.8	-0.9
Small farm east	90	-1.2	-1.3
Small farm west/south	103	-0.6	-0.8
Large farm/rural high income	185	-0.9	-1.2
Nonfarm rural low-income	85	-1.2	-1.2
Total	134	-1.0	-1.3

*Base level values in billion 1984 FMG, except for income values in thousand 1984 FMG/capita.
Source: Calculated from simulations 8 and 9 in Dorosh 1994b. The base run simulates the year 1989.

the GPMB, however, it is not clear that farmers were better off with GPMB and the subsidy than with private trade and no export tax or subsidy in these years.

In subsequent years, The Gambia again lowered groundnut prices in order to eliminate the subsidy and raise fiscal revenues for the government. However, The Gambia's low producer price for groundnuts encouraged parallel market exports to Senegal, where groundnut producer prices were kept high through government subsidies. Thus, groundnut prices were again raised in 1984/1985 and 1985/1986, only to be reduced again after world groundnut prices fell. Throughout this period, exchange rate distortions were small in The Gambia, compared with other sample countries, so indirect taxation was not very large in most years.[14] In 1989, four years after the introduction of the ERP in June 1985, groundnut marketing in The Gambia was liberalized, as the guaranteed producer price was replaced by an announced purchase price and, shortly thereafter, the GPMB's export monopoly was lifted.

Because groundnuts are grown by small farmers numbered among The Gambia's poor, taxation of groundnuts had adverse consequences for rural poverty. CGE simulations show that a reduction in the implicit export tax on groundnuts by 75 percent of the f.o.b. price increases real incomes of rural poor households by 4.4 percent (Table 5.5). This policy reduces government revenues and total savings in the economy,[15] however, leading to a decline in real investment and demand for labor-intensive urban investment decline, so the incomes of the urban poor fall by 1.1 percent.[16] In years 2 through 5 of the simulation, the implicit export tax is reduced from its base level by an average of 63.2 percent of the f.o.b. price. Investment is lower in each year, reducing urban capital and urban incomes, while the impact of reducing export taxes on rural poor household income is greater in the latter years of the simulation (e.g., 7.1 percent) since world groundnut prices are higher than in year 1. Thus, for The Gambia, the relatively large share of government revenues generated by taxes on groundnuts and the importance of investment-related labor incomes for the urban poor suggest that groundnut taxes involved a significant rural–urban trade-off (Dorosh and Lundberg 1993).

For coffee producers in Tanzania, the overvalued official exchange rate, rather than direct export taxes, has been the major source of taxation. Real producer prices of coffee were maintained at relatively stable, but very low, levels throughout the adjustment period (Figure 5.5). Between 1977 and 1988, domestic producer prices were on average 79 percent below border prices measured at the parallel exchange rate. As in Madagascar, trade and exchange rate policy reforms in 1987 and 1988 reduced the spread between parallel and official exchange rates. This reduction was offset by the decline in world prices of

---

[14] Badiane and Kinteh (1994) estimate that the divergence between the official and equilibrium exchange rates was about 20 to 30 percent in the 1984–1988 period, down from as much as 50 percent in 1980 and 1981. For the 1981–1988 period as a whole, they estimate average direct taxation at 13 percent, with total taxation of 33 percent.

[15] The model simulation assumes fixed foreign savings with a savings investment closure in which marginal propensities to save are fixed and investment adjusts to equal total savings.

[16] Note, however, that average annual incomes of the urban poor (2,530 dalasis per person) are 2.6 times greater than those of the rural poor (970 dalasis per person).

Table 5.5. *The Gambia: CGE model simulation of increased groundnut producer prices*

	Base level[a]	Percent change Year 1	Percent change Year 5
GDP	2,149	-0.1	-0.5
Consumption	1,524	1.1	1.5
Total investment	378	-6.1	-9.2
Private investment	171	-25.5	-23.8
Public investment	112	0.0	0.0
Government consumption	233	0.0	0.0
Government revenues	370	-10.4	-16.7
Real exchange rate index	100	-2.7	-4.4
Exports (mill $)	147	-0.4	-1.3
Imports (mill $)	151	-0.3	-1.3
Foreign savings (mill $)	5	0.0	0.0
Sectoral production			
Agriculture	683	0.9	1.1
Industry	329	6.1	7.3
Services	2,207	-1.8	-4.5
Public administration	232	0.0	0.1
Total production	3,403	0.6	-0.3
Household incomes			
Urban poor	2.53	-1.1	-3.6
Urban nonpoor	6.79	-1.3	-3.8
Rural poor	0.97	4.4	7.1
Rural nonpoor	1.98	3.4	6.4
Total	2.00	0.9	0.9

[a]Base level values in million dalasis, except for income values in thousand dalasis/capita.

Source: Calculated from simulation 4 and 5 in Dorosh and Lundberg 1996.

coffee, which lowered border prices at official exchange rates in 1989 and 1990, and direct taxes on coffee exports, which were not substantially reduced. Only in 1991 was the rate of direct taxation on coffee exports reduced substantially (from 29.2 to 13.2 percent of border prices), enabling a 21.3 percent increase in real producer prices.

CGE model simulations indicate that a decrease of 20 percent in the tax rate on Tanzania's export crops would lead to increases in welfare of 0.2 to 0.3 percent for the rural and urban poor, as returns from export crops increase and as real wages for unskilled labor rise by 1.0 percent in the economy overall (Sarris 1994a). Loss of tax revenues necessitates a drop in public spending, but permits a slight increase in real investment of private formal enterprises. More

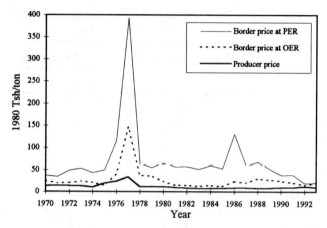

Figure 5.5. Tanzania: real coffee prices, 1970–1992. PER = parallel exchange rate; OER = official exchange rate. *Source:* Sarris and van den Brink 1993.

important for real incomes of the nonpoor, the increase in exports augments the supply of foreign exchange, thus reducing the excess demand for foreign exchange to be satisfied on the parallel market. As a result, the premium on foreign exchange in the parallel market falls, along with the rents associated with rationing of foreign exchange, so that real incomes of the rural and urban nonpoor decline.[17]

In Malawi, real incomes of small farmers suffered, both because of export crop pricing policy and institutional differences between the smallholder and estate subsector. Until reforms in 1990, the government prohibited smallholders from producing burley and flue-cured tobacco, lucrative export crops set aside for the estate subsector. During the 1970s, favorable world prices of tobacco and low levels of taxation resulted in high producer prices of burley and flue-cured tobaccos and contributed to substantial growth in exports and GDP. At the same time, other tobaccos that smallholders were permitted to grow were taxed heavily through the agricultural marketing parastatal, ADMARC.

Structural adjustment efforts in Malawi in the 1980s afforded little attention to the institutional and legal arrangements in agriculture, and instead concentrated on improving price incentives for smallholder export crops, the efficiency of the marketing parastatal (ADMARC), and, to a lesser extent, input pricing in the smallholder sector. These efforts at reforms met with only limited success, in large part because of the adverse effects of the war

---

[17] The CGE model for Tanzania simulates both the real and monetary sides of the economy. In the simulation described here, the price level, government spending, and the trade deficit are all endogenous. See Sarris 1994a for further details.

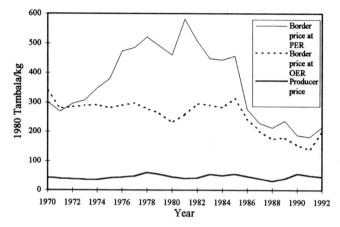

Figure 5.6. Malawi: real tobacco prices, 1970–1992. PER = parallel exchange rate; OER = official exchange rate. *Sources*: Donovan 1993; Jaeger 1992b; Sahn, Arulpragasam, and Merid 1990.

in neighboring Mozambique. As major rail lines through Mozambique were closed in the early 1980s, transport costs increased greatly, lowering export prices for Malawi's exporters. Instead of reducing direct or indirect export crop taxation, the government reduced producer prices of smallholder crops such as fire-cured tobacco (Figure 5.6). Moreover, in 1986/1987, the relative price of export crops to maize (the major food crop) declined as the influx of refugees from Mozambique led to sharp increases in maize demand and prices. Similarly, the real price of groundnuts, another major export crop, declined after 1987.

Failure to implement the envisaged reduction of taxation of smallholder export crops had adverse consequences on smallholder incomes and the economy in general. Simulations using an econometric model[18] of Malawi's agricultural sector suggest that eliminating smallholder taxes on tobacco and groundnuts would have raised production of these export crops by 65.8 percent relative to the base run. Maize production over the decade would have been approximately 5 percent below the base run, as producers would have

[18] The model, described in detail elsewhere (van Frausum and Sahn 1993), is composed of sixty stochastic equations and identities in five blocks: production, balance of payments, government finance, prices, and the monetary sector. In addition, a separate functional income distribution module was constructed that enabled the distribution of value-added among two groups of smallholders, estates, industry, construction, government, and other services, as well as between payments to labor and capital. In this classification, the poor are represented by smallholders with less than 1.5 hectares of land. These workers come from households that, according to household survey data, have incomes and expenditures per capita that are substantially less than all the others.

substituted more remunerative export crops.[19] Overall, the economy would have grown faster if the principles of export parity pricing had been adopted: GDP measured at factor cost would have been 4.4 percent higher throughout the 1980s and, despite the elimination of the export taxes, government revenue would have increased. Moreover, real incomes of the poorest smallholders would have risen by nearly 9.3 percent. Other groups of workers, including civil servants and construction workers, would lose as a consequence of such reforms, however, in part because lower maize availability leads to higher consumer prices. Likewise, the share of value-added accruing to capital would fall, possibly providing some insight into the failure to implement these important policy changes.

In the case of Zaire, policies like the overvalued exchange rate, high export duties, burdensome administrative requirements, and price controls all contributed to the generally poor performance of export agriculture. So, too, the legacy of Zairianization that led to the departure of (largely Belgian) management personnel and the deterioration of many plantations, had long-term adverse affects on export agriculture. In fact, with the exception of coffee, there is little evidence of increased production of export crops between 1970 and the years prior to Zaire's short-lived effort at reform in the mid-1980s. However, as with the other countries that followed similar practices, smuggling of export crops through parallel markets became the norm, making data on exports unreliable.

Zaire's first and most serious effort at economic reform was undertaken in 1982–1984, under the three-year Agricultural Recovery Plan. In addition to the trade and exchange rate reforms under the IMF stabilization program, price controls were eliminated, and agricultural markets were liberalized, contributing to substantial increases in real producer prices in many areas. However, implementation of reforms was uneven.[20] Regional and local authorities often proved unwilling to refrain from setting prices and taxing producers and thereby failed to encourage competition and reduce transaction costs of avoiding state harassment (Sines et al. 1987). Zaire's second, short-lived effort to reform agriculture occurred in 1987, in conjunction with the World Bank and IMF structural adjustment program. Besides the trade and exchange rate reforms that were designed to indirectly aid agriculture, the new rolling public investment program stipulated a major increase in the allocation of investment expenditures to agriculture (to 10 percent) and the supporting road network. In addition, the short-term credit ceilings that discourage agricultural lending were removed.

---

[19] The large change in export crop production in percentage terms reflects the initial small level of production relative to the size of maize production.

[20] See Tshishimbi and Glick 1993 for a fuller account of Zaire's adjustment efforts.

Any potential for achieving improved incentives for export crop production as a result of these reforms, however, was destroyed by the subsequent macro-economic and political instability. Other barriers to agricultural export growth remain as well, including high transaction costs arising from a lack of transport infrastructure, the continued regulation of export crop producers, and inadequate extension services.

Export crop policy in CFA countries

As in Ghana, Madagascar, and Tanzania, Cameroon taxed export crop producers heavily in the mid-1970s and early 1980s. Unlike other countries with discriminating policies, however, Cameroon's abundant oil revenues meant that the country was less reliant on foreign exchange earnings and tax revenues from coffee, cocoa, and other export crops. Nonetheless, the *bareme* system adversely affected Cameroon's export crop producers by setting prices and giving monopsonistic powers to export marketing parastatals, thus discouraging competition, keeping marketing costs high, and encouraging rent-seeking behavior.

Low world market prices for coffee and cocoa in the mid-1980s coincided with a sharp decline in world oil prices and Cameroon's economic crisis in the mid-1980s. In an increasingly tight fiscal situation, export crop producers could not be shielded from the world price decline through export subsidies or major reductions in marketing margins for parastatals. Instead, as part of adjustment efforts, agricultural marketing was liberalized and export crop marketing parastatals were eliminated. Moreover, the overvaluation of the CFA franc from the late 1980s through the devaluation of January 1994 worsened the effects of a decline in the dollar price of cocoa and coffee on world markets for Cameroon's producers. Thus, between 1986 and 1992, border prices of cocoa fell by 81.7 percent and real producer prices of cocoa fell 63.2 percent (Figure 5.7).

Simulations using a CGE model of Cameroon suggest that a 20 percent increase in producer prices of coffee and cocoa, achieved through a reduction in the export tax, would result in a 7 to 12 percent increase in export crop production over five years (Table 5.6). With the increase in exports, the real exchange rate would appreciate by 1.1 to 2.9 percent over its base run levels. In this simulation with nominal investment fixed and foreign savings endogenous, the trade balance improves with the increase in exports (reducing Cameroon's net borrowing). Farmers in southern Cameroon, where major export crops are grown, enjoy the largest gains in real incomes. This group includes poor farm households (21 percent of households nationwide), who enjoy a 2.7 to 5.1 percent increase in real incomes. With the decline in foreign capital inflows, however, urban households suffer declines in real incomes of 0.2 to 2.8 percent during the five years of the simulation (Subramanian 1994).

Table 5.6. *Cameroon: CGE model simulation of a reduction in the implicit tax on agricultural exports*

	Percentage change from base run				
	1985–1986	1986–1987	1987–1988	1988–1989	1989–1990
Real GDP	0.12	0.14	0.38	0.75	0.66
Real exchange rate	-2.12	-2.32	-2.90	-2.62	-1.14
Government revenue	1.43	1.70	2.20	2.61	1.50
Exports	4.15	5.31	4.96	5.52	2.96
Imports	1.49	1.49	1.90	2.35	1.35
Balance of trade	11.77	37.3	15.28	13.91	7.50
	(316)[a]	(618)	(237)	(265)	(224)
Real per capita income					
North farm poor	1.86	2.09	3.26	3.77	2.61
South farm poor	2.65	3.12	4.40	5.05	3.58
North and south farm rich	2.52	2.48	5.27	4.53	2.14
Rural nonfarm poor	-0.25	-0.30	-0.63	0.36	0.94
Rural nonfarm rich	-1.33	-1.53	-2.69	-1.65	-0.13
Urban poor	-1.30	-1.61	-2.70	-1.68	-0.24
Urban rich	-1.66	-1.83	-2.82	-1.83	-0.33

[a]Balance of trade in billion CFAF.
Source: Subramanian 1996.

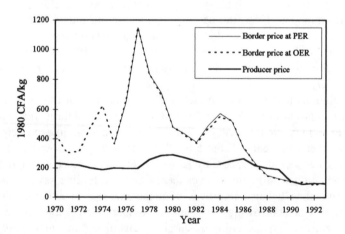

Figure 5.7. Cameroon: real cocoa prices, 1970–1992. PER = parallel exchange rate; OER = official exchange rate. *Source:* IMF 1994d.

Reforms related to agricultural exports were of minor importance in Niger because the initial distortions were small and because these exports accounted for only a small share of foreign exchange revenues, only 24 percent in 1987, even accounting for parallel market trade (Dorosh and Essama-Nssah 1991). Membership in the CFA zone helped avoid the problems of a seriously over-valued currency (at least until the late 1980s). Equally important, most trade in livestock and cowpeas, the two main agricultural exports, took place infor-mally, across the long, relatively open border with Nigeria.[21] Thus, collecting revenues and influencing domestic prices through taxation of these exports is not a viable option. Prior to the onset of the structural adjustment program in the early 1980s, export taxes of 8 percent on cattle and 20 percent on cowpeas were levied. These taxes failed to generate substantial revenues and further dis-couraged exports through legal channels (already hindered by cumbersome administrative procedures). They were finally eliminated as part of trade reforms in 1988. The monopoly of the largely ineffective cowpea and ground-nut marketing agency (SONARA) was ended in 1984, though not until the early 1990s was this parastatal finally closed (Jabara 1991).

Given the dominance of Nigeria in Niger's agricultural export trade, macro-economic policy in Nigeria has a major impact on the cowpea and livestock sectors. Between 1985 and 1988, the real exchange rate (i.e., the relative price of the CFA to naira) appreciated by 37.7 percent on the parallel market as Nigeria undertook macroeconomic reforms in response to lower world petro-leum prices. As a direct result of the fall in price in CFA terms, Niger's export revenues fell by CFAF 13 billion per year, equal to 3.5 percent of rural income in 1987 (Dorosh 1994a). In CGE simulations of a 30 percent appreciation of the CFA/naira parallel exchange rate, the volumes of exports of cowpea and livestock fall by 12.8 and 16.8 percent, respectively, and total export values in CFA terms decline by 8.7 percent (Table 5.7). With the decline in export earn-ings, the CFA per dollar real exchange rate depreciates by 8.9 percent. Largely as a result of the decline in cowpea and livestock prices and exports, real incomes of rural households fall by 2.0 to 2.3 percent (Dorosh and Essama-Nssah 1993). Nonetheless, prior to the devaluation of the CFA franc in January 1994, and in the absence of an effective way of taxing cross-border trade, Niger's government had no trade or exchange rate policy lever with which to avoid these adverse effects on rural households.

---

[21] Using figures on Nigeria's imports of cattle, Cook (1989) estimates that only about 10 percent of Niger's cattle exports to Nigeria in 1987 went through official channels. Based on this and other data, Dorosh and Essama-Nssah (1991) estimate that 80 per-cent of the value of total livestock exports and 90 percent of cowpea exports in 1987 went through parallel market channels.

Table 5.7. *Niger: CGE model simulation of an appreciation of the CFA/naira parallel exchange rate*

	Base level[a]	30% appreciation (% change)
GDP	681.5	-0.1
Consumption	518.2	-1.2
Total investment	103.2	6.6
Private investment	48.2	18.6
Public investment	55.0	0.0
Government consumption	109.0	0.0
Government revenues	65.9	10.3
Real exchange rate index	100.0	8.9
Exports	144.9	-8.7
Imports	193.8	-6.7
Foreign savings	48.9	0.0
Sectoral production		
Cereals	70.9	0.3
Export crops	23.8	-8.0
Other crops	56.8	0.2
Livestock	84.8	-0.7
Manufacturing	84.6	1.4
Total production	968.1	0.1
Household incomes		
Urban high income	414.5	0.2
Urban low income	159.9	-1.9
Semiurban	59.8	-1.4
Rural north high income	115.5	-2.3
Rural north low income	49.0	-2.0
Rural south high income	67.8	-2.3
Rural south low income	49.2	-2.1
Total	79.9	-1.7

[a]Base level values in billion 1987 CFAF, except for income values in thousand CFAF/capital.
Source: Dorosh and Essama-Nssah 1991, 1993.

General equilibrium effects of reducing export taxes:
a comparative analysis

The country histories outlined here make clear that terms-of-trade shocks and the degree of export crop tax reduction varied widely. How export crop producers were affected by economic reforms depends not only on world price movements and government policies, but also on the structures of the individual economies, especially the share of agricultural exports in foreign exchange earnings and government revenues and the distribution of export crop earnings across households.

To highlight the implications of country-specific characteristics apart from movements in terms of trade, we show in Table 5.8 the results of CGE simulations modeling the elimination of agricultural exports taxes [22] while holding foreign savings fixed. The initial level of export taxes, measured as a percentage of the producer price, ranged from 20.0 percent in The Gambia and Niger to 72.0 percent in Madagascar. In the simulations, real government revenues remain unchanged as direct taxes on all households and firms are raised by an equal percentage of income to compensate for the loss of export tax revenues. This offsetting tax increase maintains revenue neutrality in a distributionally neutral way, so that the simulation results are due to changes in export taxation and not to a change in overall fiscal balance.

Exports rise by 0.22 (The Gambia) to 1.36 percent (Cameroon) of real GDP due to the improved price incentives for export. [23] Real GDP increases slightly in each country, from 0.06 in Niger to 1.09 percent in Cameroon. Investment also rises slightly, except in Niger, where the removal of an export tax on cattle reduces expenditures on cattle as an investment good. In all countries except Tanzania, the major beneficiaries of the export tax reduction are the rural poor, who are among the major export crop producers. In Tanzania, returns to capital and land from tree crops account for only 0.4 percent of incomes for the rural poor as a group (even though the rural poor receive 37.0 percent of the total returns to capital from tree crops). Thus, increased returns from tree crops have only small effects on the incomes of the rural poor, and their real incomes rise by only 1.7 percent (before taxes) and actually fall by 0.4 percent after taxes. [24] Similarly, urban poor households would enjoy a gain of 2.0 percent in real incomes apart from the increase in direct taxes.

Urban groups also suffer small declines in real pretax incomes in The Gambia and Cameroon. In The Gambia, the real exchange rate appreciation contributes to declines in the reexport trade and formal trade sectors. In Cameroon, the large increase (4.12 percent) in direct taxes on households reduces demand for income-elastic private services, lowering returns to capital and real wages in urban areas. In general, however, elimination of export taxes leads to only

---

[22] In Niger and The Gambia, where there were no export taxes on agricultural products in the base year, the base SAM results were compared with simulations of the imposition of an ad valorem export tax equal to 20 percent of the producer price.

[23] The large increase in Cameroon results in large measure because of a shift in utilization of export crop production away from consumption and intermediate use and toward exports.

[24] Since in aggregate this large household group accounts for 39.2 percent of household incomes, their share of the direct tax increase required to offset the loss of export tax revenues is greater than their share of the increased returns to capital from export crops.

Table 5.8. *General equilibrium impacts of elimination of export taxes: model simulations*

	Percentage change[a]				
	Cameroon	Gambia	Madagascar	Niger	Tanzania
Agricultural export commodities	Coffee, cocoa	Ground- nuts	Tree crops	Cowpeas, cattle	Tree crops
Change in export tax/ producer price	-38.03	-20.00	-72.00	-20.00	-26.46
Real GDP	1.09	0.18	0.79	0.06	0.48
Consumption/GDP	0.48	-0.05	0.78	0.31	0.14
Total investment/GDP	0.62	0.23	0.02	-0.25	0.33
Government recurrent expenditures/GDP	0.00	0.00	0.00	0.00	0.00
Government revenue/GDP	0.00	0.00	0.00	0.00	0.00
Exports/GDP[b]	1.36	0.22	0.85	0.51	0.60
Imports/GDP[b]	1.36	0.22	0.85	0.51	0.60
Change in foreign savings/GDP[b]	0.00	0.00	0.00	0.00	0.00
Real exchange rate	-12.73	-1.96	-10.30	-3.07	-8.17
Real wage rates					
Skilled labor	2.02	-0.36	2.64	1.23	-1.67
Semiskilled labor	1.12	-1.28	2.30	—	—
Unskilled labor	10.01	5.46	4.65	2.19	5.96
Real incomes					
Direct tax	4.12	1.00	1.57	0.92	2.10
Urban nonpoor	-8.20	-1.96	1.72	0.63	0.36
Urban poor	-1.27	-1.97	2.67	0.79	-0.06
Rural nonpoor	2.87	2.15	0.98	0.33	0.63
Rural poor	2.24	2.25	2.16	0.81	-0.35
Small farm – export-oriented	—	—	4.93	0.64	—
Total	0.30	-0.07	1.78	0.60	0.14

[a]Percentage change relative to base simulation.
[b]Exports and imports valued at the base simulation real exchange rate.
Sources: Model simulations.

small changes in real incomes for most households, while more significantly benefiting small farmers, particularly those who produce export crops.

Cash crops, nutrition, and gender

Although the evidence indicates that higher producer prices and other incentives to increase export crop production usually benefit the poor, a concern remains that these policies may adversely affect food security and nutrition through two mechanisms. First, there may be a reduction in food production and availability due to the shift to export crops. Second, the welfare of women and children may decline even if cash cropping contributes to higher household incomes,[25] as these benefits are not shared equally within the household. This latter situation may occur, for example, to the extent that male labor and other inputs are diverted from food production to export crop production, while the burden of maintaining food production at the household level falls primarily on women (Haddad 1990; Meena 1991); or to the extent that women's direct control over income is reduced and men's preferences result in their allocating a smaller share of resources to food, or the health and nutritional needs of women and children.

Regarding the issue of food versus cash crops, there is no evidence from country-specific data on agricultural output that increasing export crop production and decreasing food production occur simultaneously. In countries showing upward trends in export crop production, in fact, this is generally accompanied by increases in food crop production. This pattern reflects in part that relative prices of export to food crops have not shifted dramatically, as discussed earlier. But more important, since factor use is not fixed, when the economic incentive structure and nonprice environment (e.g., market infrastructure, technology, credit) for agriculture improves, this will contribute to an overall increase in resources and inputs used in both food and export crop production (von Braun and Kennedy 1986; Weber et al. 1988; Lele and Adu-Nyako 1992). For example, agricultural market liberalization and real exchange rate depreciation will not only increase the incentives to produce export crops, but many food products as well since many are tradable (Dorosh and Sahn 1993).

Though trends in aggregate production statistics at the country level often show that food and cash crop output move in the same direction for the reasons already discussed, farmers do substitute between crops in response to price signals.[26] Critics worry, however, that even if higher incomes result from increased commercialization of agriculture, adverse nutritional effects may ensue. The loss of control of income by, and greater labor burdens for, women,

---

[25] The potentially adverse effects of incentives for export crops are but one aspect of structural adjustment programs criticized for their reputed effects on women and children. See Elson 1991, Due and Gladwin 1991, Mehra 1991, Nindi 1992, and Saito and Spurling 1992.

[26] Von Braun and Kennedy (1994), however, do discuss the reluctance to abandon subsistence production, even among smallholders engaged in commercial production since it represents a form of self-insurance against food insecurity in the volatile environments in which they live. This undoubtedly reduces the substitution elasticities between crops grown primarily for subsistence and the crops grown for the market. Indeed, further development of insurance and financial markets that reduce risk and transaction costs may free producers from this strategy, enabling fuller market integration and income gains from commercialization.

are given as reasons for this concern. For example, critics argue that because of a failure to identify correctly the household member responsible for crop production, some agricultural projects that provided inputs to men inadvertently reduced women's control over cash income. Projects such as the groundnut seed multiplication project in Malawi (Gladwin and McMillan 1989), the tea scheme in Tanzania (Elson 1991), and the irrigation and rice cultivation project in The Gambia (Carney 1988) caused women to lose their cash crop and/or the income generated by cash crops. In Ghana and Côte d'Ivoire, limited access to land and heavier time commitments to household work led to the erosion of female income when cash crops were integrated into existing agricultural activities (Haddad 1990).

In light of these experiences with agricultural projects, several country studies have been undertaken to determine the impact of an increase in the share of income from cash crops on nutrition. For example, in the case of Malawi, Sahn, Van Frausum, and Shively (1994) show that a shift to export crop production has no deleterious effects on nutrition, regardless of the gender of the household head.[27] In fact, the analysis suggests that the average height-for-age z-score of children younger than five years would improve by 0.36 as a result of eliminating taxation on tobacco.

Similarly, in Côte d'Ivoire, econometric analysis of household expenditure data suggests that reduced taxes on export crops during the 1970s and early 1980s would have resulted in positive nutritional benefits for the poor (Sahn 1992). This effect is attributable to two factors. First, households in the bottom two quintiles of the per capita expenditure distribution are extensively engaged in the production of export crops, resulting in higher incomes when taxation is reduced. Second, the nutritional status of households engaged in export crop production was comparable with those engaged in food crop production, controlling for other pertinent factors, including the level of income. Thus, eliminating the tax on cocoa and coffee would have not only raised incomes of households, but conferred positive nutritional benefits, indicating no adverse shift in resource control and/or utilization in the wake of changing patterns of production.

Such findings, while not universal, are consistent with the general results from other country studies reported by von Braun and Kennedy (1994). Their review indicates that cash crop production usually confers positive benefits on households in terms of increased incomes, although such benefits are not

---

[27] In Malawi, female-headed households in the densely populated southern region of the country comprise around 30 percent of households. Almost all are households without a male spouse in residence, either because the spouse is employed elsewhere (e.g., in South Africa or on estates in Malawi) or because of divorce or death of the spouse. Controlling for income and other covariates, gender of headship has no effect on nutrition, regardless of the reason for the husband being absent.

always sustained for reasons such as adverse terms-of-trade shocks. Higher incomes were also found to lead to higher spending on food, although the next link, from increased food expenditures to improved nutritional (i.e., anthropometric) outcomes among children, was weak. This weak link seems to suggest that deficits in household food consumption were not the major constraint in improving child nutrition. Instead preventative and curative health care, which in the short term was not enhanced as a result of higher incomes from commercialization, along with issues of intrahousehold allocation, seemed to be paramount. In the medium term, however, increased wealth from cash-cropping will provide the means to improve community health infrastructure, and thus nutrition (von Braun and Kennedy 1994).

While it is therefore safe to conclude that worsening food security and nutrition will generally not result from increased cash crop production, the more important point is that the underlying sector growth and welfare objectives will both be met by outward-looking agricultural policies, complemented by a broad range of investments. These include improved access to agricultural technology and extension; an enhanced road, market, and information infrastructure; promotion of self-financing rural credit schemes; and revised land tenure arrangements that encourage investment and improve security (Binswanger and von Braun 1991). At the same time, particular attention to overcoming any social or legal impediments that contribute to gender bias will reduce the extent to which women face discrimination in the access to services, land, and the general benefits of commercialization of agriculture. Such efforts to ensure that women participate in the benefits of commercialization will not only benefit the poor, but enhance overall growth objectives as well, an issue we return to at the end of this chapter.

Domestic food crop liberalization

Although often not as successful as export crop policies in affecting producer prices, government interventions in food markets in Africa are almost equally widespread. Historically, government involvement in food markets was first and foremost intended to keep consumer prices in the urban areas low and stable, thus ensuring constant and plentiful supplies of crucial wage goods. A secondary objective of state intervention was to protect the farmer from the vagaries of private marketing agents. The poor performance of agriculture coupled with the changing paradigm of development toward greater reliance on markets, however, has contributed to widespread efforts to liberalize agriculture and food markets in African countries. Reforms have fundamentally been intended to remove the restrictions that impede the transmission of market-determined prices of food crops from the farm-gate to consumers. Most notable have been attempts of adjustment programs to reduce the role of monopsonistic marketing boards responsible for procurement from farmers, processing, transportation, and even sales in retail markets.

Just as reforms of export crop pricing have wide-ranging impacts on the macroeconomy and household incomes, food crop liberalization has important sectoral, food security, and household welfare implications. Food plays a dual role, serving both as a source of income for rural producers and as a wage good for urban and rural households. The conflicts between these roles define the classic food policy dilemma that confronts efforts to liberalize markets: the need to maintain or restore incentive prices for producers, while keeping staple food prices low for urban and rural consumers. At the same time, the performance of the food sector, like export crops, is linked with both internal and external balances because, first, the large food deficits that characterize much of Africa are addressed through imports, both concessional and otherwise, and, second, government involvement in food markets has in some cases strained the treasury of African countries. The budgetary costs associated with supporting inefficient marketing parastatals, and explicitly subsidizing producers and/or consumers, have proved not only fiscally unsustainable but all too often ineffectual in achieving stated food security objectives.

From a welfare point of view, the process of state disengagement in food marketing raises two major concerns – one for farmers and the other for consumers. In the case of the former, the pertinent question regarding liberalization is whether and how private sector agents will fill the gap left by the departure of parastatal buyers. To the extent that the model of exploitative private traders and poorly integrated and inefficient markets is applicable, farmers' opportunities to sell their surplus at remunerative prices might decline. In addressing this concern, the major issues are (1) whether in fact farmers benefit, or are penalized by their reliance on parastatals; and (2) whether private markets for food commodities function well in Africa. For consumers, the question is whether liberalization will harm the poor as subsidies are removed. The key issue is whether they had access to goods at subsidized prices prior to liberalization.

In order to address these questions, we must first determine whether food is rationed at the state-determined official price. To the extent that the marketing board guarantees universal access to consumers, such that the marginal price is the same as the official price, the benefits of the subsidy will accrue to households in proportion to their consumption of the product. The distribution of costs will depend on whether the subsidy is implicit or explicit. In the case of the former, procurement at below the parity price, combined with imports as required to meet demand, will keep farm-gate prices low, thereby depressing producer incomes. If, on the other hand, an explicit subsidy from the treasury drives a wedge between the producer price and the consumer price, the financial costs are determined by who pays the taxes that finance the budget.

A further complication arises, however, when state procurement and imports fail to meet demand at the official price, a case that is not only the norm, but is also quite analogous to the discussion of foreign exchange rationing in Chapter 3. When the state intervenes to subsidize prices, rationing is likely to occur due to supply shortfalls at the official price. On the one hand, if the cost of keeping official prices low is borne by the farmer, the incentives to produce and market output are greatly reduced. On the other hand, if the treasury pays the cost of supporting parastatals that subsidize the cost of marketing, thereby allowing farmers to receive remunerative prices, the prospect arises that constrained budgetary resources will limit the amount of food procured and sold at official prices. In either case, the consequence is rationing, since demand at the official price exceeds supply. In such a case, the key consideration is who gets access to the subsidized product and who is forced into the parallel market where prices are higher than in the official market.

Before examining the critical issue of how market liberalization affects the poor, it is useful first to recognize that not all countries in sub-Saharan Africa intervened to the same extent in food markets. In fact, one can identify three categories of market intervention: (1) a laissez-faire approach to domestic food marketing with only limited roles for parastatals; (2) government involvement in setting product prices at different levels of the marketing chain for key staples, without explicit food rationing; and (3) extensive involvement not only in procurement and various efforts to administer prices, but also in the resale of goods in rationing schemes. In the remainder of this section we discuss which of the countries covered in this book fall into these three categories.

Limited parastatal involvement in food markets

In Cameroon, The Gambia, Ghana, Niger, and Zaire, government involvement in domestic food marketing has been limited and largely ineffective. Unlike the major rice-growing countries of West Africa and Madagascar, or much of eastern and southern Africa where maize is the major staple, no food grain dominates national consumption in these four countries. Instead, domestically produced root crops (e.g., cassava, yams, and sweet potatoes) and coarse grains (e.g., millet and sorghum) account for most of the food consumption, leaving food grains with a secondary role in national food supplies. This more diverse diet lessens the economy-wide implications of government interventions in any one crop. Moreover, government attempts to influence producer prices through market purchases have generally been too small to have a significant effect on market supply or prices, even for individual crops. Exceptions to the general ineffectiveness of government interventions in food markets in these countries, however, are government regulations and tariffs affecting imported rice in Cameroon, The Gambia, and Niger, which have had important impacts on consumer prices.

In Cameroon, state involvement in food markets of the traditional, or peasant farming, sector is virtually nil, despite the large size of these markets and the importance of the sector in total food consumption. These small farms, producing plantains, and roots and tubers in southern Cameroon, maize in the west, and millet and sorghum in the north, market between 25 and 50 percent of their output and account for the large majority of national food supply (Blandford and Lynch 1990).

In contrast, Cameroon's government was quite active in the production and marketing of rice in ways that had little direct benefit to the poor, at high budgetary costs. The state's role in rice policy went far beyond marketing and included capital intensive investments in irrigation projects in the north under the overall watch of the rice production and marketing parastatal Semry (Société d'Expansion et de Modernisation de la Riziculture de Yagoua) (World Bank 1989a). Despite the negligible importance of rice in the national food basket, and Cameroon's lack of comparative advantage and experience in rice production, bilateral donors and the World Bank invested very substantial resources in irrigated rice under the guise of promoting self-sufficiency and foreign exchange savings. In light of the largely metropolitan demand for rice consumption, some see this action as an urban-biased development strategy where cheap food was a crucial policy objective. Van de Walle (1989) argues, however, that the misguided production and marketing policies in the rice sector were primarily motivated by a combination of rent-seeking, misguided ideologies in terms of modernization and self-sufficiency, and weak administrative capacity.

The high costs of rice production, and the consequent accumulation of stocks because domestically produced rice was not competitive with imports, made clear the need to address the budgetary demands and institutional failure of Semry. The policy response initially involved imposing tariffs on rice imports, with part of the proceeds financing attempts to make Semry more competitive. Tax revenues, however, turned out to be very limited, largely due to the corrupt implementation of the new system and the unabated rice smuggling. Thus, the stabilization fund, undertaken in the name of reform, became corrupted itself, leading to a further call for the liberalization of the pricing and marketing of rice.

State intervention in the nonrice food sector in The Gambia, like Cameroon, has been of relatively minor importance, particularly in comparison with the active role of government in The Gambia's groundnut sector. Millet, maize, and sorghum dominate agricultural production, accounting for 85 percent of domestic grain production in 1987 (Jabara 1990), yet government policy interventions in food grains have focused on rice, a major staple for urban consumers that is imported in large quantities.[28] Prior to the Economic Recovery

---

[28] Rice imports in 1987 were nearly double domestic production of millet, maize, and sorghum (Jabara 1990), though USAID (1989) estimates that about 50 percent of this rice is reexported (mainly to Senegal).

Program (ERP) reforms, the government attempted to stabilize the retail price of rice, a major staple for urban consumers. At that time, the Gambia Produce Marketing Board (GPMB) held a monopoly on rice imports and wholesale distribution and sold rice in the wholesale market at official prices.

Rice markets were liberalized in June 1985 when all controls on rice prices were abolished and all restrictions on the participation of the private sector in rice trade and marketing were eliminated. Retail rice prices rose by 62 percent between July and December 1985 and another 77 percent by March 1986 following the liberalization and subsequent depreciation of the dalasis in January (Jabara 1990). Fortunately, a decline in world prices of rice at that time cushioned the effects of these exchange rate devaluations, helping make the adjustment program more politically palatable (Radelet 1992). For the January 1985 to December 1986 period as a whole, quarterly average rice prices rose only slightly relative to nonfood consumer prices (Jabara 1990), in part because in 1988/1989 import duties on rice, which had equaled as much as 30 percent in 1986/1987, were eliminated.

CGE model simulations of the effects of a reduction in the import tariff on rice from 30 percent to 10 percent show that real incomes of both urban poor and nonpoor households rise (by 1.1 and 0.4 percent, respectively) as the cost of one of their major consumable goods falls. Likewise, the rural poor, for whom rice constitutes an even larger share of the expenditures, enjoy a 1.4 percent increase in real incomes. Because rice is a small share of national production and rural incomes, the change in tariff has little effect on agricultural production. However, the loss of tariff revenues reduces total available savings and investment by 2.4 percent, suggesting an important potential trade-off between current consumption and future incomes (Dorosh and Lundberg 1996).

In Niger, prior to reforms, the government set producer and consumer prices of major agricultural products in official markets. However, the scale of market interventions was too small to have a significant impact on prices of millet and sorghum, the two major staples. Official producer prices were below market prices in bad harvest years; in good years between 1971 and 1983, the Office des Produits Vivriers du Niger (OPVN) purchased only 3 to 6 percent of total production (Berg and Associates 1983; Borsdorf 1979). Nonetheless, the OPVN became a substantial drain on the treasury by the early 1980s due to inefficiencies, an inadequate spread between purchase and sales prices, and the cost of maintaining a large food security stock.[29] Agricultural market reforms in 1983 and 1984 reduced the number of OPVN personnel and buying centers and ended its monopolies on cereal purchases. Two years later, OPVN's operations were limited to managing an 80,000-ton grain security stock, to be sup-

---

[29] Average annual operational losses of the OPVN between 1975 and 1983 were equal to 16.7 percent of 1983 government capital expenditures (Berg and Associates 1983; Dorosh 1994a).

plied through a bid-and-tenders system, rather than procurement at fixed official prices (Jabara 1991). These steps toward liberalization of the coarse grain
markets had little effect on consumer or producer welfare, however, since the
parastatals had little effect on market prices.[30]

Government pricing policy had a larger impact on actual prices received by
rice farmers, who cultivate paddy only on farms alongside the Niger River.
More than 75 percent of total production derives from large irrigated perimeters, and user fees paid to producers' cooperatives in the form of rice valued at
the official price enabled the government to capture a market share of approximately one-third in the mid-1980s. Official producer prices were generally
above or equal to border prices in the mid- to late 1980s, despite the lowering
of producer prices by 30 percent in 1987 in response to a fall in import prices
in world markets. Consumer prices were kept in excess of border prices
through import tariffs and other taxes on rice, equal to 33.4 percent in 1989
(Dorosh 1994a).[31]

The performance of Zaire's food crop sector, like the rest of agriculture, was
extremely poor throughout the late 1960s and 1970s. The overvalued exchange
rate, price controls, and subsidies on food imports were important contributors
to the food sector's postindependence failures. It was not until the first round
of economic reforms in 1982 that agriculture began to turn around. The recovery plan consisted of price, marketing, and exchange rate reforms with the
overall objective of increasing incentives and strengthening institutions, such
as those engaged in research, extension, and training. In practice, the implementation of these reforms across regions was uneven. Local authorities often
resisted policy change, presumably concerned about the loss of control over
commerce and a diminished ability to capture rents. Nonetheless, the elimination of price controls and the large exchange rate devaluation that occurred in
1983 did improve producer prices in many regions; where this occurred, output
increased, displaying the farmer's responsiveness to price signals. Overall,
however, while the food crop sector performed better after these partial
reforms, the magnitude of increase in output was generally disappointing. This
weak responsiveness in turn contributed to the formulation of the 1987 structural adjustment program and the 1986–1990 development plan, both of which
emphasized measures to remove institutional and infrastructural constraints in
transport and marketing, credit, and technology. The implementation of the

---

[30] Humphreys (1986) also points out how prices of staple commodities fell in Mali after
market liberalization.

[31] Prior to 1989, consumer prices were boosted by a requirement that importers purchase
minimum quantities of locally procured rice from Riz du Niger (RINI), a parastatal. In
1992, the government removed import licensing requirements for rice and abolished a
system of authorized dealers for specific commodities.

policy changes proposed under the 1987 adjustment program was very weak and so too was the overall performance of the economy. Roads to be built with the intent of reducing the exorbitant costs of transport were never completed, and maintenance of whatever roads did exist was grossly neglected (Tshishimbi and Glick 1993). Thus, overall, efforts to improve the incentives and reduce transaction costs were sporadic and partial, resulting in few benefits for producers and the rural economy.

Perhaps the only relatively positive outcome of Zaire's food policies was that open-market urban consumer prices remained stable in real terms. This reflected the substantial growth in imports that met the growing urban demand, particularly in Kinshasa. The high rate of inflation after the breakdown of reforms, however, did imply real income losses for large segments of the population. Furthermore, the fact that a country as rich in natural resources as Zaire was not able to meet the food requirements of its urban population underscores the failure of both the policies that led to Zaire's economic decline and the subsequent aborted attempts to invest in agriculture and infrastructure.

State intervention in Ghana's food markets was also limited, although the issue of the impact of liberalization, particularly on food prices and access, was of concern. We are particularly interested in understanding the impact of devaluation on prices of imported food products, as well as the indirect effects of liberalization on the costs of commodity marketing, the price level, and volatility.

Findings indicate that prices of major staple foods, both at the retail and wholesale level, declined between 1984 and 1990. In fact, the rate of decline in prices was more rapid than in the 1970s and early 1980s when prices too were falling (except for drought periods), in keeping with world price trends. Although weather may have contributed to moderating prices since the beginning of the adjustment program, another factor has been the reduction in marketing costs. Improved roads, parts for trucks, and so forth have reduced the costs of transport and thereby food. At the same time, contrary to the concerns raised over the impact of exchange rate reforms, indications are that there was a weak relationship between devaluation and increased food prices. Using an alternative model for food prices, a devaluation of 100 percent was found to translate into only an 8 percent food price increase. This is explained first by the parallel market premium prior to devaluation, as discussed in Chapter 3. However, second was the fact that in Ghana, few important commodities in the consumption bundle were traded on international markets (Alderman and Shively 1996).

Overall, the analysis of food markets in Ghana indicates that they behave efficiently. Markets are well integrated in the sense that prices are transmitted across markets and commodities relatively quickly. Furthermore, there is some evidence that price instability has been reduced concurrent with the broad set

of economic reforms. Thus, liberalization efforts in the context of broader economic reforms have not represented a threat to the food security of the poor as
mediated through higher commodity prices. Instead, liberalization has contributed to improved efficiency, reduced price volatility, and moderating
prices, with the consequent welfare gains for consumers and producer (Alderman and Shively 1996).

Government interventions without food rationing

In a number of countries in East Africa, including Tanzania and
Malawi, governments have intervened heavily in maize markets, without
resorting to extensive or explicit quantitative rationing. Liberalization efforts in
these two countries have been laconic and prolonged, largely reflecting the difficulty of abandoning government direct intervention in food markets amid
official skepticism about the role of private traders in ensuring food security.
Yet, the institutional weakness of the state grain marketing agencies contributed to enormous financial losses for these agencies, high marketing margins, and policies that benefited neither consumers nor producers.

The government of Tanzania intervened heavily in food markets, particularly after the Arusha declaration of 1967. Initially, official prices set for the
"scheduled crops" (maize, paddy, wheat, oilseeds, cashew nuts, and cotton)
varied by region as the government fixed the final delivery "into store
price." The National Milling Corporation (NMC), a parastatal given responsibility for grain marketing in 1973, subtracted off estimated marketing costs
specific to each region in determining prices paid to farmers. For the
1974/1975 crop season, the list of "scheduled crops" was expanded to
include sorghum, millet, and cassava, and "panterritorial" producer prices
were set for all "scheduled crops." Then in 1976, the government adopted
the failed policy of nationalizing village retail shops, once again in response
to the perception that private commercial trade was exploitative (Sarris and
van den Brink 1993). Shortages of consumer goods, rationing of existing
supplies, and reduced incentives for rural producers resulted (Bevan et al.
1989). Limited availability of foreign exchange in the early 1980s (due to
declining terms of trade, as well as government trade and exchange rate policies, discussed in Chapter 3) further contributed to this inadequate supply of
consumer goods, as well as to shortages in vehicles needed for the transport
of goods to and from rural areas.

As the rural marketing system broke down, it became increasingly difficult
for the NMC to provide adequate supplies of maize to urban populations. Official producer prices were below those in the parallel market reducing the
NMC's purchases, and, with official consumer prices less than parallel market
prices, there was excess demand in urban areas. Rather than substantially raise

both producer and consumer prices in the official market, Tanzania resorted to large maize imports and an explicit subsidy on maize flour (*sembe*) in 1980. Meanwhile, the *sembe* subsidy proved extremely costly, accounting for 2.2 percent of total government expenditures over a four-year period, before being abandoned in 1984. That the *sembe* subsidy was abolished without the expected urban riots or a massive public outcry suggests that most households had been relying on parallel markets rather than official markets for their maize flour (Sarris and van den Brink 1994).

With the removal of the *sembe* subsidy in 1984, private traders were allowed to buy and sell greater amounts of maize. The trade liberalization in 1985 further improved marketing efficiency by enabling own-funded imports of trucks and spare parts. Restrictions on interregional grain trade were relaxed and eventually eliminated in 1987. As a result of these reforms, consumer prices of food (an index of maize, rice, and bean prices) fell by over 50 percent in real terms in parallel markets between 1983 and 1985, raising real incomes of food-deficit poor households (Sarris and van den Brink 1993; Amani et al. 1988). Incentives for production improved as well, as rural producer prices rose in many regions and more consumers and investment goods were available in rural markets.

Nonetheless, the government attempted to maintain its system of guaranteed producer prices through purchases by the NMC through local cooperative unions. However, with good weather and improved marketing efficiency in the parallel market leading to increased market supplies, official prices of maize were higher than parallel market prices in more remote maize-producing regions over the 1985–1987 period. As a result, NMC stocks of maize in these regions accumulated, leading eventually to subsidized sales of maize flour in December 1988 and huge losses for the NMC and local cooperative unions in 1988/1989 and 1989/1990. To stem the heavy financial losses, the government of Tanzania prohibited the NMC from undertaking nonprofitable operations in 1990, virtually halting the parastatal's market activities. In its stead, private traders were gradually given more freedom, finally being legally allowed to buy crops from individual farmers in September 1990, for the first time since 1967 (Sarris and van den Brink 1994).

Despite these improvements, a survey of private grain traders in 1991 indicated that many impediments still remained to improving grain market efficiency. High on this list is the uncertainty surrounding the state's actions, which contributes to the reluctance of traders to invest in business assets, such as storage structures. Promoting state disengagement from the inappropriate roles it assumed in the past does not mean the state should not assume appropriate responsibilities. Particularly, its involvement is vital in the infrastructure (e.g., roads and information networks) that will enhance the workings of the private market (Amani, van den Brink, and Maro 1992).

As in Tanzania, the maize market in Malawi has also been liberalized. In the period prior to reform, Malawi's maize market was characterized by extensive state control, including procurement and distribution of output by the agricultural parastatal, ADMARC. Food security objectives were the purported reason for state intervention, both in terms of maintaining stable and reasonable consumer prices and in providing an outlet for smallholder producers to market their maize and other food crops. While there was little evidence of extensive taxation of maize producers, prior to reform the explicit subsidy of consumer prices was substantial. Table 5.9 shows that the markup between the price paid to farmers and the official consumer price has not been adequate to cover all the costs associated with the marketing of maize. In fact, the value of this subsidy varied between Malawi Kwacha (MK) 15.53 to 62.28 per metric ton during the 1980s, or between a total of MK 2.25 and 9.77 million, in real 1980 terms. As a share of GDP this subsidy was quite significant, being between 0.22 and 0.94 percent and, similarly, between 0.74 and 3.19 percent of total government spending.

Thus, the rate and level of explicit consumer price subsidy were high. The continued subsidization of food contributed to low and moderate prices throughout most of the decade. It was not until the 1990s, when the process of economic reform entered its second decade, that government reduced subsidies through increasing consumer prices and that private trade in maize was sanctioned and grew important in the maize market. Higher prices also ensued, although the drought in 1992 certainly contributed to these increases.

While the late 1980s witnessed reforms that allowed private trade in maize from the farm gate to the consumer, the government has been extremely slow in eliminating the crucial role of ADMARC in the maize market (Scarborough 1994). While no reliable household data enable a determination of the precise impact of the maintenance of the consumer subsidy on poverty, factors suggest that at best, ADMARC was an inefficient mechanism of promoting food security. First, throughout the past decade, long prior to liberalization, an active open market for maize purchases existed. The open-market price was, in general, substantially below (e.g., 20–75 percent) the official ADMARC price, even in the capital, Lilongwe. The divergence between official and parallel market prices increased between the post- and preharvest period, as private traders passed on the costs of intertemporal arbitrage to the consumer, while the parastatal adhered to panseasonal pricing.

There are several reasons to expect that the rural poor had only limited access to official prices. First, the quantities in which ADMARC sold maize were far greater than most of the poor could afford to purchase. Second, the distance to ADMARC distribution settlements generally reduced access for those least able to travel due to financial and related time constraints. Third, there were indications that shortages emerged, and rationing became even

Table 5.9. *ADMARC maize subsidy*

	Subsidy (1980 MK) per MT	Quantity of ADMARC sales (MT)	Total subsidy		Subsidy as % of	
			MK	1980 MK	GDP	Total expenditure
1980	55.40	136,849	7,581,435	7,581,435	0.75	2.45
1981	57.32	95,821	6,151,708	5,492,597	0.56	1.66
1982	67.76	84,212	7,018,228	5,705,876	0.56	2.17
1983	16.72	134,885	3,134,727	2,555,200	0.22	0.74
1984	31.83	174,678	9,284,136	5,559,363	0.54	1.98
1985	38.93	115,460	8,315,429	4,494,827	0.43	1.54
1986	15.35	246,860	7,995,795	3,789,476	0.36	1.35
1987	49.31	198,108	25,789,699	9,768,826	0.94	3.19
1988	62.28	102,399	20,407,097	6,377,218	0.55	2.87

Sources: Kandoole et al. n.d.; Reserve Bank of Malawi 1987, 1988.

more severe during periods of peak demand. Smallholders in rural areas would tend to be most harshly affected by such a situation, as maize availability in the major urban areas was accorded greatest priority by ADMARC. In sum, although a paucity of data precludes any precise measurement of access to the subsidized maize, it seems likely that the poor were among the beneficiaries but that the nonpoor received a disproportionate share of the benefits. After a decade of reform, progress has been made in terms of reducing the fiscal burden of state procurement and distribution. Targeted transfers for the poor will be a much less costly scheme than the universal subsidy system that existed prior to reform.

Government interventions with explicit food rationing

Madagascar, Mozambique, and Guinea all engaged extensively in direct distribution of food. In all three cases, rationing became necessary as demand exceeded the product available through official markets. A thriving parallel, or open, market was also present in these countries, providing an important source of products consumed. As indicated earlier, however, the concern that liberalization policies imply a food security risk to the poor needs to be examined, based on information about who had access to products at the administered prices.

In the case of Madagascar, prior to reform, the government banned private trade in rice, giving monopolies in rice marketing to various parastatals. Consumers in major urban centers enjoyed subsidized prices of rice in official markets supplied by imported and domestically procured rice. The subsidy was not targeted to the urban poor, however. In the capital city, Antananarivo, households in the upper expenditure quintiles purchased more subsidized rice in absolute terms, though the value of the subsidy as a share of income was greater for the urban poor (Table 5.10). Most importantly, rural households were not beneficiaries of the system since the rationing scheme was mainly limited to urban areas, even though most of Madagascar's low-income households (90 percent) live in rural areas.

To minimize the costs of domestic procurement, the government allowed only small increases in producer prices of rice while inflation accelerated in the late 1970s. As a result, producer prices fell by 33 percent in real terms between 1976 and 1982. These declining price incentives, along with fertilizer shortages and poor maintenance of existing irrigation systems, contributed to an 18.0 percent decline in per capita production of rice. Meeting subsidized urban demand thus necessitated large quantities of rice imports, reaching nearly one-quarter of total demand in 1982.

As part of broader economic reforms, the liberalization of Madagascar's rice market began in 1982. The government raised official producer prices of

Table 5.10. *Madagascar rice subsidy, 1986/1987*

	Expenditure quartile			
	1	2	3	4
Value of transfer (FMG)	14,918	20,703	20,399	24,966
Transfer as % of expenditure[a]	31.8	25.3	18.5	13.1

[a]The value of total expenditures includes the value of the transfer.
Source: Dorosh and Bernier 1994b.

paddy in 1982 and legalized private trade in most regions in 1983. Local administrative constraints on marketing persisted until the mid-1980s, but as they were removed, average real producer prices in 1987–1990 rose 30 percent relative to 1982. Real consumer prices in the official market were also increased by 31 percent between 1982 and 1985, after having fallen by 46 percent between 1975 and 1981. The official market shrank in size over time, though sales of rice on the official market continued throughout the 1980s. Reductions in rice imports and mismanagement of government stocks for official market sales led to substantial price rises in the private market in 1985 and 1986,[32] but by 1987, real rice prices were only 21.2 percent above their 1983 level (Dorosh et al. 1990).

In Mozambique, a government parastatal, AGRICOM, endeavored to control the marketing of major food crops throughout the first half of the 1980s. Producer prices for most commodities were fixed in nominal terms, and AGRICOM attempted to enforce panterritorial pricing. As a consequence, the terms of trade declined for agriculture as producer prices lagged far behind inflation. Beyond the farm gate, the government also set all margins throughout the marketing chain prior to liberalization. Traders could operate only in specific regions, with permission granted by the government, using prices published by the government. Even at the retail level, an effort was made to control prices through the establishment of government-sanctioned outlets. Practically, however, retail trade was not amenable to careful regulation, so that monopoly control ended at the wholesale level throughout most of the country. The exception, however, was Maputo, the capital city, as well as Beira, the major commercial port city. In these cases, the state instituted a far-reaching and extensive rationing system for food products at the retail level.

[32] See Shuttleworth 1989 for details of this episode.

The ration system (the Novo Sistema de Abastecimento) was designed to ensure food security in the major urban centers through the provision of key products, such as maize, rice, oil, and sugar. Consumers received ration cards and presented them to licensed retailers who sold the product at the fixed price decreed by the state. These retailers, in turn, procured the commodities from the parastatals at the official price, set significantly below import parity.

In light of the civil unrest that contributed to the decline of production and deterioration of infrastructure, the ration system relied increasingly on food imports, particularly in the form of aid from the United States. The government allocated the donated commodities to various parastatals charged with wholesaling it to licensed retail outlets, who in turn sold the product to the consumer at the rationed price. At each step, the government fixed prices and margins. Under this system there were powerful incentives for traders and parastatals to divert product to the thriving parallel market where maize and other products could be sold at considerably higher prices (Alderman, Sahn, and Arulpragasam 1991). At the same time, the treasury was forgoing substantial revenues in the form of counterpart funds from the sale of food aid. Furthermore, the system of controlled prices kept farmer incentives dismally low.

A key element of the Economic Rehabilitation Program was sectoral reforms intended to increase production through agricultural and food market liberalization, while concurrently protecting the food security needs of the population. Under the adjustment program, a combination of market liberalization and depreciation of the currency contributed to substantial increases in producer prices for food and nonfood crops alike. For example, real maize producer prices jumped from 4.0 to 6.1 meticais per kilogram between 1986 and 1992. The comparable real price increase for rice was from 5.0 to 8.3 meticais per kilogram. The improved incentive structure, coincident with a reduction in fighting, also led to substantial recovery in agriculture. Marketed maize increased by 165 percent between 1986 and 1991. Although these reforms undoubtedly contributed to higher rural incomes, the plight of the urban poor in a liberalized economy, especially in light of their having been served by the rationing system, was of major concern. Thus in the initial stages of reform, there considerable resistance to abolishing the food subsidy in Maputo and Beira.

A random sample survey of households in Maputo, conducted in 1991–1992, revealed that in fact the official price, reported by households purchasing at the ration shops, was significantly lower than the parallel market prices (Figure 5.8). Nonetheless, the subsidy was conferring relatively little benefit upon the poor (or nonpoor), because despite the price differences, the vast majority of purchases of rationed commodities was on parallel markets (Table 5.11). For example, only 7.6 and 3.0 percent of yellow maize grain and maize flour expenditures were official ration purchases. Thus, the primary ben-

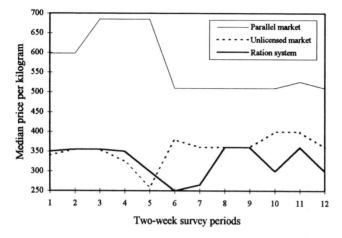

Figure 5.8. Mozambique: yellow maize flour prices in Maputo, 1992–1993 (in survey months). Price data are average biweekly prices between September 15, 1992, and March 15, 1993. *Source:* Sahn and Desai 1994.

Table 5.11. *Expenditure shares by sources of consumption for staple commodities in Maputo*

	Maize grain	Maize flour	Rice	Sugar
Parallel market	58.7	81.8	64.3	62.4
Licensed retailer	23.4	9.4	21.7	18.0
Ration	7.6	3.0	6.3	8.9
Other	10.3	5.8	7.7	8.9

Source: Sahn and Desai 1995.

eficiaries of the ration system were parastatals and traders who had access to these commodities at official prices and were able to resell them in the parallel market. These groups captured the rents associated with the subsidy, rents that represented potentially extremely large levels of forgone revenues to the treasury.

Perhaps the greatest irony in the failed subsidy program in Mozambique was that the strenuous yet unsuccessful measures to target and ration sugar, rice, and maize to households were not necessary to ensure food security and reduce poverty. More specifically, household survey results indicate that yellow maize is an inferior good and, unlike rice and sugar, is self-targeting to the poor. Furthermore, yellow maize, provided almost exclusively by food aid donors, behaves as a nontradable. This implies that increasing its supply in the open market would dampen prices on the open market. Of course, raising yellow maize imports would have a cost; however, this could have been paid for from the saving implied by selling the yellow maize at market prices and eliminating rice and sugar from the rationing system. The major concerns of such a strategy, however, were whether lowering prices of yellow maize was an effective means of poverty alleviation in Maputo, and whether there would be deleterious effects on the rural poor of adhering to such a policy.

Table 5.12 shows the results of our multimarket model simulation of the impact of increasing yellow maize imports in 1991 by 15 percent. As a result, the price of yellow maize would fall by 37.1 percent, with the increase in yellow maize consumption by the poor being 28.7 percent. Since yellow maize is an inferior product for the nonpoor, and the nonpoor have a very low price elasticity of demand, the food security benefits of reducing yellow maize prices are captured by the urban poor. An analysis of how the increase in yellow maize imports affects poverty indicates that the head count measure would fall from 34 to 11 percent of the households in Maputo, while the poverty gap would decline from 9.7 to 5.9 percent. Although this result is in part due to the income effect of lowering the price of the most important food staple, it was largely driven by the substitution effects that markedly increased yellow maize consumption. This raised calorie consumption significantly and lowered the level of expenditures required to achieve calorie adequacy and thus lowered the poverty line as defined in this model.

Among rural households, the policy change would have virtually no effect on their incomes in part because of their relatively low cross-price elasticity of demand between yellow and domestically produced white maize. In addition, most white maize consumed in the southern region of Mozambique is imported from neighboring countries, rather than being domestically produced. This latter phenomenon reflects in part the effects of war, as well as agroclimactic factors, indicating that over the long term, as rural rehabilitation occurs, the assumption of no disincentive effects must be reexamined.

Sensitivity analysis indicates the robustness of the findings that yellow maize food aid is self-targeting, with little short-term adverse effects on domestic agriculture. The prospect of changes in tastes and preferences, and significant increases in agricultural output as the war ends, may alter this scenario in the future. Nonetheless, the liberalization of domestic food markets, including the replacement of the rationing system with open-market sales of the yellow maize, clearly would confer positive benefits on the urban poor, and the treasury, while not harming rural producers (Dorosh, del Ninno, and Sahn 1995).

As with maize in Mozambique, the marketing system for rice was also under state control in Guinea. Rice is the most important staple food product in Guinea, accounting for the largest share of the consumption bundle for both urban (del Ninno 1994) and rural households. It is also the major source of agricultural income and is cultivated on more than three times as much land as

Table 5.12. *Mozambique: increased yellow maize imports: simulation results*

	Simulation (% change)				
	1	2	3	4	5
Production					
White maize	0.10	0.07	0.04	0.08	0.07
Rice	0.12	0.09	0.16	0.10	0.09
Export crops	0.23	0.17	0.26	0.18	0.17
Vegetables	-0.45	-0.36	-0.45	-0.37	-0.36
Meat	0.37	0.29	0.38	0.29	0.29
Consumption					
Yellow maize total	8.98	8.98	8.98	8.98	8.98
Urban nonpoor	0.82	8.07	0.80	0.56	8.13
Urban poor	28.71	21.70	28.73	12.50	21.64
Rural	0.00	0.00	0.00	12.49	0.00
White maize total	-0.21	-0.13	0.03	-0.36	-2.37
Urban nonpoor	1.46	1.17	1.72	0.51	-5.65
Urban poor	-0.92	-0.68	-0.66	-0.62	-7.38
Rural	-0.73	-0.54	-0.49	-0.64	-0.56
Rice	-1.77	-1.36	-1.77	-1.11	-1.36
Wheat	2.51	1.99	2.51	1.26	1.99
Nominal incomes					
Urban nonpoor	-0.43	-0.36	-0.42	-0.34	-0.36
Urban poor	-0.43	-0.36	-0.42	-0.34	-0.36
Rural	-0.40	-0.36	-0.44	-0.38	-0.36
Prices					
Yellow maize	-37.07	-30.28	-37.10	-19.63	-30.22
White maize	-0.36	-0.36	-0.67	-0.36	-0.36
Rice	-0.36	-0.36	-0.36	-0.36	-0.36
Wheat	-0.36	-0.36	-0.36	-0.36	-0.36
Vegetables	-1.55	-1.23	-1.58	-1.30	-1.23
Meat	3.80	2.94	3.84	2.93	2.93
Nonagriculture	-0.43	-0.36	-0.42	-0.34	-0.36
Real incomes					
Urban nonpoor	0.20	0.19	0.21	0.01	0.19
Urban poor	3.63	2.96	3.65	1.89	2.95
Rural	-0.07	-0.06	-0.08	2.53	-0.06
White maize	-0.86	-0.56	0.00	-1.27	-7.40

Notes: 1. Base simulation: 15 percent increase in imports sold on the Maputo market; 2. Own-price elasticity of demand for yellow maize by urban nonpoor households changed from 0.0 to -0.2. 3. Fixed white maize imports; 4. Increased rural consumption of yellow maize. 5. Increased cross-price elasticities of demand for white maize with respect to yellow maize from -0.046 to 0.150 for urban nonpoor, and from 0.004 to 0.200 for urban poor.
Source: Dorosh, del Ninno, and Sahn 1995.

the next most widespread crop, fonio. Despite the major allocation of land to rice, imports are crucial to meeting domestic demand. In the early 1990s, imports were approximately 250,000 tons and accounted for more than one-third of total supply (World Bank 1992a).

In light of rice's critical role in the food economy of Guinea, it comes as no surprise that it has been the focus of government policy, both prior and subsequent to reform. In the years prior to reform, government actively intervened in rice markets in order to keep the consumer price low. This policy involved first, the setting of official farm-gate prices that were far below world market prices. The rate of taxation on rice in the period 1981 to 1985 ranged from 43 to 72 percent. Second, restrictions were placed on the marketing of rice. Third, a rationing system was instituted in Conakry and other urban areas, through which government-procured rice was to be distributed.

Cards were distributed to eligible households. Upon presentation of the ration card to official shops, eligible households in Conakry were entitled to purchase eight kilograms per month for the household head and six kilograms per month for each additional member. For other urban areas, the ration was restricted to households with government employees, and the ration size was only four kilograms per household member. For those households with access to the subsidy, the benefits per kilogram of subsidized rice were substantial. For example, in 1980, the parallel market price for rice was GF 64 per kilogram, in contrast to an official price of GF 20.

Household survey information from 1984 provides considerable insight into who benefited from the ration system. First, the average per capita ration uptake was six kilograms per capita. The official price of GS 29 per kilogram of rice was less than one-third the parallel market price of GS 70 per kilogram, implying the mean value of transfer per capita was GS 300 per month. In Table 5.13, data on the mean value of uptake and the percent of entitled ration actually purchased are shown. The average uptake, conditional upon participating, was highest among upper-level civil servants (nine kilograms per capita) and lowest among small-scale merchants (four kilograms per capita). Overall, 17 percent of households had no access whatsoever. The categories of workers with greatest access were high-level government officials and large merchants, with 96 and 100 percent of them receiving benefits from the ration system. In contrast, one-third of the households whose head was a small-scale merchant had no access whatsoever, and among those with cards, half of the households received less than half of the entitlement. Although no data are available to show access by expenditure groups, it does seem that the subsidy was regressive, benefiting the privileged households in Conakry (Arulpragasam and Sahn 1996).

Despite the tangible benefits to the elite, even they paid a price for distortions in agriculture. They still had to purchase significant shares of rice on the parallel

Table 5.13. *Guinea: percentage of entitled ration actually purchased, by household category, 1984*

	Household head categories (%)						
	Unemployed	Low-income salaried worker	Low-level officials	High-level officials	Small-scale merchants	Large-scale merchants	Total
100	39	21	15	53	16	36	28
100 to 75	22	32	40	23	16	36	26
75 to 50	11	25	20	8	12	18	15
50 to 25	6	11	15	12	23	9	15
25 to 0	0	0	0	0	0	0	0
% without ration card	22	11	10	4	33	0	17
Total	100	100	100	100	100	100	100
Average per capita uptake of those participating (kg)	5.6	5.7	7.3	9	4	7.3	6

Source: Government of Guinea 1986.

Table 5.14. *Guinea: simulated sectoral effects of tariff increases*

	Percent change			
	Urban poor	Urban nonpoor	Rural	National
Consumption				
Local rice	13.27	15.47	0.39	
Imported rice	-15.04	-0.93	-14.58	
Cereals, roots, tubers	-2.30	-2.15	0.20	
Bread	-1.00	-2.55	-0.41	
Meat and dairy	-1.99	-0.44	0.20	
Fish	0.17	-0.66	1.04	
Vegetables	-0.17	-0.92	0.80	
Fruit	-0.26	-0.64	1.44	
Butter, oil	3.06	3.27	3.97	
Spices	-0.03	0.58	0.47	
Sugar	-2.11	-4.59	-1.21	
Beverages	-5.59	-2.79	-2.67	
Nonfood	-4.41	-2.74	-2.00	
Production				
Local rice				2.19
Cereals, roots tubers				-0.25
Meat and dairy				-0.56
Fish				0.21
Vegetables				0.18
Fruit				0.39
Butter, oil				-0.41
Spices				0.73
Consumer prices				
Local rice				7.36
Imported rice				27.27
Cereals, roots tubers				0.65
Bread				0.00
Meat and dairy				-2.78
Fish				0.84
Vegetables				0.74
Fruit				1.31
Butter, oil				0.00
Spices				3.68
Sugar				0.00
Beverages				0.00
Nonfood				-0.78

Table 5.14. *(cont.)*

	Percent change			
	Urban poor	Urban nonpoor	Rural	National
Imports				
Imported rice				-7.54
Wheat				-0.82
Butter, oil				4.32
Sugar				-0.85
Beverages				-3.13
Nonfood				-3.61
Real income				
Urban poor				-3.45
Urban nonpoor				-1.15
Rural				-1.55
Tariff revenue				72.44

Source: Arulpragasam and del Ninno 1996.

market, at much higher prices than those on world markets, an artifact of the continued control over not only domestic marketing, but imports as well. Estimates were that upward of 75 percent of the rice consumed in Conakry was from private sources, with this comparable figure being 95 percent outside the capital.

By the time market liberalization brought an end to the ration system, the parallel market was already instrumental in supplying dietary requirements of all but a handful of government officials and elite in Conakry. Thus, the income loss from eliminating the subsidy was minimal, especially to the poor. However, reform of Guinea's food markets went beyond the elimination of the subsidy and the liberalization of a domestic marketing arrangement. The government also legalized commercial rice imports and increased food aid imports, which it then sold through commercial channels at CIF prices (i.e., those including the cost of commodities, insurance, and freight), based on the liberalized exchange rate plus the requisite 10 percent tariff. These policies contributed to a substantial moderation of consumer prices of imported rice, but also exerted downward pressure on prices of local rice, an imperfect substitute for imported rice. Most Guineans, even in rural areas, purchase some rice on the market and therefore benefit as consumers of lower-priced imports. Yet, an increase in tariffs on imported rice would improve incentives for Guinean agriculture and reduce rural poverty.[33]

---

[33] How the additional revenue is spent by the government will also have important implications for the impact of tariffs on the poor. In the model simulation presented here, the marginal benefits for the revenue raised are not taken into account.

Simulation results using a multimarket model for Guinea show that imposing a 30 percent tariff on rice would lower rural incomes by 1.55 percent and urban incomes by 3.45 percent (Table 5.14). The nominal income gain of producers is outweighed by the inflation that results from the tariff. Local rice production would increase (by 2.19 percent) as would consumption of local rice (by 13.27 percent for the urban poor, 15.47 percent for urban nonpoor, and 0.39 percent for rural households), but the decline in imported rice consumption, particularly for the urban poor, would be greater. Prices of not only domestically produced rice would increase, but so too would other locally produced goods as demand for domestic crops rises following the tariff. In Conakry, the much higher price for imported rice would more importantly shift the poverty line upward. The result would be that in Conakry, the poverty head count would rise from 35.5 to 40.6 percent, with the poverty gap measure rising from 9.9 to 12.3 percent (Arulpragasam and Sahn 1996).

Thus, the model simulation indicates that the costs to the urban and rural poor of increasing tariffs on imported rice far outweigh the real income gains to rural producers. Quite simply, because imported rice is a low-cost source of calories and accounts for a large share of food consumption, policies that reduce the price of imported rice benefit the poor. Moreover, since imported and local rice are imperfect substitutes, the benefits to rural producers of high imported rice prices are small. Other approaches to raising incentives and prices for the rural producers, such as reducing marketing margins and improving technology, are preferable to raising prices of imported rice.

As shown already, interventions in food markets take a wide variety of forms in Africa and for the most part prove ineffectual in either strengthening agriculture or helping the poor. In particular, government interventions in domestic procurement, transport, storage, and sales of food commodities are both administratively difficult and financially costly. Because of weak implementation, these policies have often not achieved their food policy objectives, despite substantial budgetary costs. In contrast, policies of subsidized food imports, as in Madagascar and Mozambique, are less difficult to implement and thus have potentially wide-ranging effects on production and incomes. The CGE model simulations presented in Table 5.15 illustrate the effect of a 20 percent subsidy on imported food grains in each of five countries. As in cross-country comparisons of agricultural export tax policy, an offsetting increase in direct taxes is modeled so that real government revenues are unchanged.

Since economic structures and the importance of imported food grains vary widely in the five countries modeled, the magnitudes and signs of the simulated impacts of the food subsidy on macroeconomic and household variables also differ significantly.

Table 5.15. *General equilibrium impacts of a food subsidy: model simulations*

| | Percentage change[a] | | | | |
	Cameroon	Gambia	Madagascar	Niger	Tanzania
Real GDP	-0.01	0.26	-0.01	-0.15	0.00
Consumption/GDP	0.05	1.03	0.04	-0.09	0.01
Total investment/GDP	-0.06	-0.77	-0.05	-0.07	-0.02
Government recurrent expenditures/GDP	0.00	0.00	0.00	0.00	0.00
Government revenue/GDP	0.00	0.00	0.00	0.00	0.00
Exports/GDP[b]	0.05	1.05	0.33	0.26	0.06
Imports/GDP[b]	0.05	1.05	0.33	0.26	0.06
Change in foreign savings/GDP	0.00	0.00	0.00	0.00	0.00
Real exchange rate	0.58	4.09	3.53	3.50	0.18
Real wage rates	0.58	4.09	3.53	3.50	0.18
Skilled labor	0.15	2.45	0.37	0.25	0.10
Semiskilled labor	0.16	3.35	0.53	—	—
Unskilled labor	0.00	1.65	0.37	0.04	-0.04
Real incomes					
Direct tax	0.03	1.07	-0.12	0.47	0.01
Urban nonpoor	0.19	-0.42	-0.74	-1.15	0.00
Urban poor	-0.03	1.01	1.26	-0.56	0.03
Rural nonpoor	0.06	0.27	-0.48	-0.36	0.02
Rural poor	0.06	0.94	0.26	-0.24	0.05
Small farm — export-oriented	—	—	0.30	-0.40	—
Total	0.09	0.42	0.00	-0.48	0.03

[a]Percentage change relative to base simulation.
[b]Exports and imports valued at the base simulation real exchange rate.
Source: Model simulations.

In Madagascar, where imported rice accounted for 4.2 percent of rice supply in the simulation base year (1989), the import subsidy has a major effect on domestic incomes. The subsidy on rice results in an 87.4 percent increase in rice imports and leads to a real exchange rate depreciation of 3.53 percent to restore balance to the market for foreign exchange. Real incomes of the urban poor, for whom rice is a major food commodity, increase by 1.26 percent, while other rural rice-deficit households also enjoy small gains in real income. Large farmers and the urban nonpoor suffer a decline in real incomes as domestic rice production and real GDP fall slightly. In Niger, the increase in direct taxes on households of 0.57 percent outweighs the benefits of lower prices of rice imports for all households.[34] In The Gambia, the rice subsidy has

[34] Note that direct taxes on firms in Niger are small, so that much of the burden of the tax increase falls on households in the Niger simulation.

substantial benefits for both the rural and urban poor, who are net rice consumers, at the cost of a large drop in real investment (0.77 percent of GDP), as
direct taxes are raised by 1.07 percent to pay for the subsidy. For Tanzania and
Cameroon, levels of food grain imports are small relative to the domestic food
markets even with the 20 percent subsidy, so that this policy has only minimal
effects. It should be noted, however, that these simulations reflect short- to
medium-run effects of the subsidy. Over time, an import subsidy might lead to
larger shifts in demand patterns and, consequently, greater increases in imports
and more severe negative consequences for domestic agriculture.

In sum, our analysis of efforts at food market liberalization indicates that the
degree of reform is strongly linked to prior conditions and level of interference. For example, in most of West Africa, intervention in food markets was
relatively limited and not terribly effective or important, particularly in the case
of roots and tubers and coarse grains.[35] Liberalization thus meant relatively little for producers and even less for consumers. Many West African governments also were actively engaged in importing grains, particularly rice, with
potentially adverse effects on domestic agriculture. However, efforts to
achieve self-sufficiency in food grains by limiting access to cheap rice on
world markets and investing in irrigated rice production have been largely
unsuccessful, as exemplified by the case of Cameroon. These policies were
ineffective in alleviating poverty and diverted attention from nontraditional
exports and other strategies that would use resources more efficiently (Stryker
et al. 1994).

In contrast, many governments in eastern and southern Africa were heavily
engaged in maize marketing through procurement schemes that often discriminated against farmers and did little to help poor consumers. Eliminating the
parastatal structures responsible for grain marketing has proved much more
difficult. Despite the gradual nature of the process, liberalization has occurred
in all cases studied. Furthermore, the poor are in general not the losers,
although in some cases of remote and very thin markets (e.g., the north of
Malawi), some evidence exists that traders have been slow to pick up the slack
left behind by the disengagement of the state. Nonetheless, protecting the interests of favored urban consumers is generally a weak justification for delaying
the liberalization of food markets.

Of course, arguing against the state interference in commodity markets that
has characterized Africa does not mean governments have no role in pursuing
household food security. In fact, where feasible, it is ideal for the state to be

---

[35] The clearest exception to this rule was Guinea, where not only was marketing of all
crops, in theory, under the strict control of the state, but so too was much of the production in the state farms. In practice, the marketing agencies never gained true control,
nor did the state farms ever represent a significant share of production (Arulpragasam
and Sahn 1996).

engaged in identifying the poor and thereafter targeting transfers, whether they be in cash or kind. Where self-targeting commodities are available, government interventions via the open market can be effective. Replacing direct rationing of yellow maize food aid with open-market sales in Maputo, Mozambique, would effectively target the poor, owing to the negative income elasticity of demand for this product by the nonpoor (Dorosh, del Ninno, and Sahn 1996). Similarly, in Conakry, Guinea, imports of low-quality rice are self-targeting, eliminating the need for an expensive and inefficient rationing system (Arulpragasam 1994). Moreover, in both the Mozambique and Guinea cases, the imported commodity was an imperfect substitute for locally produced goods, limiting the disincentive effects on domestic production. In contrast, imported rice in Madagascar is of higher quality and is consumed by both poor and nonpoor households. It is also a closer substitute for domestic rice. For these reasons, an open-market subsidy on imported rice would involve large leakages to nonpoor households and could have significant disincentive effects on domestic rice producers.[36]

The differences in the country experiences noted already reinforce the need for an analytical framework that identifies avenues to increase food security with minimal cost to the treasury or to rural producers. In Guinea, like in Mozambique, greater food security can be achieved through policies that promote the increased imports of low-priced, low-quality basic staples that are imperfect substitutes for locally produced goods. In these instances, domestic producers are not threatened, at least in the short term. In the long term, this is even less likely to be a problem if countries adopt sensible strategies to promote exports as well as diversification, both from the point of view of the composition of agricultural incomes, and between agriculture and other income sources, particularly from small-scale manufacturing and services.

Improving the performance of agriculture: beyond issues of price policy

The preceding analysis of the impact of macroeconomic and market prices on output and incomes assumes only limited price responsiveness of African farmers. Therefore, the benefits to price reform shown earlier, in terms of increased output and incomes, are conservative estimates. The jury is still out, however, on what are reasonable expectations in terms of the response of aggregate output to policy change and how this response can be bolstered. More specifically, data on agricultural production in Africa paint a rather

---

[36] CGE simulations of the reverse policy (a 30 percent tax on imported rice) result in a 1.9 percent decrease in real incomes of the urban poor in the short run. Improved producer incentives lead to small increases in paddy production and in real incomes of surplus-producing farmers (Dorosh 1994b).

somber picture of trends in the past two decades. The simple unweighted average of food production per capita in the ten countries in Table 2.6 shows a decline of 12 percent between 1975–1977 and 1989–1991. Real agricultural GDP has fallen by a similar percentage while agriculture's share in GDP in Africa has remained roughly constant, on average (Table 2.5). While such data on trends in agriculture are of note, they are also of uncertain quality, reflecting the limited resources devoted to, and the difficult task of, collecting information on agriculture, especially in light of the multiple crops grcwn on smallholder plots in remote rural areas.[37] For example, the large declines in per capita food production in Cameroon, The Gambia, and Ghana shown in Table 2.6 raise some serious questions about aggregate statistics, given the general macroeconomic performance, and the absence of significant increases in real or relative food prices, in these countries. Improvements in survey data and information systems are necessary for improving agricultural policy evaluation and planning in most African countries.

Despite the possible measurement problems, lackluster performance of the agricultural sector is not only indicated but is not unexpected, given the limited improvement in producer prices following agricultural policy reform,[38] coupled with the absence of any major improvements in the institutional structures that support farmers, such as extension services and research facilities. Where the responsiveness to prices has been measured, the results are mixed. Studies find that price elasticities are low in Africa, especially for aggregate supply (see Bond 1983 for various countries; Strauss 1984 for Sierra Leone; Lecaillon and Morrisson 1985 for Burkina Faso; Singh and Janakiram 1986 for Nigeria; and Martin and Crawford 1988 for Senegal). Exceptions to this finding of low own-price elasticities, such as rice in Mali (Lecaillon and Morrisson 1986), were generally limited to single-crop response, not aggregate output. A more recent study by Block (1993), however, suggests that the agricultural sector has responded well in the cases where reforms raised producer incentives. Total factor productivity appears to have increased owing to policy reform, even though technical change, the usual driving force behind such gains, has been limited.

---

[37] See Jaeger 1992a for a more detailed discussion of the quality of African production data.

[38] Trends in producer prices are difficult to interpret, however, since the only data from prereform periods in most countries refer to official producer prices, not market prices which most farmers faced. Nevertheless, in some countries, there were substantial increases in real prices paid to farmers. Real producer prices for rice rose by 20 percent in Madagascar in the 1990s due to market liberalization and the reduction in subsidized imports (Dorosh et al. 1990). In Mozambique, economic reform and the legalization of private trade resulted in a 28 percent increase in real white maize producer prices over the same period (Dorosh and Bernier 1994a).

Table 5.16. *Government expenditures on agriculture in sub-Saharan Africa*[a]

	1976–1980	1981–1985	1986–1990	1991–1993
Cameroon	4.8	4.6	5.3[b]	—
Gambia	16.4	13.3	10.3[c]	—
Ghana	12.1	8.3	4.3	3.8[d]
Madagascar	13.3	10.3	14.6	11.9
Malawi	11.4	13.0	12.1[b]	—
Niger	6.4	4.2	5.1[b]	—
Average	10.7	9.0	8.6	7.9

[a]Percent of total government expenditure.
[b]1986-1989.
[c]1986-1988.
[d]1991-1992.
Sources: World Bank 1993e, 1994; IMF 1993b, 1994a, Jabara 1990.

A wide range of factors determines the size of the agricultural supply response including the stock of unused resources (e.g., land), the mobility of labor, the marketing infrastructure, the extent of knowledge and available information, and the degree of risk-aversion, as determined by the instability of the economic and natural environment. In most of these areas, general consensus also exists that public investments have a role in fostering aggregate output growth. In other words, certain public inputs into agriculture, including investments in research, extension, and information systems, are needed to expand the supply response and raise real incomes. In most countries, the limited available data suggest, little has changed in the share of government spending devoted to agriculture (Table 5.16). As exceptions, shares for agriculture have fallen in both The Gambia and Ghana. In Ghana, agriculture's share in government spending fell sharply in 1984, then remained relatively stable in real terms at about one-third the level of the late 1970s. Interpretation of figures from African countries on total agricultural spending is complicated, however, as they include a wide variety of expenditures, such as fertilizer subsidies, transfer payments to grain-marketing parastatals, agricultural research, provision of extension services, and salaries of government workers in capital cities.

Of the components of agricultural budgets, information is most comprehensive and reliable in the area of agricultural research. During the 1980s, the share of agricultural research expenditures in total government spending fell on average in Africa, from 0.76 percent in 1981 to 0.60 percent in 1991, as real agricultural research expenditures stagnated. Real expenditures increased during the 1980s, however, among those countries discussed in this book for which data are available: by 14.4 percent in Ghana, 3.9 percent in Niger, 3.0

percent in Madagascar, and 2.4 percent in Malawi. Of the funding for agricultural research in Africa overall, an increasing amount comes from international donors. Donor support rose from 34 percent of total agricultural research spending in 1986 to 43 percent in 1991 (Pardey, Roseboom, and Beintema 1995). Despite these efforts, however, successful adoption of improved plant varieties (e.g., flint maize in Malawi),[39] is unfortunately still the exception in much of Africa. More typical is Madagascar, where limited supply response to improved price incentives in rice was linked to low use of fertilizers and inadequate water control (Bernier and Dorosh 1993).

Likewise, the failure of agriculture to be the engine of economic recovery is also in part due to the dilapidated or limited market infrastructure. For example, one of our surveys of traders in Tanzania strongly indicated that the paucity of marketing structures and feeder roads was an impediment to reducing marketing margins. So, too, the lack of communication infrastructure hindered the activities of private traders (Amani et al. 1992). The costs of inefficient marketing are particularly evident in Guinea where the cost of transporting a kilogram of rice from Boké to Conakry in 1987 was three times as expensive as that of transporting a kilogram of rice from Bangkok to Conakry (Arulpragasam and Sahn 1996). These costs not only impede domestic commerce and production, but have large welfare costs. In fact, multimarket results indicate that reducing the marketing margins by 30 percent for food products contributes to an increase of local rice consumption by 18.5 percent in Conakry, once again raising real incomes of the urban poor, as well as the rural poor (Arulpragasam 1994). A similar story emerges from the CGE model results for Cameroon (Benjamin 1993). Thus, while dismantling of marketing parastatals that impede commerce and reduce incentives is prerequisite to rural recovery and poverty alleviation, so too are complementary efforts to lower the high transaction costs that presently face producers and consumers.

Perhaps the most contentious area for intervention by the state in terms of raising productivity and improving equity is in the area of the underlying indigenous institutions that affect the access to, and use of, land. Although access is not a major policy issue in areas without serious land scarcity, it is becoming increasingly important in the many cases where density is high and land pressures are increasing. This is nowhere more obvious than in cases such as Malawi, where we have found that the state's interference in land market transactions and the duality it imposes between estates and smallholder procedures has had deleterious consequences for the welfare of poor and the economy as a whole (Sahn and Arulpragasam 1991a, 1991b, 1993). The literature on land reform does indicate that state intervention – for example, through titling schemes – is generally not warranted or effective (Feder and Noronha

---

[39] See Simler 1994.

1987; Shipton 1987). However, the issue remains as to the adequacy of institutional arrangements governing land use and how to provide incentives, reduce uncertainty, and address asymmetric information in factor markets. The evidence in this regard is conflicting. Some argue that the inadequacy of public resources has been a major factor contributing to failed institutional arrangements in land markets (Feder and Feeny 1991). Others argue that the property rights regimes have not impeded technological change and that there is no overall problem of "missing institutions" that have slowed productivity gains or exacerbated poverty in rural areas. Instead, they believe, dangers exist for inequitable distribution of land caused by the introduction of proposed titling schemes. Thus, instead of allocating public resources to the bureaucratic implementation of cadastral survey and land titling schemes, resources should be directed toward the development of agricultural technology adapted to Africa's particular agroclimates and economic conditions and which increases labor productivity without increasing risk (van den Brink and Bromley 1992). Although these viewpoints clearly diverge, broad agreement exists that improved institutional arrangements governing access to land will lead to efficiency and, in many instances, equity gains as well.

Nonetheless, even with land reform, increasing factor productivity is the key to both sustained reductions in poverty and long-run economic growth in most African countries. For example, employing the multimarket model discussed earlier indicates that policies that would increase rice production not only have the expected positive impact on the rural households, but also improve the incomes of the urban poor in Conakry (Arulpragasam and Sahn 1996). Similar multimarket results are found for the impacts of a potential postwar recovery of agricultural production on both rural and urban households in Mozambique (Dorosh and Bernier 1994a).

Our research also indicates that investments in agriculture have the potential to spur growth in other sectors of the economy as well as through both backward and forward linkages. Increased demand for inputs such as fertilizer and transportation services generally accompanies increased agricultural production. Forward linkages are generated as higher agricultural incomes result in increased demand for both agricultural and nonagricultural products. Using a SAM-based multiplier model, Koné and Thorbecke (1994) show that investments in traditional agriculture and rural infrastructure as envisaged under Zaire's 1986/1987 Public Investment Program lead to substantial benefits for the overall economy and especially for the rural poor. Though domestic demand for traditional agriculture products is assumed fixed because of marketing constraints, investments in these rural activities, equal in magnitude to 18 percent of recurrent government expenditures, lead to increases in incomes of traditional farmers of around 2 percent. Similarly, Dorosh and Haggblade (1993) report large growth multipliers for investments in the rehabilitation of small irrigated rice perimeters in Madagascar. CGE model simulations indicate that increasing smallholder irrigated rice production in Madagascar also leads to increased real incomes of the urban poor (Dorosh 1994b).

Finally, it is critical to note that the constraints faced by small farmers that tend to reduce the benefits from reform in general, and improved price signals in particular, are especially acute for women. For example, greater restrictions on women's labor mobility in response to changing incentives stem from asymmetry in men's and women's obligations, relatively fewer female rights, and weaker bargaining positions (see, e.g., Traoré 1984 and Kennedy and Bouis 1989). Women's ability to enlarge the area of land under cultivation in response to improved incentives is also constrained by traditional patrilineal inheritance schemes (Goheen 1991; Haddad 1990), even in countries and regions where land scarcity is not a major problem.[40]

Rural poor women farmers may also have less access to agricultural implements, extension services, and credit. Formal credit facilities and extension services are oriented toward large estate farms and cash crops in the smallholder sector, in contrast to the food sector, where women are concentrated. There is evidence, furthermore, that women are less likely to be the beneficiaries of extension services, regardless of the crops grown (Quisumbing, Schwartz, and Chibawana 1992).[41] While lack of food crop research and inaccessibility to credit affect all smallholders, women receive relatively fewer productivity-enhancing inputs. For example, in parts of The Gambia women's productivity in farming is consistently estimated as 70 percent below men's. This is because, first, women tend to grow crops that result in lower net returns on their labor time. Second, however, is that labor productivity is lower for women than men for the same crop, a phenomenon explained by the lack of access to labor-saving implements among women (von Braun and Webb

---

[40] In some cases, increased production of cash crops resulted in women farmers producing food crops on lower-quality lands situated farther from villages.

[41] Koons (1989) found in Cameroon that women felt they should not ask for farm visits because they were too poor, too small, or too far away, or that visits were only for farmers who purchased inputs. Studies also show that a female extension agent and grassroots or community organizations for women increase the availability of extension information to women farmers (Gill 1987; Saito and Spurling 1992). The assumption that extension information provided to the husband will be passed on to his wife (or wives) often does not hold (Gill 1987). In many African countries, few women are full members of farmers' clubs or organizations. In Malawi, by law, married women are automatic members receiving credit indirectly through their husbands. Others – never married, divorced, or women in polygamous relationships – go to the clubs as individuals. Social stigmas set them apart from male participants (Due and Gladwin 1991). Formalizing women's clubs or organizations and redefining membership based on individual (including smallholder) farming may be one method of increasing female access to extension information.

1987). Similarly, Gladwin (1991) models how farmers choose between chemical and organic fertilizer in Malawi and Cameroon and shows that women farmers make less use of chemical fertilizer on maize because of constraints that are rooted in gender discrimination in terms of access to credit.[42] Her model also shows that women farmers are very risk-averse, and they therefore limit their use of credit in fear of defaulting on loans in bad years.

Summary

Agricultural and food policies determine to a large extent how macroeconomic policies and world market prices affect domestic producers and consumers. In a number of countries, inappropriate policies in these sectors prevent macroeconomic policy reforms from changing relative prices, improving producer incentives, and eliciting a supply response in agriculture. Given agriculture's large share in total domestic output, exports, and employment, the lack of coordination of agricultural and food policy with broader trade, exchange rate, and fiscal reforms jeopardizes macroeconomic, sectoral, and household-level objectives of adjustment. Unfortunately, state intervention in agriculture in Africa has also often overlooked the fact that farmers in Africa are private entrepreneurs, responsive to incentive structures and affected by the efficiency of markets. Lack of access to information, inputs, and technology and high transaction costs due to deteriorating infrastructure, in addition to price distortions, all work to the detriment of the poor.

Experience to date with reform is mixed. Although reductions in direct and indirect taxation of export crop producers have resulted in increased real producer prices in Ghana, Guinea, and Mozambique, falling world prices have largely offset positive effects of reforms in Madagascar, The Gambia, Tanzania, Malawi, and Cameroon. Moreover, in many countries, there has been an overall reluctance to liberalize export crop markets, even where there is a long history of successful private sector involvement in domestic food marketing (as in Cameroon and Ghana) and where cautious steps toward liberalizing food markets are taking place (as in Malawi and Tanzania). Given that most export crop producers in the countries we studied are among the poor, the uneven pace of policy reforms and their limited effectiveness in reducing explicit taxation of export crops, eliminating marketing restrictions, and depreciating real exchange rates have had adverse distributional consequences.

The effects of food crop market liberalization have also varied substantially across countries. Government attempts at influencing food markets were generally limited and ineffective in Cameroon, The Gambia, Ghana, Niger, and

---

[42] This low utilization of purchased inputs is not limited to women, however, and is characteristic of all poor farmers in most of Africa (e.g., see Sahn 1993).

Zaire, so reforms had only minor impacts on most households. Reforms succeeded in raising real incomes of large numbers of food producers in Madagascar (rice) and Mozambique (white maize); likewise, initial efforts at market liberalization in Malawi and Tanzania appear to have had overall positive effects on real incomes of most producers. Fortunately, reforms have not generally led to increases in consumer prices for urban and rural poor households (an exception here is rice-deficit small farmers in Madagascar). Rather, relatively few poor households had access to subsidized food in our sample countries, even in Mozambique, Madagascar, and Guinea, where food was rationed in an attempt to subsidize the urban poor. Thus, most poor households were little affected by price increases in official markets.[43]

Thus, overall, there is some evidence that agricultural reform, where undertaken, has worked in the favor of the poor. Yet aggregate supply response in agriculture seems to have been limited in most cases, although data problems prevent an accurate assessment. Nevertheless, all indications suggest the need for further reforms and investments that strengthen the impact of, and are complimentary to, the incomplete price reforms that have taken place to date. Any resurgence of rapid growth in agriculture will thus require more attention to microeconomic-level factors, including institutional marketing arrangements, time constraints faced by women farmers, lack of access to inputs, and local agro-ecological conditions. Understanding and overcoming these types of country- and region-specific constraints on the supply response of agriculture is crucial for sustained agricultural growth and poverty reduction.

---

[43] Again, we note exceptions to this general pattern outside our sample of countries, particularly urban Zambia and Zimbabwe.

6

Conclusion

This book has examined the impact of economic reform in Africa on income distribution and poverty. We have drawn upon a wide range of country experiences to study the implications for the poor of reform in three broad areas: trade and exchange rate, fiscal, and agricultural and food marketing policy. In general, our analysis indicates that most of the poor in most of the countries examined are small net gainers when their governments implement the types of adjustment policies discussed in this book. There are, of course, exceptions to this broad generalization. Reforms that redistribute income and resources must have losers. For policies with economy-wide effects, it is impossible that some poor households will not be among that group. Nevertheless, reforms primarily hurt those who receive rents that arise when goods are rationed, benefit from guaranteed public employment, gain a disproportionate share of subsidies on poorly targeted public services, and profit from interference in agriculture and food markets. Africa's poor rarely belong to these groups. As a result, policies that reduce or eliminate these privileges in the name of economic efficiency are not usually prejudicial to the poor.

Of the three major areas of policy reform we address in this book, exchange rate changes are the most dramatic. Even in countries where governments have had difficulty reestablishing fiscal balance and have been reluctant to pursue reforms in agricultural markets, sharp exchange rate devaluations have produced substantial changes in relative prices, to the benefit of producers of tradable goods. Although the overall growth in exports in response to such policies has been modest, evidence suggests that exports have increased in a number of countries. Beyond the macroeconomic impact on exports and the balance of payments, some critics see devaluation and the accompanying trade reforms as a nemesis of the poor, blamed for reducing employment, depressing real wages, and raising prices of vital consumer goods. Yet those impressions are based on changes in official wages and prices, often controlled in the formal sector and generally out of the poor's reach. After accounting for the fact that the economic activity of the poor largely takes place in parallel and informal markets, the results of devaluation are quite different. Drawing primarily on the model results from Cameroon, The Gambia, Madagascar, Niger, and Tanzania, we find that exchange rate reforms have been distributionally progressive. In part, this finding reflects that the poor in Africa have important direct and indirect linkages to tradable goods' production. Whether as producers of export crops as in most of the countries studied, or as low-skilled urban workers who benefit from the increased payments for their labor that accompanies a shift toward the production of tradables in the economy, many of the poor witness small increases in real incomes when the relative price of tradable goods rises.

A much more important effect on income distribution, however, is the redistribution of rents from official markets throughout the economy as a consequence of moving from rationed foreign exchange regimes to market-determined exchange rates. We have shown that, with the exception of the CFA countries in our sample, African governments rationed the existing supply of foreign exchange in order to maintain an overvalued official exchange rate. Many still do. Such rationing has two important distributional consequences. First, a parallel market for foreign exchange develops for those unable to gain access to the official market. Second, those who do gain access to foreign exchange at the official exchange rate earn a substantial rent by selling their goods at domestic prices determined on the margin by the parallel rate. An official devaluation reduces or eliminates this rent, which is by far the most important distributional consequence of devaluation for the non-CFA economies we have studied. Those households (rarely among the poor) and institutions (which rarely provide services or goods to the poor) with access to foreign exchange and imports priced at the official exchange rates do suffer large losses as a consequence of reform. The poor, on the other hand, usually benefit from the redistribution of rents that accompanies trade and exchange rate liberalization. These gains tend to be small, however, as even a very large rent will mean only a few dollars per capita when spread over the entire economy.

Fiscal policy reforms have been less dramatic than exchange rate changes. Despite a general perception that adjustment programs drastically cut government spending, such an assessment hinges on a comparison of "postadjustment" expenditures with those of a base year, like 1980, that had unusually high and clearly unsustainable levels of government spending. The same is true of social sector expenditures. Yet even if public spending were cut as part of an adjustment effort, the consequences for the poor would not be as severe as is often presumed, because government expenditures in Africa are poorly targeted. Our analysis, based on data sets from Côte d'Ivoire, Ghana, Tanzania, and the capital cities of Conakry (Guinea) and Maputo (Mozambique), finds that the poor are not the principal beneficiaries of public spending in the health and education sectors, excepting primary schools and in some cases public health clinics. Although governments should target subsidies to needy households, in most cases the poor receive a disproportionately small share of the benefits associated with expenditures on public health facilities and public schools. In most cases, the core of the problem is a strong bias of expenditures toward rationed, urban-based services, particularly hospitals and postsecondary education. The primary services that best reach the poor are also those that get lowest priority in the government budget.

Beyond the effect of adjustment policies on social services, perhaps the most politically charged fiscal policy reform within Africa has been retrenchment. Our research highlights the fact that government employment is significant in the capital cities in Africa, generally accounting for more than one-third of total employment. In rural areas, where the vast majority of the poor reside, government employment is negligible. Thus, not surprisingly, public sector workers are largely not from poor households. While this finding implies that reductions in the overstaffed public sector do not directly affect the poor, a concern exists that such retrenchment creates a new class of poor as once middle-class civil servants lose their jobs and become destitute. Whether that concern is warranted depends on the point of comparison one chooses. Surveys of retrenched workers in Ghana and Guinea, the two countries in our sample that have gone farthest in reducing the size of the public sector, suggest that redeployees do suffer significant welfare losses after retrenchment. Ghana's former civil servants had little difficulty finding new work, but their earnings fell substantially after retrenchment. In Guinea, on the other hand, former civil servants experienced lengthy unemployment spells but increased earnings if they reentered the labor market. These different experiences probably reflect the different labor market conditions prevailing in the two countries, but both cases show significant losses for redeployees as a group. At the same time, redeployees in both Ghana and Guinea have similar postretrenchment earning profiles to other people with the same human capital endowments in their respective countries. Thus, the decline in earnings of retrenched workers and their families is attributable to the loss of an earnings premium associated with public sector employment. As with foreign exchange and food market liberalizations, the most important welfare impact of public employment reform is the loss of a rent – in this case, among those engaged as public sector workers.

An equally crucial complement to the analysis of expenditure incidence is the question of who pays the taxes to fund government expenditures. Over the long run, public expenditure is obviously linked with the ability to collect revenues, even though foreign capital inflows and borrowing may permit temporary deviations between the two. Although we limit our analysis of tax incidence to the cases of Ghana and Madagascar, our findings may have broader applicability to those countries with similar tax structures. Both countries have reduced their explicit taxation of export crops and the taxation implicit in maintaining an overvalued exchange rate. Export duties are the most regressive taxes in both countries, so these policy reforms have been strongly propoor. In Ghana, the authorities have more than replaced reduced cocoa duties with broad-based taxes on income and sales, and specific excises on goods consumed largely by those at the upper end of the income distribution, most notably petroleum products. Madagascar, on the other hand, has seen a steady decline in tax revenues because it has not raised other taxes, even though the same taxes on incomes, value-added, and petroleum products (except kerosene) are also progressive there.

We also examine the impact of reforms in agriculture and food markets, given the importance of this sector in the consumption patterns and income of Africa's poor. Furthermore, many adjustment operations have focused on this sector, in light of the acute distortions that characterize agricultural policy. We initially examine the implication of reducing the extremely high levels of taxation of agricultural exports. At a sectoral level, we find that despite a decline in taxation, particularly the indirect taxation that resulted from overvalued exchange rates, the direct taxes levied on export crop producers often remain high. Distributionally, the reforms have been favorable to the poor, despite critics' skepticism as to the poor's ability to benefit from more aggressive export promotion. In all countries we examine (Cameroon, Ghana, The Gambia, Madagascar, Malawi, Niger, and Tanzania), the welfare of poor households increases as a consequence of reducing taxes on exports. This result reflects that many of the rural poor in Africa do produce export crops. Furthermore, even among households not directly engaged in export crop production, the growth of export agriculture has positive indirect effects on employment and earnings, especially in rural areas where the poor reside.

With food crops and their marketing, we focus on the effect on low-income households of liberalization policies, particularly those that eliminate consumer subsidies. Critics have largely condemned food market liberalization, which allows markets rather than government officials to set prices. Because newly established market prices are higher than previously administered ones, critics argue that the poor will surely suffer, particularly because food constitutes such an important part of their expenditures. This argument, however, presumes that the rationed product reaches poor households at the official price. Using household survey data from Guinea, Madagascar, and Mozambique, we examine who loses when governments reduce food subsidies. In all cases, the eliminated subsidies were rationed and not well targeted to the poor. Only in Madagascar did the incomes of some poor households substantially decline when food prices were decontrolled, and this was limited to the less than 10 percent of the poor residing in the capital city. The relatively privileged class of consumers, usually in public jobs, incurred the largest losses from eliminated subsidies. Likewise, marketing institutions lost from the removal of large rents associated with state intervention in food markets. On the other hand, poor farmers, who implicitly paid for subsidies through forced procurement and trade policies that depress product prices, gained from the reforms. Once again, the political economy of the rationing that public intervention generated excluded the poor from benefits that are ostensibly directed toward them.

Our results obviously diverge from the widely held view that the poor disproportionately bear the costs of adjustment. The reason our results differ from that perception lies in the fact that our analysis relies on a "with and without" rather than a "before and after" policy change comparison. As we indicate in the introduction, judging the merits of policy change requires employing the counterfactual. Our focus on evaluating the policies independent of other external and internal shocks helps us avoid two of the common pitfalls in the literature. First, critics often fail to distinguish between the impact of policy changes and the recession or external conditions that motivate their adoption. When world prices for a key export commodity collapse, the economy will suffer regardless of the policy response that the government chooses. But that suffering is not grounds for condemning the policy response, whose effects must be judged independently of the terms-of-trade shock. The right question is, after accounting for all the other positive and negative shocks affecting the economy and the welfare of the poor, Which policy produces the best outcome? We have tried to address that question.

Critics also often fail to distinguish between the receipt of adjustment loans and actual policy reform. Many countries have had adjustment programs financed by the international community. Few, however, have shown a strong commitment to correcting bad policy in the context of those programs. Those countries that actually undertake reforms often eventually reverse them. Clearly, the political economy considerations that impede the implementation and sustainability of reform are substantial, although not surprising in light of the distributional impacts uncovered in this book. It is wrong, however, to suggest that declining living standards in countries receiving loans necessarily reflect a failure of policy *design*. By focusing on the consequences of actually implementing the policies, rather than "adjustment programs" in some generic sense, we avoid the error of failing to distinguish between actual policy change and adjustment lending.

Another important way our research differs from much of the literature is in our attention to the role of rationing in official markets and the parallel markets that result. As we indicate, the implications of reform programs on the functioning of open markets in equilibrium versus controlled markets are radically different. Most research, however, has examined movements in official markets, supposing that the poor have access to them. Attention to the parallel markets, where the poor actually participate as consumers and producers, results in different conclusions. We present many examples of this throughout this book. The parallel market determines the price of most imports consumed by the poor, not the rationed official market which benefits privileged importers. The open market determines food prices most consumers face, while official, administered prices are primarily relevant to select households, usually those in the civil service and/or the capital. The public employees are also those with most access to official wages and other privileges and subsidies and are in turn adversely affected by retrenchment or declines in formal sector wage payments. In contrast, the official employment and wage statistics have little relevance to the vast majority of the poor, who are farmers and other self-employed workers. In sum, the official statistics on prices, wages, employment, and the like apparently apply to a small and relatively privileged segment of the population and thus add little to an understanding of the consequences of policy changes for the poor.

Finally, the common view that adjustment harms the poor is often based on anecdotal evidence relating to small segments of the population. It is indeed true and a legitimate cause for concern that some poor households have witnessed a decline in their living standards as a consequence of adjustment. Well-targeted government interventions may be appropriate in these cases. Yet our research suggests that the experience of these households is not representative of the effects of these policies on the large majority of the poor. Thus, rather than employ case studies of small numbers of households, we analyze the impacts of policy reform on relatively large, homogeneous groups of households (disaggregated at a minimum between poor and nonpoor and between urban and rural). So although we may conclude that average real incomes of these poor groups increase marginally as a result of economic reform, some households within these "winning" groups inevitably fail to benefit form reform. However, policy-related research should give greater weight to general patterns than to isolated occurrences.

While our main message that policy reform often shifts the distribution of welfare toward the poor diverges from the beliefs of those openly antagonistic to adjustment policies, we also recognize that economic growth has been slow in Africa. Even countries that have made policy changes have experienced only marginal economic gains in most cases. Poverty remains an overwhelming problem, perpetuated by inadequate macroeconomic performance. Exports have been slow to recover lost market shares, savings and investment remain depressed, and productivity is stagnant. Adjustment programs in Africa have thus not generated rapid and sustainable economic growth that could produce comparable gains for poor households. As we consider the future of policy reform in Africa, we believe that an understanding of this problem and its solution is the most important area for policy analysis.

Future agenda

The fact that the poverty problem in Africa's "adjusting countries" has not abated during the past decade, despite the empirical evidence indicating that the most important adjustment policies have small beneficial effects for the majority of poor households, has important implications for the future policy agenda in Africa. First, in terms of macroeconomic and sectoral reforms, we should recall that adjustment policies aim principally to improve macroeconomic balance and economic efficiency, not to redistribute income. Although we examine the criticism that adjustment policies harm the poor in Africa, and find it wanting, we are not necessarily asserting that "adjustment is good." In fact, our evidence that adjustment policies do not have adverse distributional outcomes highlights the need to address an arguably more pertinent question – why adjustment policies have not succeeded in fully achieving their macroeconomic and growth objectives. The lack of economic growth in Africa has a more pernicious effect on the poor than any of the policy reforms we have studied. While our empirical findings should alleviate concerns that macroeconomic reforms will harm the poor in Africa, the reasons for Africa's disappointing economic performance, despite supposed widespread efforts at adjustment, remain unclear. Further, understanding why African economies have not grown as rapidly as other developing areas merits greater attention. In particular, researchers need to analyze how political processes have impeded or turned back the reform agenda, the importance of achieving policy credibility in a liberalized economy, the role of a broad range of public sector actions complementary to proper macroeconomic management, and the need for institutional development and increased technical and managerial capacity.

Regarding the implementation and commitment to reform, adjustment in our sample countries has more often than not been halting, lacking the conviction of political leaders. We too often observe one-time devaluations that subsequent inflation erodes, trade reforms that governments reverse following new external shocks that require further devaluations, and declining fiscal deficits that fall prey to the political prowess of elites who have grown accustomed to capturing large rents from the state. The politics that have deterred policy makers from embracing the reform agenda, and thereafter maintaining it, are complex and are intertwined with issues of governance and social norms. While the moves toward political liberalization and democratization are manifest in Africa, both the fragility and implications of these transitions for the economic reform agenda merit serious consideration. Will political liberalization and freedom to organize and mobilize give a broader range of interest groups

254 *Structural adjustment reconsidered*

access to power? Will this have a positive effect in terms of making adjustment policies stick?

At a macroeconomic level, the paucity of African countries that have implemented reform measures with conviction complicates any analysis of the effects of such policies. It would be precipitous to condemn the underlying concept of economic liberalization in Africa, let alone the merits of restoring macroeconomic stability. Analysts lack enough examples of policy stability in a liberalized economy to suggest that policy reform does or does not work in Africa. Likewise, examples of market-based policy reforms in Africa are too rare to suggest that they, like the controlled economies they replaced, will not improve growth or reduce poverty. Thus, while the evidence indicates that adjustment programs during the 1980s failed to spur rapid growth, it is premature to declare Africa's experience with responsible macroeconomic management and market liberalization a failure. Instead, we need to examine initially the factors that impede progress in stabilizing and liberalizing African economies, then to analyze further the limitations of such a change and what complementary measures will spur rapid growth in the economy.

Thus, besides getting markets to function and macroeconomic policies in order, the role of the state in making complementary investments in human resources and infrastructure also merits closer attention. Africa's weak human resource base constitutes a major constraint on the potential for sustained development, but further exploration is necessary to determine how the state should reorient its pervasive intervention in the education and health sectors. In this book we have extensively documented inefficient and inequitable use of public resources. Moving beyond the failures of the past, we need to examine how the government can best channel efficiency- enhancing subsidies to poor households. Achieving this objective clearly requires substantial changes in the structure of public expenditure, both within and between ministries and other public sector institutions. But other options, including greater cost-recovery in public services, decentralization, and privatization also demand further investigation.

Given the failure of the state in propelling growth, more rapid growth in Africa depends on productive private sector investment. That even the most successful African economies hold weak records in promoting private investment reinforces the need to understand the role of the state as both a provider of public goods and an arbiter of incentives that will attract domestic and foreign investors. In part, this effort requires a return to older questions of economic development: where are the highest social rates of return to public expenditure? Better roads, port facilities, communications, and investment in human resources by improving access to higher education and health services will surely figure in such an analysis. But analysts must also explore more fully the complementarity between the role of the state and the private sector in the broader domain. Specific initiatives that should be accorded priority include: arriving at and enforcing credible macroeconomic policies, particularly in the areas of fiscal responsibility and policy stability; providing extension services; reducing the high administrative costs of conducting business in Africa; and enforcing a fair and manageable legal and regulatory framework. The agenda for the transformation of African governments into "developmental states" through actions complementary to responsible macroeconomic management thus has many dimensions and poses a major challenge for policy makers and researchers.

This challenge is perhaps most apparent in the need to strengthen a broad range of state and civil institutions in Africa. Even if political liberalization moves the reform agenda forward and policy makers identify appropriate complementary investments, African economies are still characterized by weak institutions that impede the articulation and implementation of the reform agenda. Clearly, much must be done to strengthen the government's capacity to manage the economy. Less well understood are the institutional and managerial limits to the community-based initiatives, which are an important aspect of many targeted poverty programs, and to the commercial functions in an economy where government cedes the commanding heights of the economy and concentrates on core functions.

We believe that the further analysis of how politics, policy stability, complementary investments, and institutional capacity affect economic growth in Africa is central to the policy agenda, even for those whose primary concern is poverty reduction. Yet another striking result of our research is that in addition to impeding growth, the prereform policy environment did little for Africa's poorest citizens. Whether this ineffectiveness is due to political structures that concentrate power or the weakness of institutional and managerial capacity among those charged with protecting the vulnerable, African governments can no doubt do a better job at redistributing services and resources to the poor. Spending, even on social services, is poorly targeted in Africa. In fact, because taxation of agriculture is so heavy, governments may actually be redistributing resources away from the poor. Both education and health expenditures could be more progressive if governments reallocated existing resources toward subsidies for rural services in primary education and primary health care. Resources could also be reallocated from wages and salaries for public employees in capital cities to capital, operations, and maintenance expenditures for legitimate primary services around the country. Thus, just as macroeconomic policy would benefit from a renewed focus on macroeconomic results, poverty policy would benefit from greater attention to improving targeted poverty policies. Effective targeting of appropriate types of interventions to alleviate poverty, however, requires local design and implementation. In contrast, centrally managed, macroeconomic policies serve only as blunt instruments in the fight against poverty. There remains no doubt, however, that even great improvement in the formulation and implementation of targeted programs and transfers will not alleviate poverty substantially. African economies do not generate enough income per capita even if it were completely equitably distributed. Thus, rapid economic growth hinges on appropriate macroeconomic and sectoral policies, as well as improved investment strategies. And to ensure that growth reduces poverty, it must utilize poor households' most abundant productive assets, labor and agricultural land.

In sum, although the evidence we have uncovered generally favors the rapid and thorough implementation of adjustment policies, it concentrates on only one dimension of the debate over them: their immediate impact on income distribution and poverty. While it would be wrong to judge adjustment policies on this single dimension, we can conclude that where the macroeconomics of adjustment policies make sense, there is usually no reason to avoid them because of their consequences for the poor. We recognize that this is not the last word in the debate over adjustment policies, nor do we claim that such initiatives have been or will be sufficient to reduce poverty substantially in Africa. But we do believe that our results should return the debate to questions that have been crowded out by the issue of adjustment and poverty: sound macroeconomic and sectoral policy, the political economy of policy implementation, institutional development, and complementary investments in physical infrastructure and human resources that will both accelerate and sustain the limited growth that has occurred in reforming African economies.

APPENDIX: STRUCTURES OF THE CGE
AND MULTIMARKET MODELS

Adjustment policies affect household incomes and consumption through numerous channels, including changes in relative prices of commodities, returns to factors of production (labor, capital, and land), levels of savings, investment and foreign capital inflows, and government expenditures. SAM-based CGE models provide the best analytical framework for understanding these complex pathways and mapping the effects of macroeconomic and sectoral policies to households (Scobie 1989). These models require substantial amounts of data, however, especially for constructing the base year social accounting matrix. Thus, we used an alternative methodology, multimarket models, to analyze impacts of price policies in Guinea and Mozambique. These models focus on food production, consumption, trade, and prices and require data only on the base levels of these variables and elasticities of supply and demand of major commodities.

The CGE models

In five of the countries of our sample (Cameroon, The Gambia, Madagascar, Niger, and Tanzania), national accounts tables, household surveys, and other statistical information were sufficient to construct SAMs. Detailed sets of national accounts including input–output tables and institutional income and expenditure accounts (équilibres resources-emplois) underly the 1984 Madagascar SAM (Dorosh et al. 1991) and the 1987 Niger SAM (Dorosh and Essama-Nssah 1991). Less detailed national accounts supplemented by a national household budget survey formed the basis of the 1985 Cameroon SAM (Gauthier and Kyle 1991; Subramanian 1994). In constructing the 1990 Gambia SAM, Jabara, Lundberg, and Sireh Jallow (1992) relied heavily on a household survey to supplement the more rudimentary Gambian national accounts. Finally, lack of reliable data from the 1980s necessitated using the 1976 input–output table as the basis for the Tanzania SAM (Sarris 1994).

Appendix Table A.1. *Summary of CGE model structures*

	Cameroon	Gambia	Madagascar	Niger	Tanzania
Activities					
Agriculture	4	5	10	5	5
Mining	1	0	0	1	0
Industry	4	2	9	5	4
Services	4	9	8	9	6
Total	13	16	27	20	15
Commodities	13	17	15	14	16
Noncompetitive					
imports	No	Yes	No	No	Yes
Household groups					
Urban	2	2	3	3	3
Rural	5	2	4	4	3
Labor types	4	2	3	2	8
Agroecological					
zones	2	1	3	2	1
Consumption		Constant		Constant	
functions	LES[a]	shares	LES[a]	shares	LES[a]
Year of base					
SAM	1984/1985	1989/1990	1984	1987	1976

[a]Linear Expenditure System.

Sources: Dorosh 1996; Dorosh and Lundberg 1996; Dorosh, Essama-Nssah, and Samba-Mamadou 1996; Sarris 1996; and Subramanian 1996.

Appendix Table A.1 summarizes the structures of the SAMs and CGE models. Each of the SAMs includes incomes and expenditures for several groups of households. The disaggregation varies by country, but in all cases contains poor and nonpoor households in both rural and urban areas. In Cameroon, Madagascar, and Niger, rural poor households are also grouped according to agro-ecological zones, thus helping to isolate the effects of policies on farmers growing particular crops (e.g., export crops in Madagascar).

All five CGE models are neoclassical in structure, with prices adjusting to clear markets, as in Dervis, deMelo, and Robinson (1982). As outlined in Chapter 3, each of the models specifies value-added in production as a CES (constant elasticity of substitution) function of labor of various skill types and sector-specific fixed capital. Elasticities of substitution in the CES production functions are chosen so as to give inelastic supply responses to output price changes, particularly in tradeable agriculture sectors.[1] The Gambia and Niger

[1] For example, elasticities of supply in agriculture in Madagascar range from 0.3 to 0.5; for The Gambia, elasticities of supply are 0.8 for export crops and rice, and 1.5 for coarse grains, fruits, and vegetables. For all crop sectors in Niger, the elasticity of supply is 1.0.

models calculate consumption of each commodity as a fixed value share of total expenditures, implying unitary price elasticities of demand for all commodities. The Cameroon, Madagascar, and Tanzania models use the more flexible, linear expenditure system (LES) specification for household consumption with implied elasticities calibrated using econometric estimates of demand parameters where available.

Apart from the structures of the economies considered, the major differences between the models are in the equations for external trade and government investment.[2] Only the Tanzania model contains explicit equations for parallel markets for all exports and imports. For The Gambia and Niger, world prices of some commodities reflect cross-border trade, rather than official transactions. Parallel market exports are not modeled in Madagascar or Cameroon. In general, all the CGE models allow for substitution of domestic products for imports, the exceptions being noncompetitive imports in The Gambia (most of which are reexported) and Tanzania (mainly capital goods). Finally, government investment is not modeled separately from private investment in the Cameroon model. In the other models, government investment is exogenous in most simulations, and is fixed in real terms.

Comparative static simulations of external shocks and policy changes show that the models approximate historical changes reasonably well. In addition, base runs of dynamic versions of these models approximated historical changes in major economic variables.[3] Appendix Tables A.2 to A.16 describe the structure of production and trade, household income sources, and household expenditure patterns in the five models. Further details regarding the behavior of the models, model equations, and model parameters are found in Dorosh (1996), Dorosh and Lundberg (1996), Dorosh, Essama-Nssah, and Samba-Mamadou (1996), Sarris (1996), and Subramanian (1996).

The multimarket models

In Guinea and Mozambique, lack of detailed and reliable national accounts data precluded building SAMs. Nonetheless, household surveys conducted by Cornell University in Conakry, Guinea, and Maputo, Mozambique provide detailed information on expenditures and prices paid, enabling econometric estimation of demand parameters for poor and nonpoor households (Appendix Tables A.17 and A.18, Dorosh, del Ninno, and Sahn 1996; Arulpragasam and del Ninno 1996). In addition to base data from the surveys and

---

[2] The Tanzania CGE model used for the simulations in this book was adapted from Sarris (1996) and excludes the financial variables and equations of the original model.

[3] These dynamic simulations are essentially sequences of comparative static solutions where capital stock is determined from the previous year's capital and investment, labor supply growth is exogenous, and values of exogenous variables (such as government spending and foreign savings) are set to historical levels.

Appendix Table A.2. *Cameroon: production and trade, 1984/1985 (billion FCFA)*

	Production	Value-added	Exports	Imports	Elasticity of substitution
Food agriculture	677.0	501.9	6.1	14.9	0.8
Export agriculture	467.7	308.7	273.8	14.4	0.8
Forestry	191.2	69.2	31.5	0.0	0.4
Estate sector	36.2	24.0	20.7	1.1	0.9
Food processing (private)	331.5	55.0	17.7	24.5	0.9
Food processing (public)	39.3	6.3	2.2	3.0	0.9
Manufacturing (private)	1,032.1	299.6	95.2	599.1	1.1
Manufacturing (public)	186.7	71.2	8.9	31.8	1.1
Construction	587.5	351.0	0.0	0.0	0.4
Services (private)	2,005.8	1,319.3	71.1	21.9	0.4
Services (public)	249.9	153.9	12.8	4.0	0.4
Public administration	376.2	252.2	0.0	0.0	0.4
Oil	968.4	724.8	721.3	12.6	3.0
Total	7,149.6	4,137.1	1,261.5	727.3	—

Source: Subramanian 1996.

the demand parameter estimates, sectoral level data on production and trade comprise the core quantitative information for modeling the effects of policy changes on households.

The Guinea and Mozambique models are essentially identical in structure; see Dorosh, del Ninno and Sahn (1996) and Arulpragasam and del Ninno (1996). Each model determines the level of domestic production of agricultural commodities given rural prices; nonagricultural production is fixed exogenously. Rural prices, in turn, are linked to urban consumer prices by a fixed marketing margin. Consumption of both urban and rural households is a function of household income and consumer prices. (For rural households, the consumer price is equal to the producer price.) With nonagricultural output fixed, nonagricultural income varies with the price of nonagricultural goods in the models. Agricultural incomes are determined by quantities produced and their prices.

In general, domestic prices of traded goods are determined by world prices, the exchange rate, tariffs, and marketing margins. Net imports adjust so that total supply equals demand. For nontraded goods, net imports are set to the

Appendix Table A.3. *Cameroon: sources of household income and savings rates, 1984/1985*

	North farm poor	South farm poor	Farm nonpoor	Nonfarm rural poor	Nonfarm rural nonpoor	Urban poor	Urban nonpoor
			(%)				
Labor							
Agriculture & informal sector	77.1	84.5	48.2	42.1	6.5	20.1	2.2
Formal unskilled	19.9	5.2	16.8	32.1	11.4	35.0	6.8
Skilled	0.0	5.4	19.9	16.4	33.6	28.4	25.1
Highly skilled	0.0	1.8	3.2	9.4	25.1	16.6	14.4
Agricultural capital	3.0	3.0	11.2	0.0	0.0	0.0	0.0
Nonagricultural capital	0.0	0.0	0.0	0.0	23.4	0.0	47.0
Transfers from government	0.0	0.0	0.8	0.0	0.0	0.0	4.5
Total	100.0	100.0	100.0	100.0	100.0	100.0	100.0
Number of households	159,273	322,327	523,077	127,503	241,394	11,053	155,647
Per capita income ('000 CFAF)	164.8	148.0	480.2	160.3	749.3	310.2	852.8

261

Appendix Table A.4. *Cameroon: household budget shares, 1984/1985*

	North farm poor	South farm poor	Farm nonpoor	Nonfarm rural poor	Nonfarm rural nonpoor	Urban poor	Urban nonpoor
				(%)			
Food agriculture	37.8	27.6	23.0	21.7	15.3	13.4	12.2
Export agriculture	1.4	8.0	4.6	6.5	4.1	3.2	2.3
Forestry	0.6	0.8	1.7	5.6	4.1	13.3	7.4
Estate sector	0.1	0.6	0.4	0.5	0.3	0.3	0.2
Food processing (private)	9.1	13.0	8.9	14.4	11.4	11.3	12.0
Food processing (public)	1.1	1.5	1.1	1.7	1.3	1.3	1.4
Manufacturing (private)	27.8	18.7	29.7	19.6	32.3	19.6	27.2
Manufacturing (public)	3.1	2.1	3.3	2.2	3.6	2.2	3.0
Construction	0.8	0.3	0.5	0.3	0.4	0.9	0.6
Services (private)	12.3	21.3	19.6	21.2	19.5	27.4	25.6
Services (public)	2.0	3.5	3.3	3.5	3.3	4.6	4.3
Public administration	0.0	0.0	0.0	0.0	0.0	0.0	0.0
Oil	3.9	2.6	4.1	2.7	4.5	2.7	3.8
Total	100.0	100.0	100.0	100.0	100.0	100.0	100.0
	(175.9)ᵃ	(318.7)	(984.9)	(137.8)	(636.4)	(22.7)	(576.8)
Marginal propensity to save	4.0	4.0	14.2	4.0	21.8	4.0	21.8

ᵃTotal expenditures in billion 1984/1985 CFAF.
Source: Subramanian 1996.

Appendix Table A.5. *The Gambia: production and trade, 1989/1990 (million dalasis)*

	Production	Value-added	Imports	Exports	Elasticity of substitution
Groundnuts	199.4	158.5	0.0	71.0	2.0
Rice	48.3	43.1	91.3	0.0	2.0
Coarse grains	114.1	101.7	30.8	0.0	2.0
Fruits, vegetables	103.3	90.3	25.8	35.9	2.0
Livestock, forestry	201.6	149.8	15.6	24.4	0.9
Groundnut products	117.0	22.9	0.0	86.0	2.0
Manufacturing	231.0	88.5	14.1	17.0	0.9
Construction	183.9	74.2	0.0	0.0	0.9
Transportation, communication	292.0	158.6	0.0	43.2	0.9
Informal trade	71.5	61.0	0.0	0.0	0.4
Formal trade	253.7	196.9	0.0	0.0	0.4
Reexports	723.1	200.0	0.0	723.2	2.0
Private services	390.8	139.0	0.0	207.3	0.7
Public services	231.8	153.8	0.0	0.0	0.4
Urban housing	95.0	95.0	0.0	0.0	0.4
Rural housing	89.2	89.2	0.0	0.0	0.4
Noncompetitive imports	0.0	0.0	1,191.0	0.0	2.0
Total	3,345.9	1,822.3	1,368.5	1,207.8	—

Source: Dorosh and Lundberg 1996.

Appendix Table A.6. The Gambia: income shares, 1989/1990

	Urban poor	Urban nonpoor	Urban total	Rural poor	Rural nonpoor	Rural total	Gambia total
			(%)				
Labor income							
Skilled	41.6	40.8	41.2	2.5	5.7	4.0	24.0
Unskilled	42.1	24.5	32.7	66.6	44.3	56.2	43.6
Entrepreneurial income	5.5	24.4	15.6	3.7	4.8	4.2	10.3
Housing	7.2	6.7	6.9	12.1	9.5	10.9	8.8
Land rents	0.9	0.2	0.5	6.7	15.1	10.6	5.2
Interest received	0.5	0.6	0.5	0.4	0.1	0.2	0.4
Transfers	2.2	2.9	2.6	8.0	20.5	13.8	7.8
Total	100.0	100.0	100.0	100.0	100.0	100.0	100.0
Population ('000)	172.9	74.1	247.0	430.5	184.5	615.0	862.0
Per capita income ('000 dalasis/person)	2.55	6.80	3.83	1.01	2.05	1.33	2.04

Source: Dorosh and Lundberg 1996.

264

Appendix Table A.7. *The Gambia: household budget shares,*
1989/1990

	Urban poor	Urban nonpoor	Rural poor	Rural nonpoor
		(%)		
Groundnuts	1.0	1.1	3.0	1.9
Rice	11.6	4.7	16.3	12.6
Coarse grains	8.0	6.6	11.9	9.7
Fruits, vegetables	7.1	6.8	6.0	5.5
Livestock, forestry	12.9	11.3	12.4	11.6
Groundnut products	3.9	2.3	3.1	2.4
Manufacturing	9.4	11.3	9.1	8.5
Construction	0.0	0.0	0.0	0.0
Transportation, communications	6.2	8.4	2.6	2.3
Informal trade	0.0	0.0	0.0	0.0
Formal trade	0.0	0.0	0.0	0.0
Reexports	0.0	0.0	0.0	0.0
Private services	11.0	14.1	8.2	8.1
Public services	0.5	0.4	0.5	0.7
Urban housing	12.3	13.4	0.0	0.0
Rural housing	0.0	0.0	10.9	12.4
Noncompetitive imports	16.1	19.6	16.0	24.2
Total expenditures	100.0	100.0	100.0	100.0
	(364.2)*	(374.8)	(424.6)	(348.3)
Marginal propensity to save	7.4	11.1	2.6	8.4

*Total expenditures in million dalasis.
Source: Dorosh and Lundberg 1996.

base level of imports, and the models solve for the consumer prices that clear the markets, equating supply and demand.

The numeraire in these models is the price index of nontraded goods, which is computed from the price of nontraded agriculture and nontraded nonagricultural goods. The exchange rate adjusts so that exogenous foreign capital inflows equal the excess of import demand over export supply. Since food imports represent only a small fraction of total imports in both Guinea and Mozambique, only minor adjustments in the exchange rate result in the model simulations shown in this book.

The only major difference in the models is the treatment of food aid imports of yellow maize in Mozambique. For this commodity, import levels are exogenous and the domestic market price adjusts to equilibrate supply and demand. This specification reflects the widespread leakages of rationed yellow maize to parallel markets, as described in Chapter 5.

Appendix Table A.8. *Madagascar: production and trade, 1984 (billion FMG)*

	Production	Gross value-added	Exports	Imports	Elasticity of Substitution
Paddy	168.2	119,036	0.0	0.0	2.0
Small farm irrigated		44,227			
Large farm irrigated		58,947			
Upland		15,682			
Other food crops	237.9	197,855	2.0	3.7	0.9
Export crops	43.3	37,573	35.2	0.0	5.0
Small farms		27,283			
Large farms		10,290			
Industrial crops	14.2	11,680	0.0	0.0	2.0
Small farms		8,030			
Large farms		3,650			
Livestock and forestry	250.1	202,565	10.1	0.0	0.9
Informal sector		189,548			
Formal sector		13,017			
Mining, energy, and water	80.2	31,969	7.4	66.3	0.9
Rice milling	170.0	3,807	0.0	18.0	5.0
Informal sector		0			
Formal sector		3,807			
Other food processing	322.2	59,944	12.9	8.6	0.9
Informal sector		12,118			
Formal sector		47,826			

Textiles	73.5	24,545	6.7	11.3	0.9
Informal sector		4,391			
Formal sector		20,154			
Other industry	122.6	44,447	1.8	130.9	0.7
Informal sector		10,664			
Formal sector		33,783			
Construction	88.2	42,752	0.0	0.0	0.4
Informal sector		5,339			
Formal sector		37,413			
Transportation, communication	266.6	160,758	33.8	24.5	0.4
Informal sector		130,818			
Formal sector		29,940			
Commerce	346.8	331,933	0.0	0.0	0.4
Informal sector		219,161			
Formal sector		112,772			
Services, private	298.0	188,787	3.4	26.0	0.4
Public administration	180.4	130,301	0.0	0.0	0.4
Total	2,662.1	1,587,954	113.5	289.2	n.a.

Source: Dorosh 1996.

Appendix Table A.9. *Madagascar: household income shares, 1984*

	Urban nonpoor	Urban middle	Urban poor	Small farmer plateau	Small farmer east coast	Small farmer west/south	Rural nonpoor	Rural nonfarm poor	All households
Highly skilled labor	0.404	0.000	0.000	0.000	0.000	0.000	0.000	0.000	0.071
Skilled labor	0.014	0.584	0.000	0.000	0.000	0.000	0.068	0.000	0.082
Unskilled labor	0.006	0.248	0.681	0.711	0.708	0.621	0.308	0.575	0.401
Informal capital	0.000	0.168	0.319	0.077	0.076	0.067	0.406	0.425	0.190
Land: plateau	0.000	0.000	0.000	0.213	0.000	0.000	0.000	0.000	0.027
Land: east coast	0.000	0.000	0.000	0.000	0.215	0.000	0.000	0.000	0.029
Land: west/south	0.000	0.000	0.000	0.000	0.000	0.312	0.000	0.000	0.032
Land: large farm	0.000	0.000	0.000	0.000	0.000	0.000	0.218	0.000	0.068
Dividends	0.292	0.000	0.000	0.000	0.000	0.000	0.000	0.000	0.051
Rents	0.284	0.000	0.000	0.000	0.000	0.000	0.000	0.000	0.050
Total	1.000	1.000	1.000	1.000	1.000	1.000	1.000	1.000	1.000

Source: Dorosh 1996.

Appendix Table A.10. *Madagascar: household budget shares, 1984*

	Urban nonpoor	Urban middle	Urban poor	Small farmer plateau	Small farmer east coast	Small farm west/south	Rural nonpoor	Rural nonfarm poor
	(%)							
Paddy	0.00	0.00	0.00	0.00	0.00	0.00	0.00	0.00
Other food crops	6.32	11.31	12.97	28.22	20.37	22.55	21.26	26.33
Export crops	0.00	0.00	0.00	0.00	3.27	0.12	0.37	0.00
Industrial crops	0.00	0.00	0.00	0.00	2.07	2.69	0.45	0.00
Livestock/fishing	0.66	1.63	1.85	3.01	5.02	5.02	9.65	5.02
Mines/energy/water	3.08	7.70	8.85	0.45	0.45	0.45	0.54	0.45
Rice	3.63	17.44	23.68	18.64	15.32	12.96	12.00	19.42
Processed food	14.33	14.47	12.76	19.50	23.32	26.03	24.34	18.60
Textiles	3.01	2.93	3.09	6.74	6.74	6.74	7.54	6.75
Manufactures	25.00	8.13	4.70	3.09	3.09	3.09	3.08	3.09
Construction	3.56	1.57	3.09	0.00	0.00	0.00	0.00	0.00
Transportation, communications	10.00	3.71	2.26	12.64	12.64	12.64	13.12	12.64
Commerce	0.00	0.00	0.00	0.00	0.00	0.00	0.00	0.00
Private services	30.02	30.61	26.33	7.70	7.70	7.70	7.65	7.70
Public services	0.40	0.49	0.42	0.00	0.00	0.00	0.00	0.00
Total	100.00	100.00	100.00	100.00	100.00	100.00	100.00	100.00
	(178.54)*	(169.07)	(34.27)	(198.67)	(210.60)	(161.83)	(479.86)	(46.14)
Marginal propensity to save	15.0	5.0	2.0	2.0	2.0	2.0	10.0	2.0

*Total expenditures in billion FMG.

Source: Dorosh 1996.

Appendix Table A.11. *Niger: production and trade, 1987 (billion CFAF)*

	Domestic production	Value-added	Exports	Imports	Elasticity of substitution
Grains	70.93	64.21	1.62	11.61	2.0
Export crops	23.82	18.31	14.12	0.21	2.0
Other crops	56.84	53.16	2.71	6.44	0.9
Livestock	84.77	83.44	11.57	1.50	2.0
Forestry, fish	23.38	22.32	0.09	0.41	0.9
Mining	91.19	43.95[a]	85.51	6.17	2.0
Meat processing	53.93	9.49[a]	0.11	0.12	0.9
Food processing	17.19	7.05	1.35	20.02	0.9
Formal	10.28	3.57			
Informal	6.91	3.48			
Manufacturing	84.55	41.41	13.91	141.14	0.7
Formal	56.88	22.26			
Informal	27.67	19.15			
Construction	55.83	20.67	0.00	0.00	0.4
Formal	37.30	14.58			
Informal	18.53	6.09			
Trade	165.83	123.78	0.00	0.00	0.4
Formal	31.18	18.93	·		
Informal	134.65	104.86			
Transportation, communication	56.60	34.17	0.00	4.85	0.4
Formal	25.10	16.39			
Informal	31.50	17.78			
Private services	76.92	58.93	0.00	5.75	0.4
Formal	16.58	10.75			
Informal	60.34	48.18			
Public services	82.12	73.96	0.00	0.00	0.4
Total	943.92	654.85	131.00	198.21	—

[a]For value-added only, mining and meat processing subsectors include both formal and informal activities.

Sources: Dorosh and Essama-Nssah 1991; Dorosh, Essama-Nssah, and Samba-Mamadou 1996.

Appendix Table A.12. *Niger: revenue shares by household, 1987*

	Urban nonpoor	Urban poor	Semiurban	Rural north nonpoor	Rural north poor	Rural south nonpoor	Rural south poor
Factor income shares							
Skilled labor	0.769	0.000	0.000	0.000	0.000	0.000	0.000
Unskilled labor	0.057	0.499	0.746	0.375	0.884	0.639	0.881
Informal capital	0.174	0.481	0.218	0.458	0.057	0.229	0.031
Land: north nonpoor	0.000	0.007	0.012	0.167	0.000	0.000	0.000
Land: north poor	0.000	0.003	0.006	0.000	0.059	0.000	0.000
Land: south nonpoor	0.000	0.007	0.013	0.000	0.000	0.131	0.000
Land: south poor	0.000	0.003	0.005	0.000	0.000	0.000	0.088
Total	1.000	1.000	1.000	1.000	1.000	1.000	1.000
Population							
In thousands	228.0	451.5	344.3	729.6	2188.8	1660.1	1414.2
% of total	3.2	6.4	4.9	10.4	31.2	23.7	20.2
Total income							
In million CFAF	94.5	72.2	20.6	84.3	107.3	112.6	69.6
% of total	16.8	12.9	3.7	15.0	19.1	20.1	12.4
Per capita income							
CFAF/person	414.5	159.9	59.8	115.5	49	67.8	49.2

Source: Dorosh, Essama-Nssah, and Samba-Mamadou 1996.

271

Appendix Table A.13. *Niger: household budget shares, 1987 (%)*

	Urban nonpoor	Urban poor	Semiurban	Rural north nonpoor	Rural north poor	Rural south nonpoor	Rural south poor
Cereals	11.07	16.22	17.74	10.41	24.57	15.03	19.58
Export crops	0.66	0.98	1.43	0.84	1.98	1.21	1.58
Other food crops	7.56	11.17	15.77	4.01	9.48	22.02	28.69
Livestock	0.56	0.83	11.45	29.59	3.68	12.55	1.62
Forestry products	2.53	3.72	2.48	2.55	2.79	2.28	2.25
Mining	2.70	1.66	0.00	0.00	0.00	0.00	0.00
Meat	10.69	6.14	11.06	11.38	12.44	10.15	10.01
Processed food	5.13	7.03	7.31	7.53	8.23	6.71	6.62
Manufactures	40.62	34.52	12.21	12.56	13.73	11.20	11.05
Construction	0.61	0.65	0.25	0.26	0.28	0.23	0.23
Commerce	3.04	4.48	5.19	5.34	5.84	4.76	4.70
Transportation, communication	2.04	2.99	5.57	5.73	6.27	5.11	5.04
Private services	12.34	8.83	9.45	9.73	10.63	8.67	8.56
Public services	0.43	0.79	0.08	0.08	0.08	0.08	0.08
Total	100.00	100.00	100.00	100.00	100.00	100.00	100.00
	(178.54)ᵃ	(169.07)	(34.27)	(198.67)	(210.60)	(161.83)	(479.86)
Marginal propensity to save	10.0	3.0	3.0	10.0	3.0	10.0	3.0

ᵃTotal expenditures in million CFAF.

Source: Dorosh, Essama-Nssah, and Samba-Mamadou 1996.

272

Appendix Table A.14. *Tanzania: production and trade levels, 1976 (million Tsh)*

	Value-added[a]	Official imports	Parallel imports	Official exports	Parallel exports	Elasticity of substitution
Cereals	2,147.2	20.7	5.4	0.0	0.0	2.0
Other staples	1,729.5	0.8	0.2	43.9	11.0	0.8
Other food crops	1,796.1	0.0	0.0	1.7	0.4	0.8
Export and cash crops	1,602.5	58.1	15.2	1,232.2	308.1	2.0
Livestock, fishing	2,501.6	34.4	9.0	62.6	15.7	2.0
Food processing	612.0	170.1	44.7	45.8	11.5	1.5
Other consumer goods	548.4	125.9	33.0	114.5	28.6	0.5
Other manufacturing, mining, utilities	1,829.2	1,051.0	276.0	804.2	201.1	0.5
Household industries	254.7	0.0	0.0	0.0	0.0	1.5
Construction	791.1	209.4	55.0	0.0	0.0	0.5
Commerce	2,813.7	54.4	14.3	439.2	109.8	0.5
Transportation, communication	3,946.1	240.8	63.2	589.1	147.3	0.5
Health and education	1,490.3	172.9	45.4	0.0	0.0	0.5
Other services	1,629.4	536.2	140.8	654.5	163.6	0.5
Public administration	842.1	60.1	120.4	0.0	0.0	1.5
Noncompetitive imports	0.0	2,121.0	120.4	0.0	0.0	—
Total	24,533.9	4,855.6	822.8	3,987.8	997.0	—

[a]Value-added at factor cost.
Source: Sarris 1996.

273

Appendix Table A.15. *Tanzania: sources of household income, 1976*

	Rural poor	Rural middle	Rural nonpoor	Urban poor	Urban middle	Urban nonpoor
			(%)			
Wages						
Public unskilled	0.5	3.1	2.6	3.4	9.4	6.6
Public skilled	0.8	5.4	4.4	6.0	16.3	11.6
Parastatal unskilled	0.3	2.0	1.6	2.2	6.0	4.3
Parastatal skilled	0.3	2.2	1.8	2.4	6.5	4.6
Formal unskilled	0.6	2.3	1.9	4.2	6.8	4.8
Formal skilled	0.7	2.4	1.9	4.7	7.1	5.1
Informal unskilled	51.6	42.1	28.6	34.5	24.4	14.9
Informal skilled	1.8	3.0	2.9	4.4	5.5	4.4
Unincorporated capital						
Nonagriculture	21.1	18.1	32.7	14.5	12.1	27.6
Cereals	1.7	0.7	0.5	0.6	0.1	0.0
Other staple crops	1.5	0.6	0.2	0.5	0.0	0.0
Other food crops	1.2	0.7	0.5	0.3	0.0	0.0
Export crops	0.4	1.0	0.7	0.0	0.0	0.0
Livestock	6.5	7.5	4.7	9.1	2.3	0.0
Household transfers	0.3	0.0	0.0	6.8	0.0	0.0
Private enterprises	10.1	8.0	13.5	4.3	2.5	14.5
Interest income	0.0	0.1	0.2	0.0	0.1	0.2
Government	0.0	0.2	0.5	1.3	0.2	0.8
Foreign transfers	0.5	0.6	0.7	0.6	0.7	0.6
Total income	100.0	100.0	100.0	100.0	100.0	100.0
Population (millions)	11.01	3.14	0.75	0.67	0.99	0.56
Per capita income ('000 Tsh/person)	798.8	1,490.0	2,711.3	870.5	2,253.9	7,423.7

Sources: Sarris 1994b, 1996.

Appendix Table A.16. *Tanzania: household budget shares, 1976*

	Rural poor	Rural middle	Rural nonpoor	Urban poor	Urban middle	Urban nonpoor
			(%)			
Cereals	15.2	9.5	5.3	10.9	5.9	3.3
Other staples	14.9	6.2	4.2	8.6	3.7	2.1
Other food crops	9.9	7.1	5.2	7.5	6.5	4.8
Export and cash crops	0.1	0.2	0.2	0.2	0.3	0.2
Livestock, fishing	10.6	10.7	7.5	14.6	12.4	8.9
Food processing	7.5	10.3	10.6	12.3	15.5	13.5
Other consumer goods	7.0	9.0	9.2	5.6	5.0	4.0
Other manufacturing, mining, utilities	5.6	6.9	7.9	5.6	7.0	8.4
Household industries	6.5	6.9	3.7	4.6	2.3	0.9
Construction	0.1	0.1	0.1	0.1	0.1	0.1
Commerce	12.3	16.6	14.4	17.6	19.4	15.8
Transportation, communication	5.7	10.4	18.4	7.1	13.8	21.6
Health and education	1.5	1.6	3.3	0.4	0.5	1.4
Other services	0.4	0.7	1.3	1.4	3.3	5.4
Public administration	0.0	0.0	0.0	0.0	0.0	0.0
Noncompetitive imports	2.6	3.6	8.6	3.6	4.3	9.6
Total	100.0	100.0	100.0	100.0	100.0	100.0
	(7,967.4)[a]	(3,813.4)	(1,439.6)	(519.0)	(1,624.1)	(2,221.5)
Savings rate	3.0	7.6	11.8	2.3	11.4	26.6

[a]Billion 1976 TSh. Includes transfers abroad.
Sources: Sarris 1994a, 1996.

Appendix Table A.17. *Conakry, Guinea: demand elasticities*

	Income elasticities			Own-price elasticities		
	Poor	Nonpoor	All	Poor	Nonpoor	All
Local rice	0.644	0.594	0.652	-1.893	-2.020	-1.874
Imported rice	0.338	-0.531	0.069	-0.592	-0.151	-0.455
Other coarse grains	1.069	1.068	1.062	-0.857	-0.859	-0.872
Bread	0.510	0.265	0.397	-0.673	-0.523	-0.604
Meat	1.317	1.230	1.239	-0.930	0.955	0.952
Fish	0.408	0.098	0.314	-0.727	-0.610	-0.692
Vegetables	0.515	0.308	0.460	-0.644	-0.510	-0.608
Fruit	1.152	1.102	1.114	-0.968	-0.980	-0.977
Butter and oil	0.467	0.227	0.396	-0.823	-0.751	-0.801
Spices	0.325	-0.092	0.193	-0.697	-0.522	-0.642
Sugar	0.381	0.070	0.248	-0.543	-0.319	-0.447
Beverages	1.584	1.323	1.420	-1.304	-1.171	-1.221
Nonfoods	1.473	1.374	1.437	-1.207	-1.066	-1.041

Source: Arulpragasam and Sahn 1996.

Appendix Table A.18. *Mozambique: urban poor and rural demand elasticities*

					Price			
Quantity	Yellow maize	White maize	Rice	Wheat	Vegetables	Meat	Nonagriculture	Income
Yellow maize	-0.552	0.013	0.080	0.014	0.213	0.034	0.026	0.172
White maize	0.004	-0.856	0.016	0.051	0.232	-0.102	0.145	0.510
Rice	0.019	-0.012	-0.668	0.143	-0.237	-0.276	-0.020	1.052
Wheat	-0.065	0.009	0.152	-1.077	-0.047	-0.097	0.228	0.897
Vegetables	0.054	0.031	-0.034	0.013	-0.617	-0.043	0.045	0.551
Meat	-0.166	-0.095	-0.321	-0.176	-0.491	-0.219	-0.514	1.980
Nonagriculture	-0.138	-0.018	-0.033	0.010	-0.189	-0.078	-0.977	1.423

Source: Dorosh, del Ninno, and Sahn 1996.

REFERENCES

ACC/SCN. 1992. *Second report of the world nutrition situation*. Rome: Administrative Coordinating Committee/Sub-Committee on Nutrition.

Alderman, Harold. 1991. *Downturn and economic recovery in Ghana: Impacts on the poor*. Monograph No. 10. Ithaca, NY: Cornell Food and Nutrition Policy Program.

Alderman, Harold, Sudarshan Canagarajah, and Stephen Younger. 1993. *Consequences of permanent lay-off from civil service: Results from a survey of retrenched workers in Ghana*. Working Paper No. 35. Ithaca, NY: Cornell Food and Nutrition Policy Program.

——— 1994. "Consequences of permanent lay-off from civil service: Results from a survey of retrenched workers in Ghana." In *Employment reform in Africa*, ed. D. L. Lindauer and B. Nunberg. Washington, DC: World Bank.

——— 1995. "A comparison of Ghanaian civil servants' earnings before and after adjustment." *Journal of African Economies*. 4(2): 259–288.

Alderman, Harold, David E. Sahn, and Jehan Arulpragasam. 1991. "Food subsidies and exchange rate distortions in Mozambique." *Food Policy*. 16(5): 395–404.

Alderman, Harold, and Gerald Shively. 1996. "Price movements and economic reform in Ghana: Implications for food security." In *Economic reform and the poor in Africa*, ed. David E. Sahn, 436–473. Oxford: Clarendon Press.

Amani, H. K. R., S. M. Kapunda, N. H. I. Lipumba, and B. J. Ndulu. 1988. "Effects of market liberalization on food security in Tanzania." In *Southern Africa: Food security policy options*, ed. M. Rukuni and R. Bernsten. Harare: University of Zimbabwe/Michigan State University Food Security Research Project.

Amani, H. K. R., Rogier van den Brink, and W. E. Maro. 1992. *Tolerating the private sector: Grain trade in Tanzania after adjustment*. Working Paper No. 32. Ithaca, NY: Cornell Food and Nutrition Policy Program.

Appleton, Simon, Paul Collier, and Paul Horsnell. 1990. *Gender, education, and employment in Côte d'Ivoire*. Social Dimensions of Adjustment Working Paper No. 8. Washington, DC: World Bank.

Arulpragasam, Jehan. 1994. "The effects of trade and exchange policies in food markets, household food consumption and urban poverty in Guinea Maritime: A multi-market analysis." Ithaca, NY: Cornell Food and Nutrition Policy Program. Photocopy.

Arulpragasam, Jehan, and Carlo del Ninno. 1996. "Do cheap imports harm the poor? Rural-urban tradeoffs in Guinea." In *Economic reform and the poor in Africa*, ed. David E. Sahn, 366–397. Oxford: Clarendon Press.

Arulpragasam, Jehan, and David E. Sahn. 1994. "Policy failure and the limits of rapid reform: Lessons from Guinea." In *Adjusting to policy failure in African economies*, ed. David E. Sahn, 53–95. Ithaca, NY: Cornell University Press.

——— 1996. Economic transition in Guinea: *Implications for growth and poverty*. New York: New York University Press.

Azam, Jean-Paul, and J. J. Faucher. 1988. "The case of Mozambique." In *The supply of manufactured goods and agricultural development*. Development Centre Paper. Paris: Organization for Economic Cooperation and Development.

Azam, Jean-Paul, and Christian Morrisson. 1994. *The Political Feasibility of Adjustment in Côte d'Ivoire and Morocco*. Development Centre Paper. Paris: Organization for Economic Cooperation and Development.

Badiane, Ousmane, and Sambouh Kinteh. 1994. *Trade pessimism and regionalism in African countries: The case of groundnut exporters*. Research Report No. 97. Washington, DC: International Food Policy Research Institute.

Bagachwa, Mboya S. D., Alexander Sarris, and Platon Tinios. 1993. *Small scale urban enterprises in Tanzania: Results from a 1991 survey*. Working Paper No. 44. Ithaca, NY: Cornell Food and Nutrition Policy Program.

Balassa, Bela. 1990. "Incentive policies and export performance in sub-Saharan Africa." *World Development*. 18(3): 383–391.

Bates, Robert H. 1981. *Markets and states in tropical Africa: The political basis of agricultural policies*. Berkeley: University of California Press.

——— 1994. "The impulse to reform in Africa." In *Economic change and political liberalization in sub-Saharan Africa*, ed. Jennifer A. Widner. Baltimore: Johns Hopkins University Press.

Benjamin, Nancy. 1993. *Income distribution and adjustment in an agricultural economy: A general equilibrium analysis of Cameroon*. Working Paper No. 41. Ithaca, NY: Cornell Food and Nutrition Policy Program.

Benjamin, Nancy C., and Shantayanan Devarajan. 1986. "Oil revenues and the Cameroonian economy." In *The political economy of Cameroon*, ed. Michael G. Schatzberg and I. William Zartman. New York: Praeger Special Studies.

Berg, Elliot, and Associates. 1983. *Joint program assessment of grain marketing in Niger*. Report prepared for USAID/Niger and the Government of Niger. Alexandria, VA: Elliot Berg and Associates.

Berg, Elliot, Graeme Hunter, Tom Lenaghan, and Malaika Riley. 1994. *Trends in living standards in Latin America and Africa in the 1980s: UNICEF myths and statistical realities*. Bethesda, MD: Development Alternatives Incorporated.

Bernier, René, and Paul A. Dorosh. 1993. *Constraints on rice production in Madagascar: The farmer's perspective*. Working Paper No. 34. Ithaca, NY: Cornell Food and Nutrition Policy Program.

Berthélemy, J. C. 1988. "The case of Madagascar." In *The supply of manufactured goods and agricultural development*. Development Centre Paper. Paris: OECD Development Centre.

Bevan, David, Paul Collier, and Jan Willem Gunning. 1990. *Controlled open economies: A neoclassical approach to structuralism*. New York: Oxford University Press.

Bevan, David, Paul Collier, Jan Willen Gunning, Peter Horsnell, and A. Bigsten. 1989. *Peasants and governments: An economic analysis*. Oxford: Clarendon Press.

Bhagwati, Jagdish. 1978. *Anatomy and consequences of exchange control regimes.* Cambridge, MA: Ballinger Pub. Co. for National Bureau for Economic Research (NBER).

1988. "Export-promoting trade strategy: Issues and evidence." *World Bank Research Observer.* 3(1): 27–57.

Bhatia, Rattan J. 1985. *The West African monetary union.* Occasional Paper No. 35. Washington, DC: International Monetary Fund.

Binswanger, Hans, and Joachim von Braun. 1991. "Technological change and commercialization in agriculture: The effect on the poor." *World Bank Research Observer.* 6(1): 57–80.

Blandford, David, Deborah Friedman, Sarah Lynch, Natasha Mukherjee, and David E. Sahn. 1994. "Oil boom and bust: The harsh realities of adjustment in Cameroon." In *Adjusting to policy failure in African economies,* ed. David E. Sahn, 131–163. Ithaca, NY: Cornell University Press.

Blandford, David, and Sarah Lynch. 1990. *Structural adjustment and the poor in Cameroon.* Washington, DC: Cornell Food and Nutrition Policy Program.

Block, Stephen A. 1993. "Agricultural productivity in sub-Saharan Africa." Ph.D. thesis. Cambridge, MA: Harvard University.

Boateng, E. Oti, Kodwo Ewusi, Ravi Kanbur, and Andrew McKay. No date. "A poverty profile for Ghana, 1987–1988." Social Dimensions of Adjustment in sub-Saharan Africa Working Paper No. 5. Washington, DC: World Bank.

Bond, M. 1983. "Agricultural responses to prices in sub-Saharan Africa." Staff Paper No. 30. Washington, DC: International Monetary Fund.

Borsdorf, Roe. 1979. *Marketing profile: Cereals and cash crops.* Vol. 2, P. F. Niger Agricultural Sector Assessment. Niamey: United States Agency for International Development (USAID).

Bourguignon, F., W. H. Branson, and J. de Melo. 1989a. *Adjustment and income distribution: A counterfactual analysis.* National Bureau of Economic Research Working Paper. Cambridge, MA.

1989b. *Macroeconomic adjustment and income distribution: A macro-micro simulation model.* Development Centre Technical Papers No. 1. Paris: Organization for Economic Cooperation and Development.

Bourguignon, François, and Christian Morrisson. 1989. *External trade and income distribution.* Paris: Organization for Economic Cooperation and Development.

Bruno, Michael, Martin Ravallion, and Lyn Squire. 1995. "Equity and growth in developing countries: Old and new perspectives on the policy issues." Prepared for the IMF Conference on Income Distribution and Sustainable Growth. Draft.

Callaghy, Thomas M., and John Ravenhill, eds. 1993. *Hemmed in: Responses to Africa's economic decline.* New York: Columbia University Press.

Carney, Judith A. 1988. "Struggles over land and crops in an irrigated rice scheme: The Gambia." In *Agriculture, women and land: The African experience,* ed. Jean Davison. Boulder, CO: Westview Press.

Chacholiades, Miltiades. 1978. *International trade theory and policy.* Auckland: McGraw-Hill.

Chen, Shaohua, Gaurav Datt, and Martin Ravallion. 1993. "Is poverty increasing in the developing world?" Poverty and Human Resources Division. Policy Research Department. Washington, DC: World Bank.

Cleaver, Kevin, and W. Graeme Donovan. 1994. "Agriculture, poverty and policy reform in sub-Saharan Africa." Printed for African Studies Association meeting. Washington, DC: World Bank. Draft.

Colclough, Christopher. 1991. "Wage flexibility in sub-Saharan Africa: Trends and explanations." In *Towards social adjustment: Labor market issues in structural adjustment*, ed. G. Standing and V. Tokman. Geneva: International Labour Organisation.

Collier, Paul. 1991. "Africa's external economic relations: 1960–90." *African Affairs*. 90(360): 339–356.

Cook, Andy. 1989. "Nigerian markets for livestock and meat: Prospects for Niger." Niamey: United States Agency for International Development. Photocopy.

Corden, W. M. 1984. "The normative theory of international trade." In *Handbook of international economics*, vol. 1, ed. R. W. Jones and P. B. Kenen. Amsterdam: Elsevier Science Publishers.

Cornell Food and Nutrition Policy Program. 1990. *Conakry Household Welfare Survey, 1989–1990*. Ithaca, NY: Cornell University.

1992. *CFNPP Labor Retrenchment Survey, Ghana*. Ithaca, NY: Cornell University.

Cornia, G. A. 1994. "Neglected issues in the decline of Africa's agriculture: Land tenure, land distribution and R&D constraints." In *From adjustment to development in Africa: Conflict, controversy, convergence, consensus?*, ed. G. A. Cornia and G. K. Helleiner. New York: St. Martin's Press.

Cornia, G. A., R. Jolly, and F. Stewart. 1987. *Adjustment with a human face*. Vol. 2. Oxford: Clarendon Press for UNICEF.

Cornia, G. A., R. van der Hoeven, and D. Lall. 1992. In *Africa's recovery in the 1990s: From stagnation and adjustment to human development*, ed. G. A. Cornia, R. van der Hoeven, and T. Mkandawire. New York: St. Martin's Press.

Cuddington, J. 1992. "Long-run trends in 26 primary commodity prices: A disaggregated look at the Prebisch-Singer hypothesis." *Journal of Development Economics*. 39(2): 207–227.

Deaton, Angus, and John Muellbauer. 1980. *Economics and consumer behavior*. Cambridge: Cambridge University Press.

de Merode, Louis. 1992. "Implementing civil service pay and employment reform in Africa: The experiences of Ghana, The Gambia, and Guinea." Draft.

del Ninno, Carlo. 1994. *Welfare and poverty in Conakry: Assessment and determinants*. Working Paper No. 66. Ithaca, NY: Cornell Food and Nutrition Policy Program.

Dervis, Kemal, Jaime de Melo, and Sherman Robinson. 1982. *General equilibrium models for development policy*. Washington, DC: World Bank.

Devarajan, Shantayanan, and Jaime de Melo. 1987. "Evaluating participation in African monetary unions: A statistical analysis of the CFA zones." *World Development*. 15(4): 483–496.

1990. *Membership in the CFA zone: Odyssean journey or Trojan horse?* Working Paper No. 482. Washington, DC: World Bank.

Devarajan, Shantayanan, and D. Rodrik. 1991. *Do the benefits of fixed exchange rates outweigh their costs? The Franc zone in Africa*. Working Paper No. 3727. Cambridge, MA: National Bureau of Economic Research.

Dollar, David. 1992. "Outward-oriented developing economies really do grow more rapidly: Evidence from 95 LDCs, 1976–1985." *Economic Development and Cultural Change*. 40(3): 523–544.

Donovan, Graeme. 1993. "Malawi – Structural adjustment and agriculture." World Bank Sector Study. Washington, DC: World Bank.

Dornbusch, Rudiger. 1974. "Tariffs and nontraded goods." *Journal of International Economics*. 4(May): 177–185.

Dorosh, Paul. 1994a. "Economic fallout from a uranium boom: Structural adjustment in Niger." In

Adjusting to policy failure in African economies, ed. David E. Sahn, 164–195. Ithaca, NY: Cornell University Press.

1994b. *Structural adjustment, growth and poverty in Madagascar: A CGE analysis.* Monograph No. 17. Ithaca, NY: Cornell Food and Nutrition Policy Program.

1996. "Rents and exchange rates: Redistribution through trade liberalization in Madagascar." In *Economic reform and the poor in Africa*, ed. David E. Sahn, 29–61. Oxford: Clarendon Press.

Dorosh, Paul, and René Bernier. 1991. "Memorandum on the monitoring of export crop prices in Madagascar." Ithaca, NY: Cornell Food and Nutrition Policy Program.

1994a. *Agricultural and food policy issues in Mozambique: A multi-market analysis.* Working Paper No. 63. Ithaca, NY: Cornell Food and Nutrition Policy Program.

1994b. "Staggered reforms and limited success: Structural adjustment in Madagascar." In *Adjusting to policy failure in African economies*, ed. David E. Sahn, 332–365. Ithaca, NY: Cornell University Press.

Dorosh, Paul A., René Bernier, Armand Roger Randrianarivony, and Christian Rasolomanana. 1991. *A social accounting matrix for Madagascar: Methodology and results.* Working Paper No. 6. Ithaca, NY: Cornell Food and Nutrition Policy Program.

Dorosh, Paul, René Bernier, and Alexander Sarris. 1990. *Macroeconomic adjustment and the poor: The case of Madagascar.* Monograph No. 9. Ithaca, NY: Cornell Food and Nutrition Policy Program.

Dorosh, Paul, Carlo del Ninno, and David E. Sahn. 1995. "Poverty alleviation in Mozambique: A multi-market analysis of the role of food aid." *Agricultural Economics.* 13: 1156.

1996. "Market liberalization and the role of food aid in Mozambique." In *Economic reform and the poor in Africa*, ed. David E. Sahn. Oxford: Clarendon Press.

Dorosh, Paul A., and B. Essama-Nssah. 1991. *A social accounting matrix for Niger: Methodology and results.* Working Paper No. 18. Ithaca, NY: Cornell Food and Nutrition Policy Program.

1993. *External shocks, policy reform and income distribution in Niger.* Working Paper No. 40. Ithaca, NY: Cornell Food and Nutrition Policy Program.

Dorosh, Paul A., B. Essama-Nssah, and Ousmane Samba-Mamadou. 1996. "Terms of trade and the real exchange rate in the CFA zone: Implications for income distribution in Niger." In *Economic reform and the poor in Africa*, ed. David E. Sahn, 147–182. Oxford: Clarendon Press.

Dorosh, Paul, and Steven Haggblade. 1993. "Agriculture-led growth: Foodgrains versus export crops in Madagascar." *Agricultural Economics.* 9: 165–180.

Dorosh, Paul A., and Mattias K. A. Lundberg. 1993. *A general equilibrium analysis of adjustment and the poor in Gambia.* Working Paper No. 46. Ithaca, NY: Cornell Food and Nutrition Policy Program.

1996. "More than just peanuts (groundnuts): Aid flows and policy reform in The Gambia." In *Economic reform and the poor in Africa*, ed. David E. Sahn, 398–435. Oxford: Clarendon Press.

Dorosh, Paul A., and David E. Sahn. 1993. *A general equilibrium analysis of the effect of macroeconomic adjustment on poverty in Africa.* Working Paper No. 39. Ithaca, NY: Cornell Food and Nutrition Policy Program.

Forthcoming. A general equilibrium analysis of the effect of macroeconomic adjustment on poverty in Africa." *Journal of Policy Modeling.*

Due, Jean M., and Christina Gladwin. 1991. "Impacts of structural adjustment programs on African women farmers and female-headed households." *American Journal of Agricultural Economics.* 73(5): 1431–1439.

Edwards, Sebastian. 1988. *Exchange rate misalignment in developing countries.* Baltimore, MD: Johns Hopkins University Press.

———. 1989. *Real exchange rates, devaluation, and adjustment: Exchange rate policy in developing countries.* Cambridge, MA: MIT Press.

———. 1993. "Openness, trade liberalization, and growth in developing countries." *Journal of Economic Literature.* 31: 1358–1393.

Elson, Diane. 1991. "Gender and adjustment in the 1990's: An update on evidence and strategies." Presented at the Inter-Regional Meeting on Economic Distress: Structural Adjustment and Women, Lancaster House, London, June 13–14.

Ethier, W. 1983. *Modern international economics.* London: Norton.

Feder, Gershon, and David Feeny. 1991. "Land tenure and property rights: Theory and implications for development policy." *World Bank Economic Review.* 5(1): 135–153.

Feder, Gershon, and Raymond Noronha. 1987. *Land rights systems and agricultural development in sub-Saharan Africa.* Washington, DC: World Bank.

Fields, Gary. 1989. "Changes in poverty and inequality in developing countries." *World Bank Research Observer.* 4(2): 87–102.

Folbre, Nancy. 1986. "Hearts and spades: Paradigms of household economics." *World Development.* 14(2S): 245S–255S.

Frenkel, J., and M. Khan. 1990. "Adjustment policies and economic development." *American Journal of Agricultural Economics.* 72: 815–820.

Gallagher, Mark. 1991. "A scorecard of African economic reforms." *Fletcher Forum of World Affairs.* 15(1): 57–76.

Gauthier, Madeleine, and Steven Kyle. 1991. *A social accounting matrix for Cameroon.* Working Paper No. 4. Ithaca, NY: Cornell Food and Nutrition Policy Program.

Gelb, Alan. 1986. "Adjustments to windfall gains: A comparative analysis of oil-exporting countries." In *Natural resources and the macroeconomy,* ed. J. P. Neary and S. van Wijnbergen. Cambridge, MA: MIT Press.

Ghura, Dhaneshwar, and Thomas J. Grennes. 1993. "The real exchange rate and macroeconomic performance in sub-Saharan Africa." *Journal of Development Economics.* 42(1): 155–174.

Gill, Dhara S. 1987. "Effectiveness of agricultural extension services in reaching rural women: A synthesis of studies from five African countries." Rome: Food and Agricultural Organization.

Gladwin, Christina H. 1991. "Fertilizer subsidy removal programs and their potential impacts on women farmers in Malawi and Cameroon." In *Structural adjustment and African women farmers,* ed. C. H. Gladwin. Gainesville: University of Florida Press.

Gladwin, C., and D. McMillan. 1989. "Is a turnaround in Africa possible without helping African women to farm?" *Economic Development and Cultural Change.* 37(2): 345–364.

Glewwe, Paul. 1988. "The distribution of welfare in Côte d'Ivoire in 1985." Living Standard Measurement Study Working Paper No. 29. Washington, DC: World Bank.

Glick, Peter, and David E. Sahn. 1993. *Labor force participation, sectoral choice, and earnings in Conakry, Guinea.* Working Paper No. 43. Ithaca, NY: Cornell Food and Nutrition Policy Program.

———. 1997. "Gender and education impacts on employment and earnings in West Africa: Evidence from Guinea." *Economic Development and Cultural Change.*

Goheen, Miriam. 1991. "The ideology and political economy of gender: Women and land in Nso, Cameroon." In *Structural adjustment and African women farmers,* ed. Christina Gladwin. Gainesville: University of Florida Press.

Government of Côte d'Ivoire. 1985. "Côte d'Ivoire living standards survey." Data tapes, Abijan, Côte d'Ivoire.

Government of Ghana. 1987. "Ghana living standards survey." Data tapes, Accra, Ghana.

Government of Guinea. 1986. "Enquête légère sur la consommation des ménages de la ville de Conakry, 30/09/84–3/11/84." Conakry, Guinea: Minstére du Plan et de la Coopération International. Photocopy.

Government of Guinea. 1994. "Enquête integrale sur les conditions de vie des manages." Conakry, Guinea: Minstére du Plan/ Minstére des Finances. Photocopy.

Government of Madagascar. 1993. "Enquête permanente auprès des ménages 1993." Data tapes, Antananarivo, Madagascar.

Government of Mozambique/Cornell Food and Nutrition Policy Program. 1992. "Maputo food security survey." Data tapes, Mozambique: Food Security Department, Ministry of Commerce.

Government of Niger. 1993. *Annuaire Statistique: Edition 1992–1993.* Niamey, Niger: Ministère des Finances et du Plan, Direction Generale du Plan, Direction de la Statistique et des Comptes Nationaux.

Government of Tanzania/World Bank. 1995. "Tanzania human resource development survey." Data tapes, Dar Es Salaam, Tanzania.

Greenaway, David, and Chris Milner. 1990. "Industrial incentives, domestic resource costs and resource allocation in Madagascar." *Applied Economics.* 22: 805–821.

Greer, J., and Erik Thorbecke. 1986. "A methodology for measuring food poverty applied to Kenya." *Journal of Development Economics.* 24(1): 59–74.

Grootaert, Christian. 1995. "Analyzing poverty and policy reform: The experience of Côte d'Ivoire." Washington, DC: World Bank. Photocopy.

Guillaumont, Patrick, and Sylviane Guillaumont. 1984. *Zone franc et developpement Africain.* Paris: Economica.

Guillaumont, Patrick, Sylviane Guillaumont, and Patrick Plane. 1988. "Participating in African monetary unions: An alternative evaluation." *World Development.* 16(5): 569–576.

Haddad, Lawrence. 1990. "Gender and economic adjustment in Ghana and Côte d'Ivoire: Executive summary." Washington, DC: International Food Policy Research Institute. Draft.

Haggblade, Steven, Peter Hazell, and James Brown. 1989. "Farm-nonfarm linkages in rural sub-Saharan Africa." *World Development.* 17(8): 1173–1201.

Helleiner, G. K. 1992. "Introduction." *Trade policy, industrialization, and development: New perspectives*, ed. G.K. Helleiner, Oxford: Clarendon Press.

——— 1994. "Introduction." In *Trade policy and industrialization in turbulent times*, ed. G. K. Helleiner. London: Routledge.

Hoddintot, John. 1993. *Wages and unemployment in urban Côte d'Ivoire.* Working Paper No. 93.3. Oxford: Centre for the Study of African Economies.

Horton, Susan, Ravi Kanbur, and Dipak Mazumdar. 1994. "Labor markets in an era of adjustment: An overview." In *Labor markets in an era of adjustment: An overview*, ed. S. Horton, R. Kanbur, and D. Mazumdar. Washington, DC: World Bank.

Humphreys, Charles P. 1986. "Mali: Cereals policy reform in the Sahel." A Report prepared for the Organization For Economic Cooperation and Development/Club du Sahel/CILSS.

Husain, Ishrat, and Rashid Faruqee. 1993. *Adjustment in Africa: Lessons from country case studies.* Washington, DC: World Bank.

International Monetary Fund (IMF). Various years a. *Government finance statistics yearbook.* Washington, DC: IMF.

Various years b. *International financial statistics.* Washington, DC: IMF.

1989. "Madagascar – Recent economic developments." Washington, DC: IMF. Photocopy.

1992a. "The Gambia – Background paper and statistical appendix." Washington, DC: IMF. Photocopy.

1992b. "Republic of Mozambique – Statistical annex." Washington, DC: IMF. Photocopy.

1993a. "The Gambia – Statistical annex." Washington, DC: IMF. Photocopy.

1993b. "Ghana – Recent economic developments." Washington, DC: IMF. Photocopy.

1993c. "Madagascar – Statistical annex." Washington, DC: IMF. Photocopy.

1993d. "Niger – Recent economic developments." Washington, DC: IMF. Photocopy.

1994a. "Malawi – Background paper." Washington, DC: IMF. Photocopy.

1994b. "Tanzania – Recent economic developments." Washington, DC: IMF. Photocopy.

1994c. "Zaire – Recent economic developments." Washington, DC: IMF. Photocopy.

1994d. "Cameroon – Background papers and statistical appendix." Washington, DC: IMF. Photocopy.

Jabara, Cathy. 1990. *Economic reform and poverty in The Gambia.* Monograph No. 8. Ithaca, NY: Cornell Food and Nutrition Policy Program.

1991. *Structural adjustment and stabilization in Niger: Macroeconomic consequences and social adjustment.* Monograph No. 11. Ithaca, NY: Cornell Food and Nutrition Policy Program.

1994. "Structural adjustment in a small, open economy: The case of Gambia." In *Adjusting to policy failure in African economies*, ed. David E. Sahn, 302–331. Ithaca, NY: Cornell University Press.

Jabara, Cathy L., Mattias Lundberg, and Abdoulie Sireh Jallow. 1992. *A social accounting matrix for Gambia.* Working Paper No. 20. Ithaca, NY: Cornell Food and Nutrition Policy Program.

Jaeger, William K. 1992a. "The causes of Africa's food crisis." *World Development.* 20(11): 1631–1645.

1992b. *The effects of economic policies on African agriculture.* World Bank Discussion Papers No. 147. Washington, DC: World Bank.

Jamal, Vali. 1993. "Surplus extraction and the African agrarian crisis in historical perspective." In *Economic crisis and Third World agriculture*, ed. Ajit Singh and Hamid Tabatabai. Cambridge: Cambridge University Press.

Jamal, Vali, and John Weeks. 1993. *Africa misunderstood or whatever happened to the rural-urban gap?* London: Macmillan and International Labour Organization.

Jebuni, Charles, and Wayo Seini. 1992. *Agricultural input policies under structural adjustment: Their distributional implications.* Working Paper No. 31. Ithaca, NY: Cornell Food and Nutrition Policy Program.

Jimenez, Emmanuel. 1989. "Social sector pricing policy revisited: A survey of some recent controversies." *Proceedings of the World Bank annual conference on development economics.* Washington, DC: World Bank.

Jones, Ronald W., and J. Peter Neary. 1984. "The positive theory of international trade." In *Handbook of international economics*, vol. 1, ed. R. W. Jones and P. B. Kenen. Amsterdam: Elsevier Science Publishers.

Kandoole, B. F., et al. No date. "ADMARC's cost structure." Malawi Government/World Bank Study. Mimeographed copy.

Karp-Toledo, Elaine. 1991. "Les fonds d'emploi – Sont-ils efficaces? Une evaluation socio-economique de la Dire/FNE au Senegal." Draft.

Kennedy, Eileen, and Lawrence Haddad. 1994. "Are preschoolers from female-headed households less malnourished? A comparative analysis of results from Ghana and Kenya." *Journal of Development Studies.* 30(3): 680–695.

Kiguel, Miguel, and Stephen A. O'Connell. 1995. "Parallel exchange rates in developing countries." *World Bank Research Observer.* 10(1): 21–52.

Kingsbury, David S. 1992. "Compensatory social programs and structural adjustment: A review of experience." Bethesda, MD: Development Alternatives.

Koné, Solomane, and Erik Thorbecke. 1994. "Macroeconomic policies and poverty alleviation in Zaire: A social accounting matrix (SAM) approach." Ithaca, NY: Cornell Food and Nutrition Policy Program. Photocopy.

Koons, A. S. 1989. "Reaching rural women in the Northwest Province. A presentation of more ways in which women are not men." Draft paper for the Conference on Development in Cameroon: The Role of Food and Agriculture. Gainesville: University of Florida.

Krueger, Anne O. 1974. "The political economy of the rent-seeking society." *American Economic Review.* 64(3): 291–303.

——— 1978. *Foreign trade regimes and economic development: Liberalization attempts and consequences.* Cambridge, MA: Ballinger Pub. Co. for National Bureau for Economic Research (NBER).

Krueger, Anne O., Maurice Schiff, and Alberto Valdes. 1988. "Agricultural incentives in developing countries: Measuring the effect of sectoral and economywide policies." *World Bank Economic Review.* 2(3): 255–271.

Krumm, Kathie L. 1993. "A medium-term framework for analyzing the real exchange rate, with applications to the Philippines and Tanzania." *World Bank Economic Review.* 7(2): 219–245.

Kyle, Steven. 1994. "Structural adjustment in a country at war: The case of Mozambique." In *Adjusting to policy failure in African economies*, ed. David E. Sahn, 234–259. Ithaca, NY: Cornell University Press.

Lane, C. E. 1989. *The effectiveness of monetary policy in Côte d'Ivoire.* Working Paper No. 30. London: Overseas Development Institute.

Lecaillon, J., and C. Morrisson. 1985. *Economic policies and agricultural performance: The case of Burkina Faso.* Paris: Organization for Economic Cooperation and Development.

——— 1986. *Economic policies and agricultural performance: The case of Mali.* Paris: Organization for Economic Cooperation and Development.

Lele, Uma, and Kofi Adu-Nyako. 1992. "Approaches to uprooting poverty in Africa." *Food Policy.* 17(2): 95–108.

León, Javier, and Raimundo Soto. 1995. *Structural breaks and long-run trends in commodity prices.* Policy Research Working Paper No. 1406. Washington, DC: World Bank.

Levy, Victor, and John Newman. 1989. "Wage rigidity: Micro and macro evidence on labor market adjustment in the modern sector." *World Bank Economic Review.* 3(1): 97–117.

Lewis, Jeffrey D., and Malcolm F. McPherson. 1994. "Macroeconomic management: To finance or adjust." In *Asia and Africa: Legacies and opportunities in development*, ed. David L. Lindauer and Michael Romer, 99–149. San Francisco: Institute for Comtemporary Studies Press.

Lindauer, David, and B. Nunberg, eds. 1994. *Rehabilitating government: Pay and employment reform in Africa.* Washington, DC: World Bank.

Lipton, Michael, and Martin Ravallion. 1995. "Poverty and policy." In *Handbook of development economics*, vol. 3, ed. Jere Behrman and T. N. Srinivasan. Amsterdam: North-Holland.

Lipumba, N. H. I. 1993. "Economic adjustment, policy performance, and development in Tanzania." In *Policies for growth and development in Africa*. A collection of papers presented at the Second Regional Conference of the International Center for Economic Growth. Africa Correspondent Institutes. Abidjan, Côte d'Ivoire April 20–24.

Little, Ian, Tibor Scitovsky, and Maurice Scott. 1970. *Industry and trade in some developing countries*. London: Oxford University Press for Organization for Economic Cooperation and Development.

Lynch, Sarah. 1991. *Income distribution, poverty, and consumer preferences in Cameroon*. Working Paper No. 16. Ithaca, NY: Cornell Food and Nutrition Policy Program.

Martin, F., and E. Crawford. 1988. "Analysis of alternative producer price policies in Senegal using a micro-macro modelling approach." East Lansing: Michigan State University. Mimeographed copy.

Meena, Ruth. 1991. "The impact of structural adjustment programs on rural women in Tanzania." In *Structural adjustment and African women farmers*, ed. C. Gladwin. Gainesville: University of Florida Press.

Meerman, Jacob. 1979. *Public expenditure in Malaysia: Who benefits and why*. Oxford: Oxford University Press for the World Bank.

Mehra, Rekha. 1991. "Can structural adjustment work for women farmers?" *American Journal of Agricultural Economics*. 73(5): 1440–1447.

Mellor, John W., Christopher L. Delgado, and Malcolm J. Blackie, eds. 1987. *Accelerating food production in sub-Saharan Africa*. Baltimore: Johns Hopkins University Press for International Food Policy Research Institute.

Mills, Bradford. 1994. *The impact of gender discrimination on the job search strategies of redeployed public sector workers*. Working Paper No. 51. Ithaca, NY: Cornell Food and Nutrition Policy Program.

Mills, Bradford, and David E. Sahn. 1993a. "Characteristics of small scale enterprises and proprietors in Conakry." Guinea Bulletin No. 9. Ithaca, NY: Cornell Food and Nutrition Policy Program.

1993b. *Is there life after public service: The fate of retrenched workers in Conakry, Guinea*. Working Paper No. 42. Ithaca, NY: Cornell Food and Nutrition Policy Program.

1995. "Reducing the size of the public sector work force: Institutional constraints and human consequences in Guinea." *Journal of Development Studies*. 31(4): 505–528.

Mills, Bradford, David E. Sahn, E. E. Walden, and Stephen Younger. 1994. *Public finance and public employment: An analysis of public sector retrenchment programs in Guinea and Ghana*. Working Paper No. 52. Ithaca, NY: Cornell Food and Nutrition Policy Program.

MOA/MSU/UA Research Team. 1992. *The determinants of household income and consumption in rural Nampula province: Implications for food security and agricultural policy reform*. Working Paper No. 6. Mozambique: Ministry of Agriculture.

Mosley, Paul, Jane Harrigan, and John Toye. 1991. *Aid and power*. London: Routledge.

Mosley, Paul, and John Weeks. 1993. "Has recovery begun? 'Africa's adjustment in the 1980s' revisited." *World Development*. 21(10): 1583–1606.

Mukui, John Thinguri. 1994. "Kenya: Poverty profiles, 1982–92." Consultant report prepared for the Office of the Vice-President and Ministry of Planning and National Development, Nairobi, Kenya. Unpublished manuscript.

Nashashibi, Karim, and Stefania Bazzoni. 1993. *Alternative exchange rate strategies and fiscal performance in sub-Saharan Africa*. IMF Working Paper. Washington, DC: IMF.

Ndongko, Wilfred A. 1986. "The political economy of development in Cameroon: Relations between the state, indigenous business, and foreign investors." In *The political economy of Cameroon*, ed. Michael G. Schatzberg and I. William Zartman. New York: Praeger Publishers.

Ndulu, Bennno J., and Joseph J. Semboja. 1994. "Trade and industrialization in Tanzania: A review of experience and issues." In *Trade policy and industrialization in turbulent times*, ed. G. K. Helleiner. London: Routledge.

Nindi, B. C. 1992. "Gender, exploitation development and agricultural transformation in sub-Saharan Africa." *Eastern Africa Economic Review*. 8(2): 123–134.

Nunberg, Barbara. 1994. "Experience with civil service reform: An overview." In *Rehabilitating government: Pay and employment in Africa*, ed. D. Lindauer and B. Nunberg. Washington, DC: World Bank.

Omolehinwa, Eddy, and Emery M. Roe. 1989. "Boom and bust budgeting: Repetitive budgetary processes in Nigeria, Kenya and Ghana." *Public Budgeting and Finance*. 9(2): 43–65.

Pardey, Philip G., Johannes Roseboom, and Nienke M. Beintema. 1995. "Investments in African agricultural research." Environment and Production Technology Division Discussion Paper No. 14. The Hague, The Netherlands, and Washington, DC: International Service for National Agricultural Research and International Food Policy Research Institute. Photocopy.

Pinto, Brian. 1990. "Black market premia, exchange rate unification, and inflation in sub-Saharan Africa." *World Bank Economic Review*. 3(3): 321–338.

Prebisch, Raúl. 1950. *The economic development of Latin America and its principal problems.* New York: United Nations.

Pryor, Frederic L. 1988. *Income distribution and economic development in Malawi: Some historical statistics*. World Bank Discussion Paper No. 36. Washington, DC: World Bank.

    1990. *The political economy of poverty, equity, and growth: Malawi and Madagascar*. Oxford: Oxford University Press for the World Bank.

Quisumbing, Agnes, L. Schwartz, and C. Chibawana. 1992. "Women in agriculture: Issues and strategies." Working Paper Draft.

Radelet, Steven C. 1992. "Reform without revolt: The political economy of economic reform in The Gambia." *World Development*. 20(8): 1087–1099.

Ravallion, Martin. 1994. *Poverty comparisons*. Fundamentals of Pure and Applied Economics 56. Switzerland: Harwood Academic Publishers.

Reinhart, C., and P. Wickham. 1994. "Commodity prices: Cyclical weakness or secular decline?" *IMF Staff Papers*. 41(2): 175–213.

Reserve Bank of Malawi. 1987. *Financial and economic review*. 19(2).

    1988. *Financial and economic review*. 20(4).

Sahn, David E. 1992. "Public expenditure in sub-Saharan Africa during a period of economic reforms." *World Development*. 20(5): 673–693.

    1993. "A preliminary analysis of labor force participation and sectoral choice among women in Maputo, Mozambique." Ithaca, NY: Cornell Food and Nutrition Policy Program. Photocopy.

    ed. 1994. *Adjusting to policy failure in African economies*. Ithaca, NY: Cornell University Press.

    ed. 1996. *Economic reform and the poor in Africa*. Oxford: Clarendon Press.

Sahn, David E., and Jehan Arulpragasam. 1991a. *Development through dualism? Land tenure policy and poverty in Malawi*. Working Paper No. 9. Ithaca, NY: Cornell Food and Nutrition Policy Program.

1991b. "The stagnation of smallholder agriculture in Malawi: A decade of structural adjustment." *Food Policy.* 16(3): 219–234.

1993. "Land tenure, dualism, and poverty in Malawi." In *Including the poor,* ed. Jacques van der Gaag and Michael Lipton, 306–334. Washington, DC: World Bank.

Sahn, David E., Jehan Arulpragasam, and Lemma Merid. 1990. *Policy reform and poverty in Malawi: A survey of a decade of experience.* Monograph No. 7. Ithaca, NY: Cornell Food and Nutrition Policy Program.

Sahn, David E., and René Bernier. 1993. *Evidence from Africa on the intrasectoral allocation of social sector expenditures.* Working Paper No. 45. Ithaca, NY: Cornell Food and Nutrition Policy Program.

1995. "Have structural adjustments led to health sector reform in Africa?" *Health Policy* 32(1–3): 193–214.

Sahn, David E., and Carlo del Ninno. 1994. *Living standards and the determinants of poverty and income distribution in Mozambique.* Working Paper No. 56. Ithaca, NY: Cornell Food and Nutrition Policy Program.

Sahn, David E., and Jaikishan Desai. 1994. *The emergence of parallel markets in a transition economy: The case of Mozambique.* Working Paper No. 53. Ithaca, NY: Cornell Food and Nutrition Policy Program.

1995. "The emergence of parallel markets in a transition economy: The case of Mozambique." *Food Policy.* 20(2): 83–98.

Sahn, David E., Paul A. Dorosh, and Stephen D. Younger. 1994. *Economic reform in Africa: A foundation for poverty alleviation.* Working Paper No. 72. Ithaca, NY: Cornell Food and Nutrition Policy Program.

Sahn, David E., Yves Van Frausum, and Gerald Shively. 1994. "Modeling the nutritional and distributional effects of taxing export crops." *Economic Development and Cultural Change.* 42(4): 773–793.

Saito, Katrine A., and Daphne Spurling. 1992. *Developing agricultural extension for women farmers.* World Bank Discussion Paper No. 156. Washington, DC: World Bank.

Sapsford, D., P. Sarkar, and H. W. Singer. 1992. "The Prebisch-Singer terms of trade controversy revisited." *Journal of International Development.* 4(5): 315–332.

Sarris, Alexander. 1994a. "Macroeconomic policy and household incomes: A dynamic general equilibrium analysis for Tanzania." Ithaca, NY: Cornell Food and Nutrition Policy Program. Photocopy.

1994b. *A social accounting matrix for Tanzania.* Working Paper No. 62. Ithaca, NY: Cornell Food and Nutrition Policy Program.

1996. "Macroeconomic policies and household welfare in Tanzania." In *Economic reform and the poor in Africa,* ed. David E. Sahn, 104–146. Oxford: Clarendon Press.

Sarris, Alexander H., and Rogier van den Brink, eds. 1993. *Economic policy and welfare during crisis and adjustment in Tanzania.* New York: New York University Press for the Cornell Food and Nutrition Policy Program.

1994. "From forced modernization to Perestroika: Crisis and adjustment in Tanzania." In *Adjusting to policy failure in African economies,* ed. David E. Sahn, 260–301. Ithaca, NY: Cornell University Press.

Scarborough, Vanessa. 1994. "Malawi agricultural sector memorandum: Agricultural pricing and marketing issues." Working Paper No. 7. Washington, DC: World Bank. Draft.

Schneider, Hartmut, Winifred Weekes-Vagliani, Paolo Groppo, Sylvie Lambert, Akiko Suwa, and Nghia Nguyen Tinh. 1992. *Adjustment and equity in Côte d'Ivoire.* Paris: Organization for Economic Cooperation and Development.

Scobie, Grant M. 1989. *Macroeconomic adjustment and the poor: Toward a research policy.* Monograph No. 1. Ithaca, NY: Cornell Food and Nutrition Policy Program.

Selowsky, Marcelo. 1979. *Who benefits from government expenditures? A case study of Colombia.* New York: Oxford University Press for the World Bank.

Sen, Binayak. 1994. "Adjustment, poverty and inequality: Insights from a cross-country analysis with household expenditure survey data." Washington, DC: Operations Evaluation Department, World Bank. Draft.

Shipton, Parker. 1987. *The Kenyan land tenure reform: Misunderstandings in the public creation of private property.* Developmental Discussion Paper No. 239. Cambridge, MA: Harvard Institute for International Development.

Shoven, John B., and John Whalley. 1992. *Applying general equilibrium.* Cambridge. Cambridge University Press.

Shuttleworth, Graham. 1989. "Policies in transition: Lessons from Madagascar." *World Development.* 17(3): 397–408.

Simler, Kenneth. 1994. *Agricultural policy and technology options in Malawi: Modelling smallholder responses and outcomes.* Working Paper No. 49. Ithaca, NY: Cornell Food and Nutrition Policy Program.

Sines, Richard, Christopher Pardy, Mary Reintsma, and E. Scott Thomas. 1987. *Impact of Zaire's economic liberalization program on the agricultural sector: A preliminary assessment.* Washington, DC: Robert Nathan Associates and United States Agency for International Development.

Singer, Hans W. 1950. "The distribution of gains between investing and borrowing countries." *American Economic Review.* 40(2): 473–485.

Singh, Ajit, and Hamid Tabatabai. 1993. *Economic crisis and Third World agriculture.* Cambridge: Cambridge University Press.

Singh, I., and S. Janakiram. 1986. "Agricultural household modeling in a multicrop environment: Case studies in Korea and Nigeria." In *Agricultural household models: Extensions, applications, and policy,* ed. I. Singh, L. Squire, and J. Strauss. Baltimore: Johns Hopkins University Press for the World Bank.

SPA. 1994. "Status Report for The Gambia." April 1994 Multidonor Meeting.

Stewart, Frances. 1992. *Alternative development strategies in sub-Saharan Africa.* New York: St. Martin's Press.

———. 1994. "Are short-term policies consistent with long-term development needs in Africa." In *From adjustment to development in Africa: Conflict, controversy, convergence, consensus?* ed. Giovanni Andrea Cornia and Gerald K. Helleiner. New York: St. Martin's Press.

Stolper, W., and Samuelson, P. 1941. "Protection and real wages." *Review of Economic Studies.* 19(1): 58–73.

Strauss, J. 1984. "Joint determination of food consumption and production in rural Sierra Leone." *Journal of Development Economics.* 14(1): 77–103.

Stryker, Dirck, et al. 1994. "Linking macroeconomic and sectoral policies and investments with the alleviation of poverty in sub-Saharan Africa." Cambridge: Associates for International Resources and Development. Photocopy.

Subramanian, Shankar. 1994. *Structural adjustment and income distribution in Cameroon.* Working Paper No. 67. Ithaca, NY: Cornell Food and Nutrition Policy Program.

———. 1996. "Vulnerability to price shocks under alternative policies in Cameroon." In *Economic reform and the poor in Africa,* ed. David E. Sahn, 62–103. Oxford: Clarendon Press.

Tabatabai, Hamid. 1993. *Poverty and food consumption in urban Zaire.* Working Paper No. 47. Ithaca, NY: Cornell Food and Nutrition Policy Program.

Taylor, Lance. 1993. *The rocky road to reform: Adjustment, income distribution, and growth in the developing world.* Cambridge, MA: MIT Press.

Thomas, Vinod, and John Nash. 1991. "Reform of trade policy: Recent evidence from theory and practice." *World Bank Research Observer.* 6(2): 219–240.

Tinios, P., A. H. Sarris, H. K. R. Amani, W. E. Maro, and S. Zografakis. 1994. "The structure of households in Tanzania in 1991: Results from a national household survey." Working Paper No. 59. Ithaca, NY: Cornell Food and Nutrition Policy Program. Photocopy.

Traoré, Aminata. 1984. "Women's access to resources in the Ivory Coast: Women and land in Adioukrou district." In *Rural development and women in Africa.* Geneva: International Labour Organisation.

Tshishimbi, wa Bilenga, and Peter Glick. 1993. *Stabilization and structural adjustment in Zaire.* Monograph No. 16. Ithaca, NY: Cornell Food and Nutrition Policy Program.

United Nations. Various years. *International trade statistical yearbook.* New York: United Nations.

United Nations Development Programme (UNDP). 1993. *Human development report.* New York: Oxford University Press for United Nations Development Programme.

United Nations Development Programme and World Bank. 1989. *African economic and financial data.* New York and Washington, DC: UNDP and World Bank.

United Nations Economic Commission for Africa (UNECA). 1989. *Statistics and politics – ECA preliminary observations on the World Bank report.* Addis Ababa: United Nations Economic Commission in Africa.

United States Agency for International Development (USAID). 1989. "Food needs assessment for The Gambia, 1989–90." Banjul: USAID. Mimeographed copy.

van de Walle, Nicolas. 1989. "Rice politics in Cameroon: State commitment, capability, and urban bias." *Journal of Modern African Studies.* 27(4): 579–599.

——— 1994. "Neopatrimonialism and democracy in Africa, with an illustration from Cameroon." In *Economic change and political liberalization in sub-Saharan Africa,* ed. Jennifer A. Widner. Baltimore: Johns Hopkins University Press.

van den Brink, Rogier, and Daniel W. Bromley. 1992. *The enclosures revisited: Privatization, titling, and the quest for advantage in Africa.* Working Paper No. 19. Ithaca, NY: Cornell Food and Nutrition Policy Program.

Van Frausum, Yves, and David E. Sahn. 1993. "An econometric model for Malawi: Measuring the effects of external shocks and policies." *Journal of Policy Modeling.* 15(3).

von Braun, Joachim, and E. Kennedy. 1986. "Commercialization of subsistence agriculture: Income and nutritional effects in developing countries." Washington, DC: International Food Policy Research Institute.

——— 1994. *Agricultural commercialization, economic development and nutrition.* Baltimore: Johns Hopkins University Press.

von Braun, J., and D. Puetz. 1987. An African fertilizer crisis: Origin and economic effects in the Gambia. Food Policy 12 (November): 337–348.

von Braun, J., and P. J. R. Webb. 1987. "The impact of new crop technology on the agricultural division of labor in a West African setting." Washington, DC: International Food Policy Research Institute.

Wagoa, J. H. 1992. "Adjustment policies in Tanzania, 1981–9: The impact on growth, structure, and human welfare." In *Africa's recovery in the 1990s: From stagnation and adjust-*

ment to human development, ed. G. A. Cornia, R. van der Hoeven, and T. Mkandawire. New York: St. Martin's Press.

Weber, Michael, et al. 1988. "Informing food security decisions in Africa: Empirical analysis and policy dialogue." Staff Paper 88–50. East Lansing: Michigan State University.

Widner, Jennifer A., ed. 1994. *Economic change and political liberalization in sub-Saharan Africa*. Baltimore: Johns Hopkins University Press.

Willame, Jean-Claude. 1986. "The practices of a liberal political economy: Import and export substitution in Cameroon (1975–1981)." In *The political economy of Cameroon*, ed. Michael G. Schatzberg and I. William Zartman. New York: Praeger Publishers.

Wilson, Ernest J., III. 1993. "French support for structural adjustment programs in Africa." *World Development*. 21(3): 331–347.

World Bank. Various years. *World debt tables*. Washington, DC: World Bank.

   1981. "Accelerated development in sub-Saharan Africa: An agenda for action." Washington, DC: World Bank.

   1984. "Madagascar: Current economic situation and prospects." Report No. 5154-MAG. Washington, DC: World Bank. Photocopy.

   1986. "The democratic republic of Madagascar: Country economic memorandum." Report No. 5996-MAG. Washington, DC: World Bank. Photocopy.

   1988. "Mozambique agricultural sector survey." Report No. 7094-MOZ. Washington, DC: World Bank.

   1989a. *Cameroon agricultural sector report*. Vols. 1–2. Washington, DC: World Bank.

   1989b. *Tanzania public expenditure review*. Report No. 7559-TA. Washington, DC: World Bank.

   1990. "Malawi country economic memorandum: Growth through poverty reduction." Washington, DC: World Bank.

   1992a. "Republic of Guinea agricultural sector review." Washington, DC: Agriculture and Operations Division, Occidental and Central Africa Department, World Bank. Draft.

   1992b. "Mozambique education sector expenditure, management and financing review." Report No. 11000-MOZ. Washington, DC: World Bank.

   1993a. *Adjustment in sub-Saharan Africa: Selected findings from OED evaluations*. Report No. 12155. Washington, DC: World Bank.

   1993b. *African development indicators*. Washington, DC: World Bank.

   1993c. *Uganda: Growing out of poverty*. A World Bank Country Study. Washington, DC: World Bank.

   1993d. *World development report*. New York: Oxford University Press.

   1993e. *Africa Development Indicators* (STARS: Socio-economi time series access retrieval system).

   1994a. "Lesotho poverty assessment." World Bank Report No. 13171 LS. Washington, DC: World Bank.

   1994b. "Poverty indicators for selected countries." Washington, DC: World Bank. Photocopy.

   1994c. "Special program of assistance: Launching the third phase." Washington, DC: World Bank.

   1994d. *World tables 1994*. Baltimore, MD: Johns Hopkins University Press for the World Bank.

   1994e. *Tanzania role of government: Public expenditure review*. Vols. 1–2. Report No. 12601-TA. Washington, DC: World Bank.

   1995a. "The social impact of adjustment operations." Report No. 14776. Washington, DC: World Bank.

1995b. "Status report on poverty in sub-Saharan Africa." Washington, DC: World Bank. Photocopy.

1995c. *World tables 1995*. Baltimore, MD: Johns Hopkins University Press for the World Bank.

1995d. "Poverty in Ghana: Understanding the past and anticipating the future, a synthesis of the first phase of the extended poverty study." Washington, DC: World Bank. Photocopy.

World Bank and United Nations Development Programme. 1989. *Africa's adjustment and growth in the 1980s*. Washington, DC, and New York: World Bank and United Nations Development Programme.

Yitzhaki, Shlomo. 1983. "On an extension of the Gini inequality index." *International Economic Review*. 24(3): 617–628.

Yitzhaki, Shlomo, and Joel Slemrod. 1991. "Welfare dominance: An application to commodity taxation." *American Economic Review*. 81(3): 480–496.

Younger, Stephen. 1992. *Testing the link between devaluation and inflation: Time series evidence from Ghana*. Working Paper No. 24. Ithaca, NY: Cornell Food and Nutrition Policy Program.

1993. *Estimating tax incidence in Ghana: An exercise using household data*. Working Paper No. 48. Ithaca, NY: Cornell Food and Nutrition Policy Program.

1996a. "Estimating tax incidence in Ghana: An exercise using household data." In *Economic reform and the poor in Africa*, ed. David E. Sahn, 231–253. Oxford: Clarendon Press.

1996b. "Labor market consequences of retrenchment for civil servants in Ghana." In *Economic reform and the poor in Africa*, ed. David E. Sahn, 185–202. Oxford: Clarendon Press.

Younger, Stephen, Sudarshan Canagarajah, and Harold Alderman. 1994. *A comparison of Ghanian civil servants' earnings before and after adjustment*. Working Paper No. 64. Ithaca, NY: Cornell Food and Nutrition Policy Program.

Younger, Stephen, and David E. Sahn. 1995. "Macroeconomic adjustment policies and poverty in the Caribbean." Report prepared for the World Bank. Ithaca, NY: Cornell Food and Nutrition Policy Program. Photocopy.

Younger, Stephen, David E. Sahn, Steven Haggblade, and Paul A. Dorosh. 1996. "Tax incidence in Madagascar: An analysis using household data." Report prepared for the World Bank. Ithaca, NY: Cornell Food and Nutrition Policy Program. Photocopy.

Index